PH

PHANTASY DEGR

Episode 2: Madosa Guild

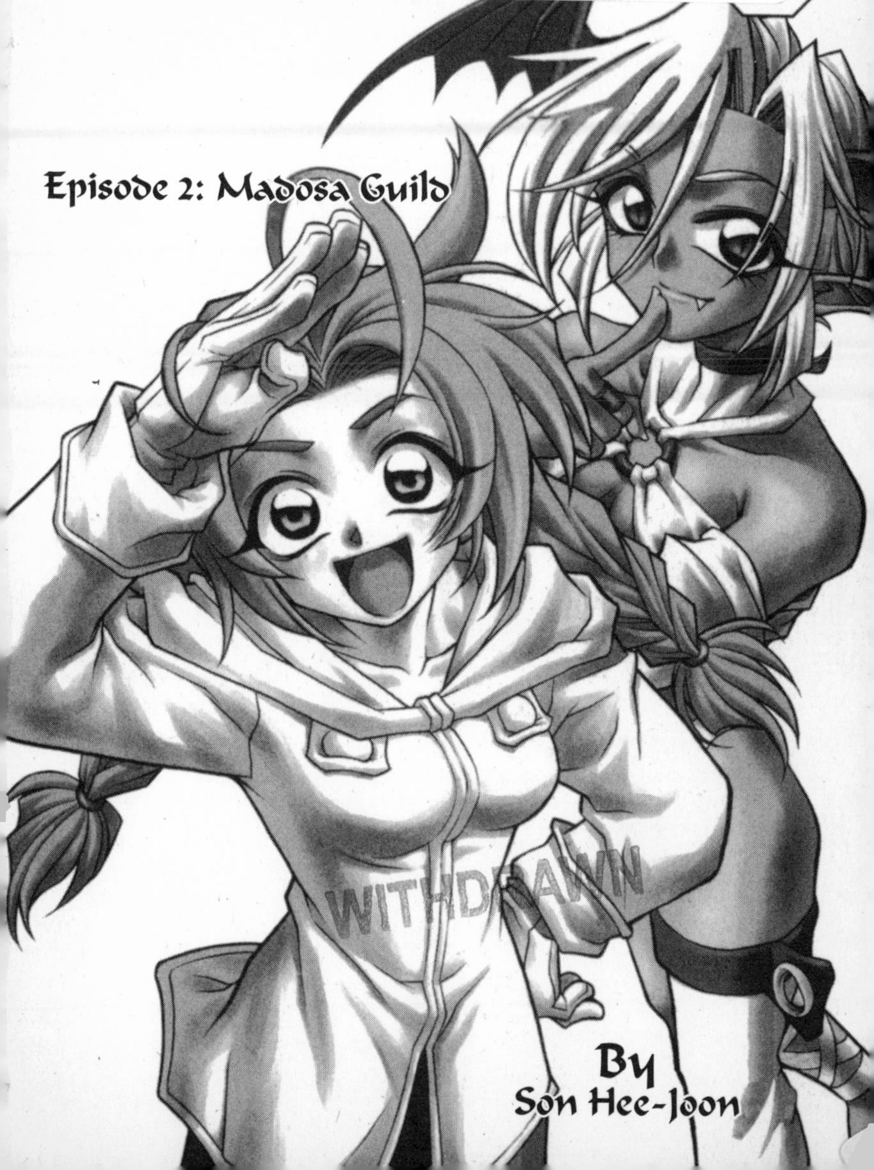

By
Son Hee-Joon

PhD: Phantasy Degree Vol. 2
Created by Son Hee-Joon

Translation - Sarah Kim
English Adaptation - Adam Arnold
Copy Editor - Aaron Sparrow
Retouch and Lettering - Jason Milligan and Alex Madrigal
Production Artist - James Dashiell
Cover Design - Raymond Makowski

Editor - Paul Morrissey
Digital Imaging Manager - Chris Buford
Pre-Press Manager - Antonio DePietro
Production Managers - Jennifer Miller and Mutsumi Miyazaki
Art Director - Matt Alford
Managing Editor - Jill Freshney
VP of Production - Ron Klamert
Editor-in-Chief - Mike Kiley
President and C.O.O. - John Parker
Publisher and C.E.O. - Stuart Levy

A  Manga

TOKYOPOP Inc.
5900 Wilshire Blvd. Suite 2000
Los Angeles, CA 90036

E-mail: info@TOKYOPOP.com
Come visit us online at www.TOKYOPOP.com

ISBN: 1-59532-320-1

First TOKYOPOP printing: April 2005
10 9 8 7 6 5 4 3 2 1
Printed in the USA

PhD
PHANTASY DEGREE

Volume 2

By
SON HEE-JOON

HAMBURG // LONDON // LOS ANGELES // TOKYO

Previously in...

PhD
PHANTASY DEGREE

MOST MUMMIES I'VE SEEN ARE ROTTING IN SARCOPHAGUSES, AND THEY'RE LIVELIER THAN YOU! DO MUMMIES EVEN EAT FLESH? I THOUGHT THAT'S WHAT ZOMBIES DID. AT LEAST ZOMBIES CAN INSPIRE SOME FEAR.

HEY, YOU! WITH THE BABY FANGS! YOU'RE NOT EVEN A PURE-BLOODED VAMPIRE, ARE YOU? I BET YOU WERE BITTEN BY ANOTHER VAMPIRE, RIGHT?

Mm-hmm.

AND YOU, GOAT BOY! ARE YOU SUPPOSED TO BE A DEMON? WITH HORNS THAT STUBBY, YOU'RE NOTHING BUT AN IMPOTENT IMP! HONESTLY, ARE YOU EVEN CAPABLE OF CASTING MAGIC?

WHAT A BUNCH OF SAD SACKS! PATHETIC!

YOU'RE A BUNCH OF DEMON SCHOOL SLACKERS, AREN'T YOU? JUST A GROUP OF BELOW-AVERAGE BEELZEBUBS! AM I RIGHT?

A spunky, fearless girl named Sang searches for the Demon School Hades...and a legendary ring contained within its walls. When she encounters a group of misfit monsters that are playing hooky from school, her hunt is over. They reluctantly take her to Hades, where Sang meets Notra, a female monster who's wearing a very special ring! But before Sang can snatch Notra's ring, a group of humans from the Madosa Guild attack the school! A deadly battle ensues, and Sang fights alongside her new beastly buddies...

Table of Contents

Madosa Guild

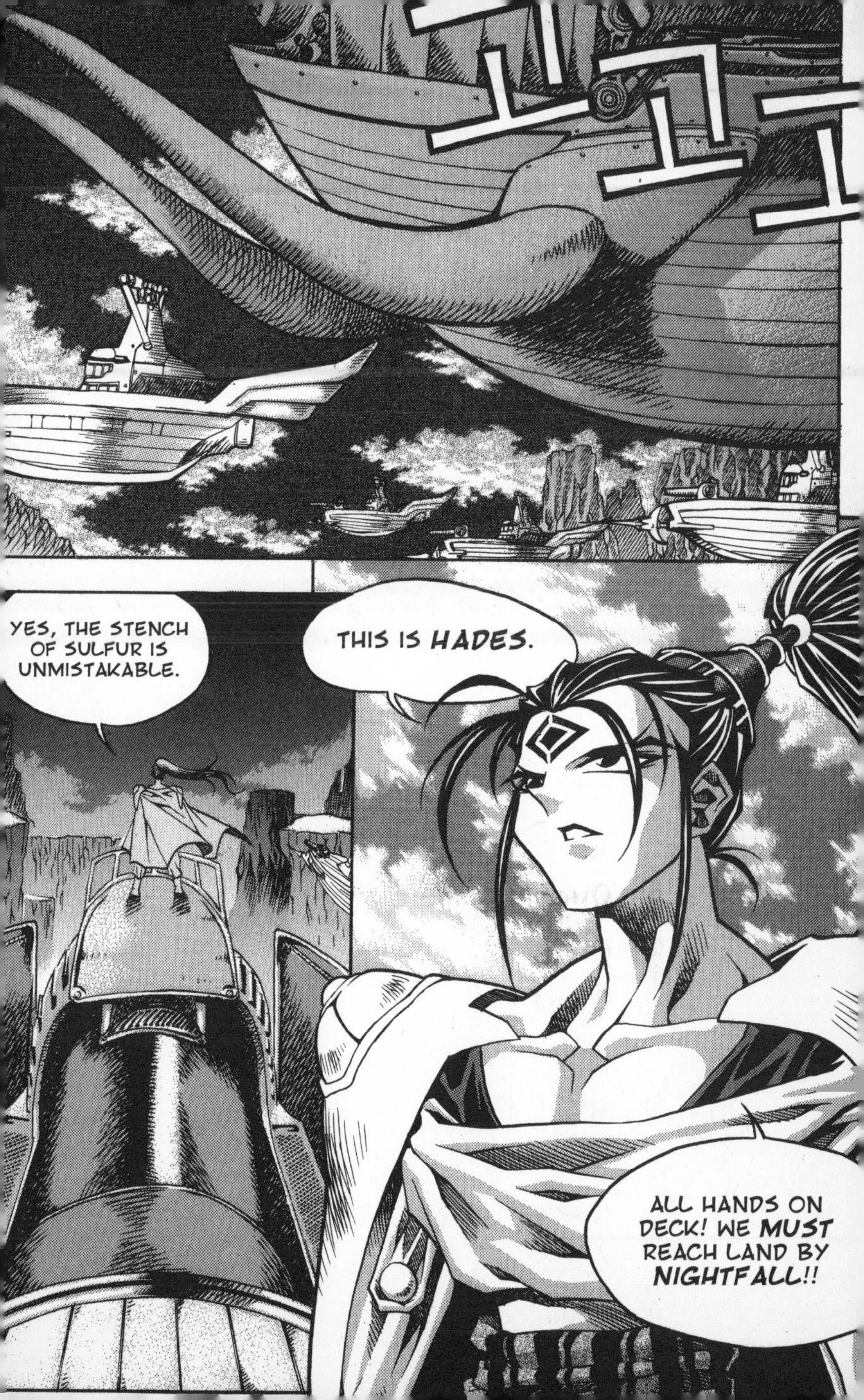
YES, THE STENCH OF SULFUR IS UNMISTAKABLE.
THIS IS HADES.
ALL HANDS ON DECK! WE MUST REACH LAND BY NIGHTFALL!!

Quest 11

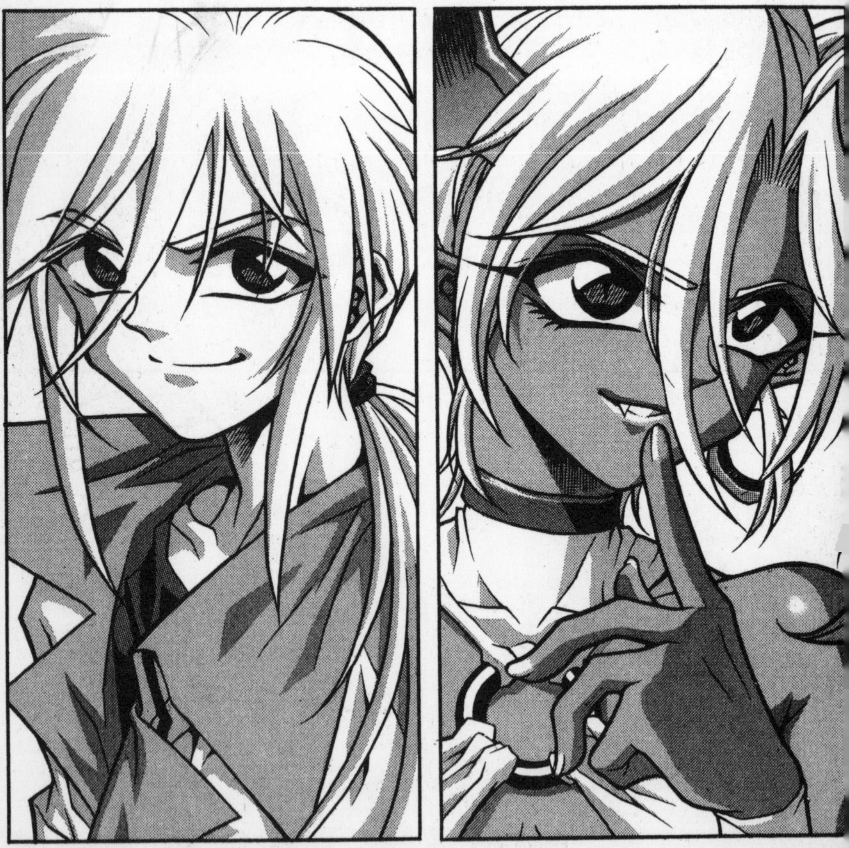

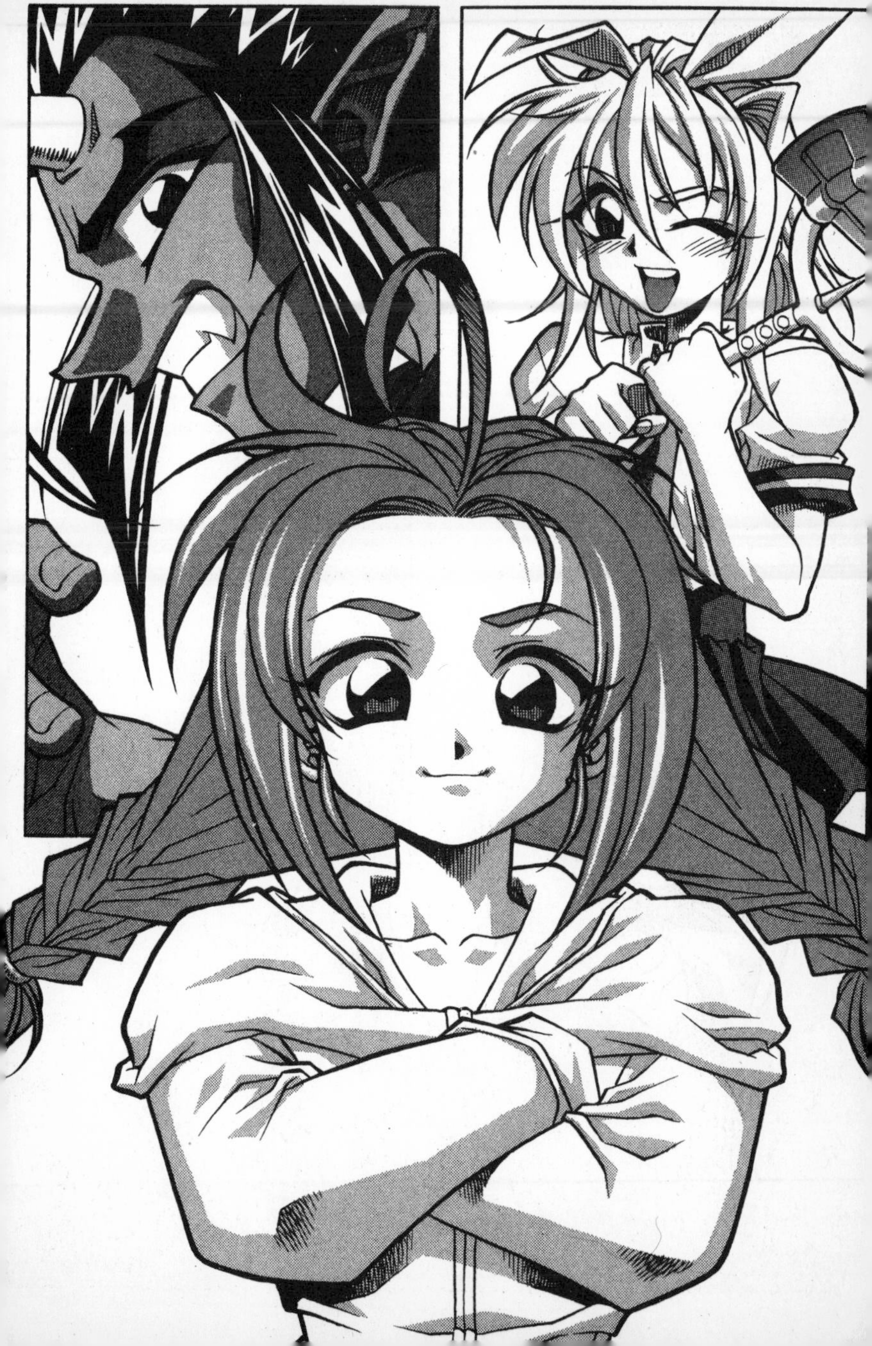

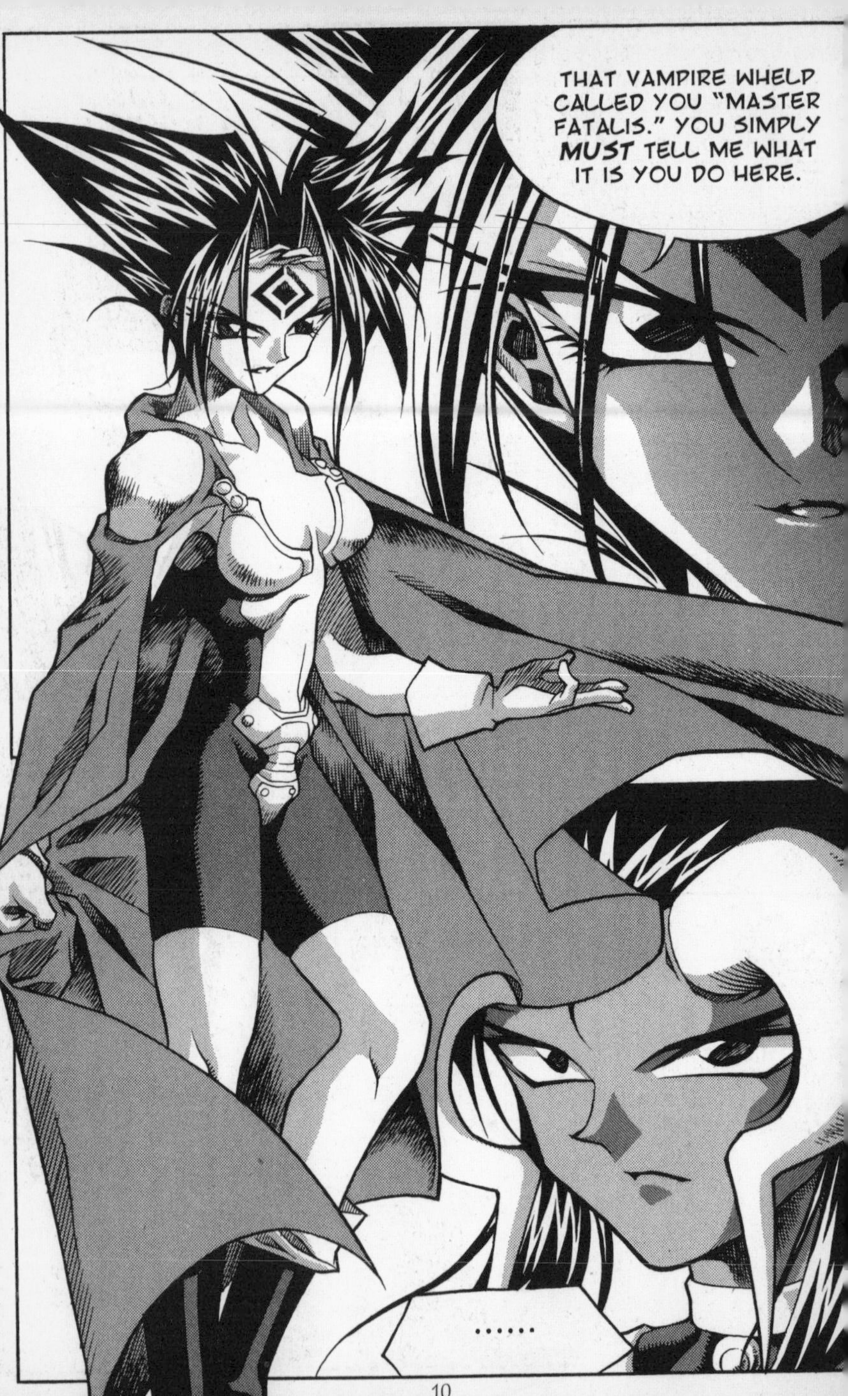
THAT VAMPIRE WHELP CALLED YOU "MASTER FATALIS." YOU SIMPLY MUST TELL ME WHAT IT IS YOU DO HERE.
......

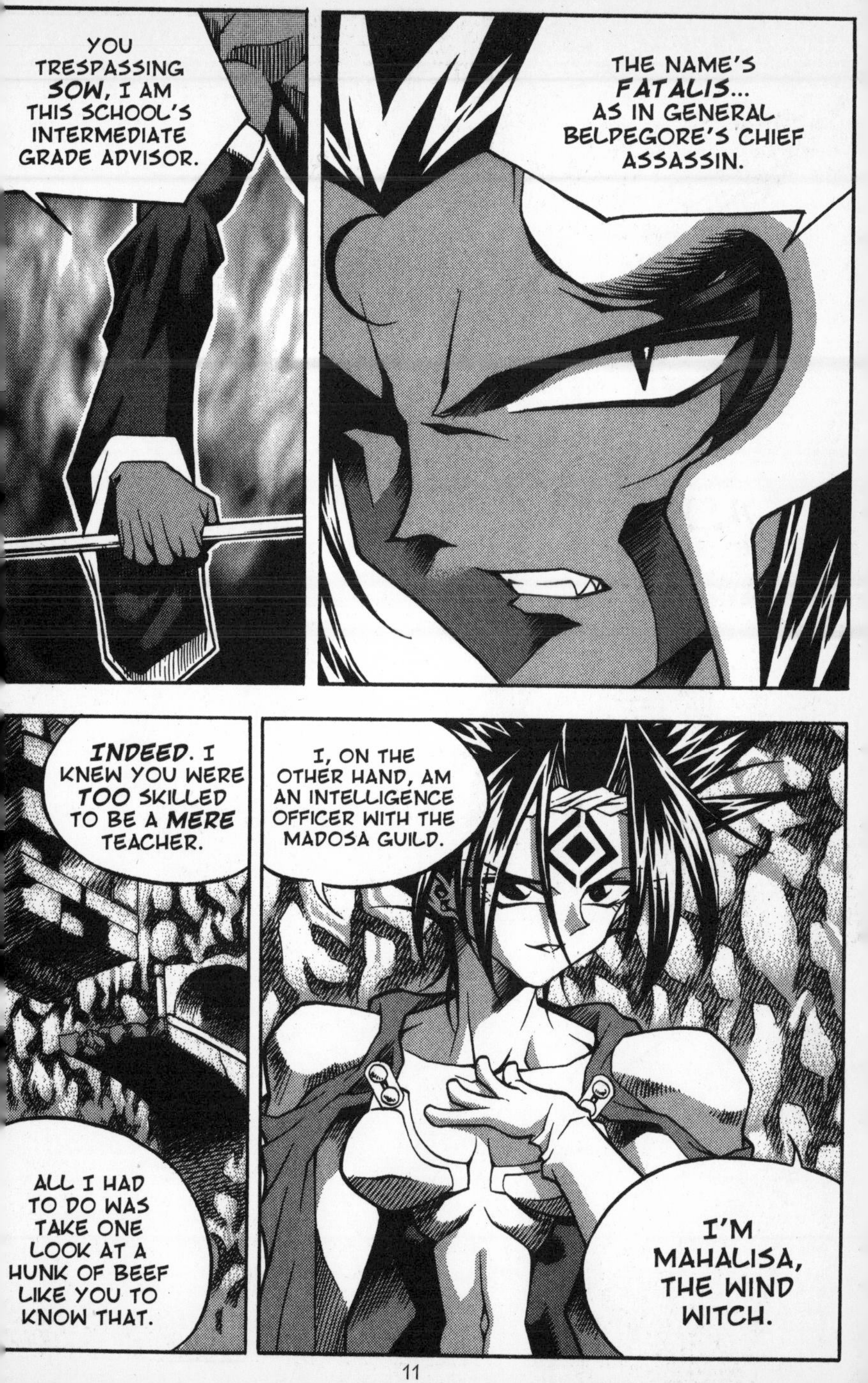

YOU TRESPASSING SOW, I AM THIS SCHOOL'S INTERMEDIATE GRADE ADVISOR.
THE NAME'S FATALIS... AS IN GENERAL BELPEGORE'S CHIEF ASSASSIN.
INDEED. I KNEW YOU WERE TOO SKILLED TO BE A MERE TEACHER.
ALL I HAD TO DO WAS TAKE ONE LOOK AT A HUNK OF BEEF LIKE YOU TO KNOW THAT.
I, ON THE OTHER HAND, AM AN INTELLIGENCE OFFICER WITH THE MADOSA GUILD.
I'M MAHALISA, THE WIND WITCH.

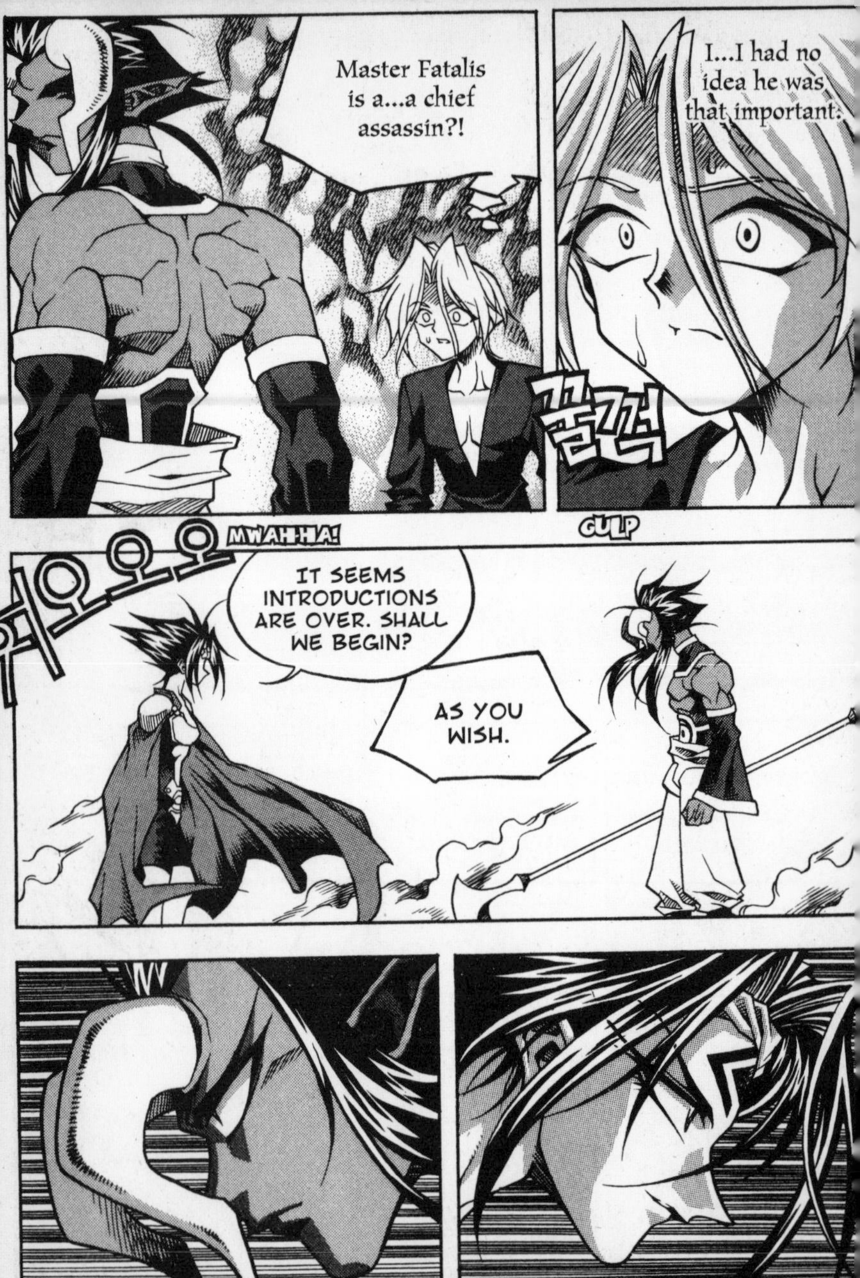

Master Fatalis is a...a chief assassin?!
I...I had no idea he was that important.
MWAHHA!
GULP
IT SEEMS INTRODUCTIONS ARE OVER. SHALL WE BEGIN?
AS YOU WISH.

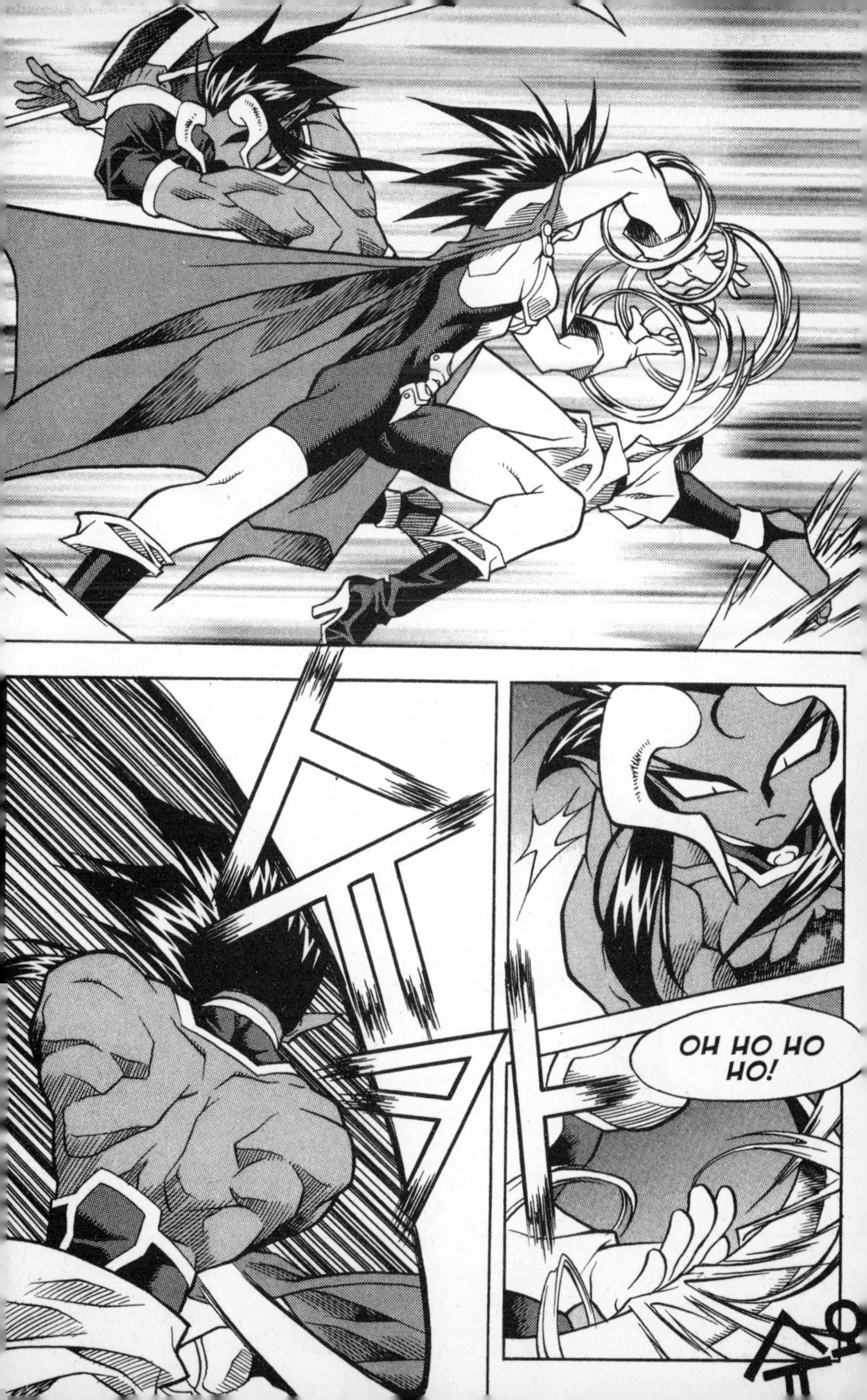
OH HO HO HO!

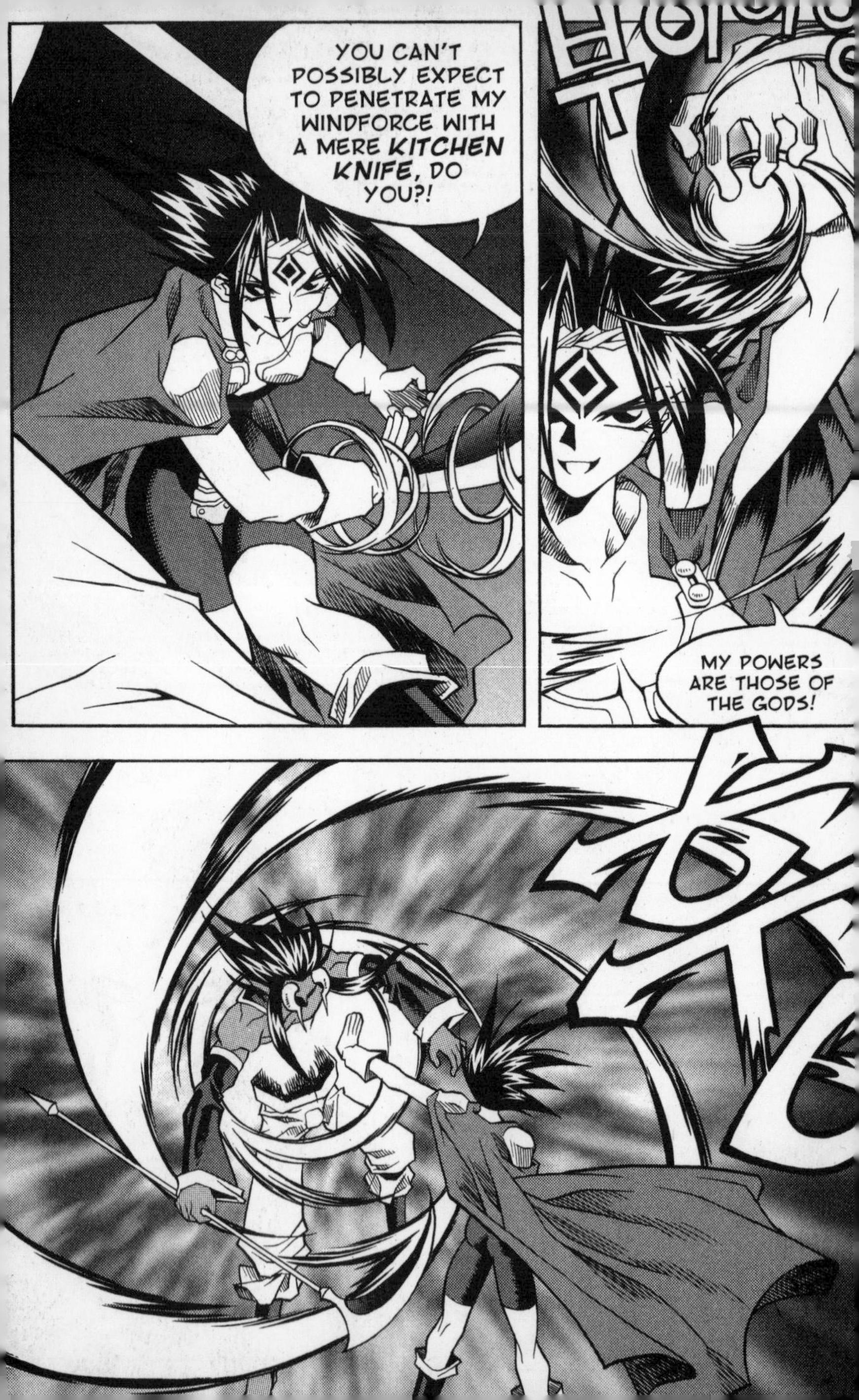
YOU CAN'T POSSIBLY EXPECT TO PENETRATE MY WINDFORCE WITH A MERE **KITCHEN KNIFE**, DO YOU?!
MY POWERS ARE THOSE OF THE GODS!

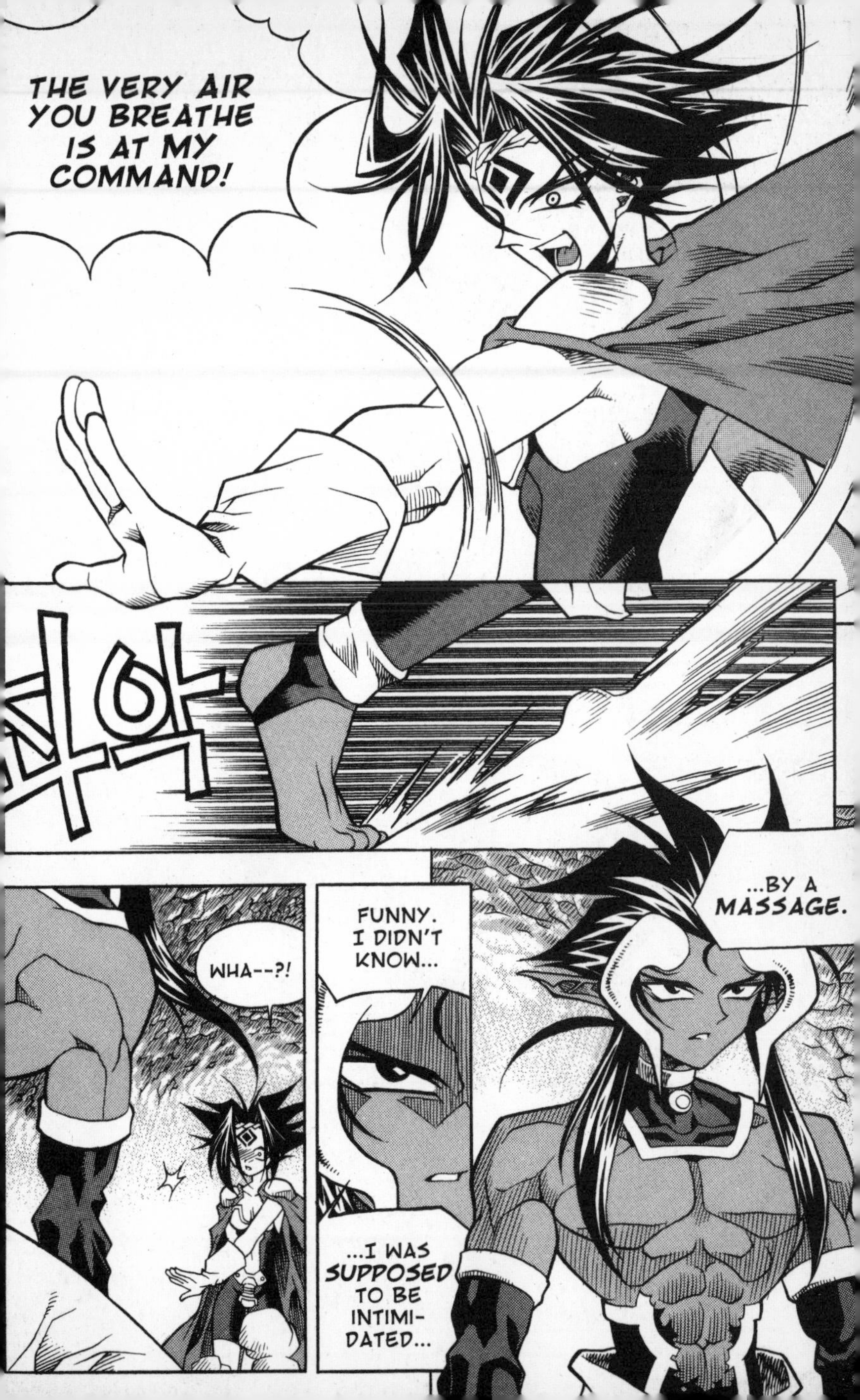
THE VERY AIR YOU BREATHE IS AT MY COMMAND!
WHA--?!
FUNNY. I DIDN'T KNOW...
...I WAS SUPPOSED TO BE INTIMIDATED...
...BY A MASSAGE.

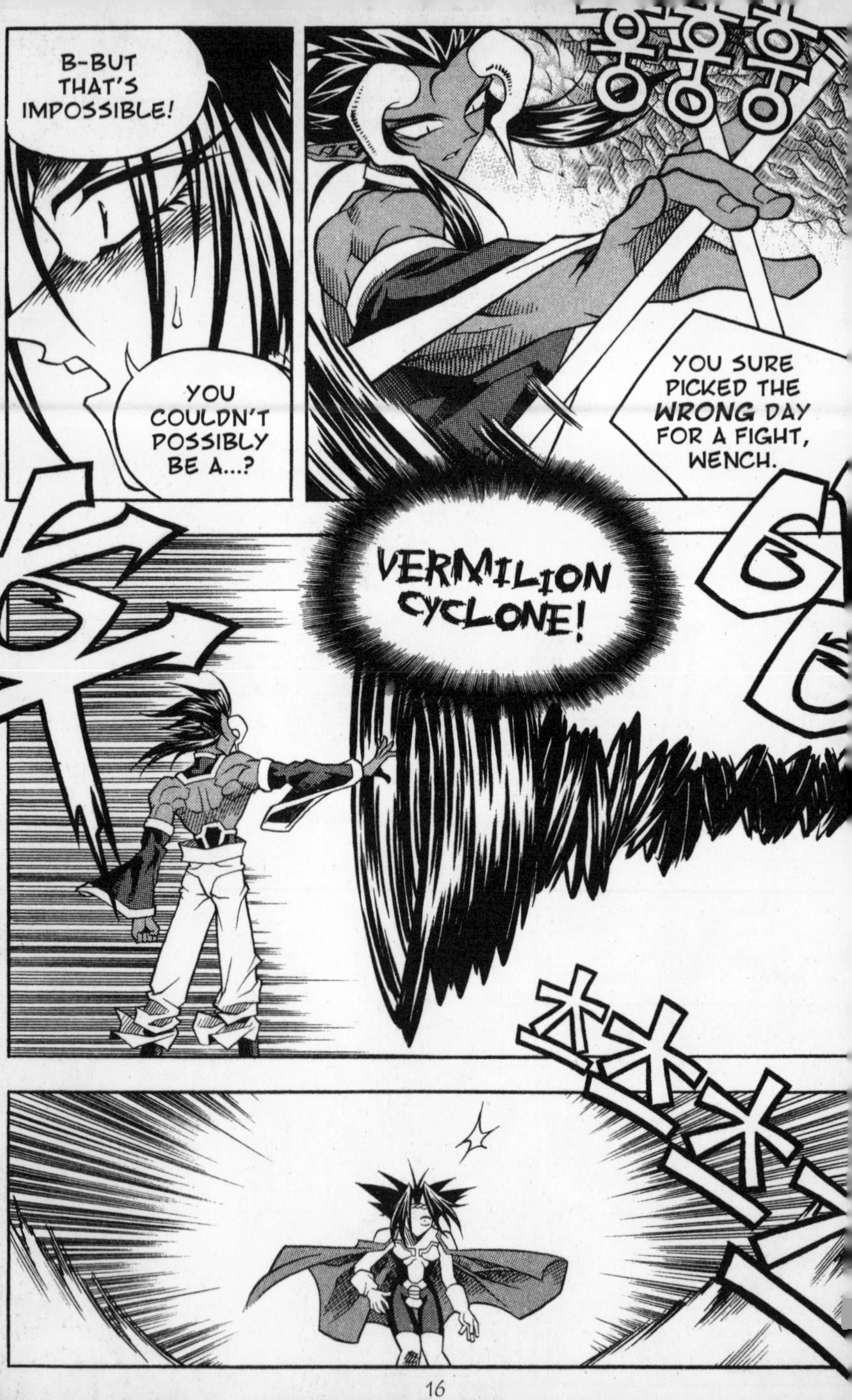
B-BUT THAT'S IMPOSSIBLE!
YOU COULDN'T POSSIBLY BE A...?
흥흥흥
YOU SURE PICKED THE **WRONG** DAY FOR A FIGHT, WENCH.
VERMILION CYCLONE!

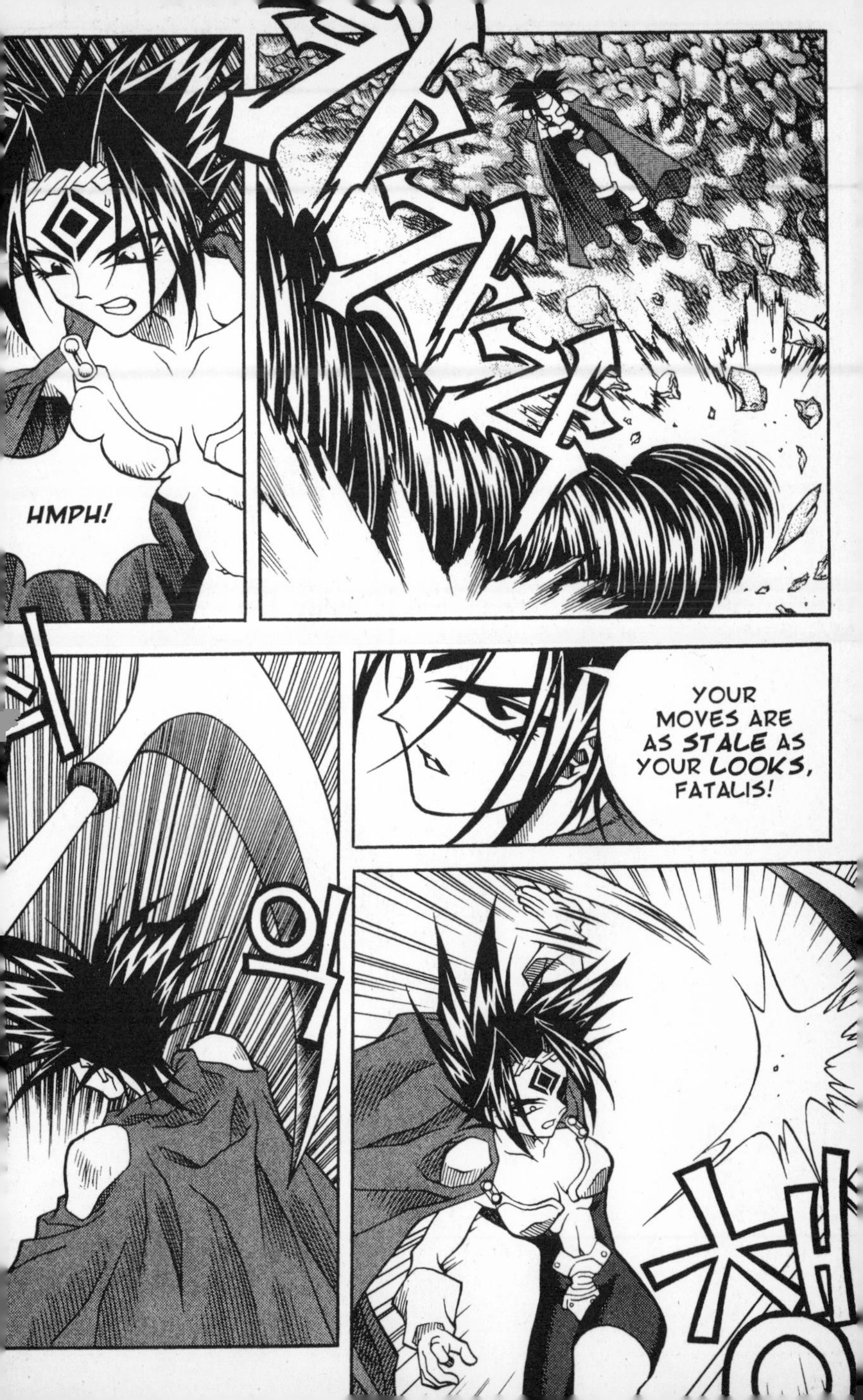
HMPH!
YOUR MOVES ARE AS STALE AS YOUR LOOKS, FATALIS!

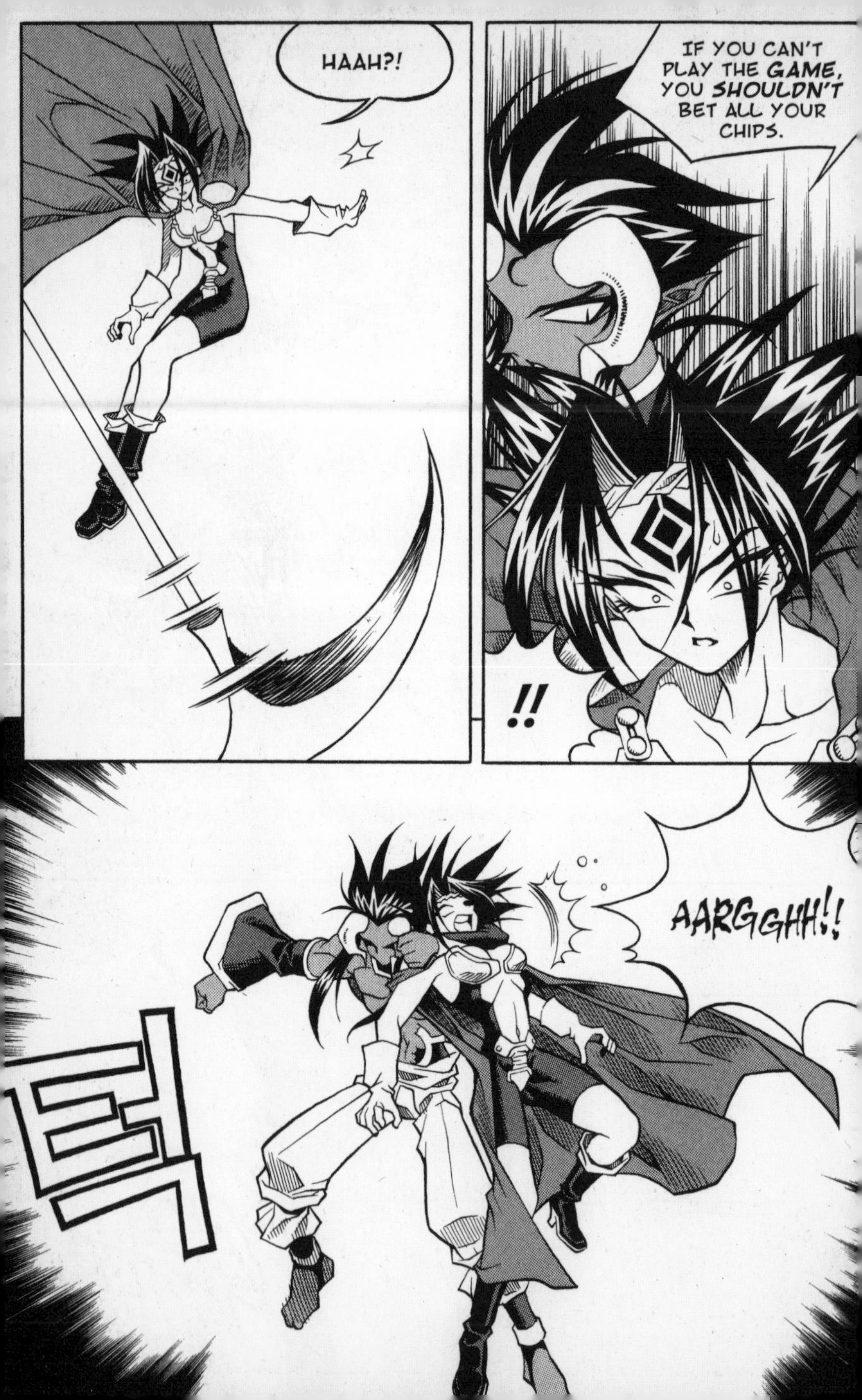
HAAH?!
IF YOU CAN'T PLAY THE GAME, YOU SHOULDN'T BET ALL YOUR CHIPS.
!!
AARGGHH!!

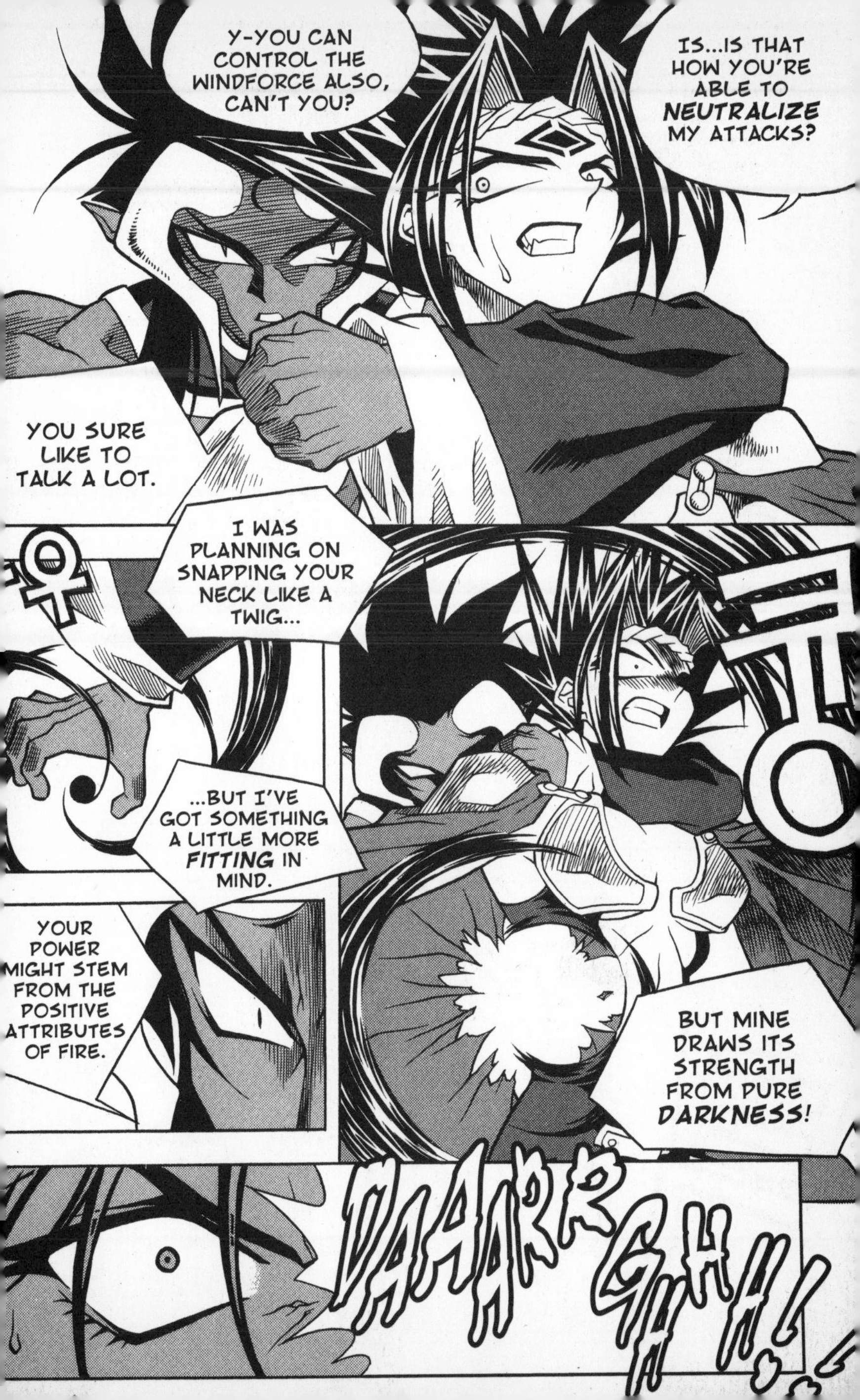
Y-YOU CAN CONTROL THE WINDFORCE ALSO, CAN'T YOU?
IS...IS THAT HOW YOU'RE ABLE TO **NEUTRALIZE** MY ATTACKS?
YOU SURE LIKE TO TALK A LOT.
I WAS PLANNING ON SNAPPING YOUR NECK LIKE A TWIG...
...BUT I'VE GOT SOMETHING A LITTLE MORE **FITTING** IN MIND.
YOUR POWER MIGHT STEM FROM THE POSITIVE ATTRIBUTES OF FIRE.
BUT MINE DRAWS ITS STRENGTH FROM PURE **DARKNESS**!
DAARRGHHA!!

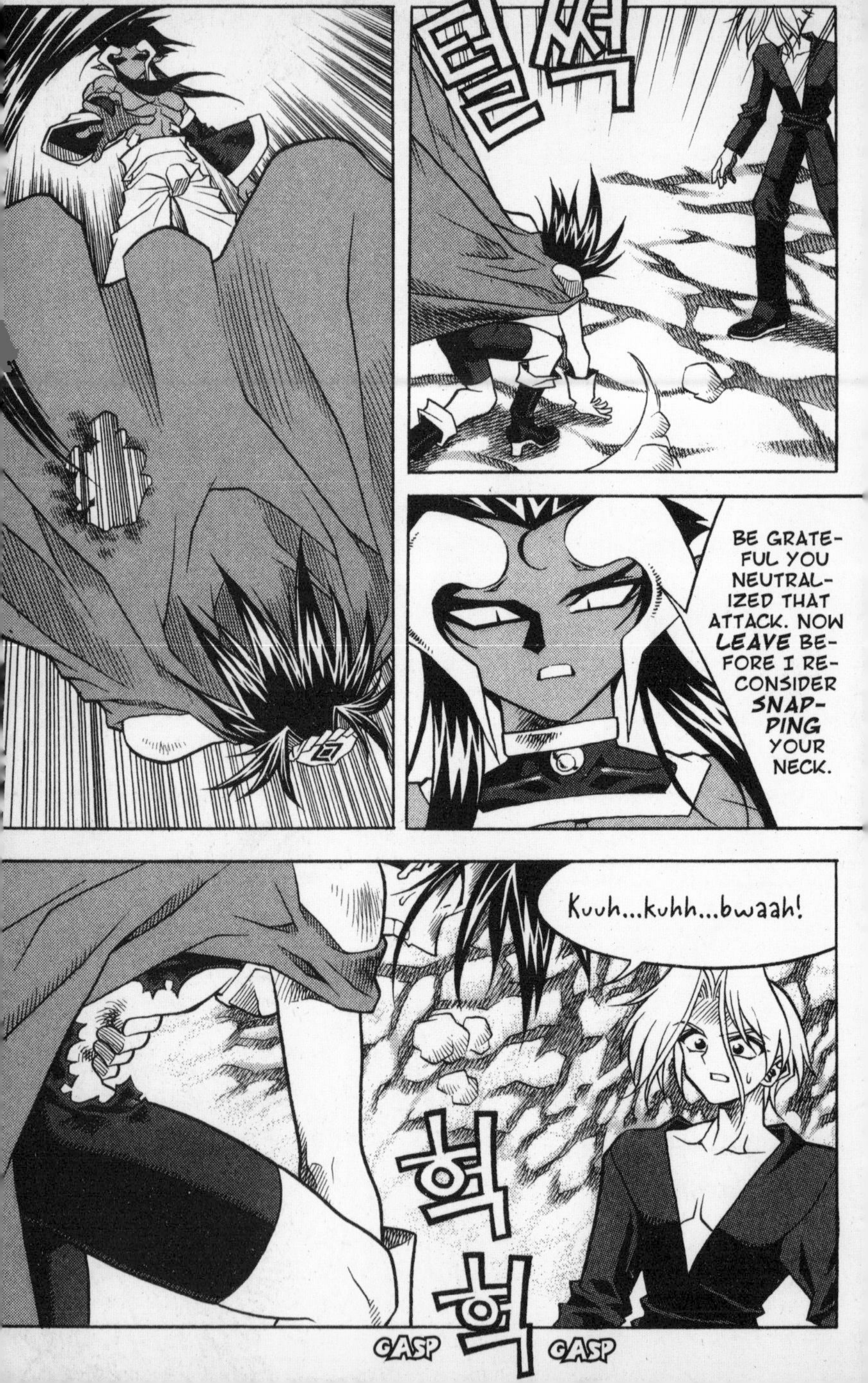
털썩
BE GRATEFUL YOU NEUTRALIZED THAT ATTACK. NOW **LEAVE** BEFORE I RECONSIDER ***SNAPPING*** YOUR NECK.
Kuuh...kuhh...bwaah!
헉 헉
GASP GASP

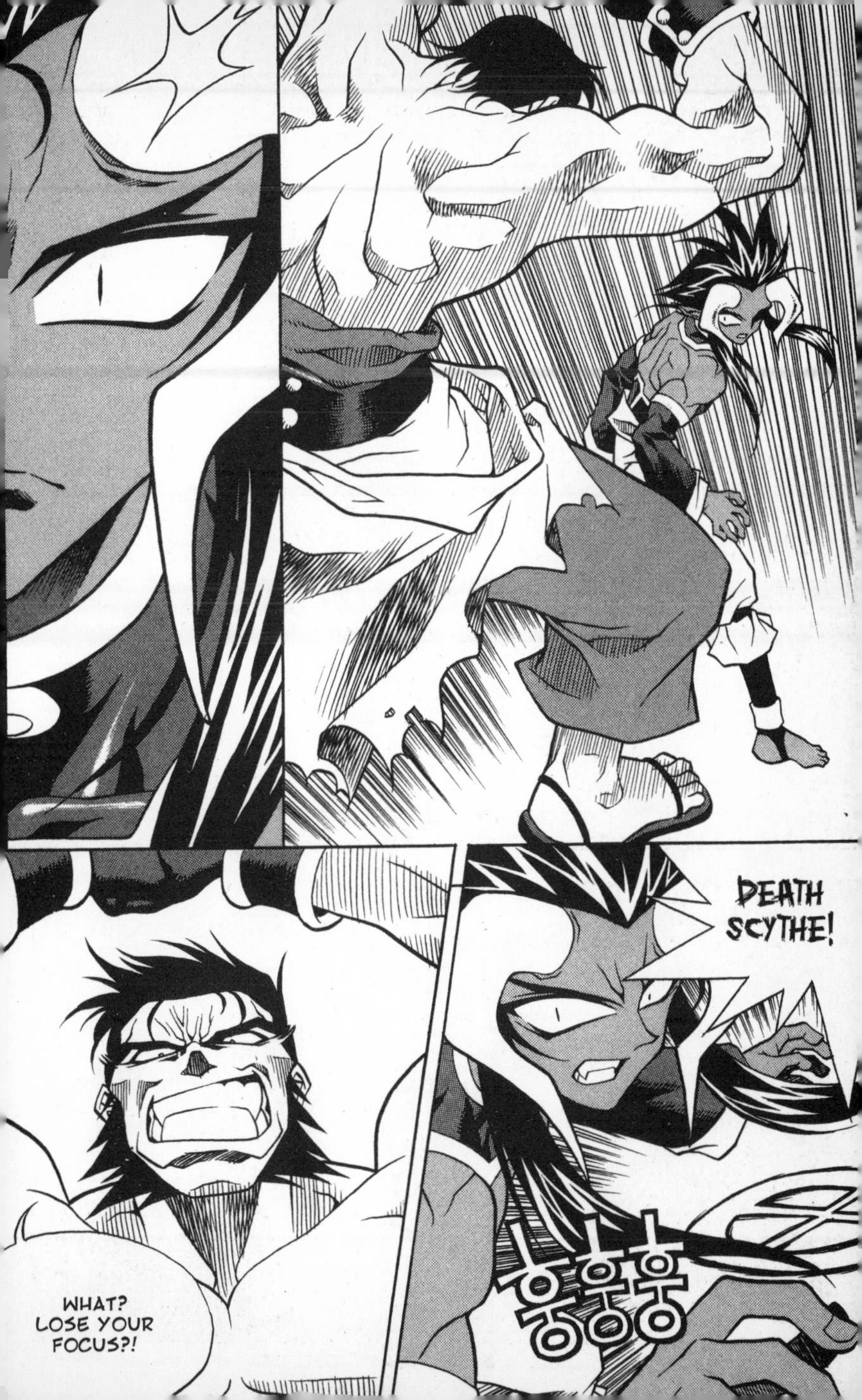
WHAT? LOSE YOUR FOCUS?!
DEATH SCYTHE!
훙훙훙

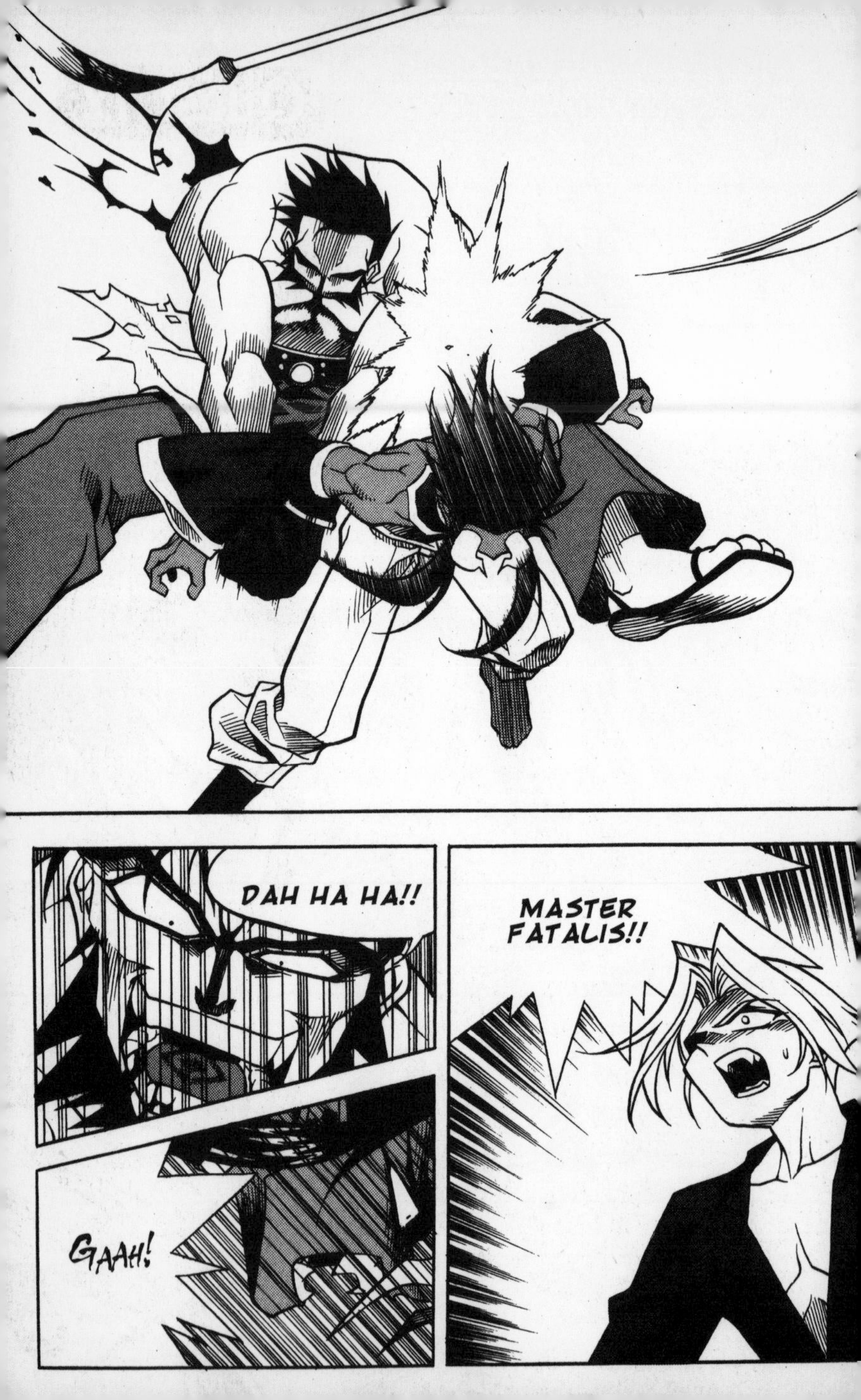
DAH HA HA!!
GAAH!
MASTER FATALIS!!

Quest 12

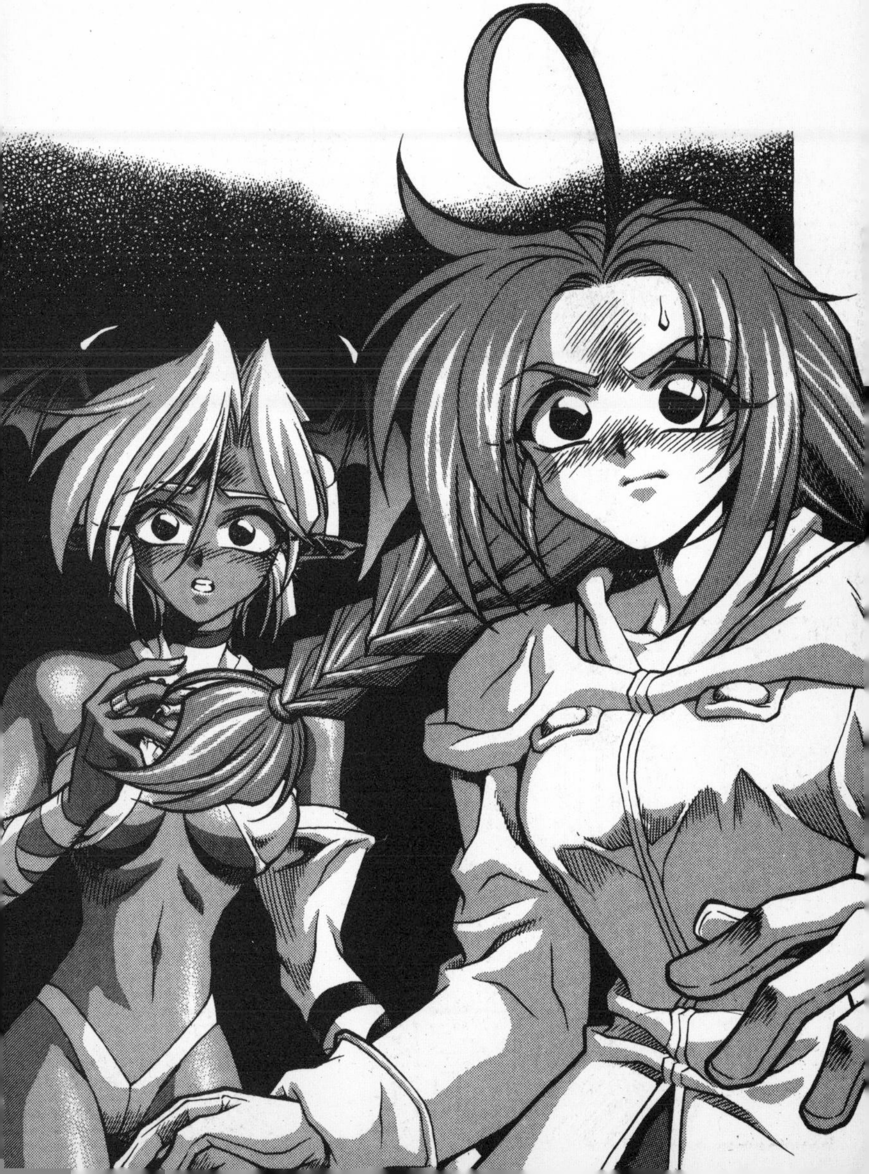

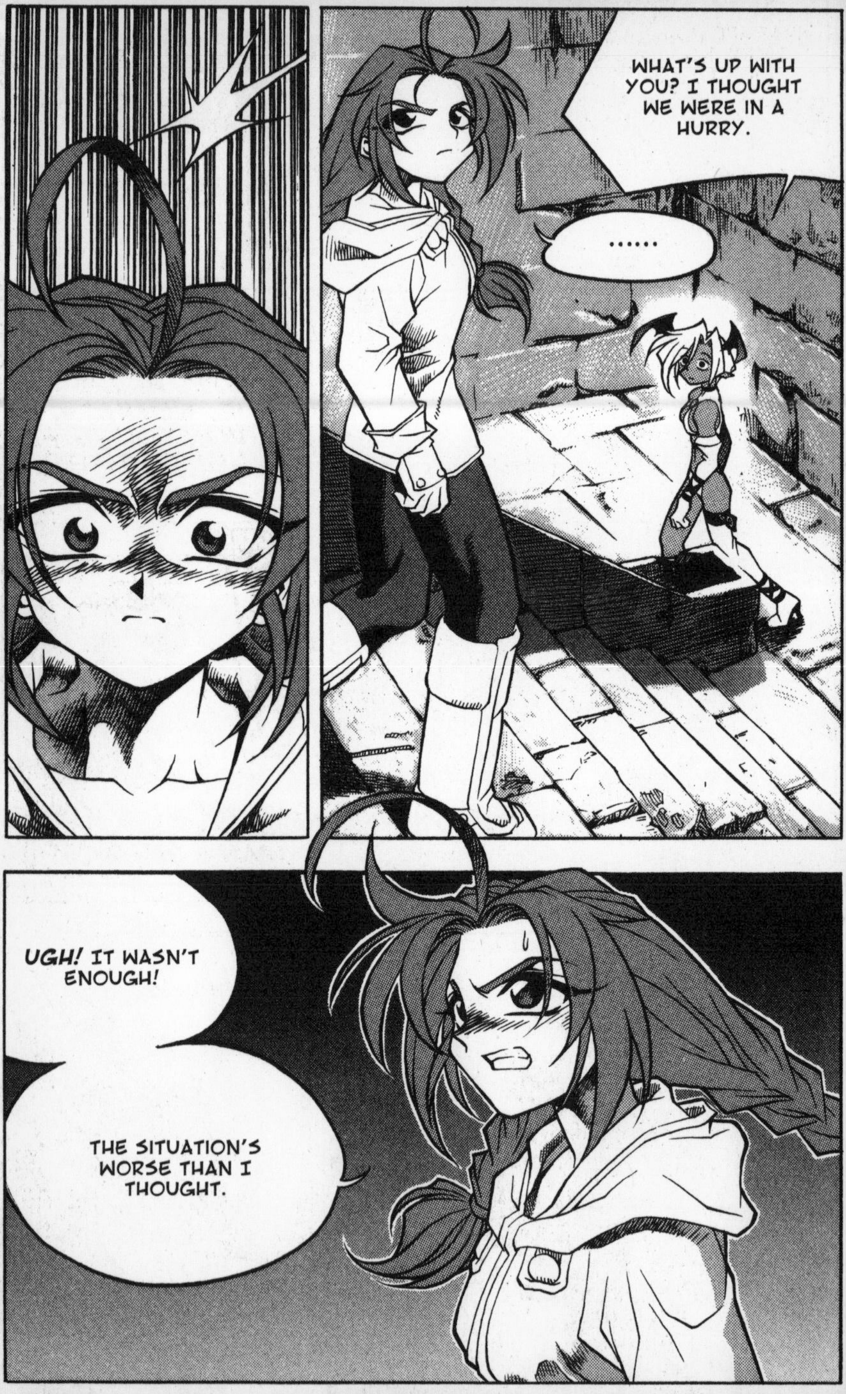
WHAT'S UP WITH YOU? I THOUGHT WE WERE IN A HURRY.
......
UGH! IT WASN'T ENOUGH!
THE SITUATION'S WORSE THAN I THOUGHT.

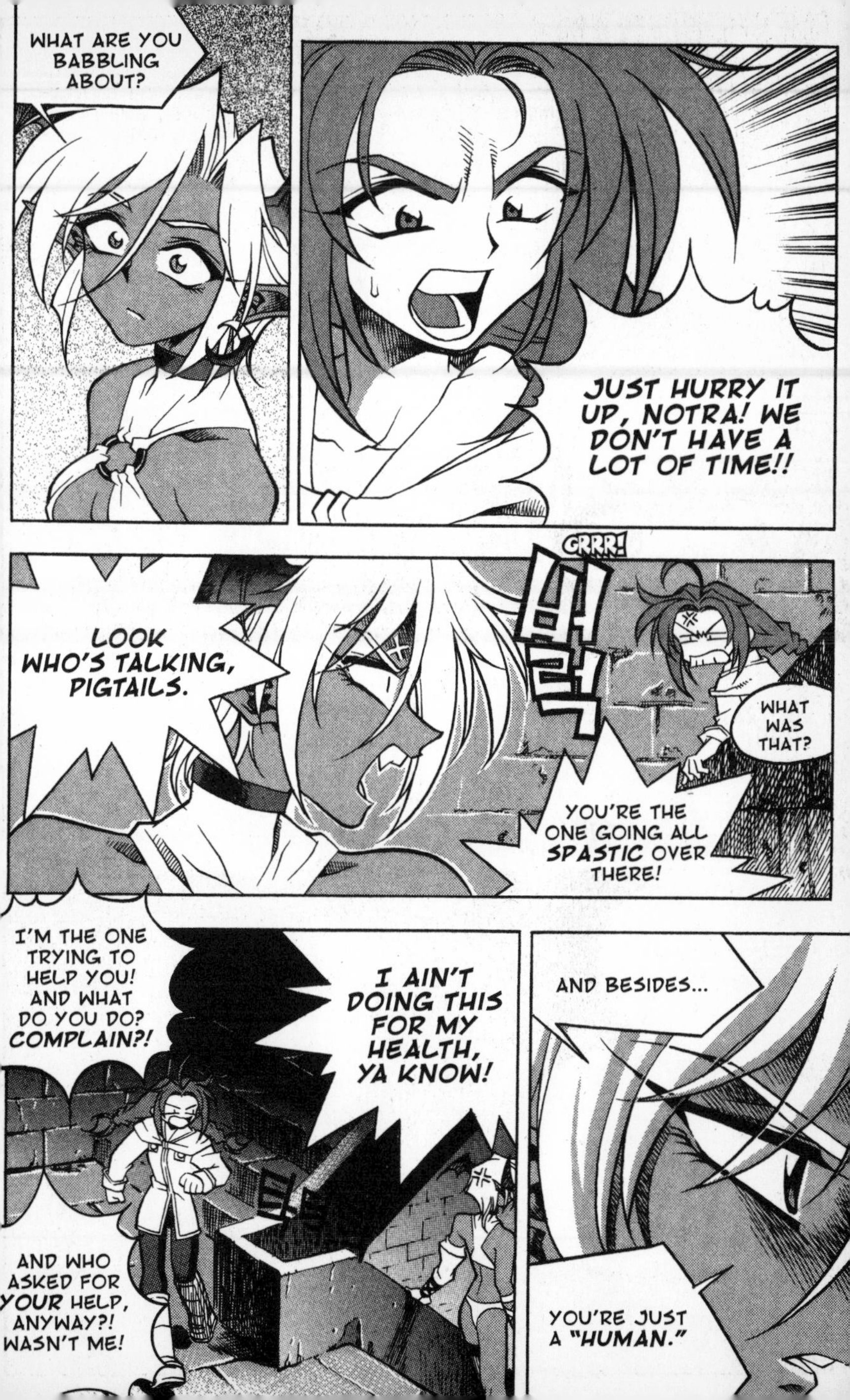
WHAT ARE YOU BABBLING ABOUT?
JUST HURRY IT UP, NOTRA! WE DON'T HAVE A LOT OF TIME!!
LOOK WHO'S TALKING, PIGTAILS.
YOU'RE THE ONE GOING ALL SPASTIC OVER THERE!
GRRR!
WHAT WAS THAT?
I'M THE ONE TRYING TO HELP YOU! AND WHAT DO YOU DO? COMPLAIN?!
I AIN'T DOING THIS FOR MY HEALTH, YA KNOW!
AND WHO ASKED FOR YOUR HELP, ANYWAY?! WASN'T ME!
AND BESIDES...
YOU'RE JUST A "HUMAN."

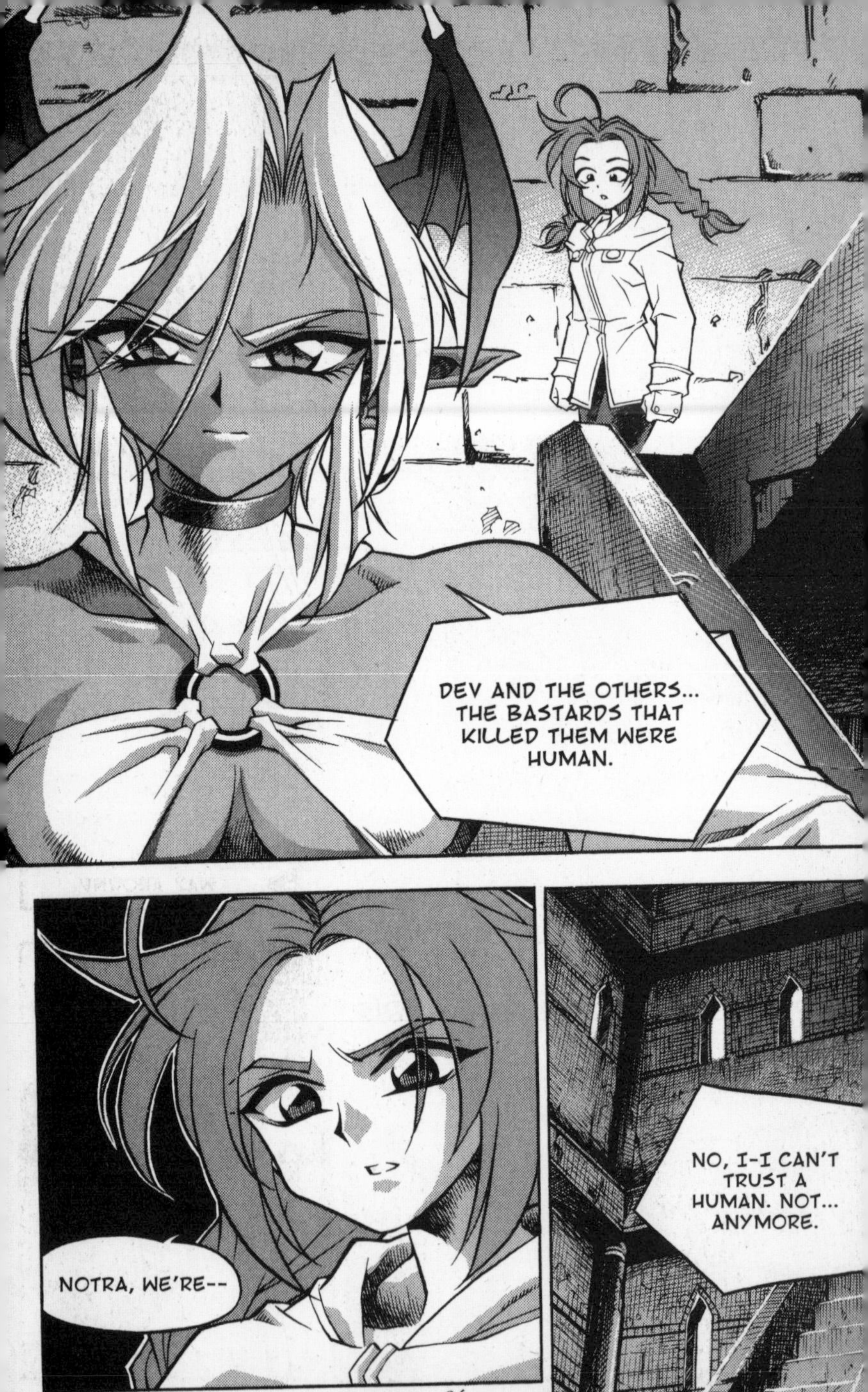
DEV AND THE OTHERS... THE BASTARDS THAT KILLED THEM WERE HUMAN.
NOTRA, WE'RE--
NO, I-I CAN'T TRUST A HUMAN. NOT... ANYMORE.

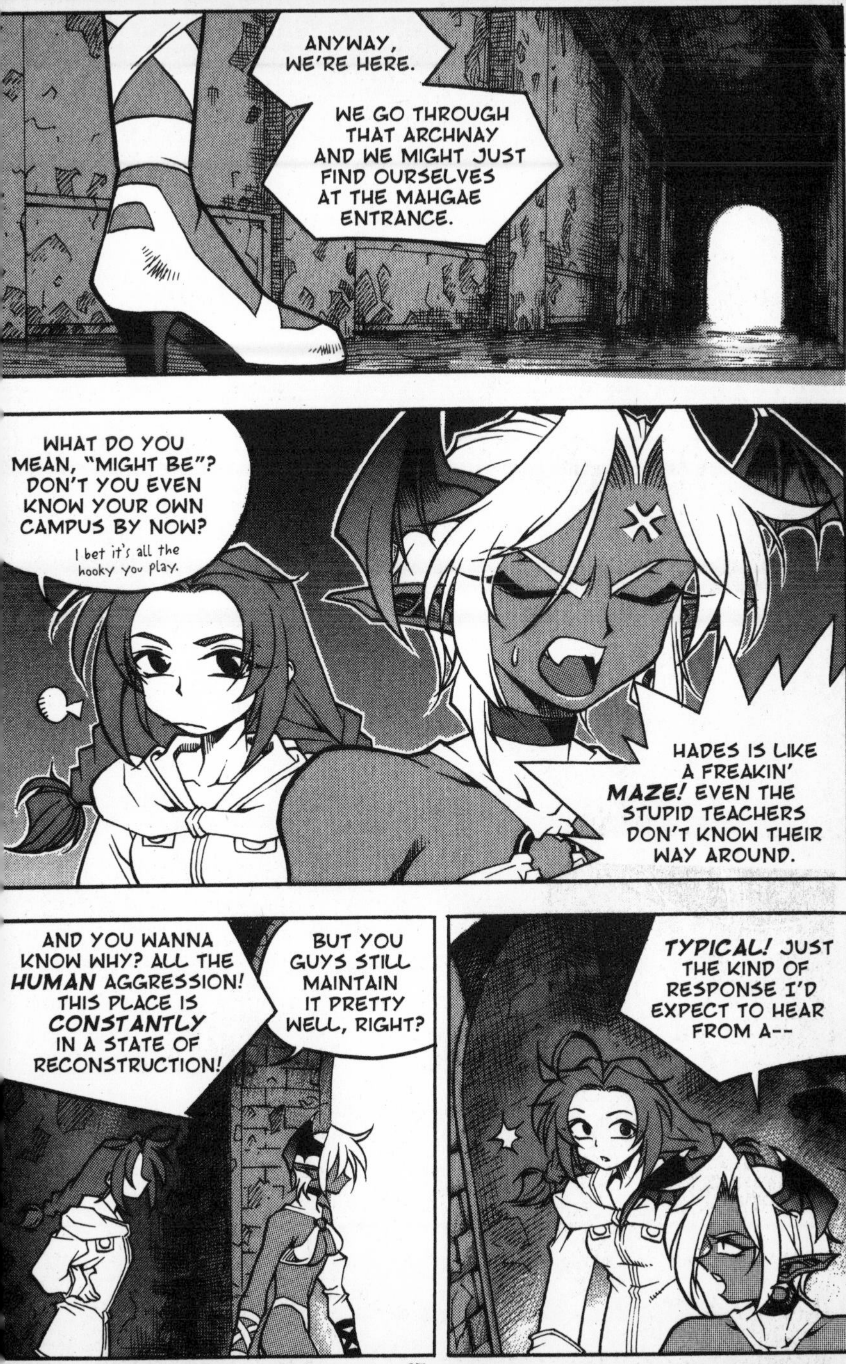
ANYWAY, WE'RE HERE.
WE GO THROUGH THAT ARCHWAY AND WE MIGHT JUST FIND OURSELVES AT THE MAHGAE ENTRANCE.
WHAT DO YOU MEAN, "MIGHT BE"? DON'T YOU EVEN KNOW YOUR OWN CAMPUS BY NOW?
I bet it's all the hooky you play.
HADES IS LIKE A FREAKIN' MAZE! EVEN THE STUPID TEACHERS DON'T KNOW THEIR WAY AROUND.
AND YOU WANNA KNOW WHY? ALL THE HUMAN AGGRESSION! THIS PLACE IS CONSTANTLY IN A STATE OF RECONSTRUCTION!
BUT YOU GUYS STILL MAINTAIN IT PRETTY WELL, RIGHT?
TYPICAL! JUST THE KIND OF RESPONSE I'D EXPECT TO HEAR FROM A--

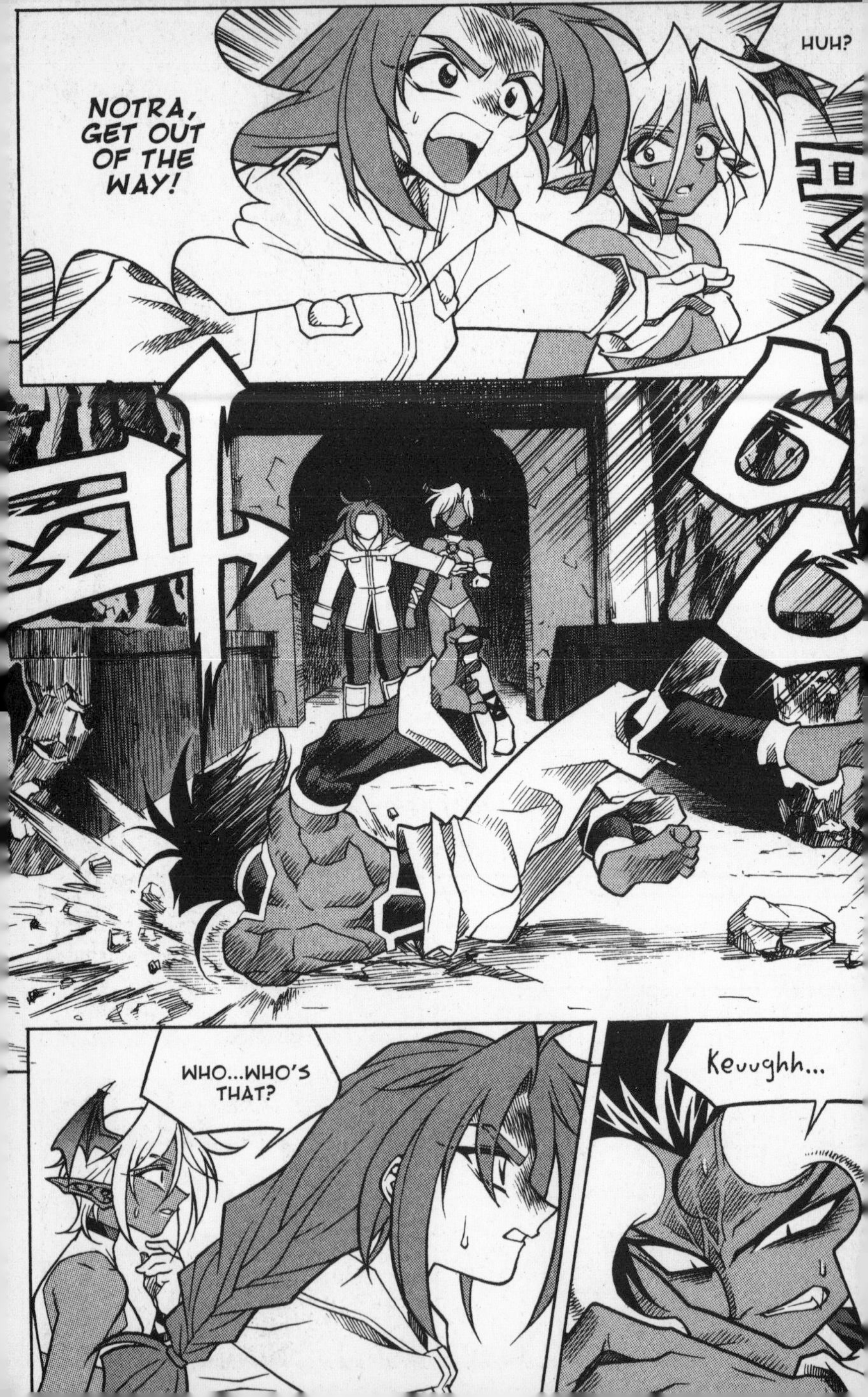
NOTRA, GET OUT OF THE WAY!
HUH?
WHO...WHO'S THAT?
Keuughh...

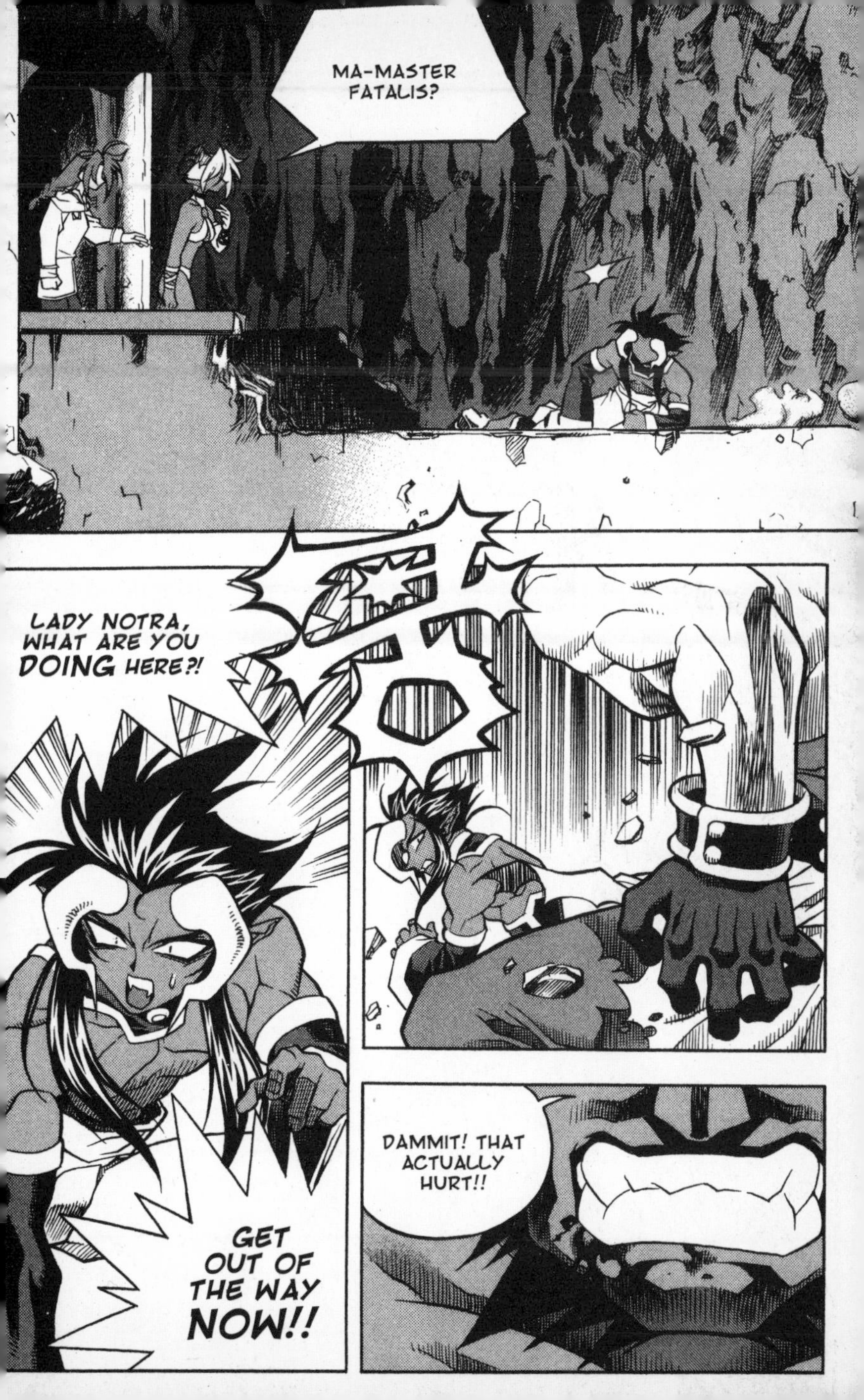
MA-MASTER FATALIS?
LADY NOTRA, WHAT ARE YOU DOING HERE?!
GET OUT OF THE WAY NOW!!
DAMMIT! THAT ACTUALLY HURT!!

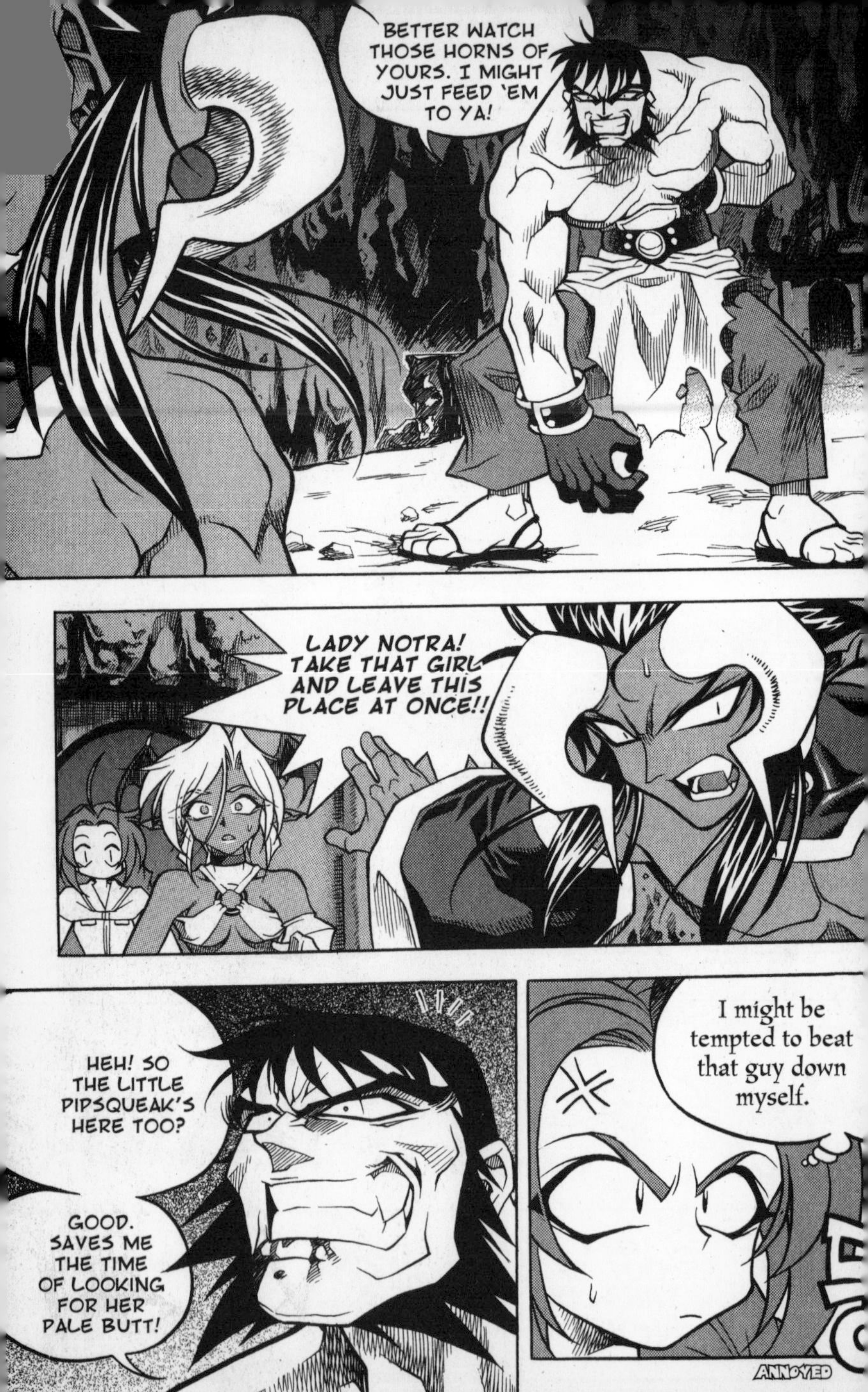

BETTER WATCH THOSE HORNS OF YOURS. I MIGHT JUST FEED 'EM TO YA!
LADY NOTRA! TAKE THAT GIRL AND LEAVE THIS PLACE AT ONCE!!
HEH! SO THE LITTLE PIPSQUEAK'S HERE TOO?
GOOD. SAVES ME THE TIME OF LOOKING FOR HER PALE BUTT!
I might be tempted to beat that guy down myself.
ANNOYED

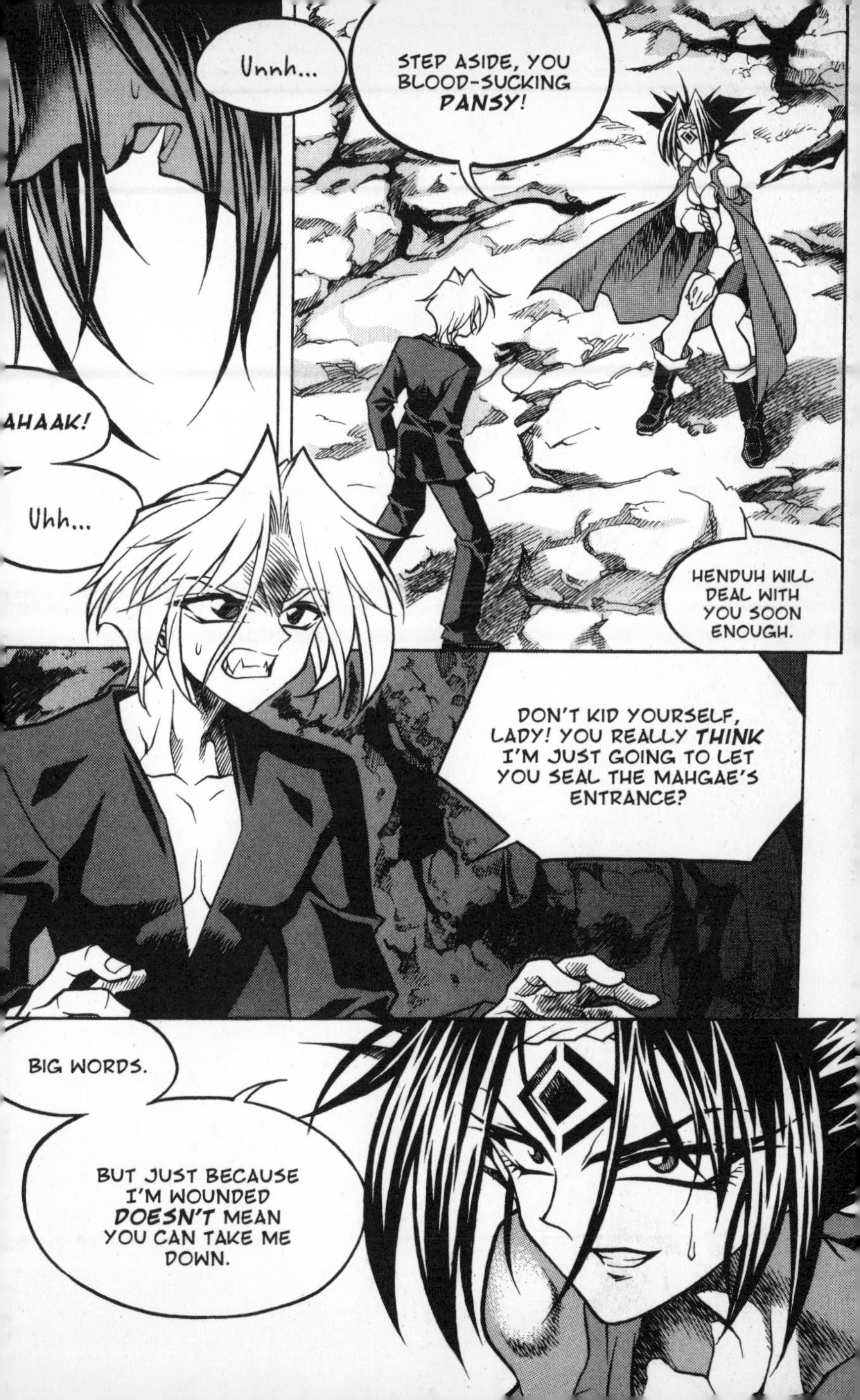
Unnh...
STEP ASIDE, YOU BLOOD-SUCKING PANSY!
AHAAK!
Uhh...
HENDUH WILL DEAL WITH YOU SOON ENOUGH.
DON'T KID YOURSELF, LADY! YOU REALLY THINK I'M JUST GOING TO LET YOU SEAL THE MAHGAE'S ENTRANCE?
BIG WORDS.
BUT JUST BECAUSE I'M WOUNDED DOESN'T MEAN YOU CAN TAKE ME DOWN.

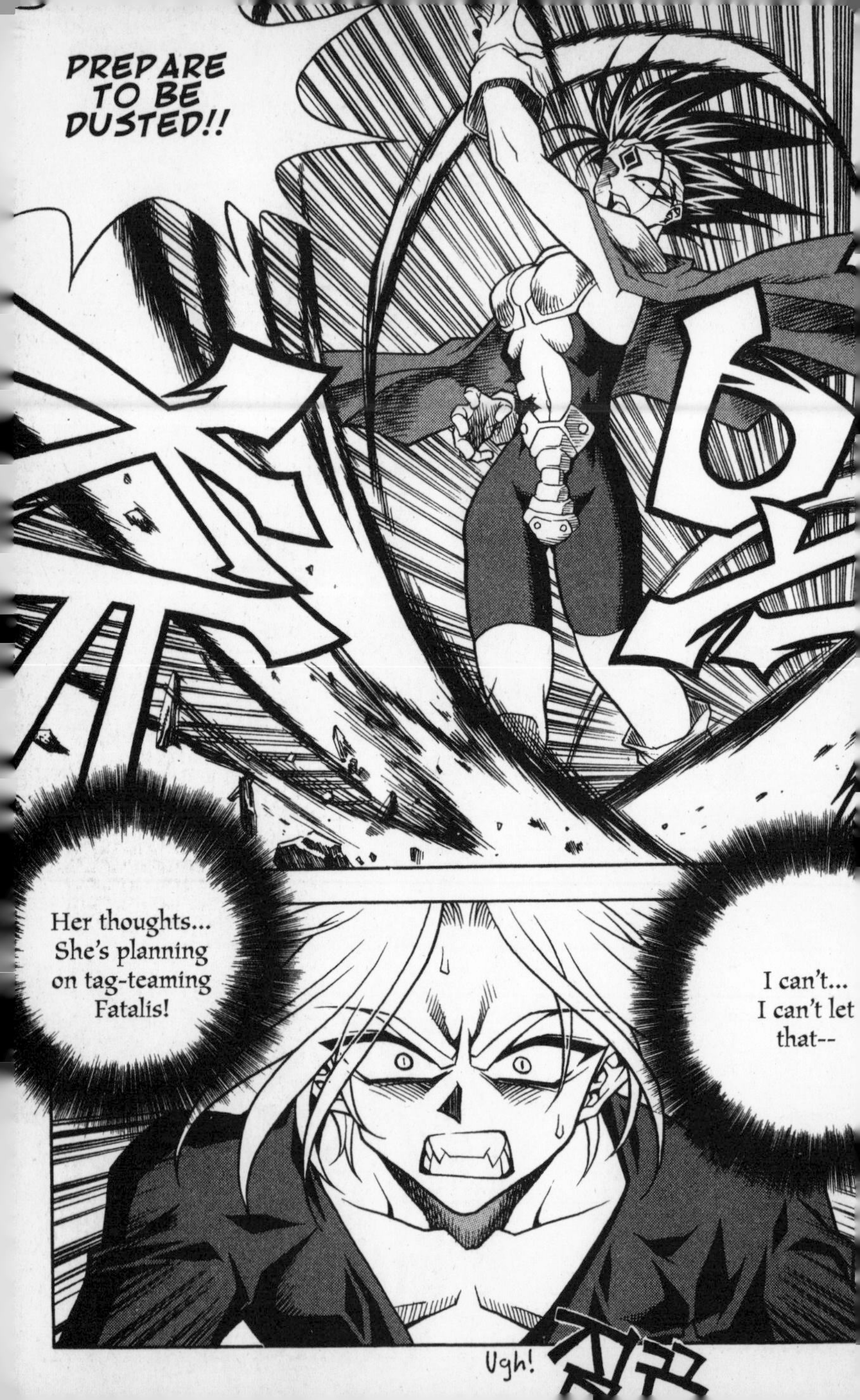
PREPARE TO BE DUSTED!!
Her thoughts... She's planning on tag-teaming Fatalis!
I can't... I can't let that--
Ugh!

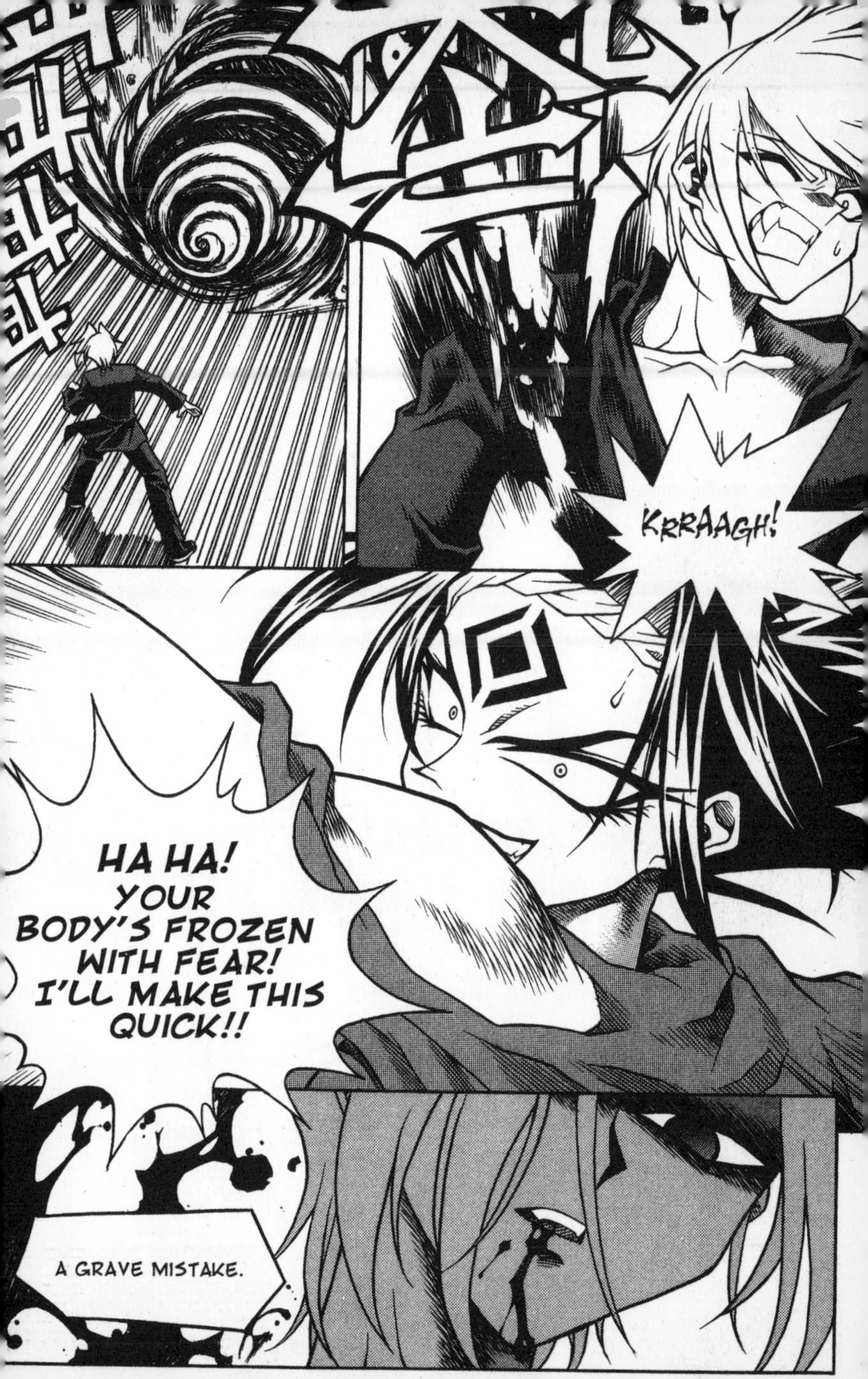
KRRAAGH!
HA HA! YOUR BODY'S FROZEN WITH FEAR! I'LL MAKE THIS QUICK!!
A GRAVE MISTAKE.

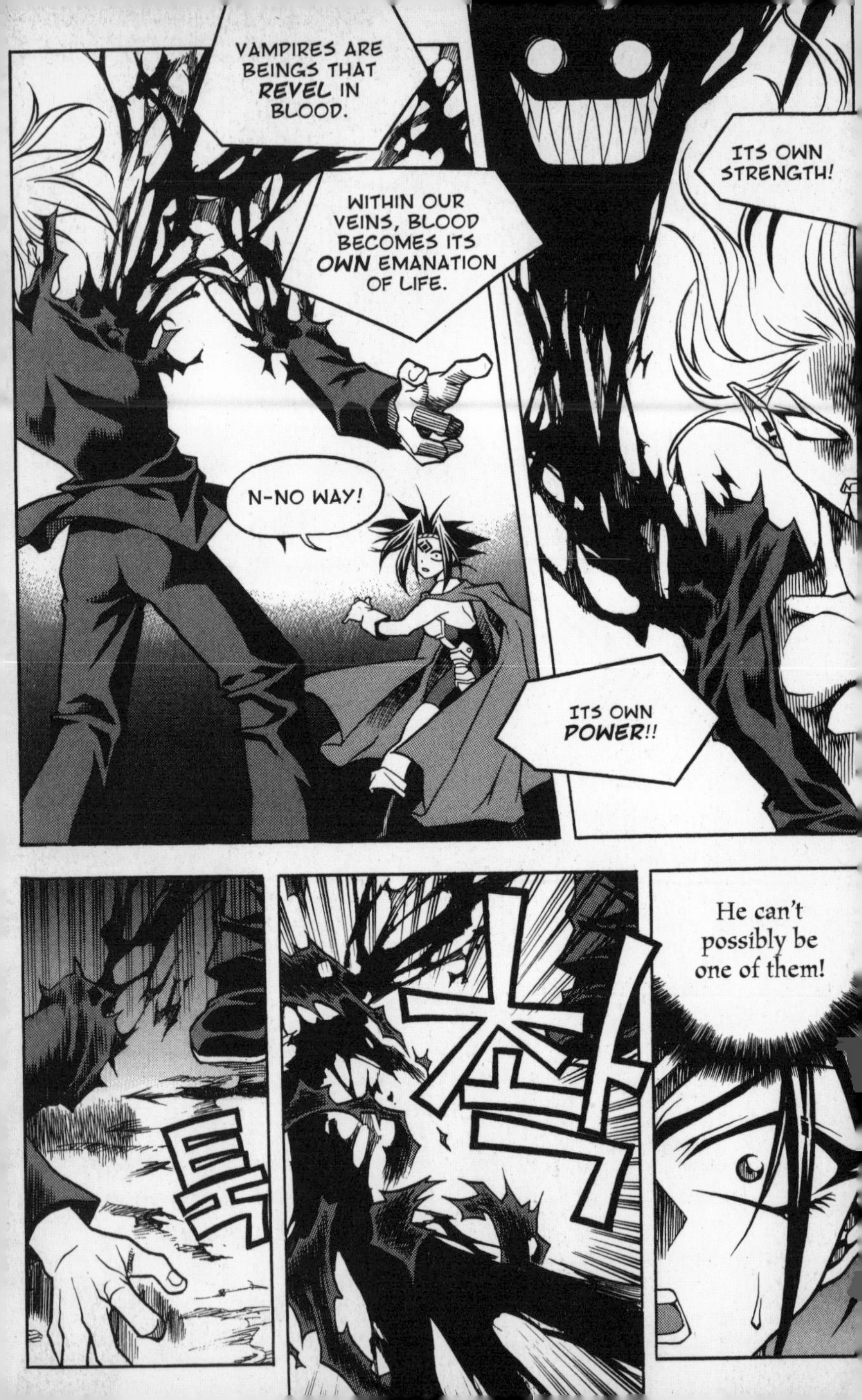
VAMPIRES ARE BEINGS THAT REVEL IN BLOOD.
WITHIN OUR VEINS, BLOOD BECOMES ITS OWN EMANATION OF LIFE.
N-NO WAY!
ITS OWN STRENGTH!
ITS OWN POWER!!
He can't possibly be one of them!

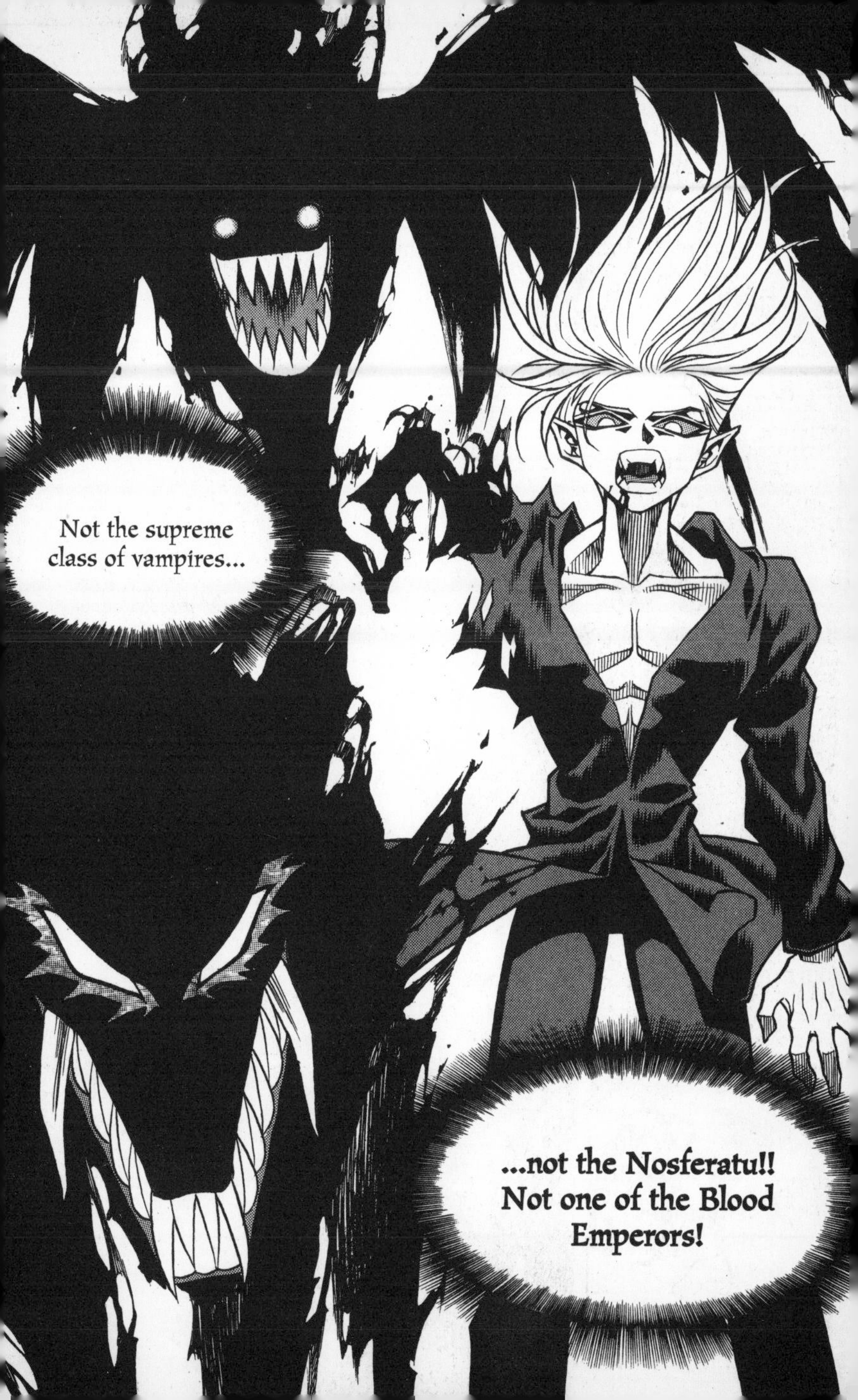
Not the supreme class of vampires...
...not the Nosferatu!! Not one of the Blood Emperors!

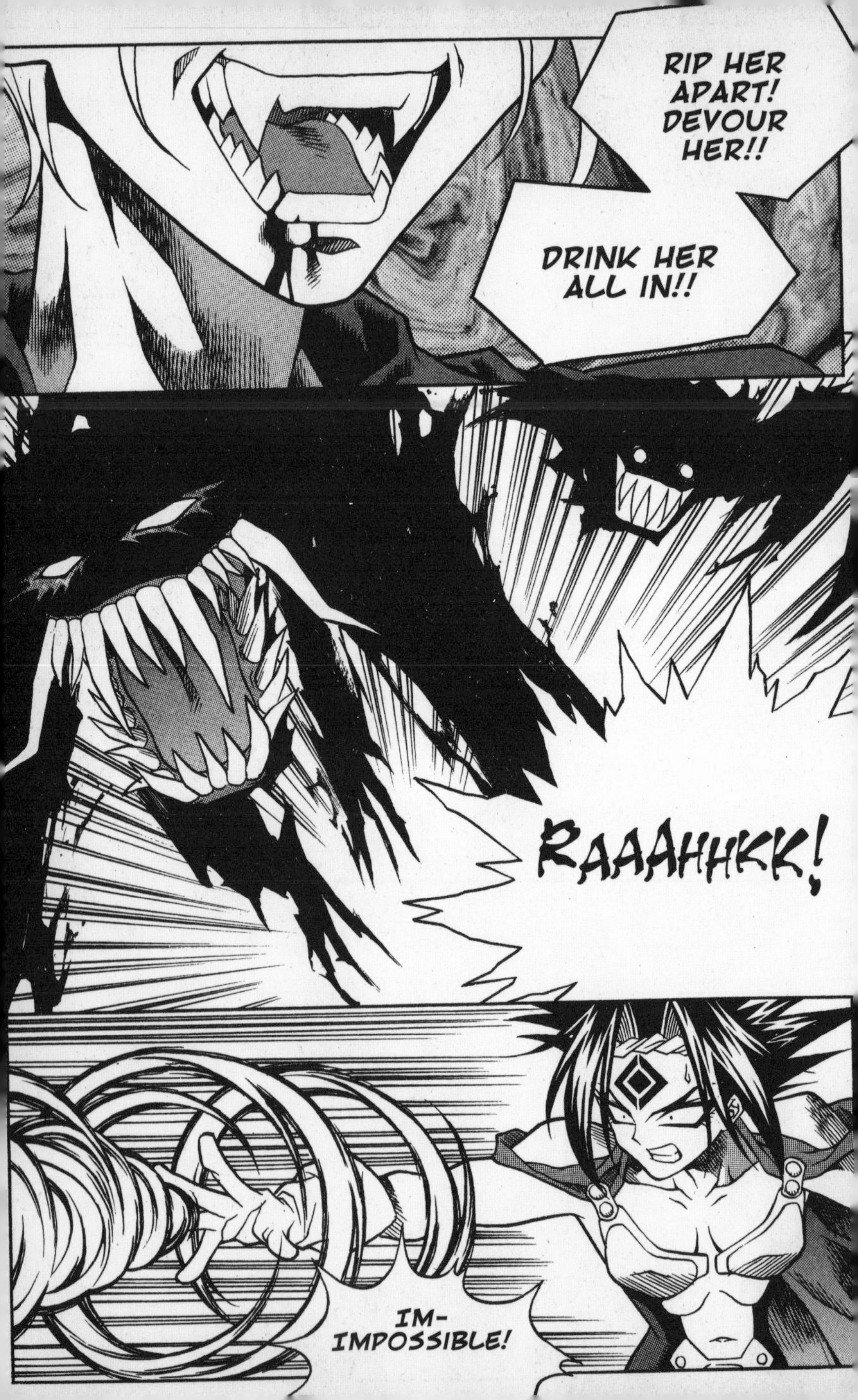
RIP HER APART! DEVOUR HER!!
DRINK HER ALL IN!!
RAAAHHKK!
IM-IMPOSSIBLE!

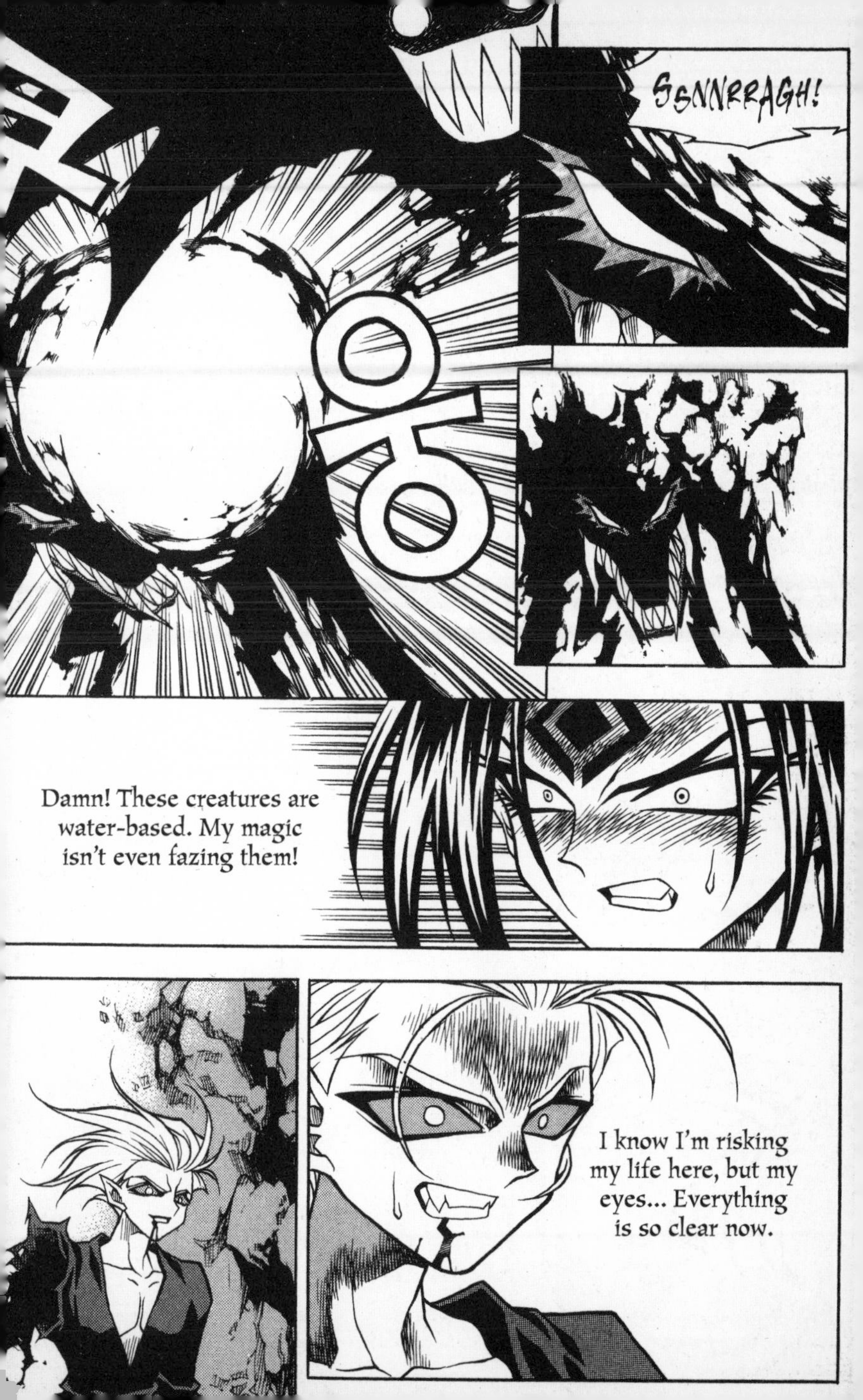
SSNNRRAGH!
Damn! These creatures are water-based. My magic isn't even fazing them!
I know I'm risking my life here, but my eyes... Everything is so clear now.

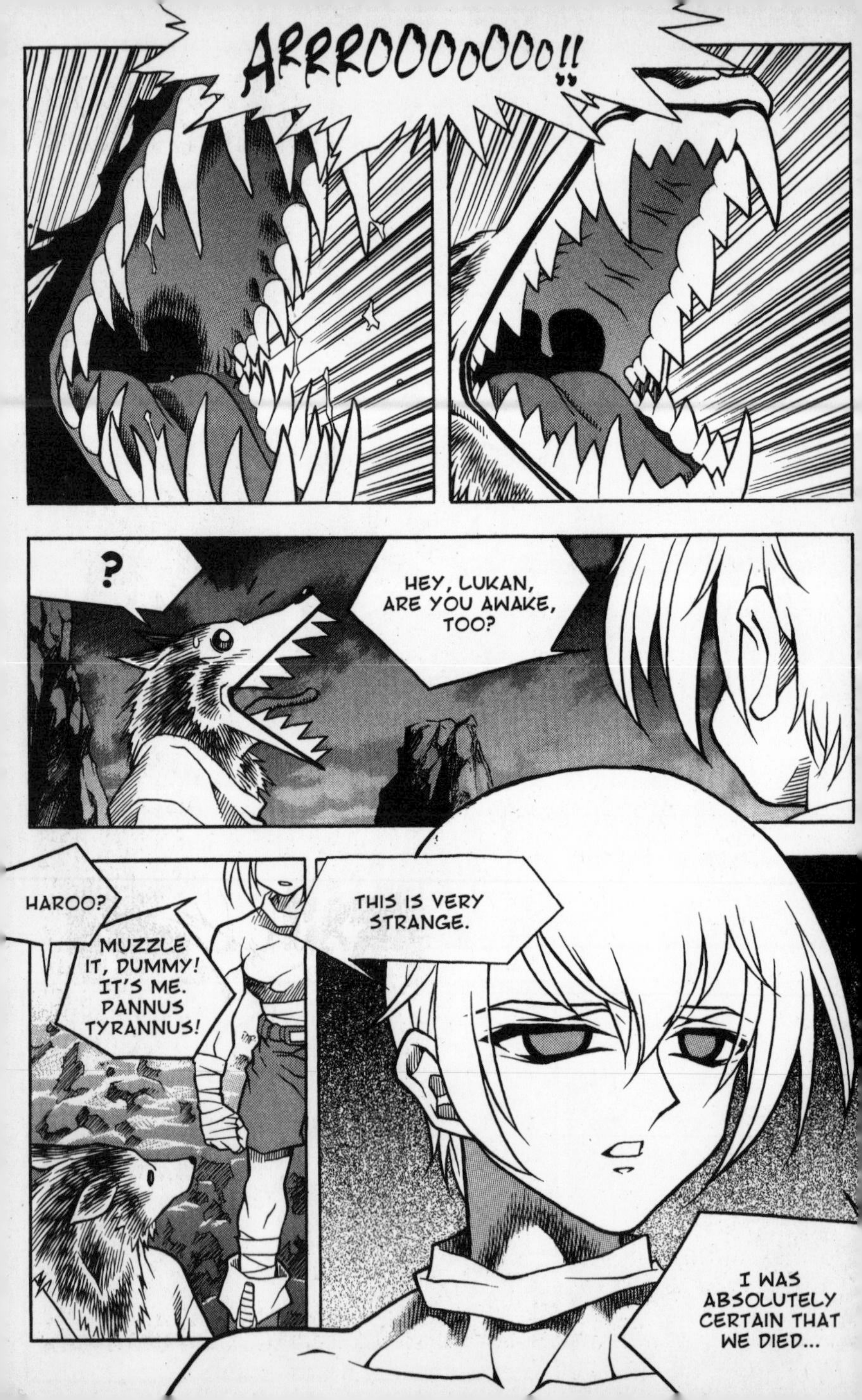
ARRROOOOOOO!!
?
HEY, LUKAN, ARE YOU AWAKE, TOO?
HAROO?
MUZZLE IT, DUMMY! IT'S ME. PANNUS TYRANNUS!
THIS IS VERY STRANGE.
I WAS ABSOLUTELY CERTAIN THAT WE DIED...

Quest 13

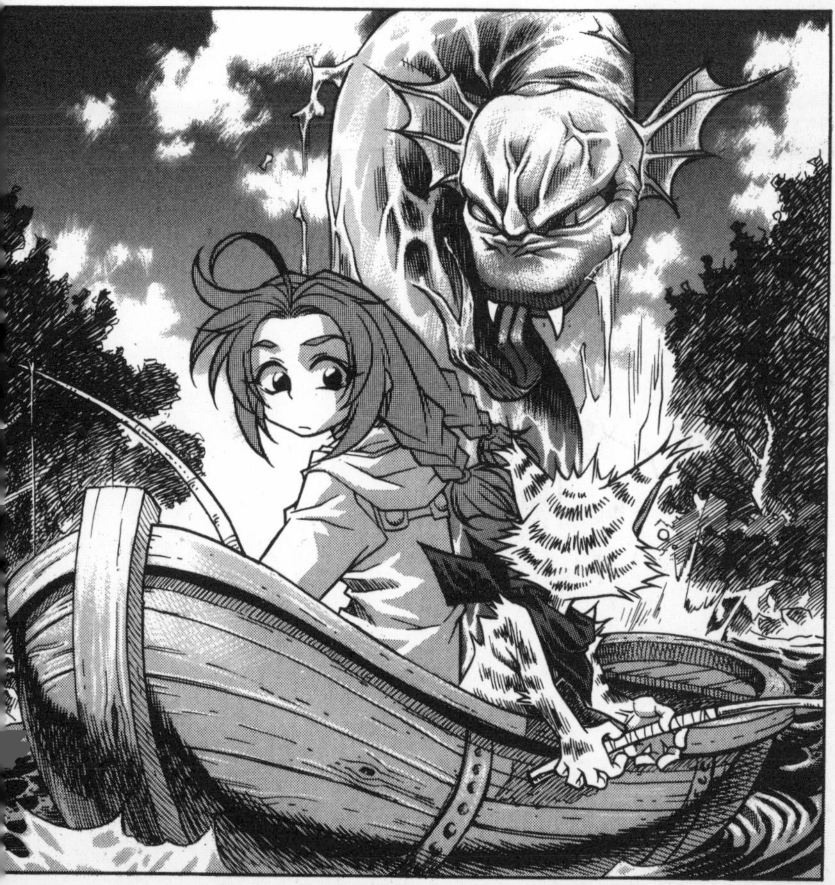

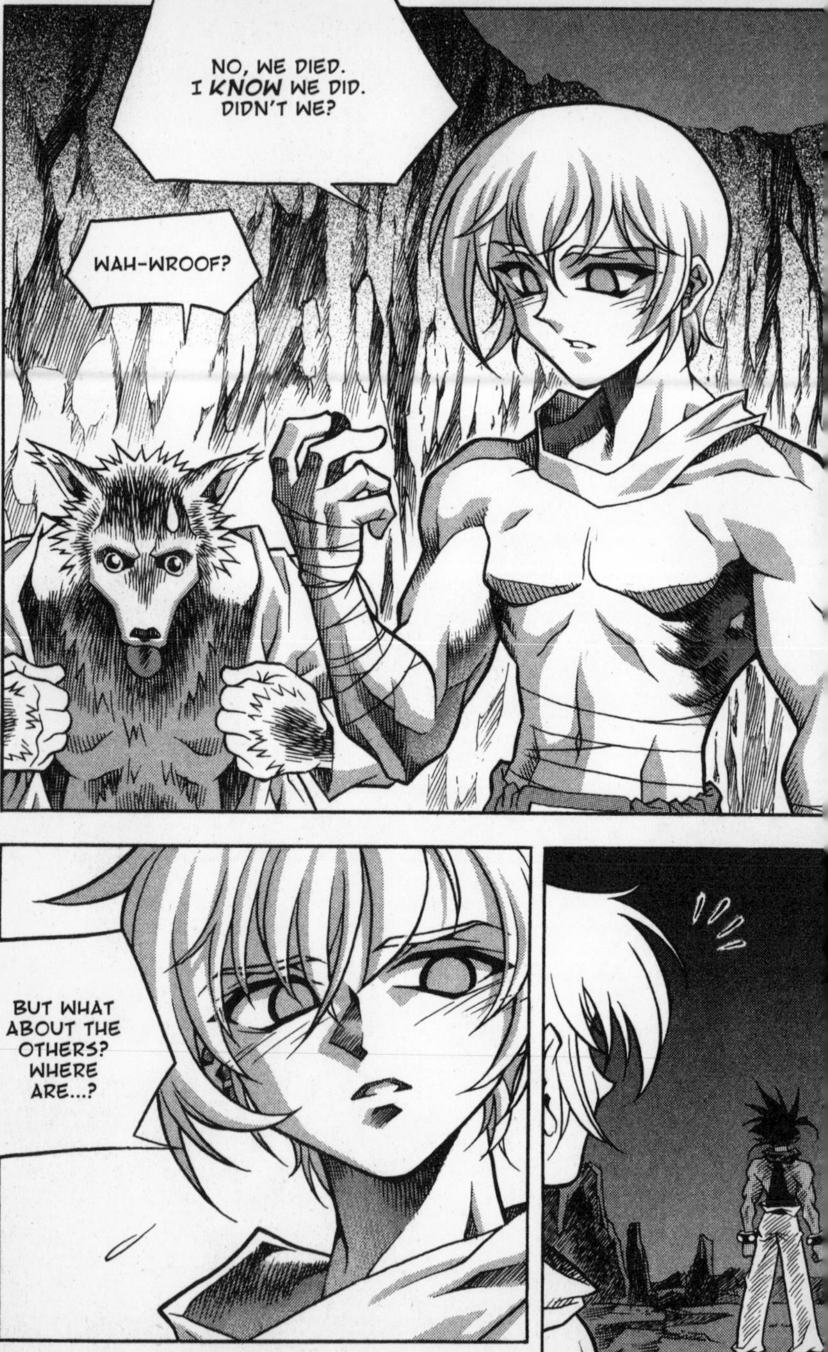
NO, WE DIED. I KNOW WE DID. DIDN'T WE?
WAH-WROOF?
BUT WHAT ABOUT THE OTHERS? WHERE ARE...?

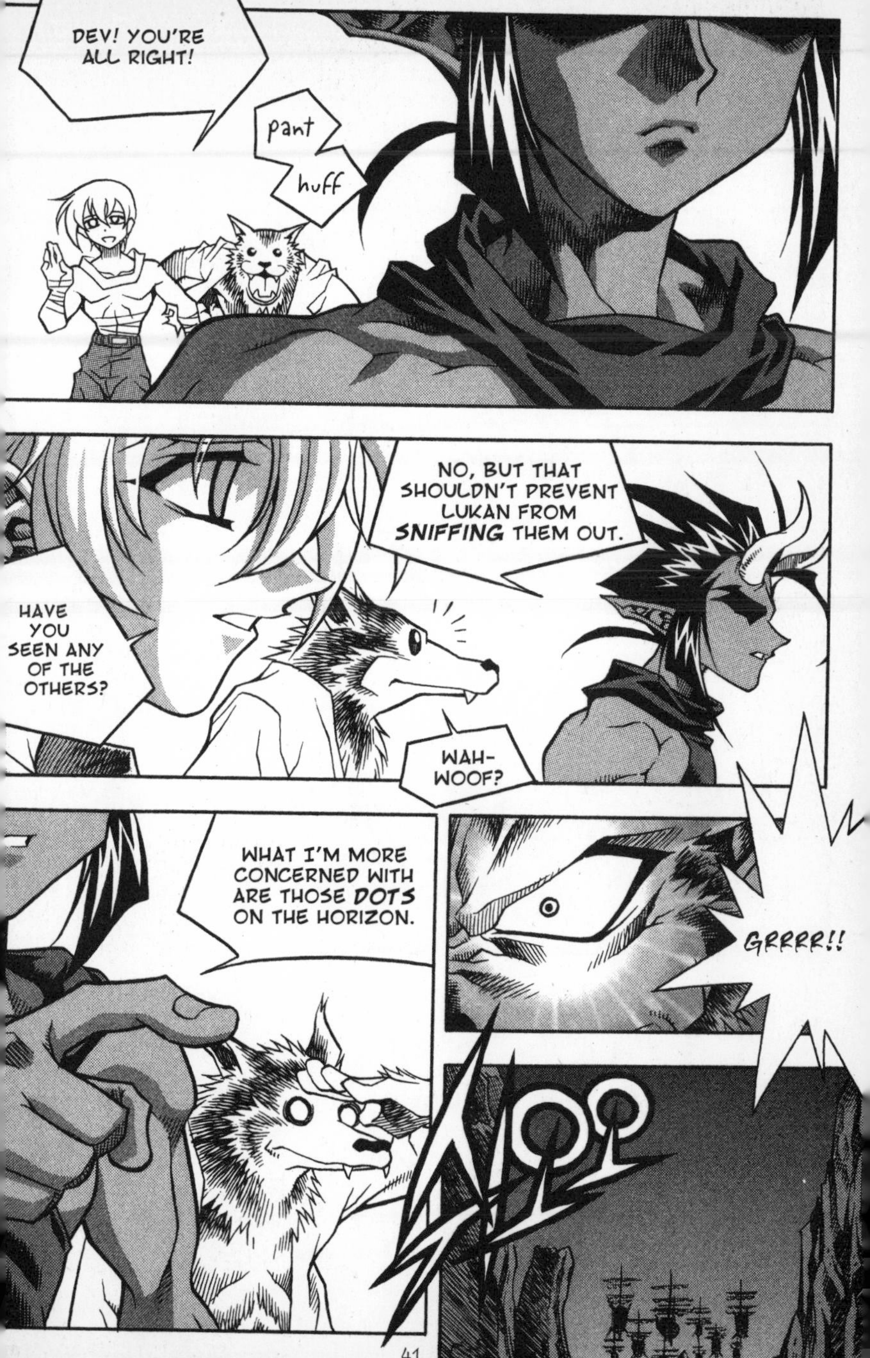
DEV! YOU'RE ALL RIGHT!
pant
huff
HAVE YOU SEEN ANY OF THE OTHERS?
NO, BUT THAT SHOULDN'T PREVENT LUKAN FROM SNIFFING THEM OUT.
WAH-WOOF?
WHAT I'M MORE CONCERNED WITH ARE THOSE DOTS ON THE HORIZON.
GRRRR!!
AROO

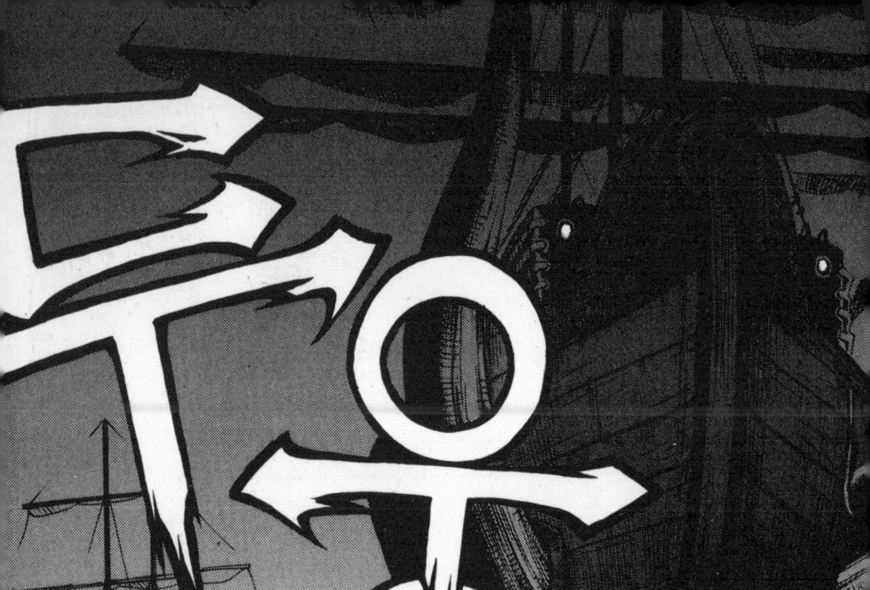

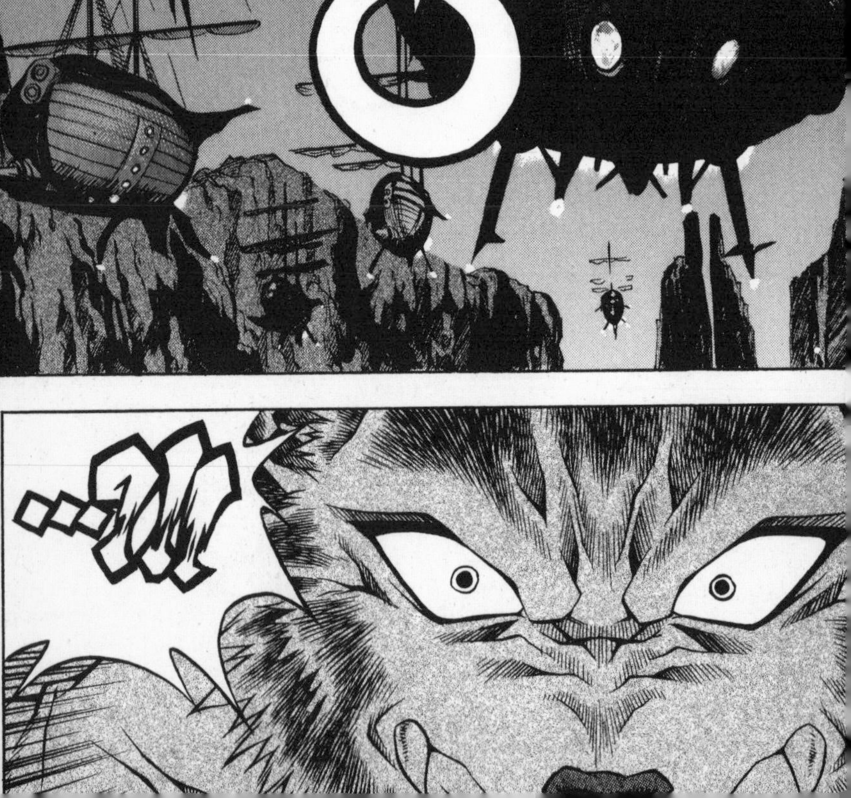
...?!

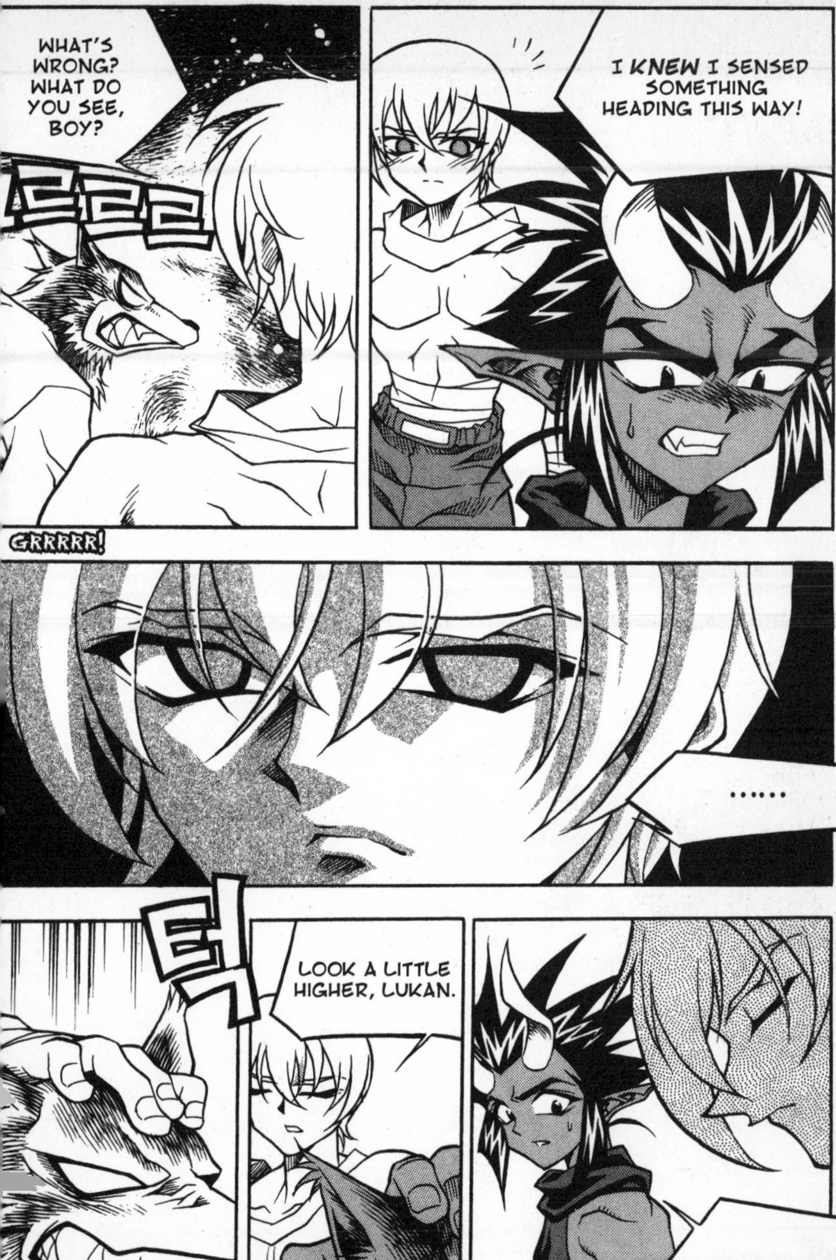
WHAT'S WRONG? WHAT DO YOU SEE, BOY?
GRRR
I KNEW I SENSED SOMETHING HEADING THIS WAY!
GRRRRR!
......
E!
LOOK A LITTLE HIGHER, LUKAN.
PANNUS, WHA-WHAT ARE YOU DOING?

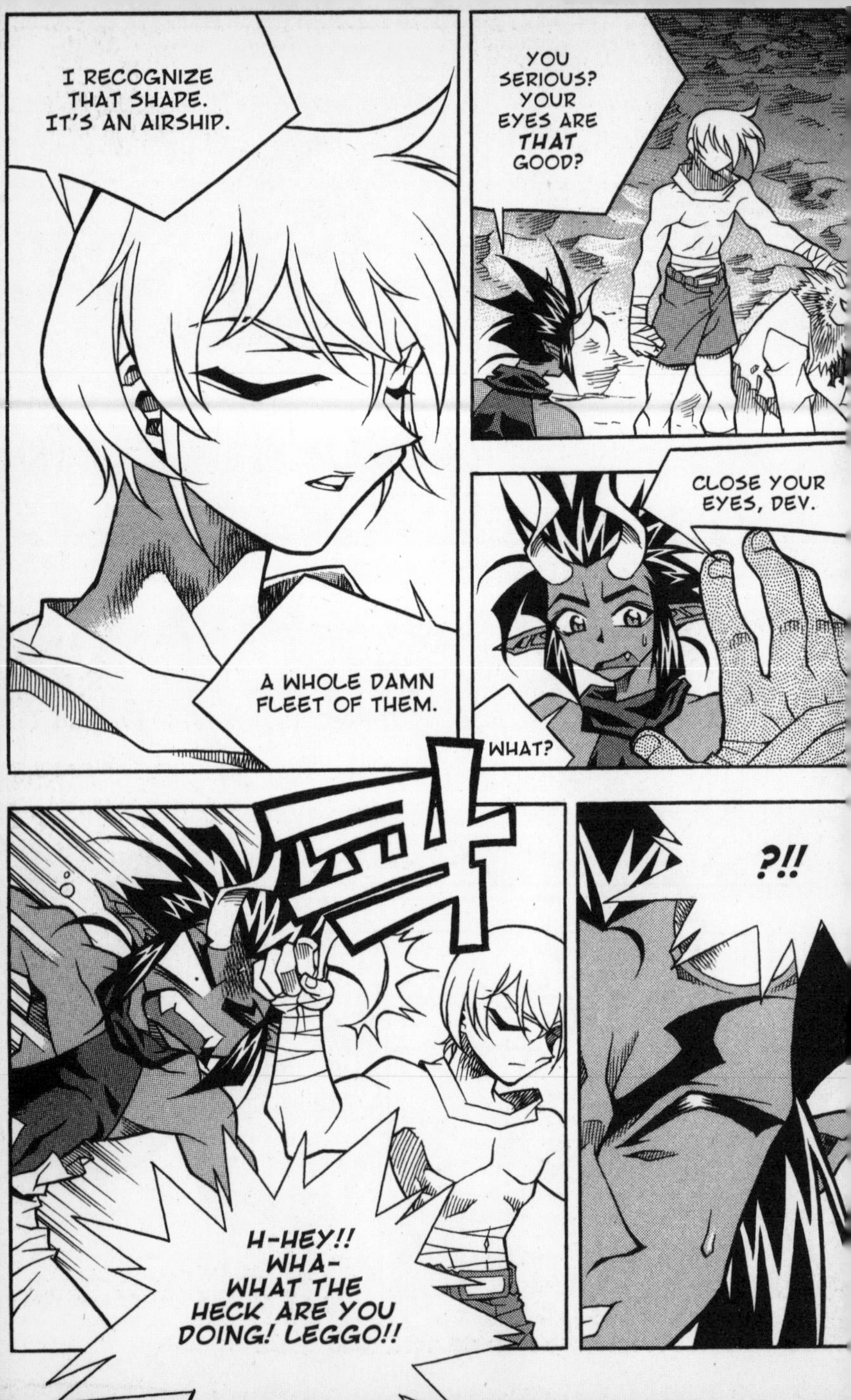
I RECOGNIZE THAT SHAPE. IT'S AN AIRSHIP.
A WHOLE DAMN FLEET OF THEM.
YOU SERIOUS? YOUR EYES ARE THAT GOOD?
CLOSE YOUR EYES, DEV.
WHAT?
H-HEY!! WHA- WHAT THE HECK ARE YOU DOING! LEGGO!!
?!!

AH, I SEE NOW.

SO IT *IS* AN AIRSHIP.

LOOKS LIKE **MORE** HUMANS ARE ON THE WAY.

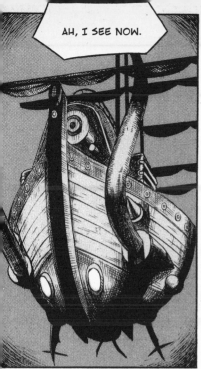

FOCUS IN ON THE BOW, LUKAN. CAN YOU MAKE OUT THAT FIGURE?

WROOF!

WAIT... THAT MARK ON HIS FOREHEAD...

I'D SAY CLASSES JUST GOT CANCELLED...*AGAIN*.

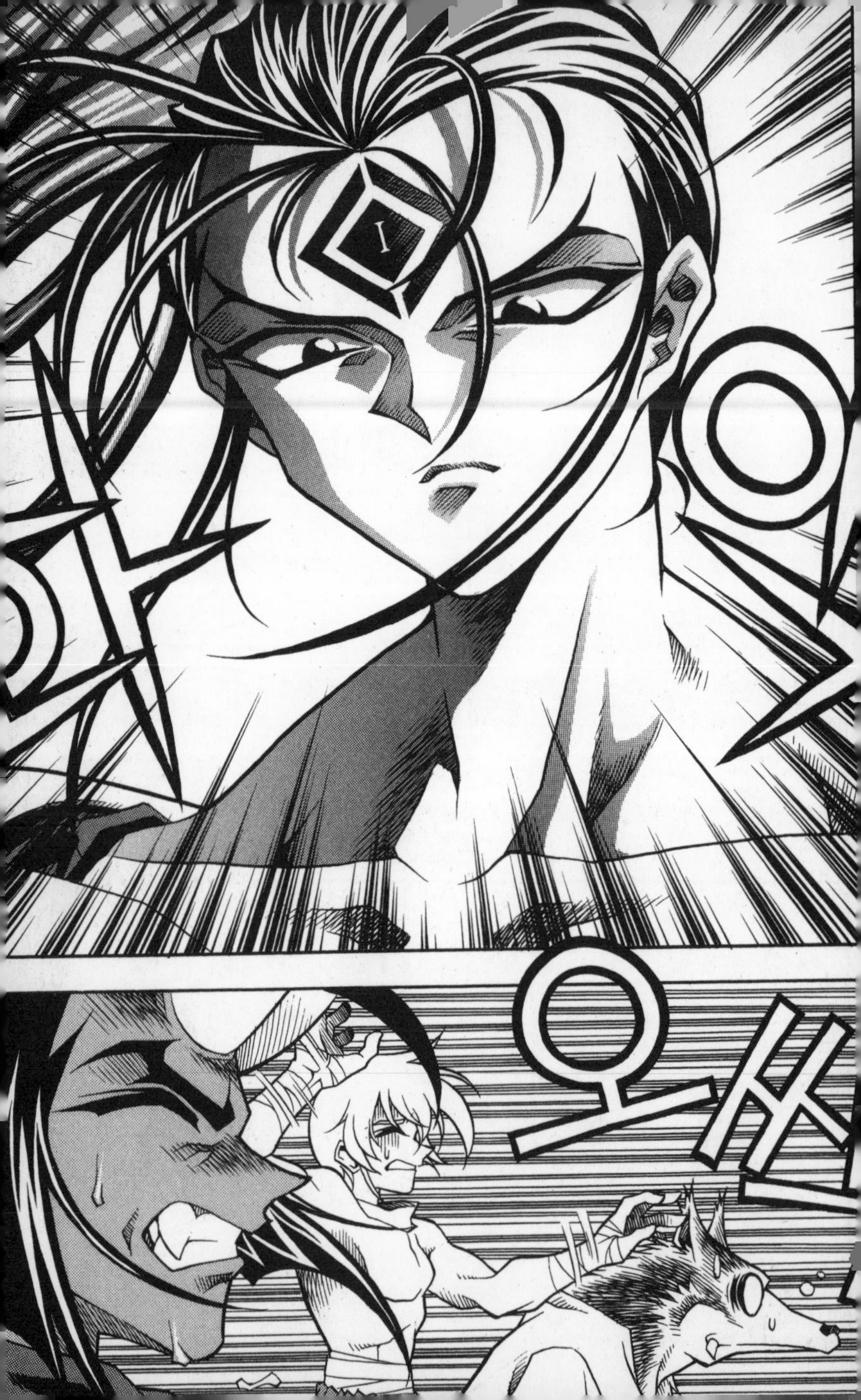

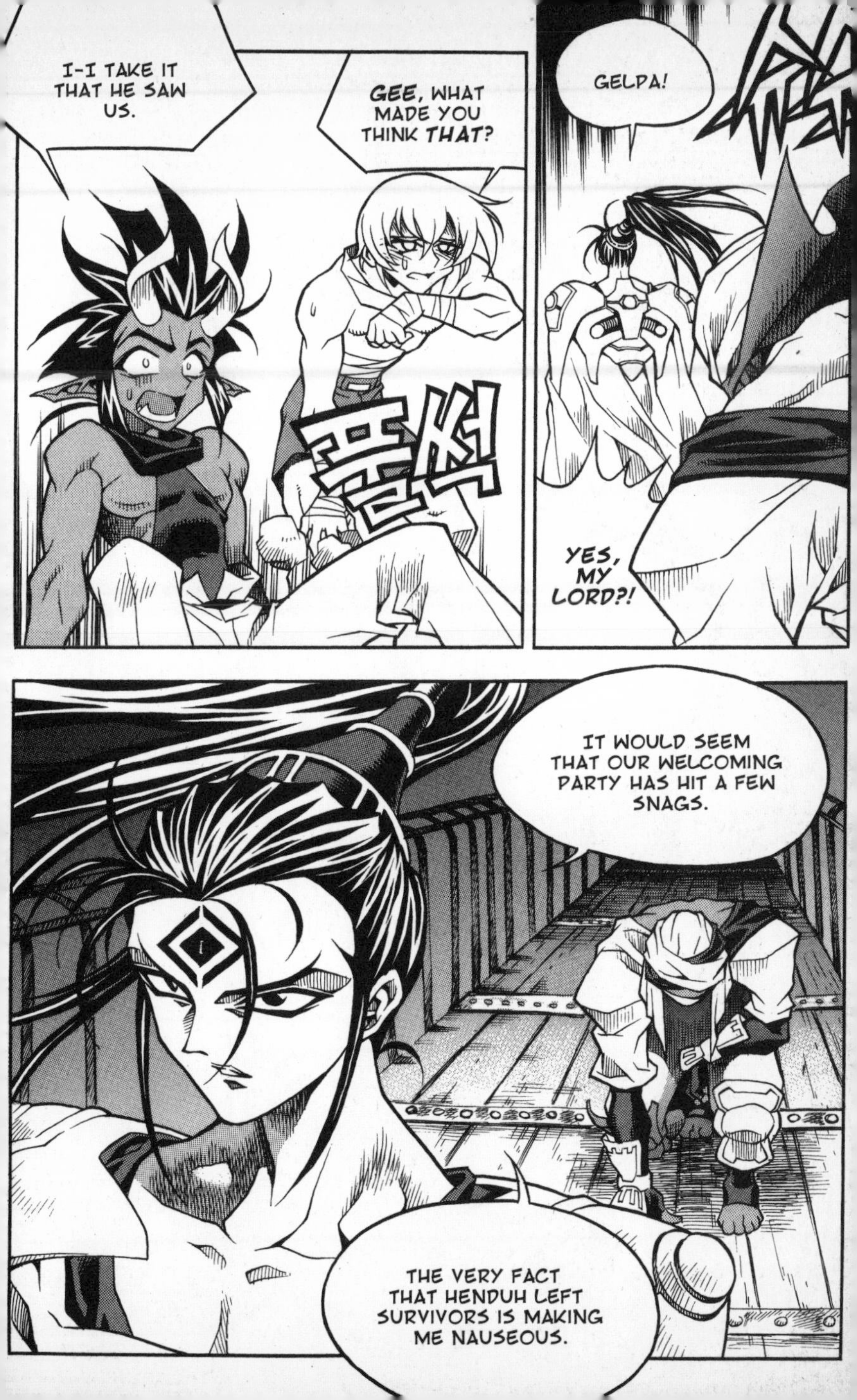
I-I TAKE IT THAT HE SAW US.
GEE, WHAT MADE YOU THINK THAT?
GELDA!
YES, MY LORD?!
IT WOULD SEEM THAT OUR WELCOMING PARTY HAS HIT A FEW SNAGS.
THE VERY FACT THAT HENDUH LEFT SURVIVORS IS MAKING ME NAUSEOUS.

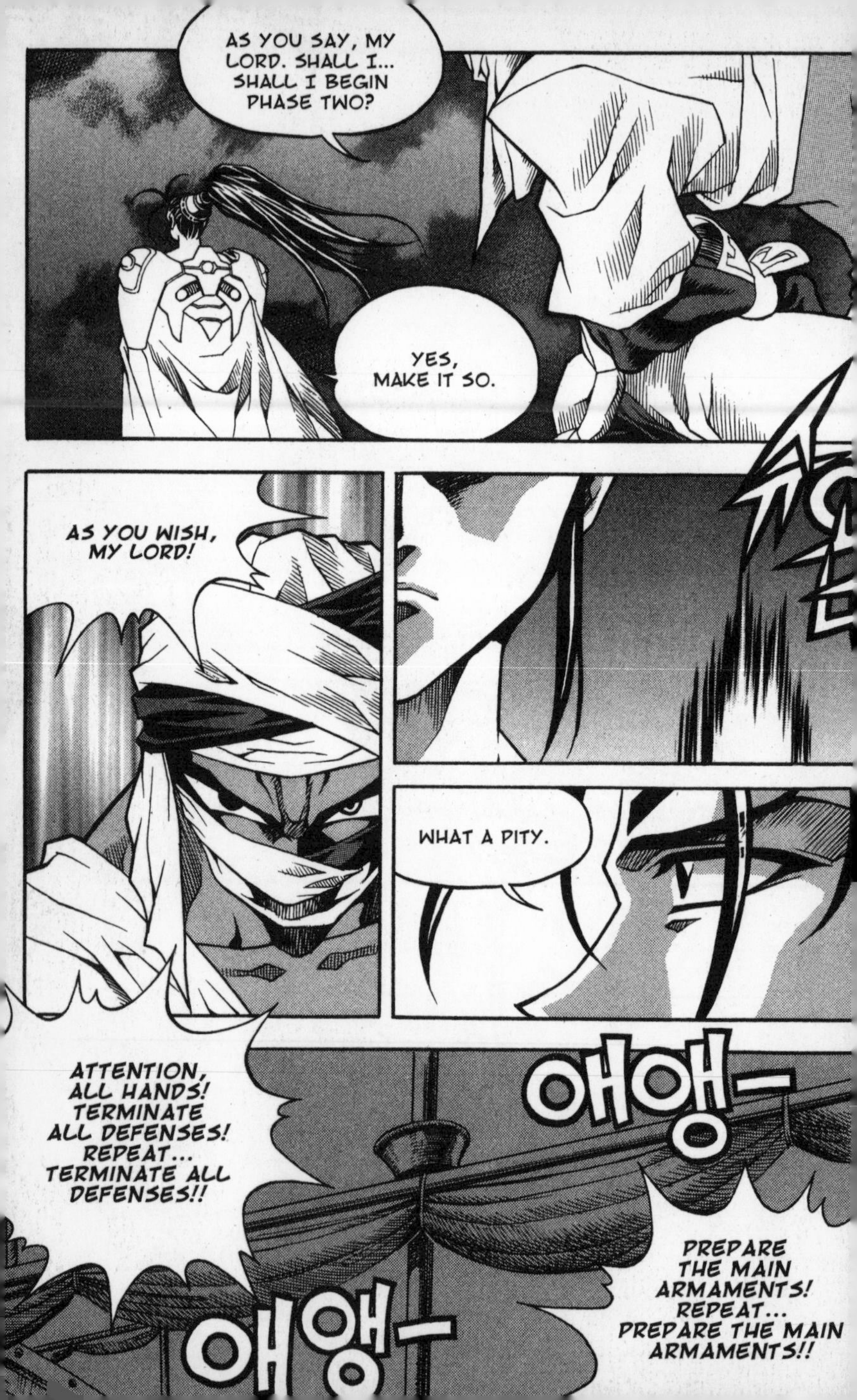
AS YOU SAY, MY LORD. SHALL I... SHALL I BEGIN PHASE TWO?
YES, MAKE IT SO.
AS YOU WISH, MY LORD!
WHAT A PITY.
ATTENTION, ALL HANDS! TERMINATE ALL DEFENSES! REPEAT... TERMINATE ALL DEFENSES!!
OHOH-
PREPARE THE MAIN ARMAMENTS! REPEAT... PREPARE THE MAIN ARMAMENTS!!
OHOH-

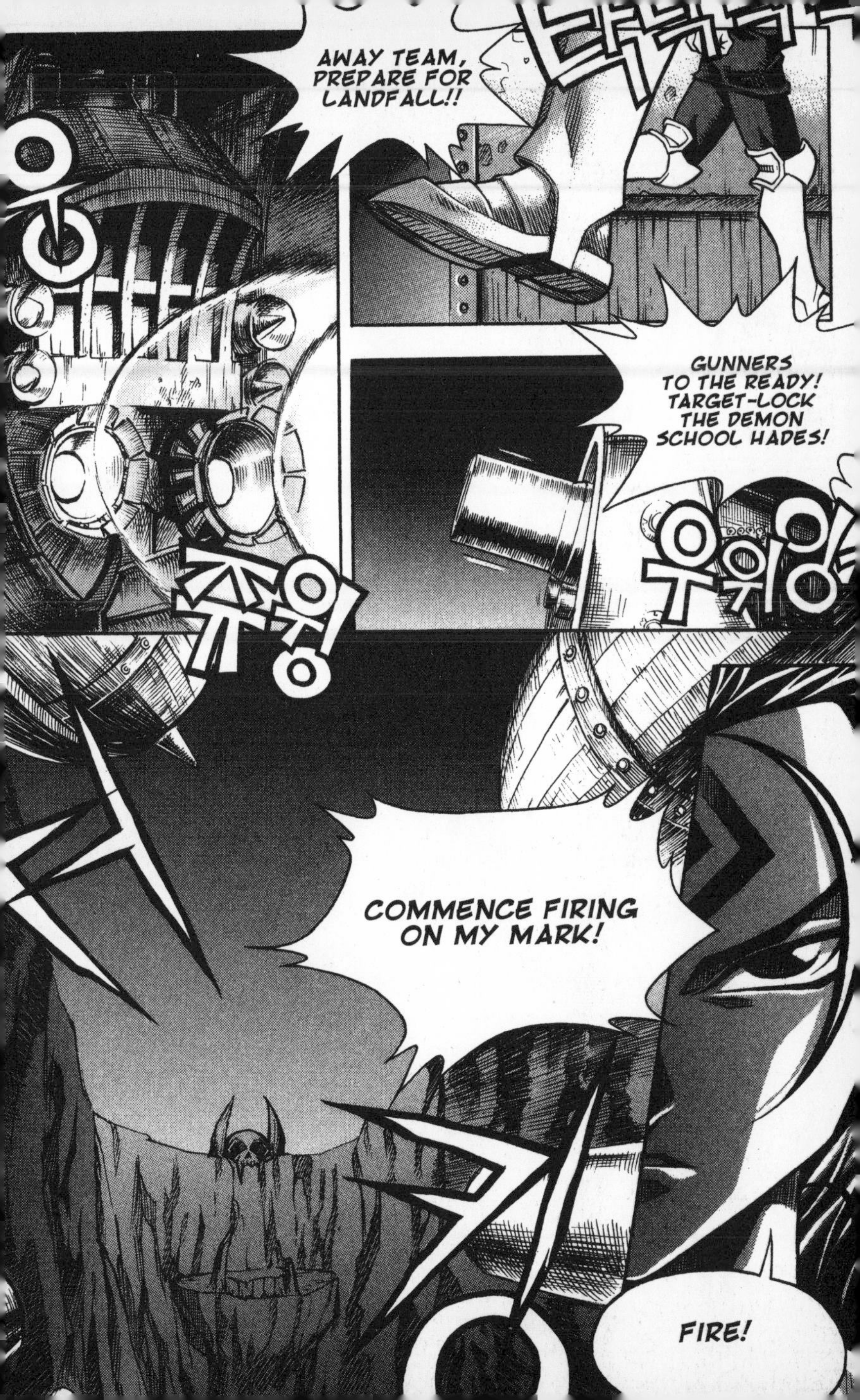
AWAY TEAM, PREPARE FOR LANDFALL!!
GUNNERS TO THE READY! TARGET-LOCK THE DEMON SCHOOL HADES!
COMMENCE FIRING ON MY MARK!
FIRE!

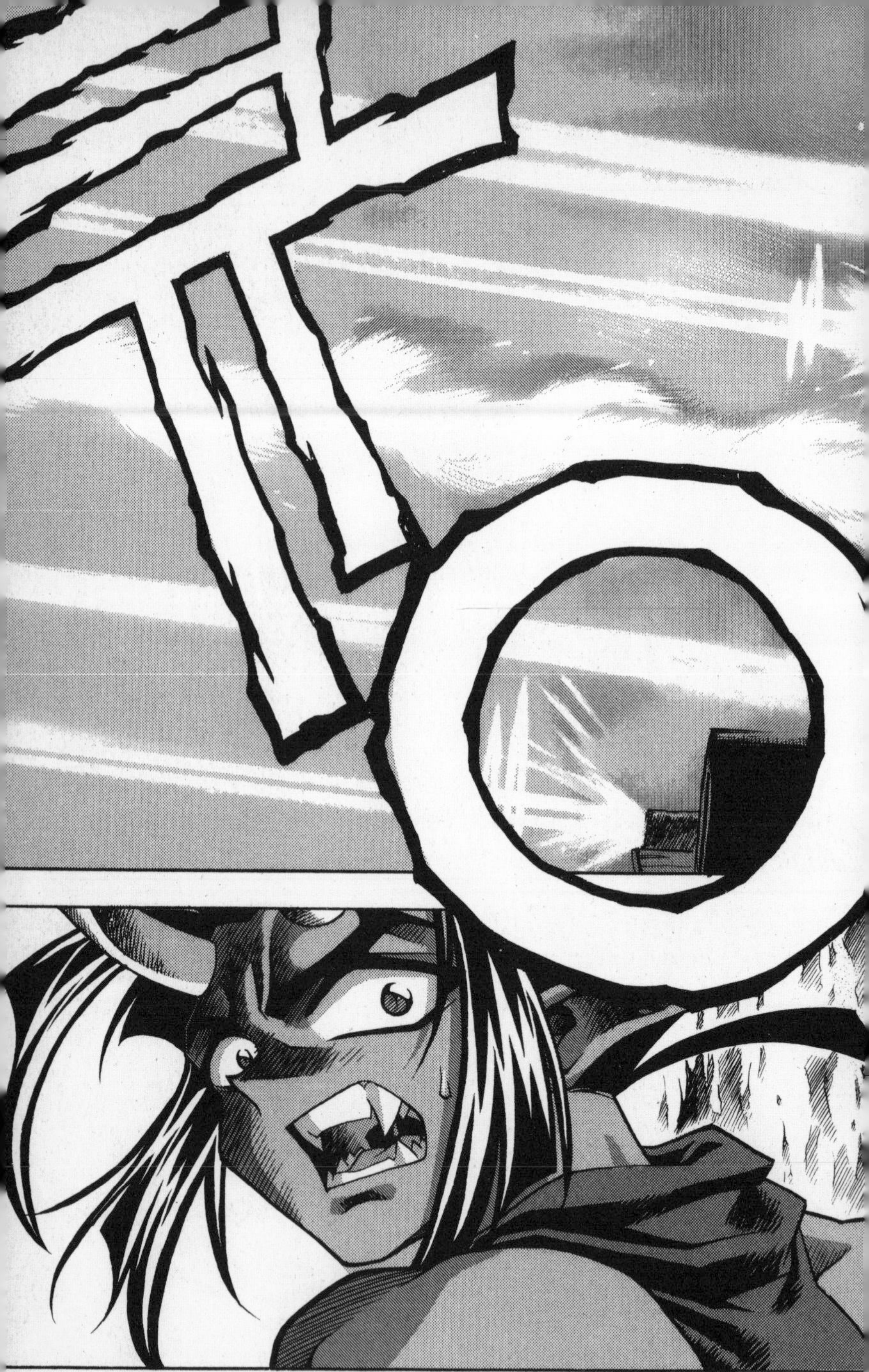

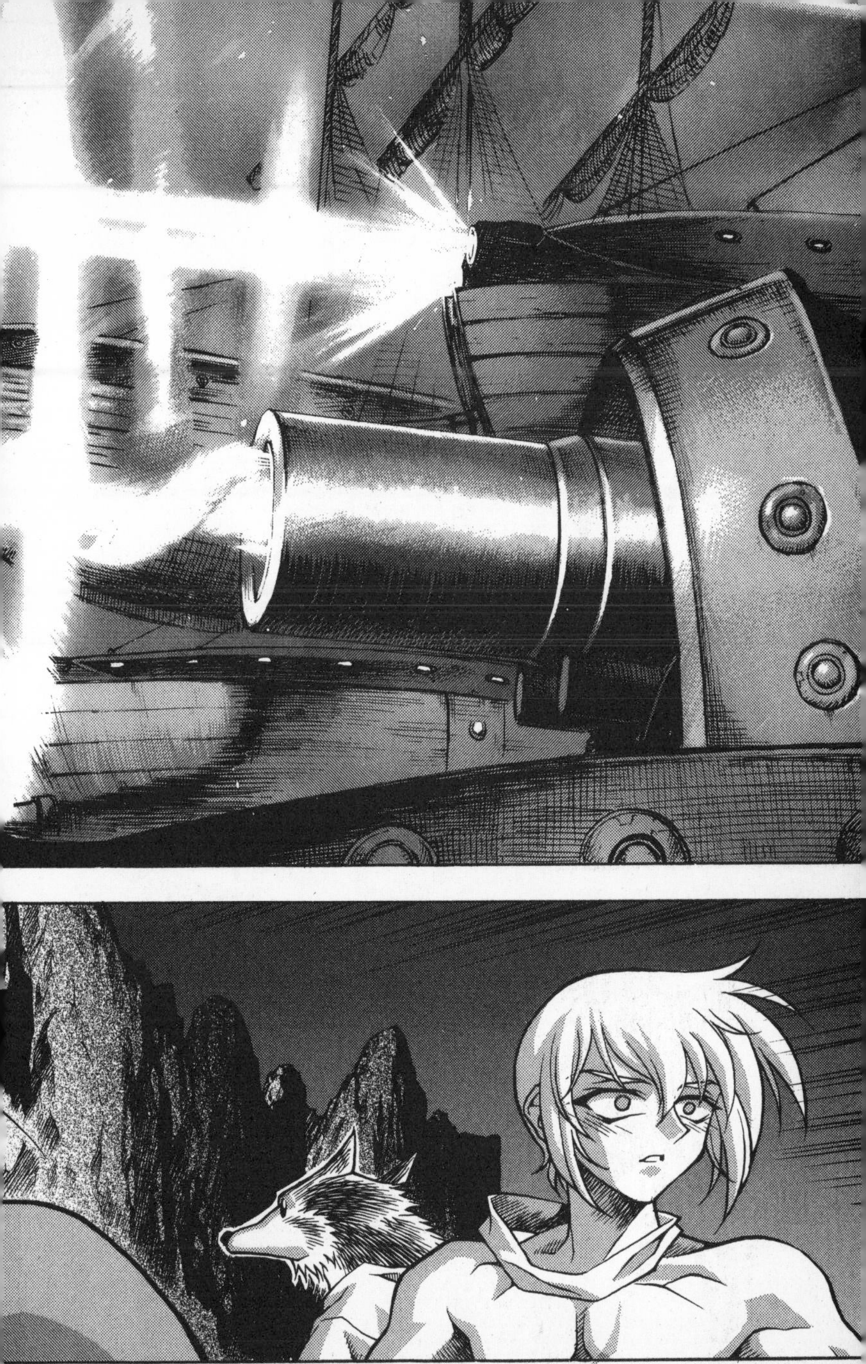

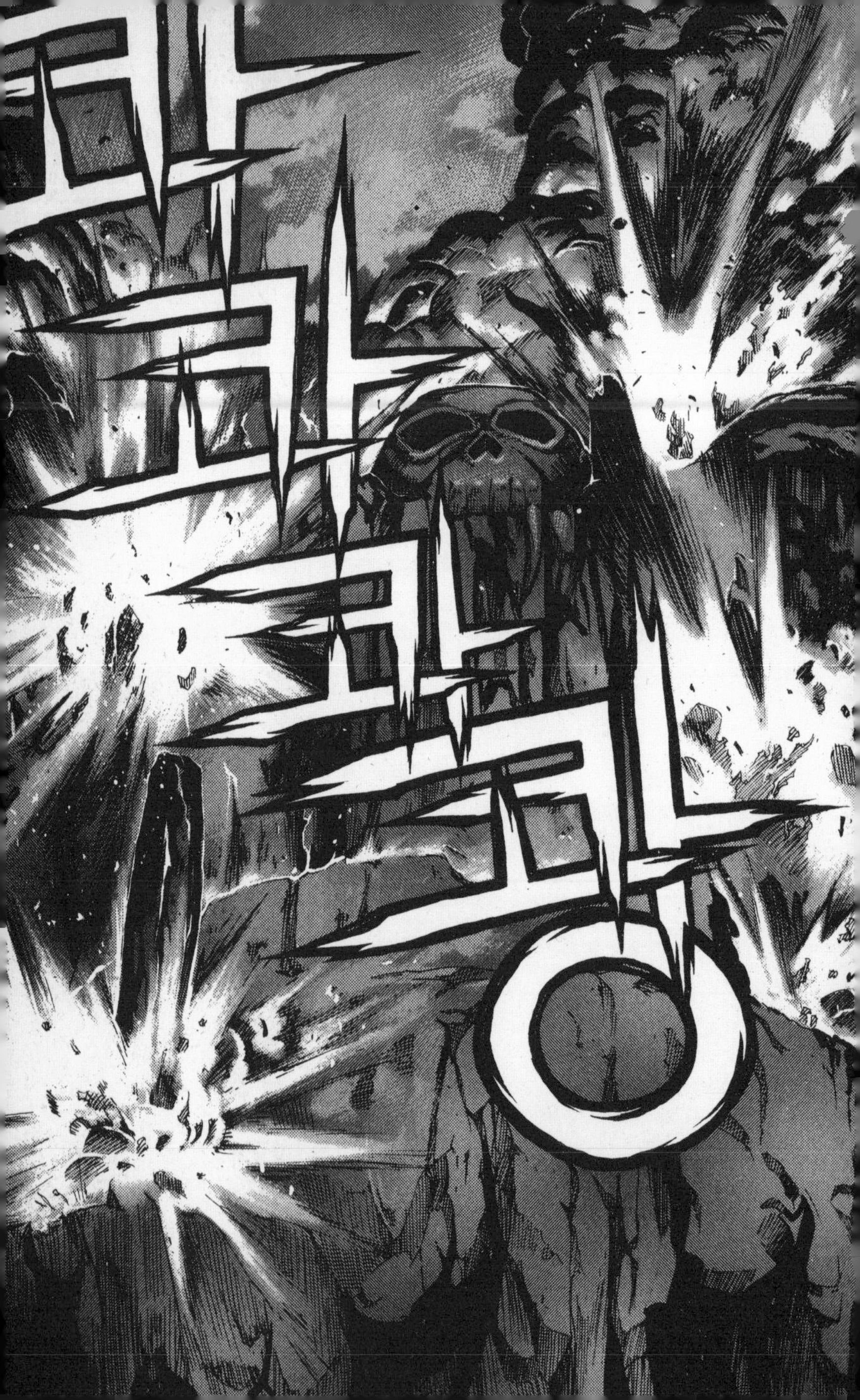

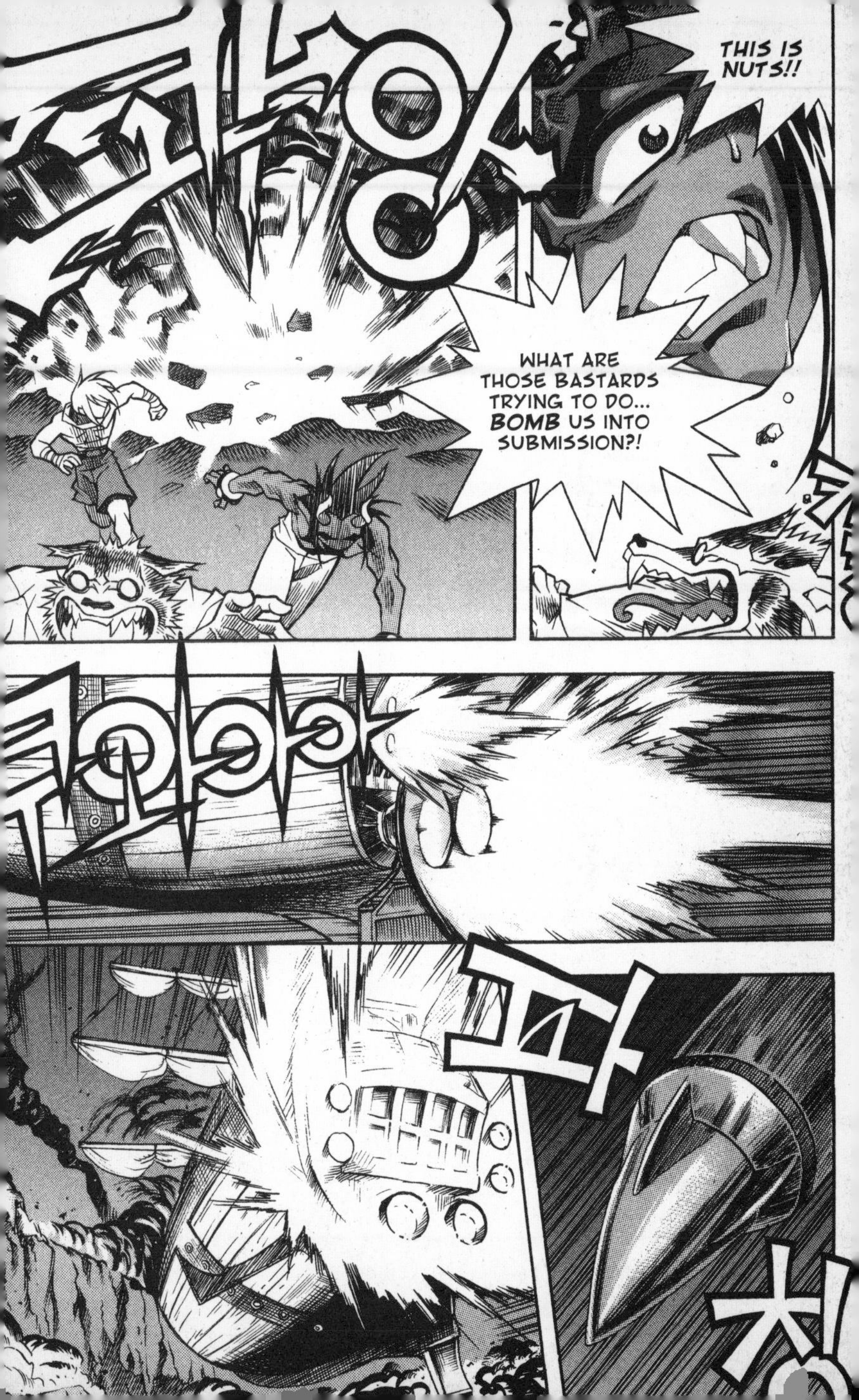

WHAT ARE THOSE BASTARDS TRYING TO DO... **BOMB** US INTO SUBMISSION?!
THIS IS NUTS!!

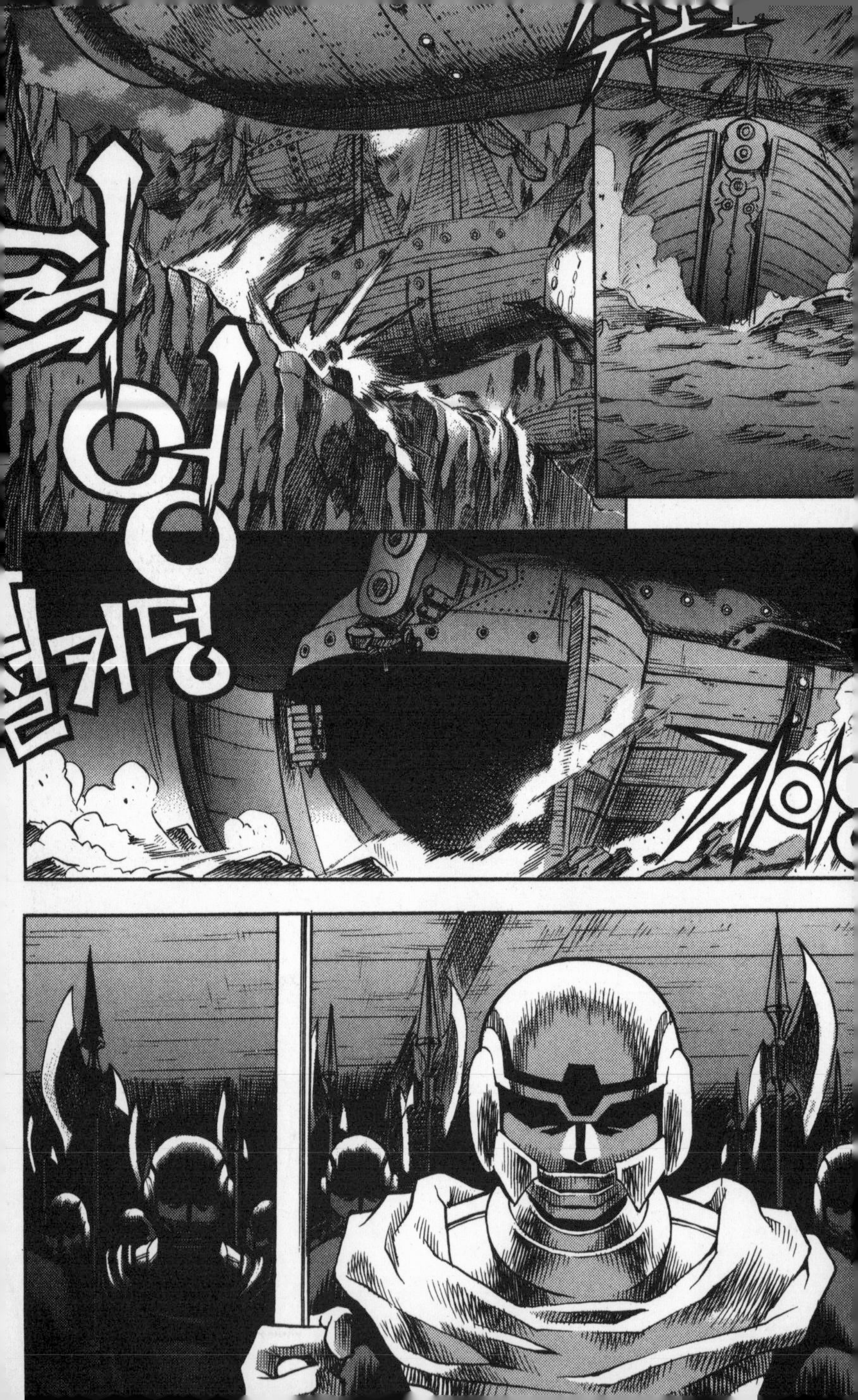
철커덩

Quest 14

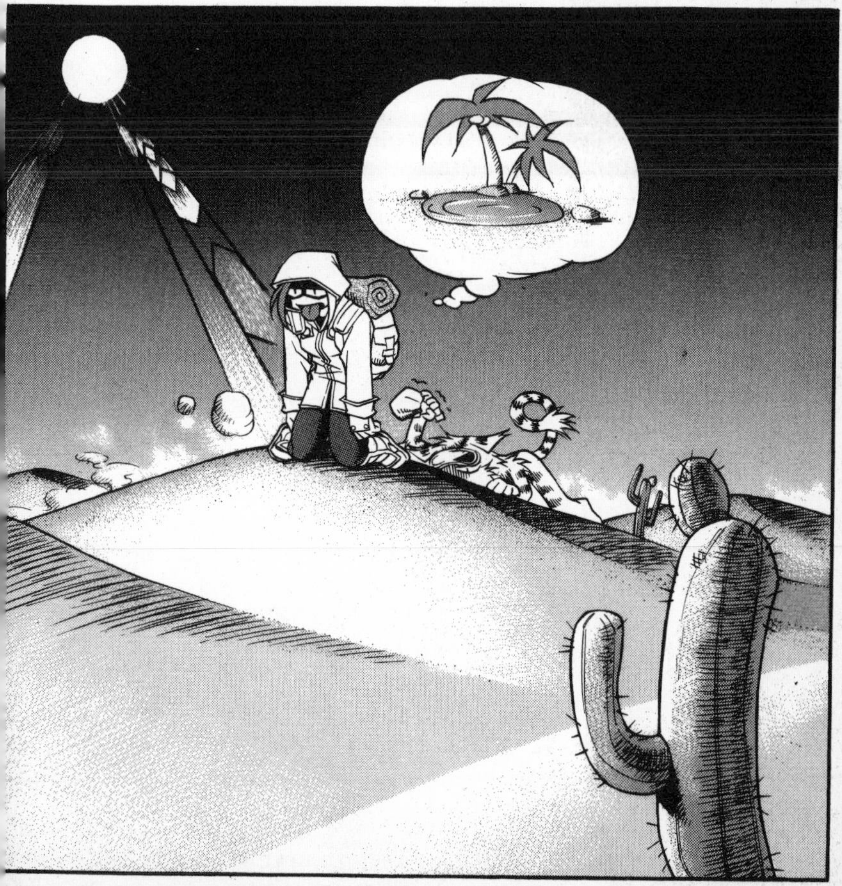

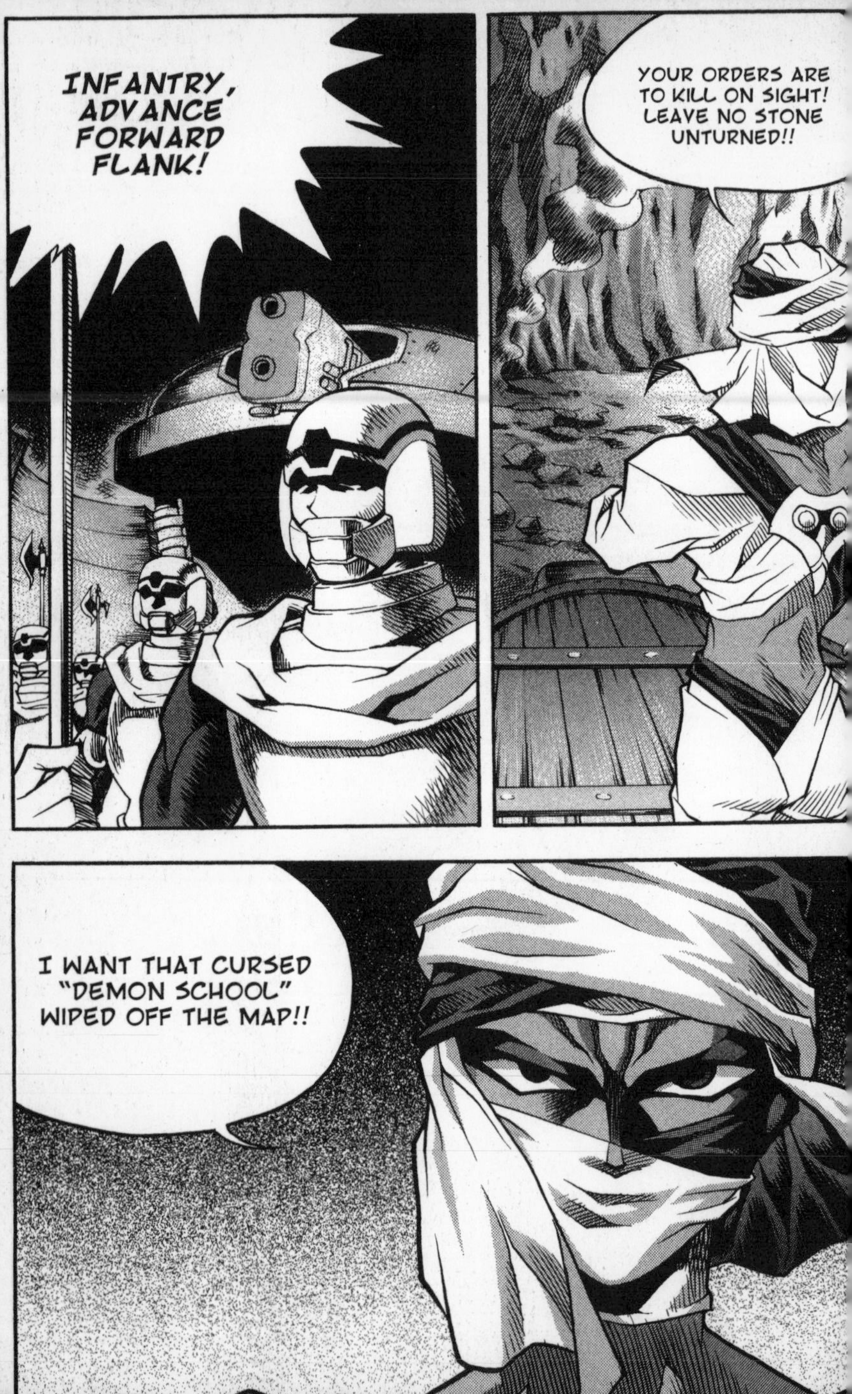
INFANTRY, ADVANCE FORWARD FLANK!
YOUR ORDERS ARE TO KILL ON SIGHT! LEAVE NO STONE UNTURNED!!
I WANT THAT CURSED "DEMON SCHOOL" WIPED OFF THE MAP!!

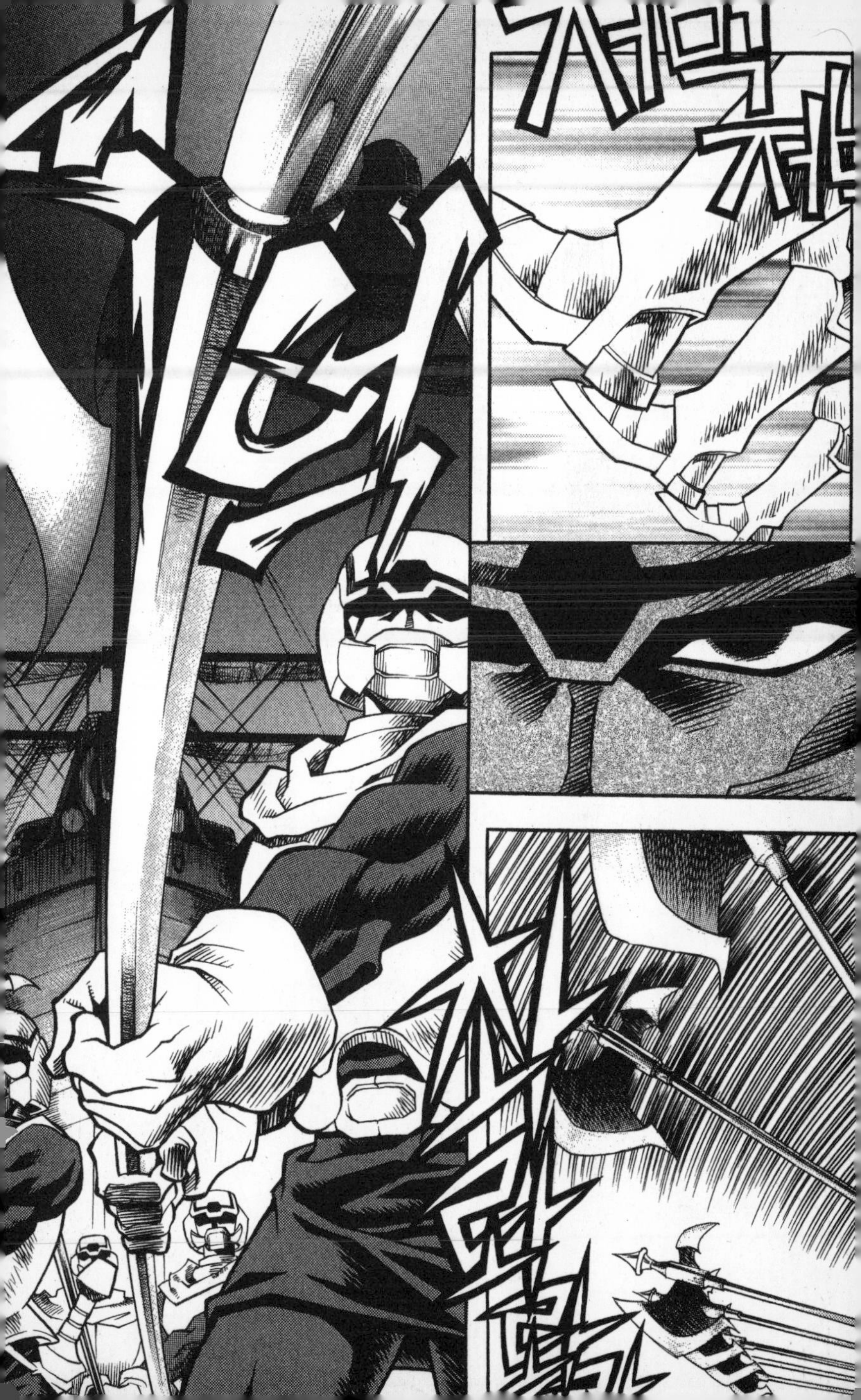

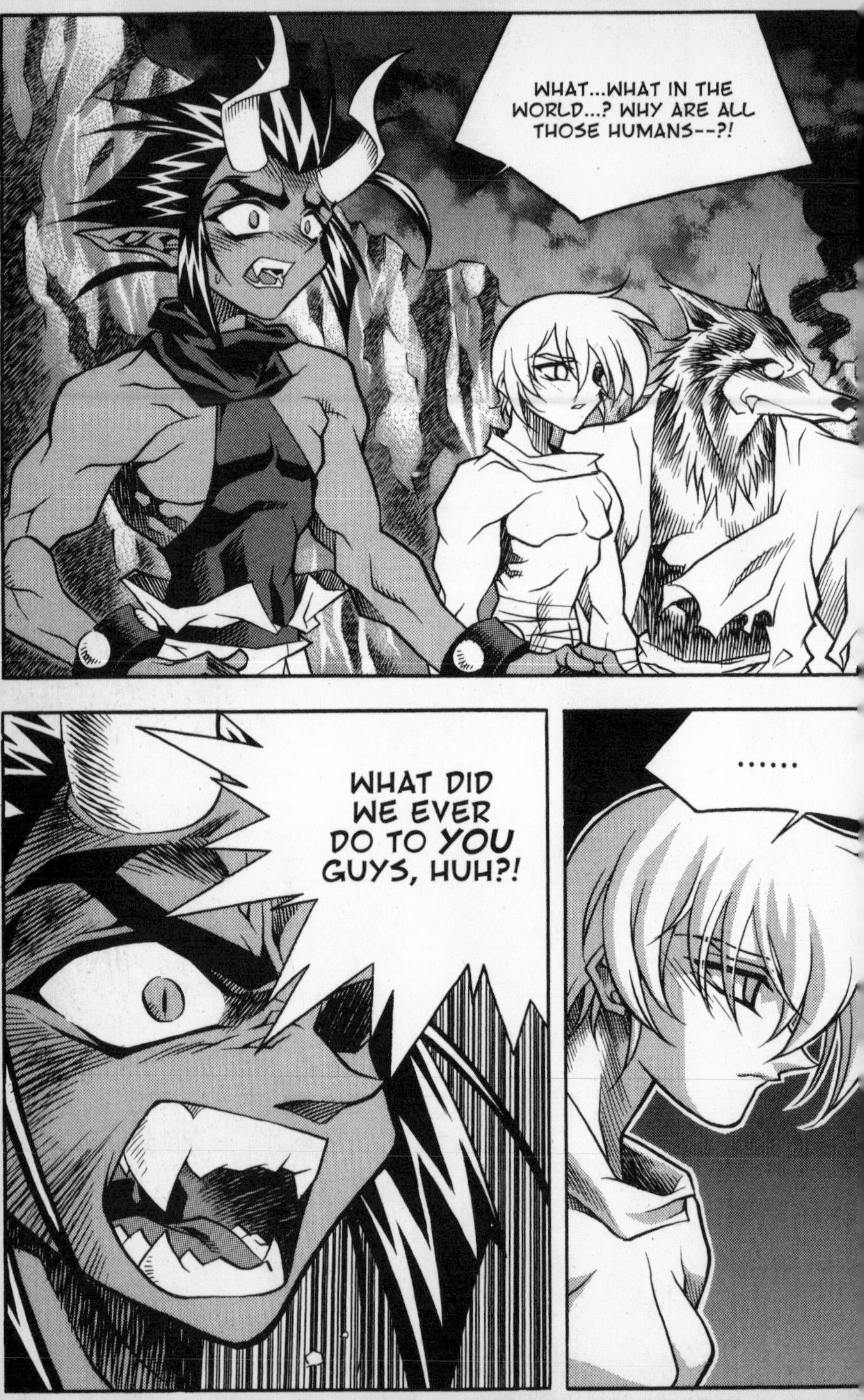
WHAT...WHAT IN THE WORLD...? WHY ARE ALL THOSE HUMANS--?!
WHAT DID WE EVER DO TO YOU GUYS, HUH?!
......

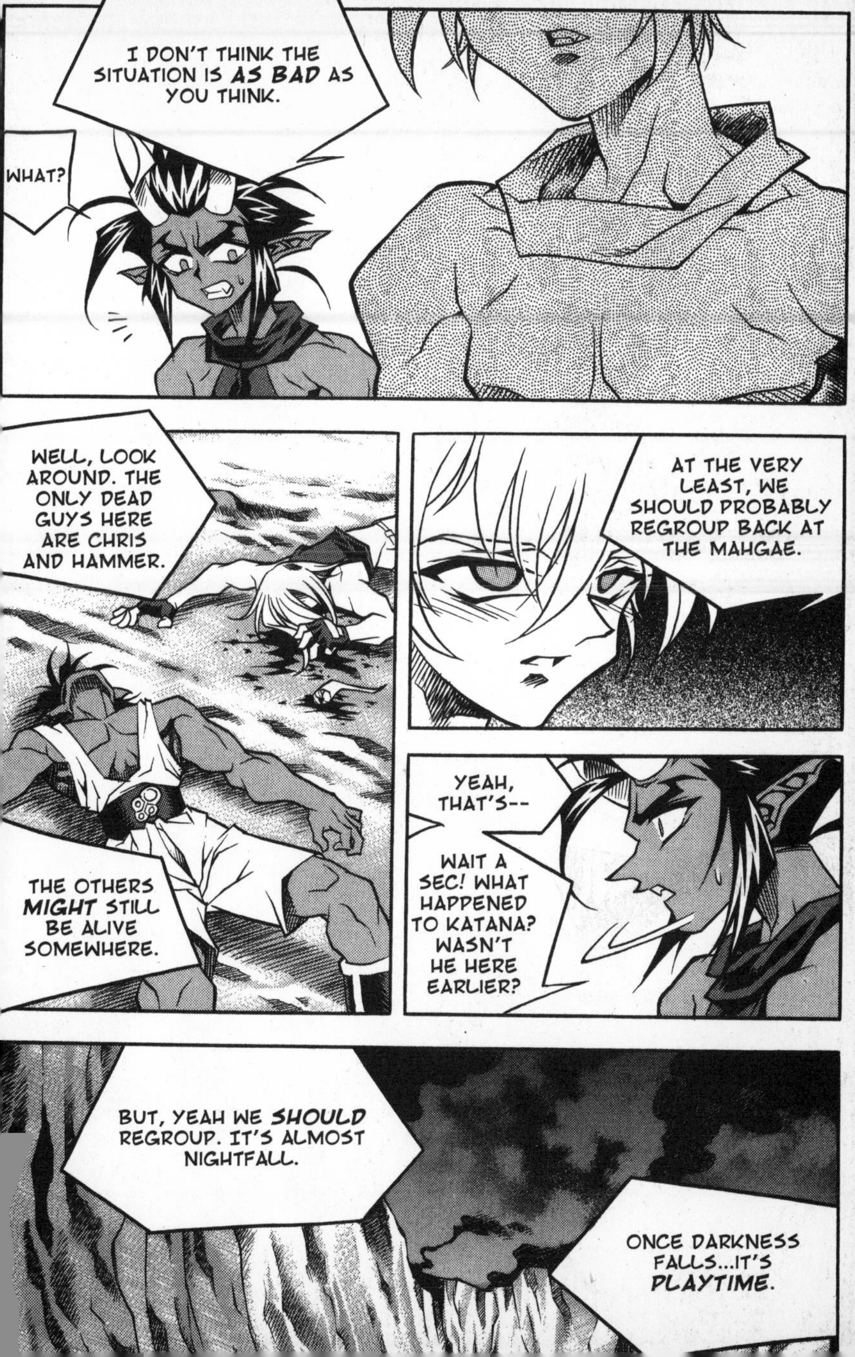
I DON'T THINK THE SITUATION IS AS BAD AS YOU THINK.
WHAT?
WELL, LOOK AROUND. THE ONLY DEAD GUYS HERE ARE CHRIS AND HAMMER.
THE OTHERS MIGHT STILL BE ALIVE SOMEWHERE.
AT THE VERY LEAST, WE SHOULD PROBABLY REGROUP BACK AT THE MAHGAE.
YEAH, THAT'S--
WAIT A SEC! WHAT HAPPENED TO KATANA? WASN'T HE HERE EARLIER?
BUT, YEAH WE SHOULD REGROUP. IT'S ALMOST NIGHTFALL.
ONCE DARKNESS FALLS...IT'S PLAYTIME.

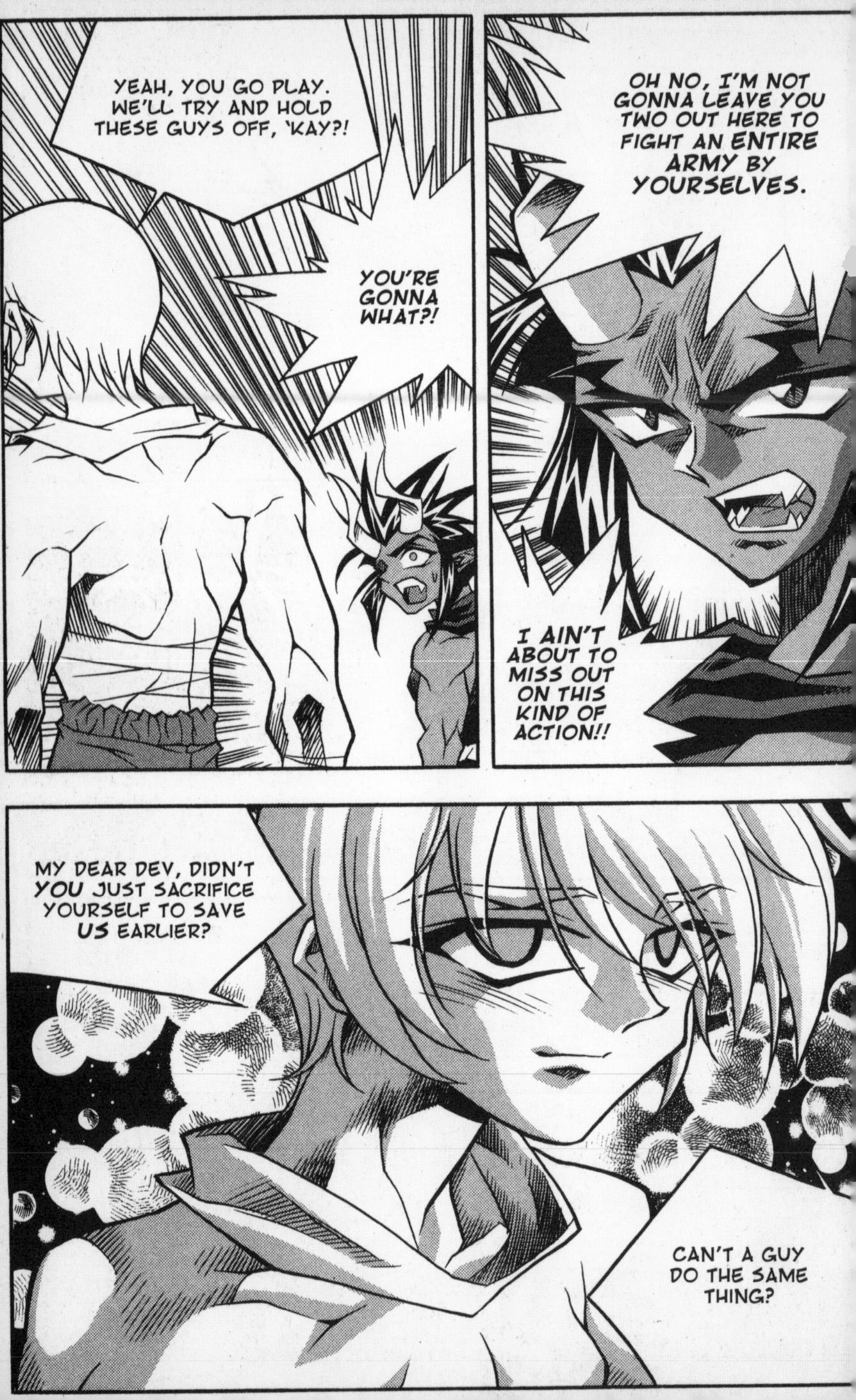
YEAH, YOU GO PLAY. WE'LL TRY AND HOLD THESE GUYS OFF, 'KAY?!
YOU'RE GONNA WHAT?!
OH NO, I'M NOT GONNA LEAVE YOU TWO OUT HERE TO FIGHT AN ENTIRE ARMY BY YOURSELVES.
I AIN'T ABOUT TO MISS OUT ON THIS KIND OF ACTION!!
MY DEAR DEV, DIDN'T YOU JUST SACRIFICE YOURSELF TO SAVE US EARLIER?
CAN'T A GUY DO THE SAME THING?

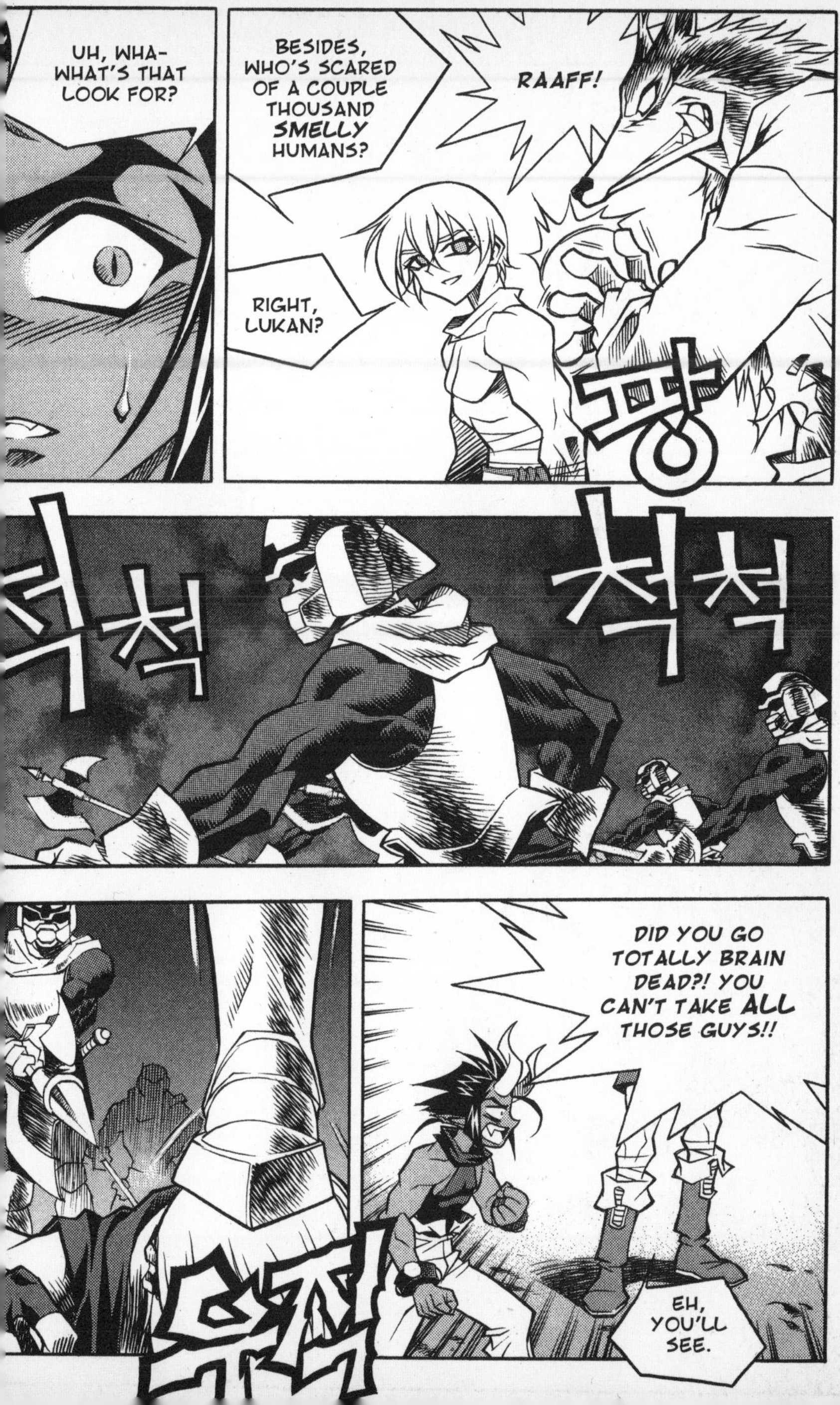
UH, WHA- WHAT'S THAT LOOK FOR?
BESIDES, WHO'S SCARED OF A COUPLE THOUSAND SMELLY HUMANS?
RAAFF!
RIGHT, LUKAN?
펑
척척
척척
DID YOU GO TOTALLY BRAIN DEAD?! YOU CAN'T TAKE ALL THOSE GUYS!!
EH, YOU'LL SEE.

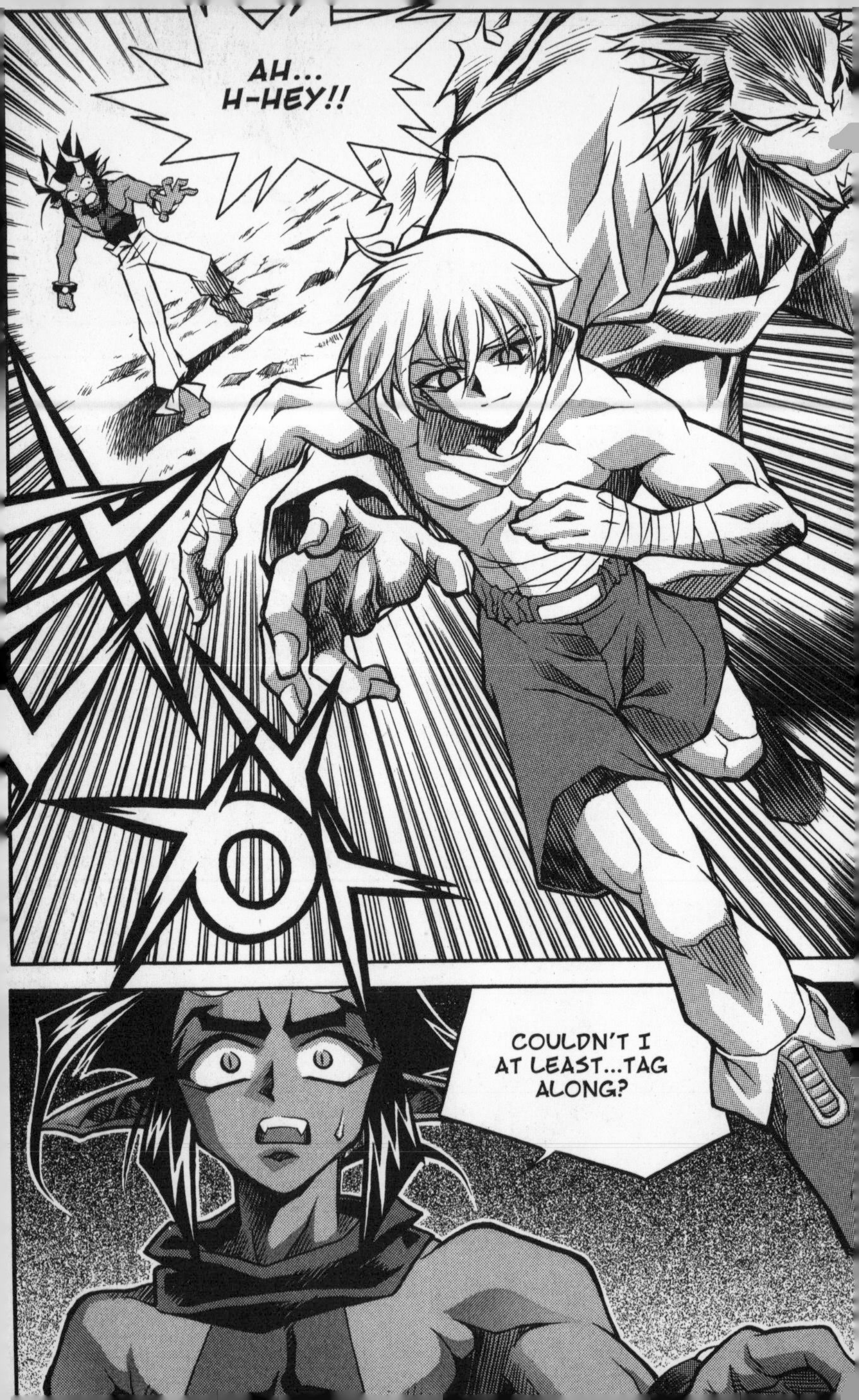
AH... H-HEY!!
COULDN'T I AT LEAST...TAG ALONG?

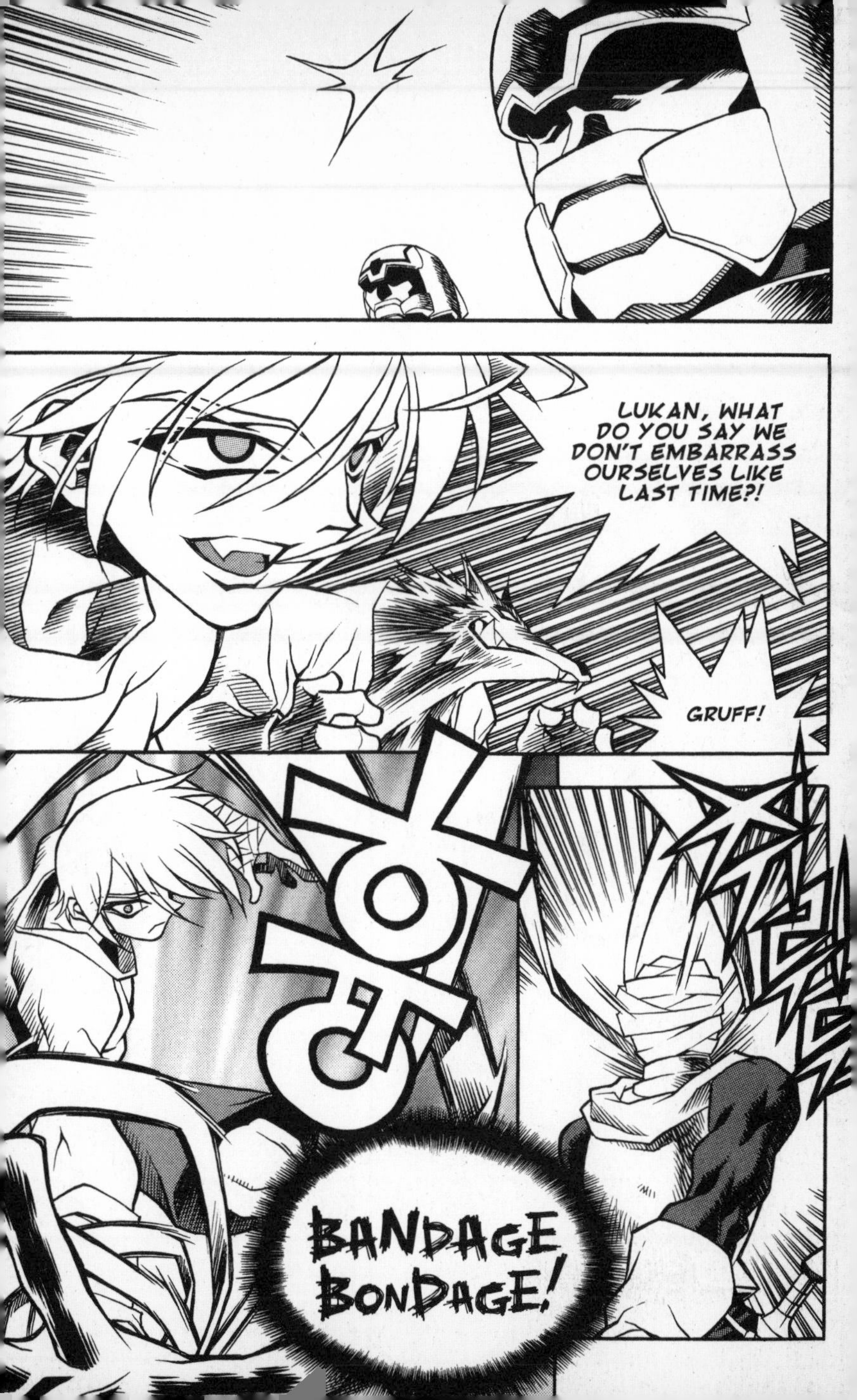
LUKAN, WHAT DO YOU SAY WE DON'T EMBARRASS OURSELVES LIKE LAST TIME?!
GRUFF!
BANDAGE BONDAGE!

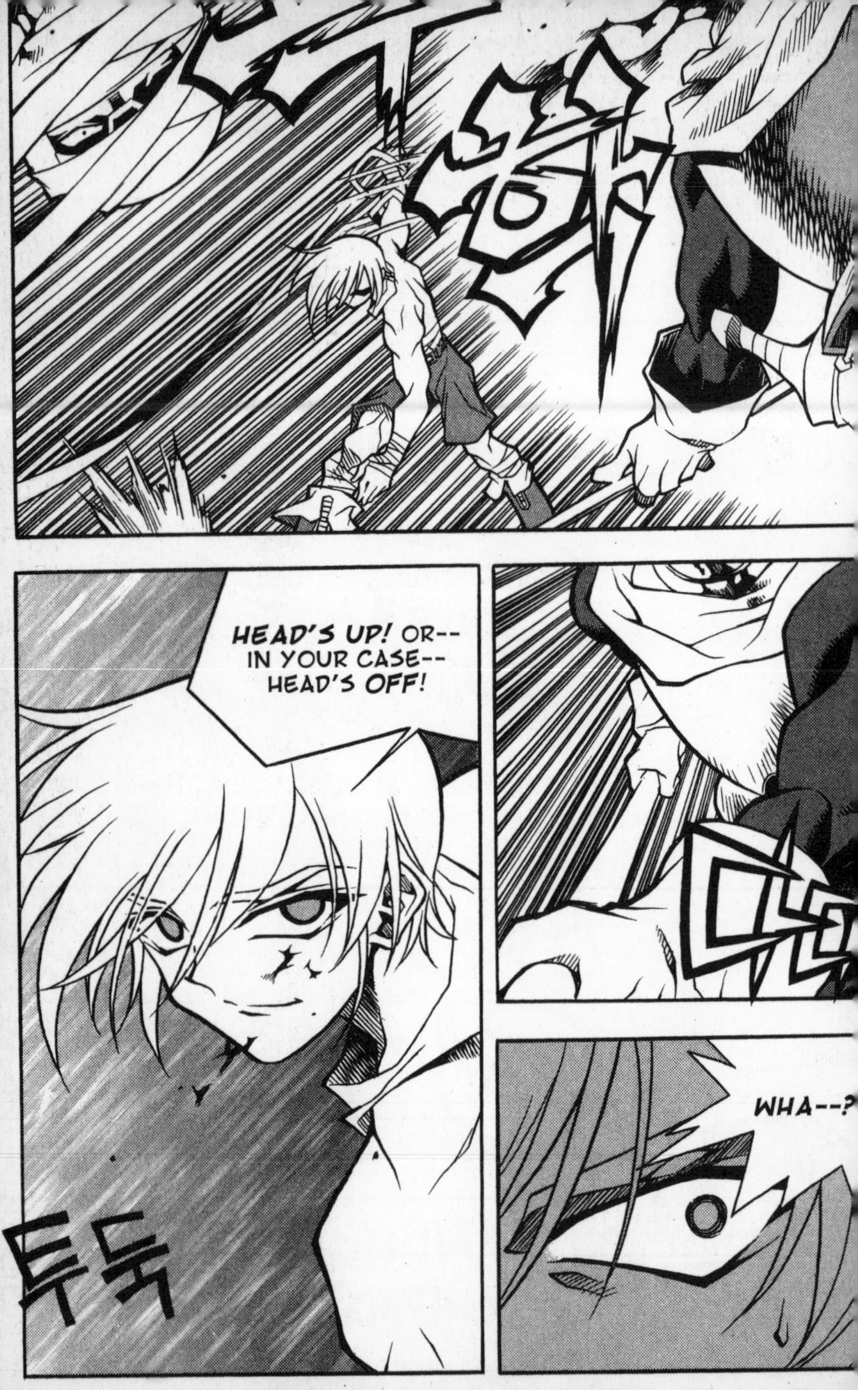
HEAD'S UP! OR-- IN YOUR CASE-- HEAD'S OFF!
두둑
WHA--?

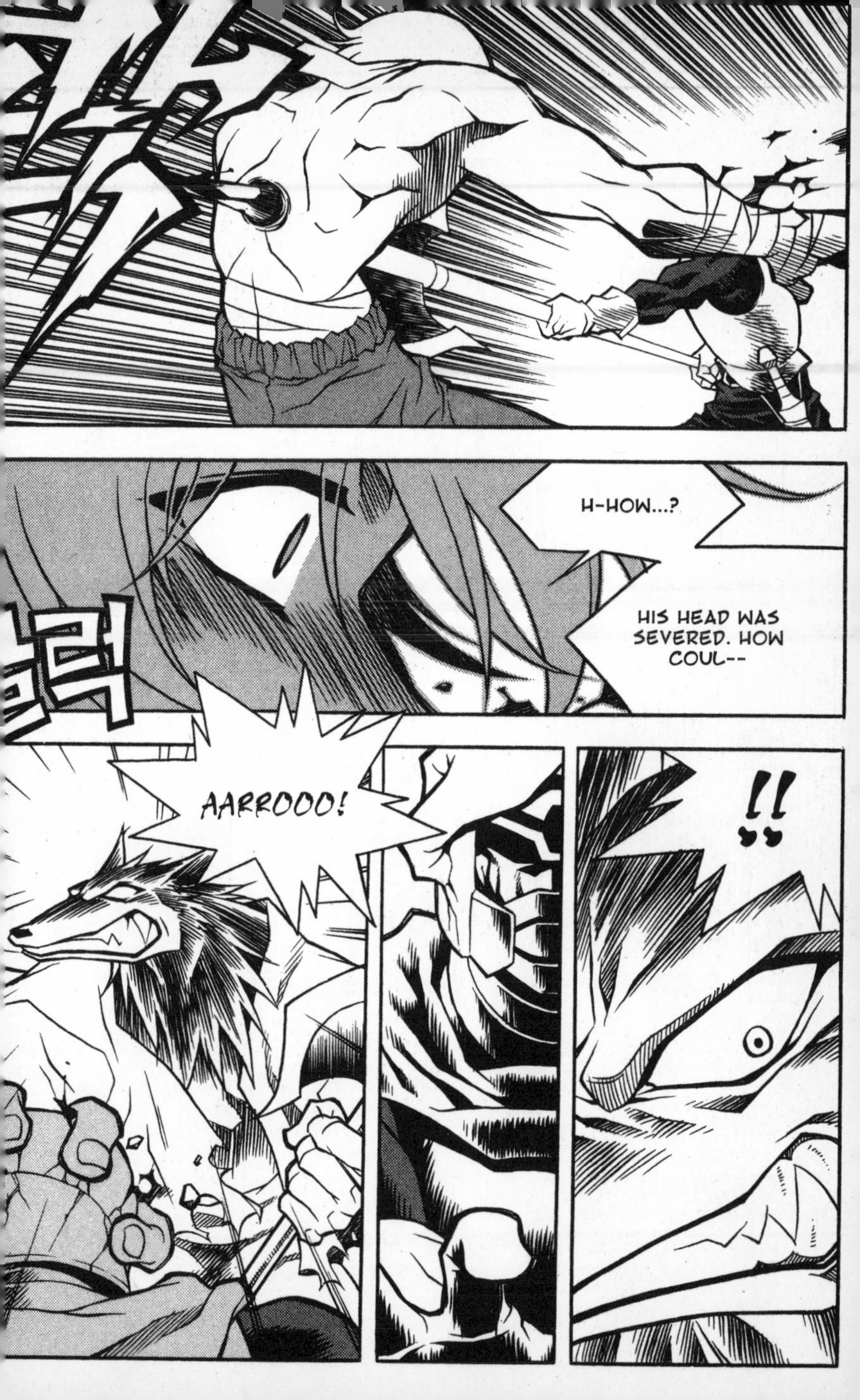
H-HOW...?
HIS HEAD WAS SEVERED. HOW COUL--
AARROOO!
!!

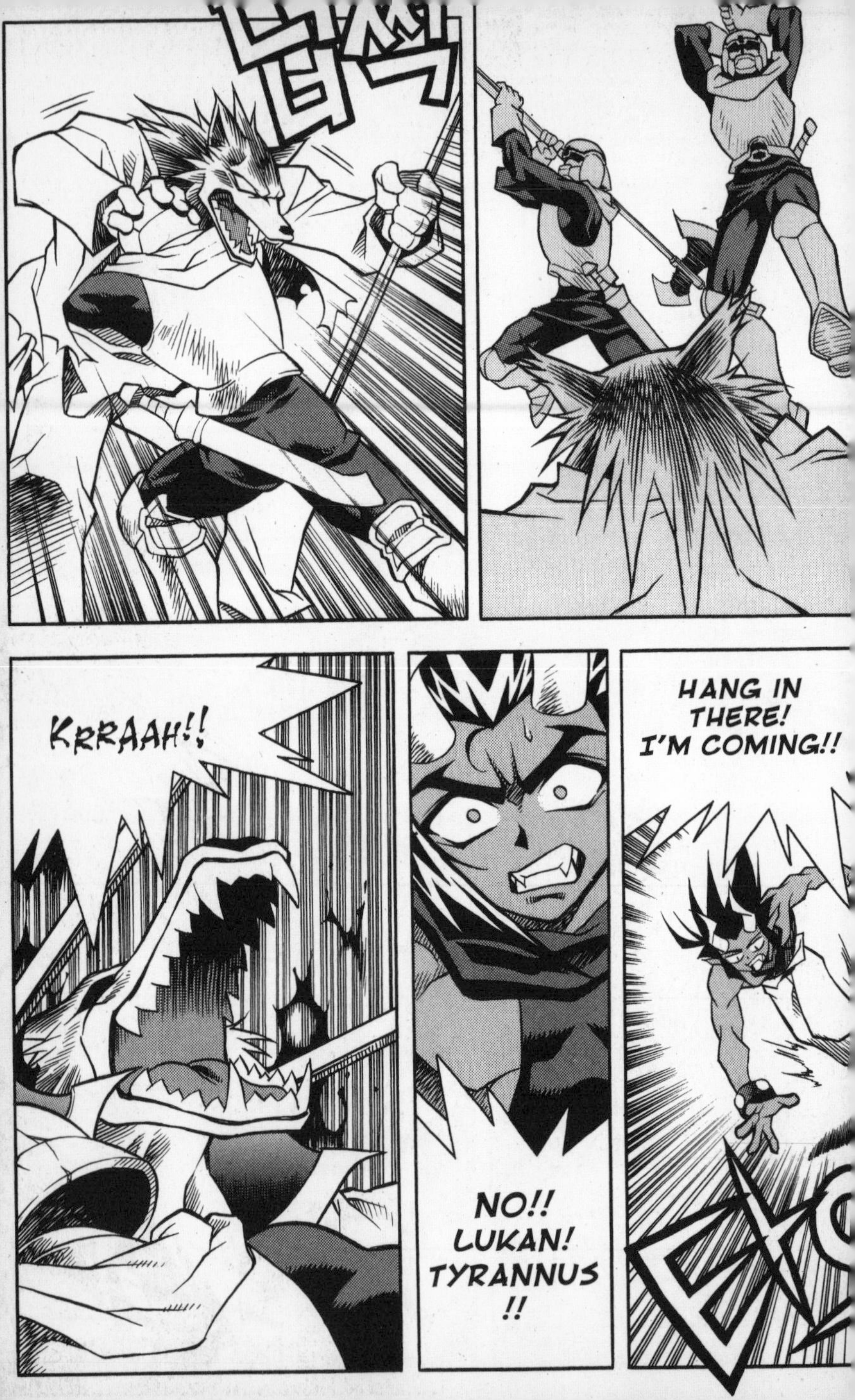
KRRAAH!!
NO!! LUKAN! TYRANNUS !!
HANG IN THERE! I'M COMING!!

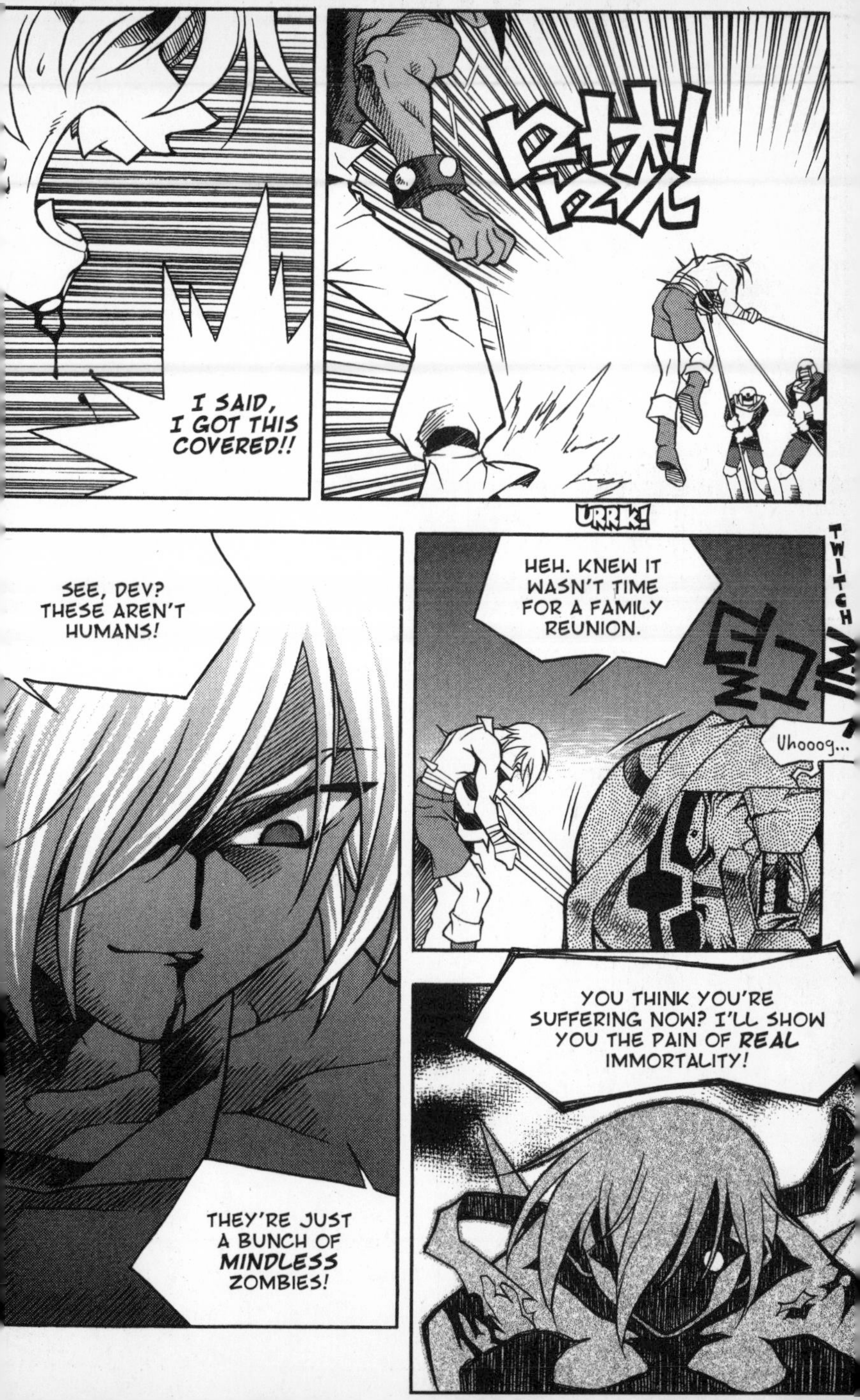
I SAID, I GOT THIS COVERED!!
URRK!
SEE, DEV? THESE AREN'T HUMANS!
THEY'RE JUST A BUNCH OF **MINDLESS** ZOMBIES!
HEH. KNEW IT WASN'T TIME FOR A FAMILY REUNION.
TWITCH
Uhooog...
YOU THINK YOU'RE SUFFERING NOW? I'LL SHOW YOU THE PAIN OF **REAL** IMMORTALITY!

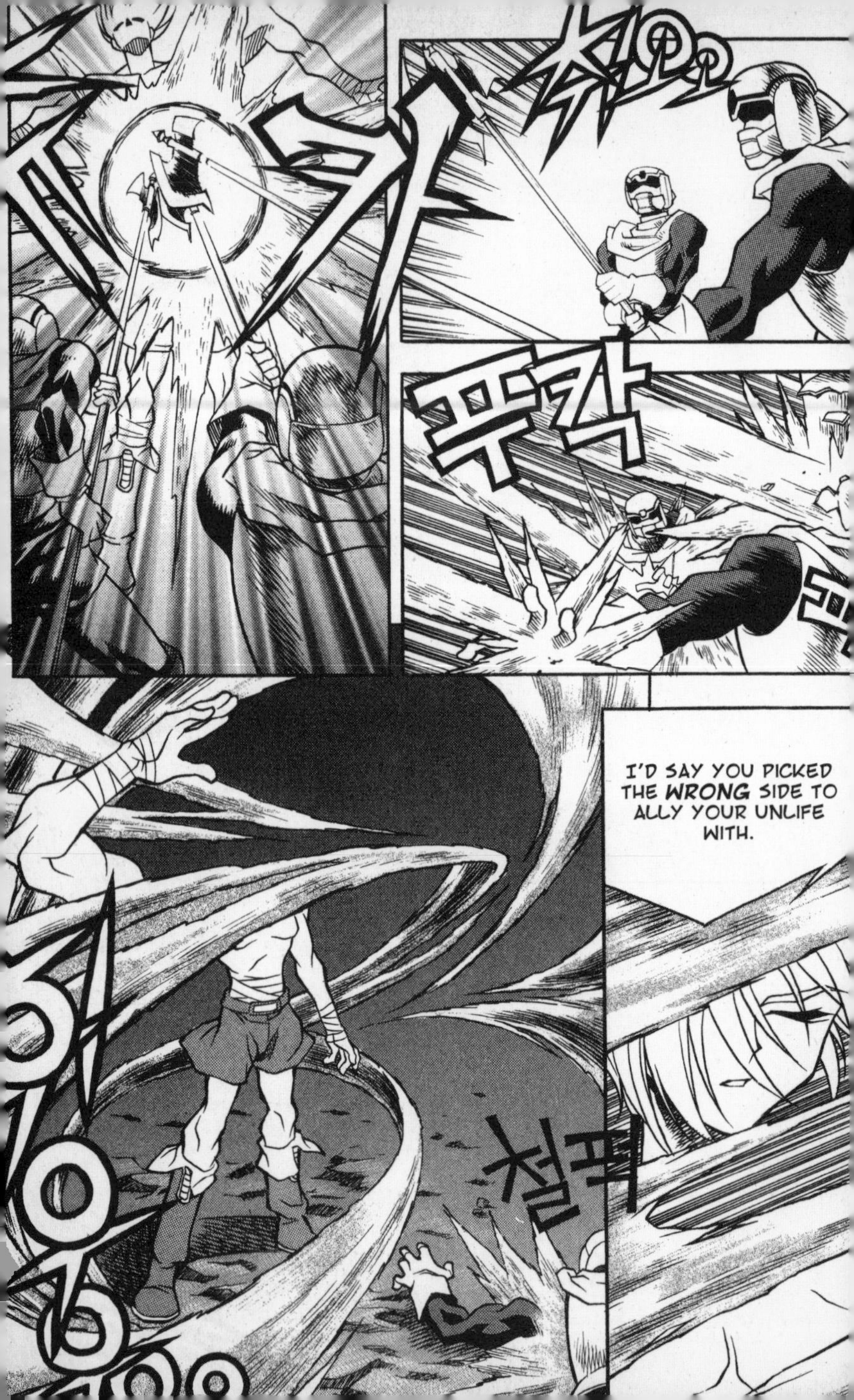
푸각
I'D SAY YOU PICKED THE WRONG SIDE TO ALLY YOUR UNLIFE WITH.

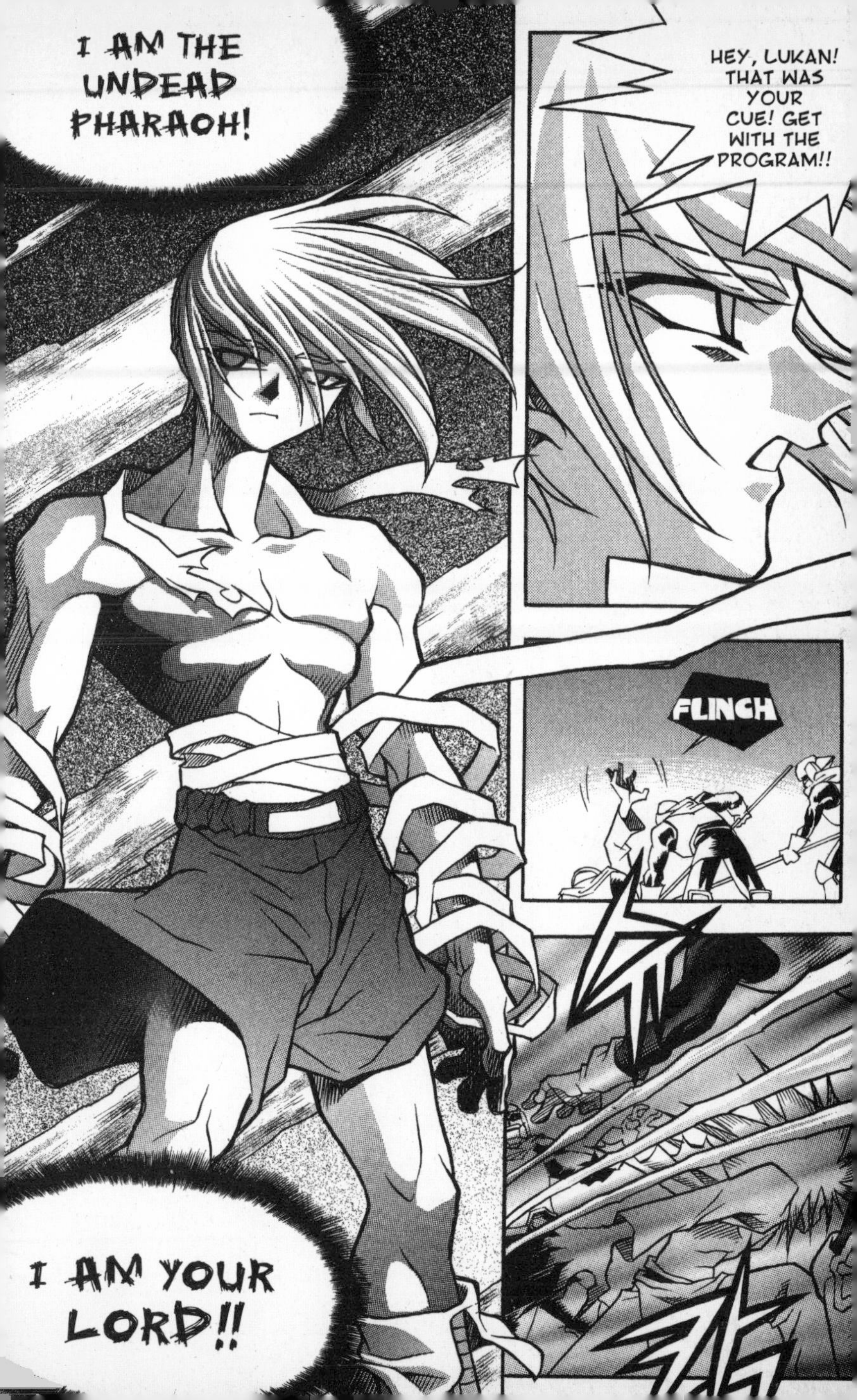
I AM THE UNDEAD PHARAOH!
I AM YOUR LORD!!
HEY, LUKAN! THAT WAS YOUR CUE! GET WITH THE PROGRAM!!
FLINCH

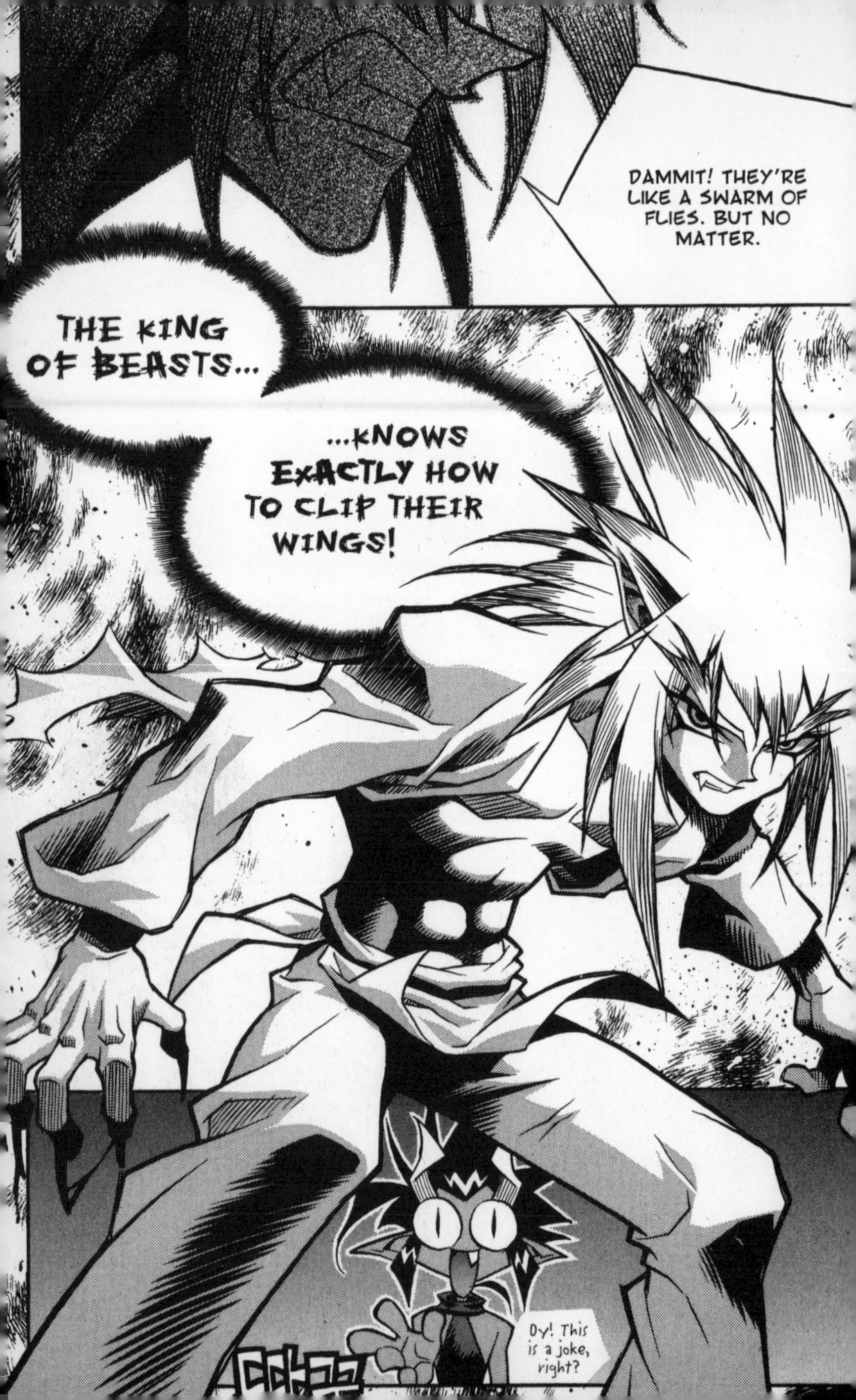
DAMMIT! THEY'RE LIKE A SWARM OF FLIES. BUT NO MATTER.
THE KING OF BEASTS...
...KNOWS EXACTLY HOW TO CLIP THEIR WINGS!
Oy! This is a joke, right?

Quest 15

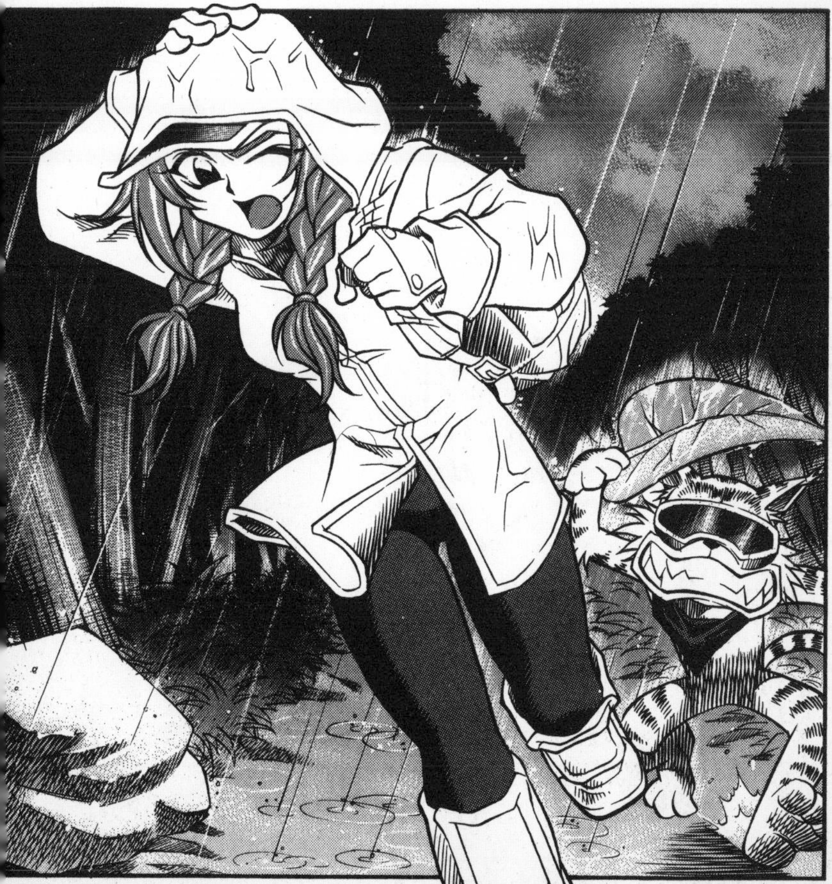

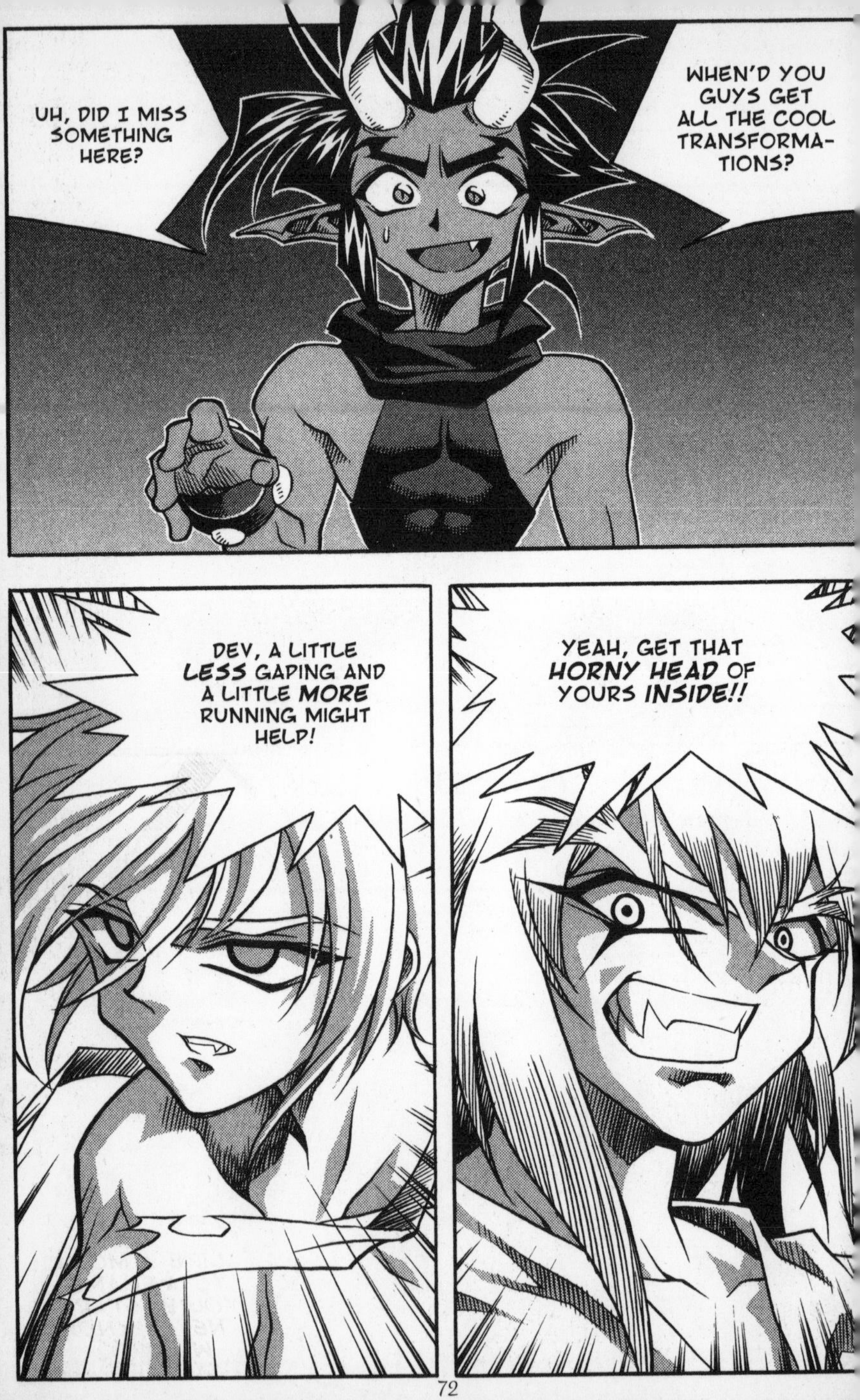
UH, DID I MISS SOMETHING HERE?
WHEN'D YOU GUYS GET ALL THE COOL TRANSFORMA-TIONS?
DEV, A LITTLE **LESS** GAPING AND A LITTLE **MORE** RUNNING MIGHT HELP!
YEAH, GET THAT **HORNY HEAD** OF YOURS **INSIDE!!**

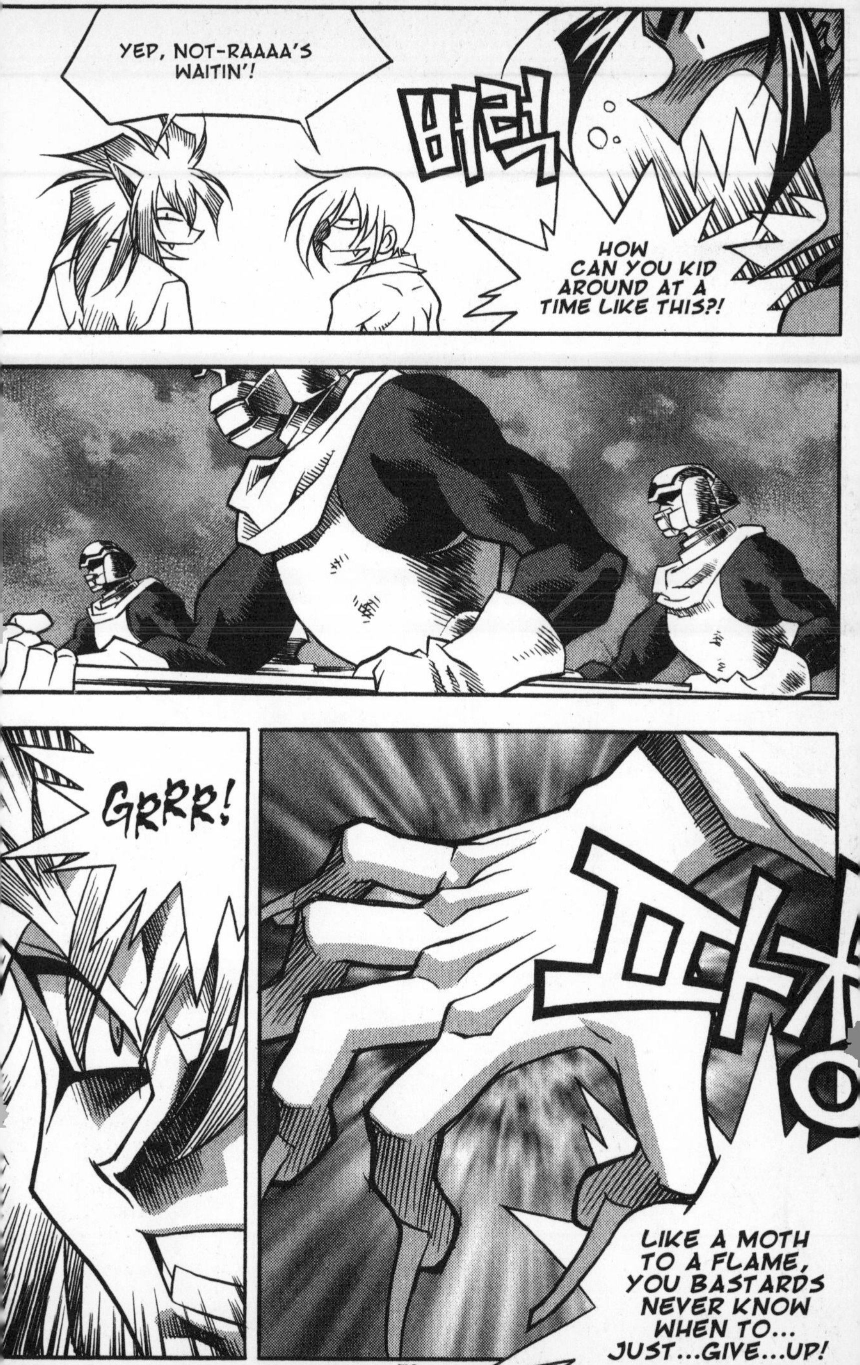
YEP, NOT-RAAAA'S WAITIN'!
HOW CAN YOU KID AROUND AT A TIME LIKE THIS?!
GRRR!
LIKE A MOTH TO A FLAME, YOU BASTARDS NEVER KNOW WHEN TO... JUST...GIVE...UP!

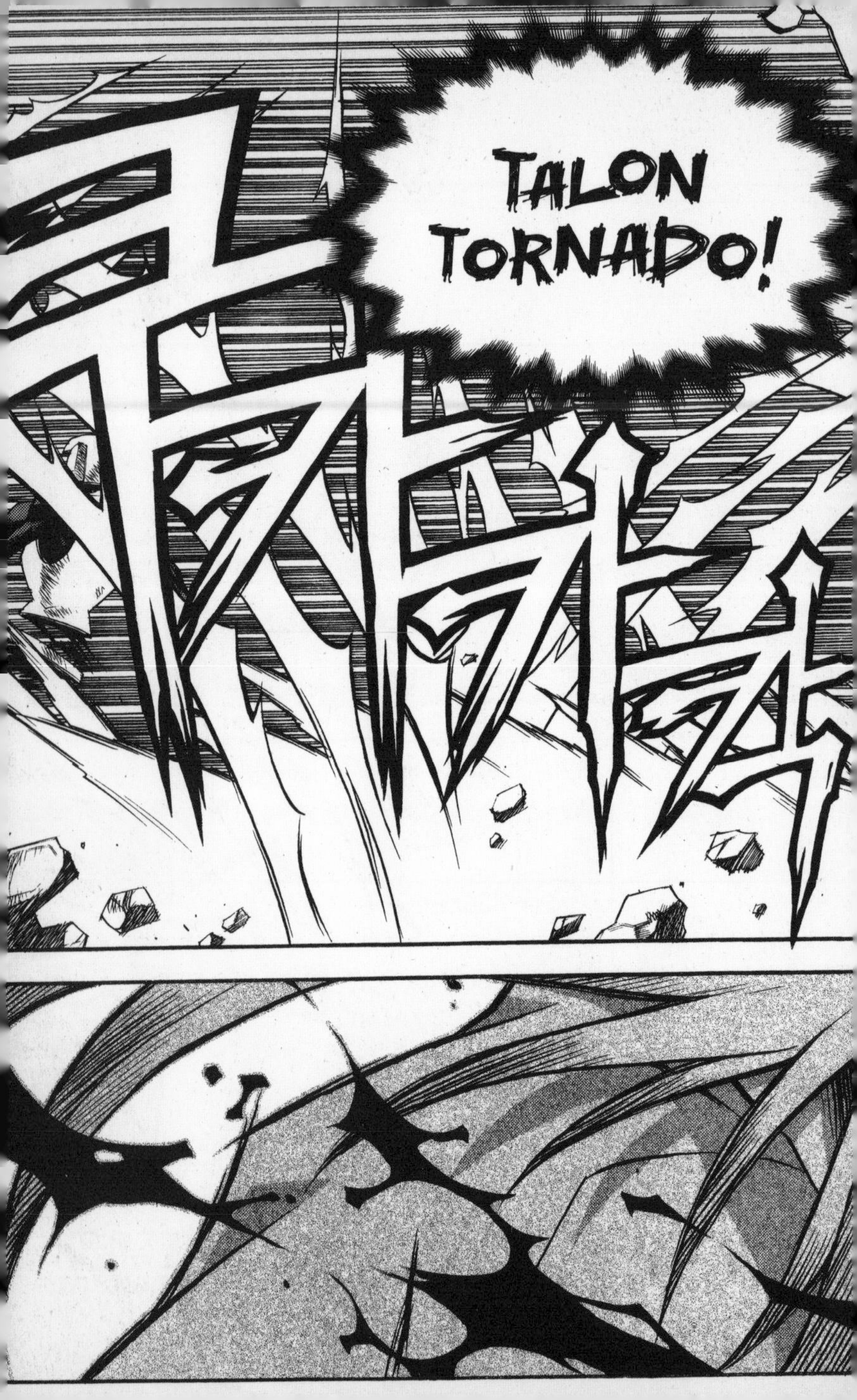
TALON TORNADO!

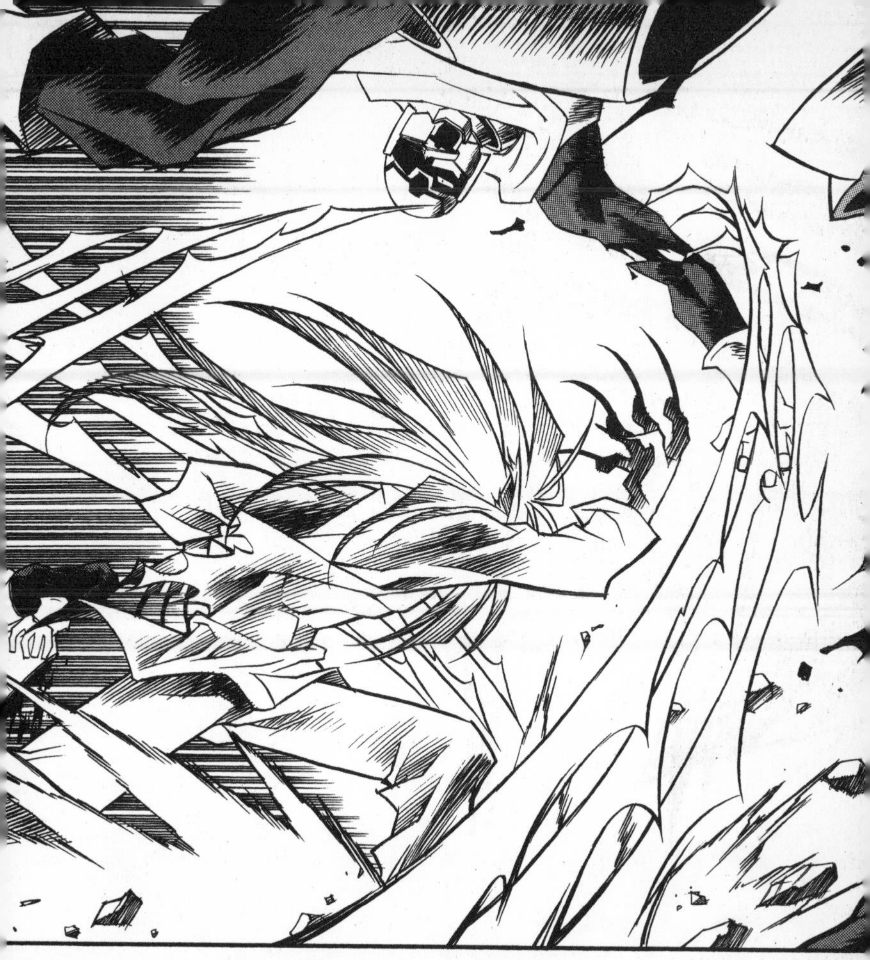

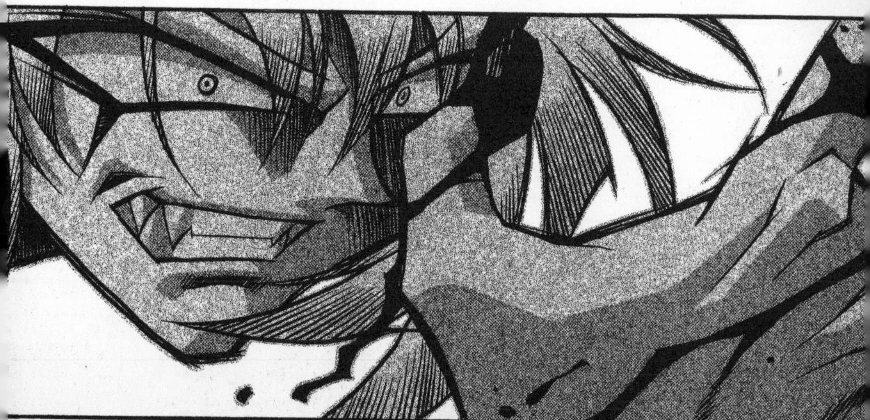

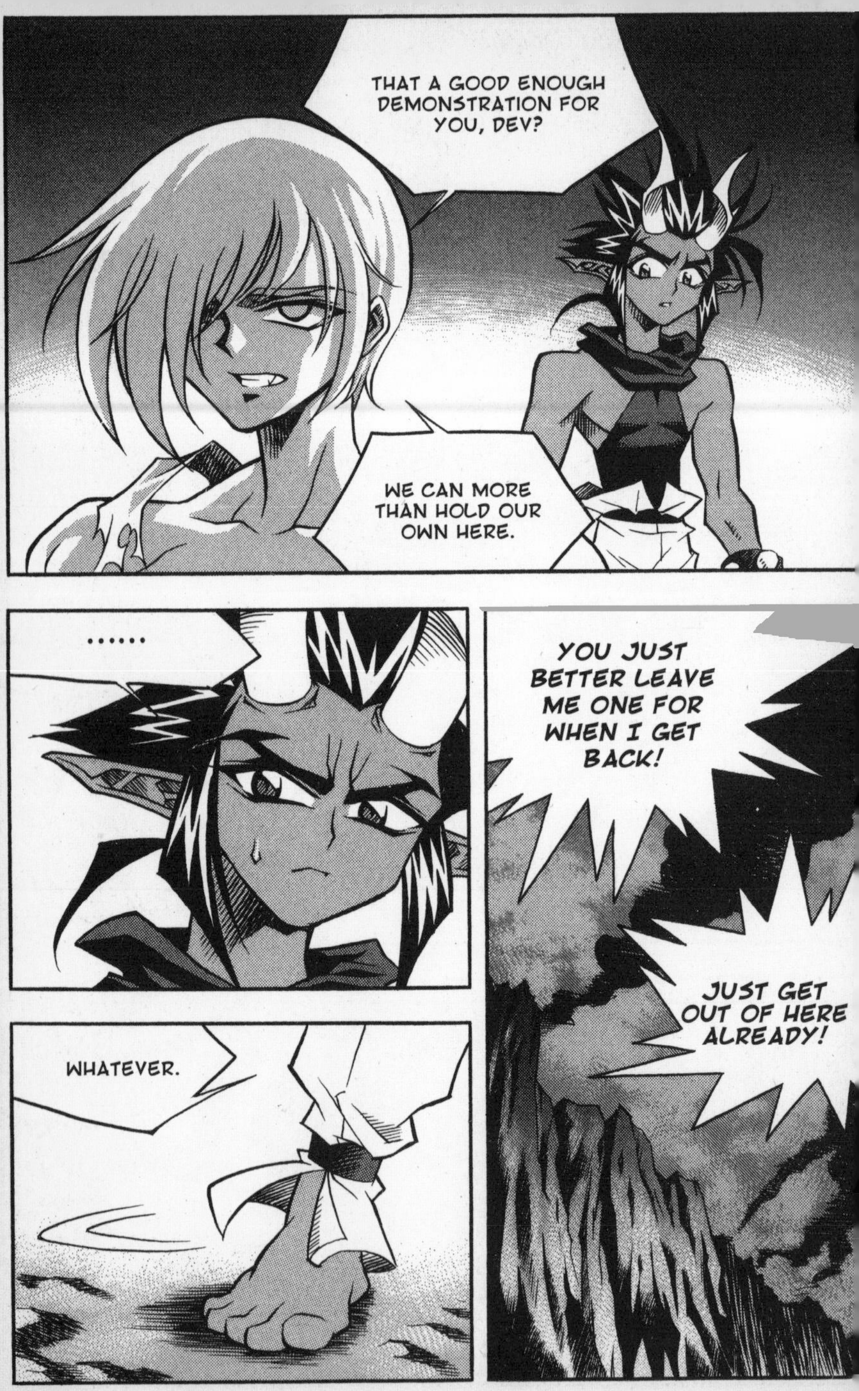
THAT A GOOD ENOUGH DEMONSTRATION FOR YOU, DEV?
WE CAN MORE THAN HOLD OUR OWN HERE.
......
WHATEVER.
YOU JUST BETTER LEAVE ME ONE FOR WHEN I GET BACK!
JUST GET OUT OF HERE ALREADY!

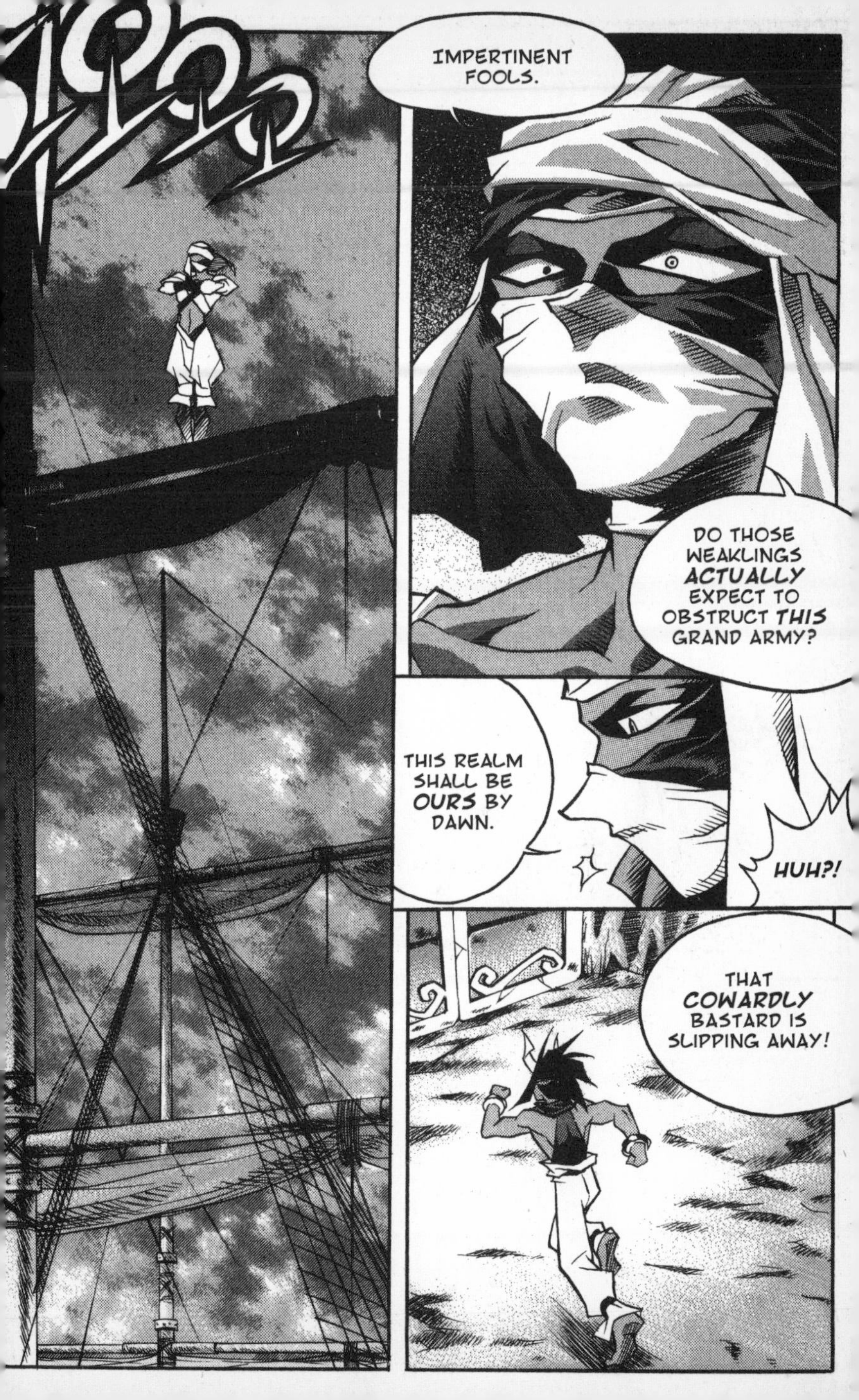
IMPERTINENT FOOLS.
DO THOSE WEAKLINGS *ACTUALLY* EXPECT TO OBSTRUCT *THIS* GRAND ARMY?
THIS REALM SHALL BE *OURS* BY DAWN.
HUH?!
THAT *COWARDLY* BASTARD IS SLIPPING AWAY!

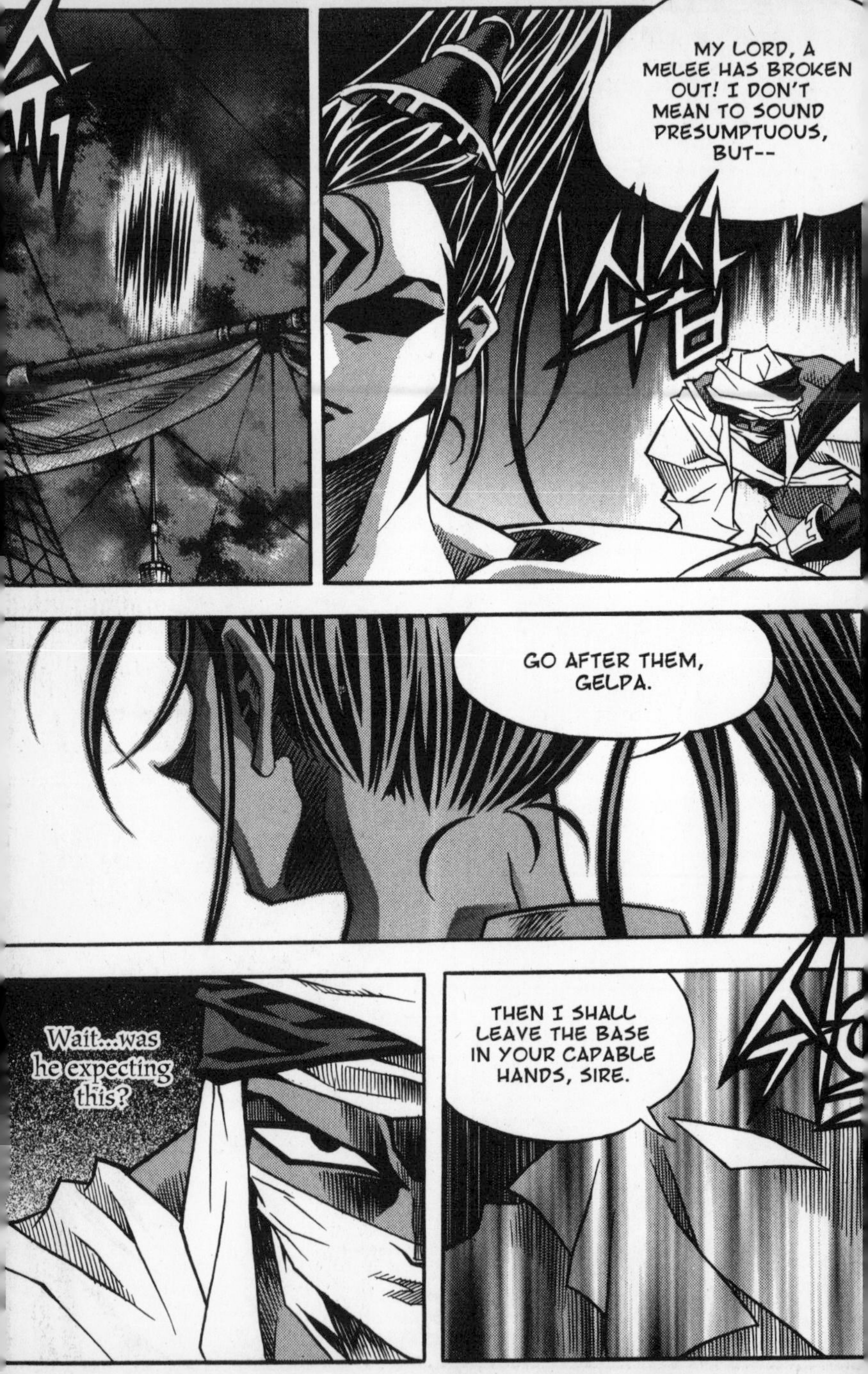
MY LORD, A MELEE HAS BROKEN OUT! I DON'T MEAN TO SOUND PRESUMPTUOUS, BUT--
GO AFTER THEM, GELPA.
Wait...was he expecting this?
THEN I SHALL LEAVE THE BASE IN YOUR CAPABLE HANDS, SIRE.

OUR ARMY OF ZOMBIES WILL BE NOTHING MORE THAN A BLOODY MESS WITH THAT *DAMNABLE* UNDEAD PHARAOH AND BEAST KING IN OUR MIDST.

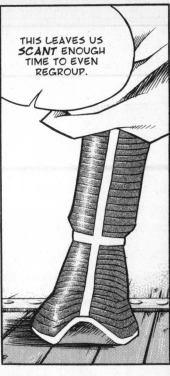

THIS LEAVES US *SCANT* ENOUGH TIME TO EVEN REGROUP.

WE MAY NEED *ANOTHER* SET OF HIGH-RANKING MEMBERS OF THE MADOSA GUILD ONCE THIS IS OVER.

HMPH! IT SEEMS AS THOUGH I *MUST* DIRTY MY HANDS IN THIS AFFAIR.

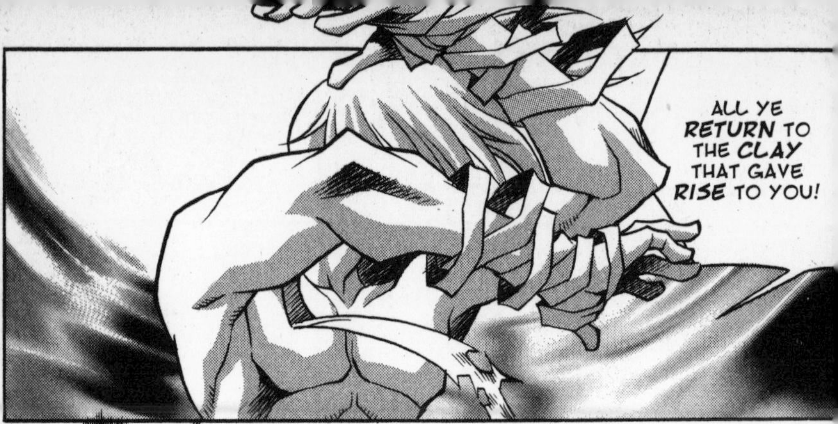
ALL YE RETURN TO THE CLAY THAT GAVE RISE TO YOU!

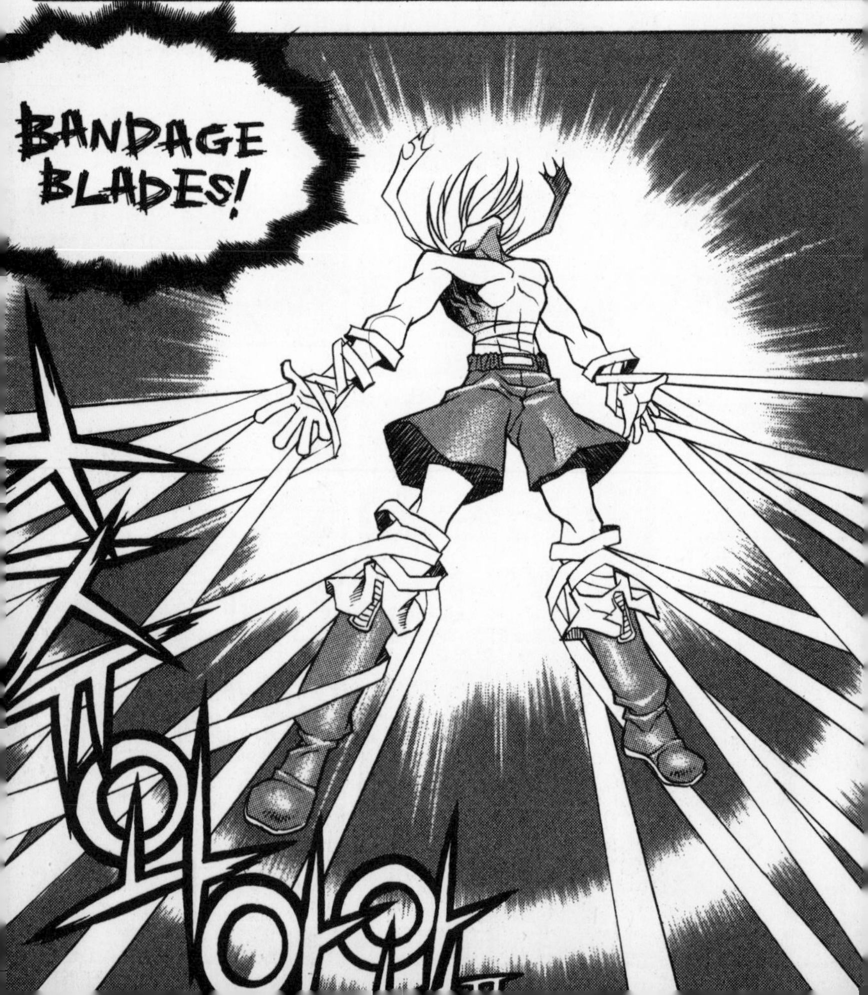
BANDAGE BLADES!

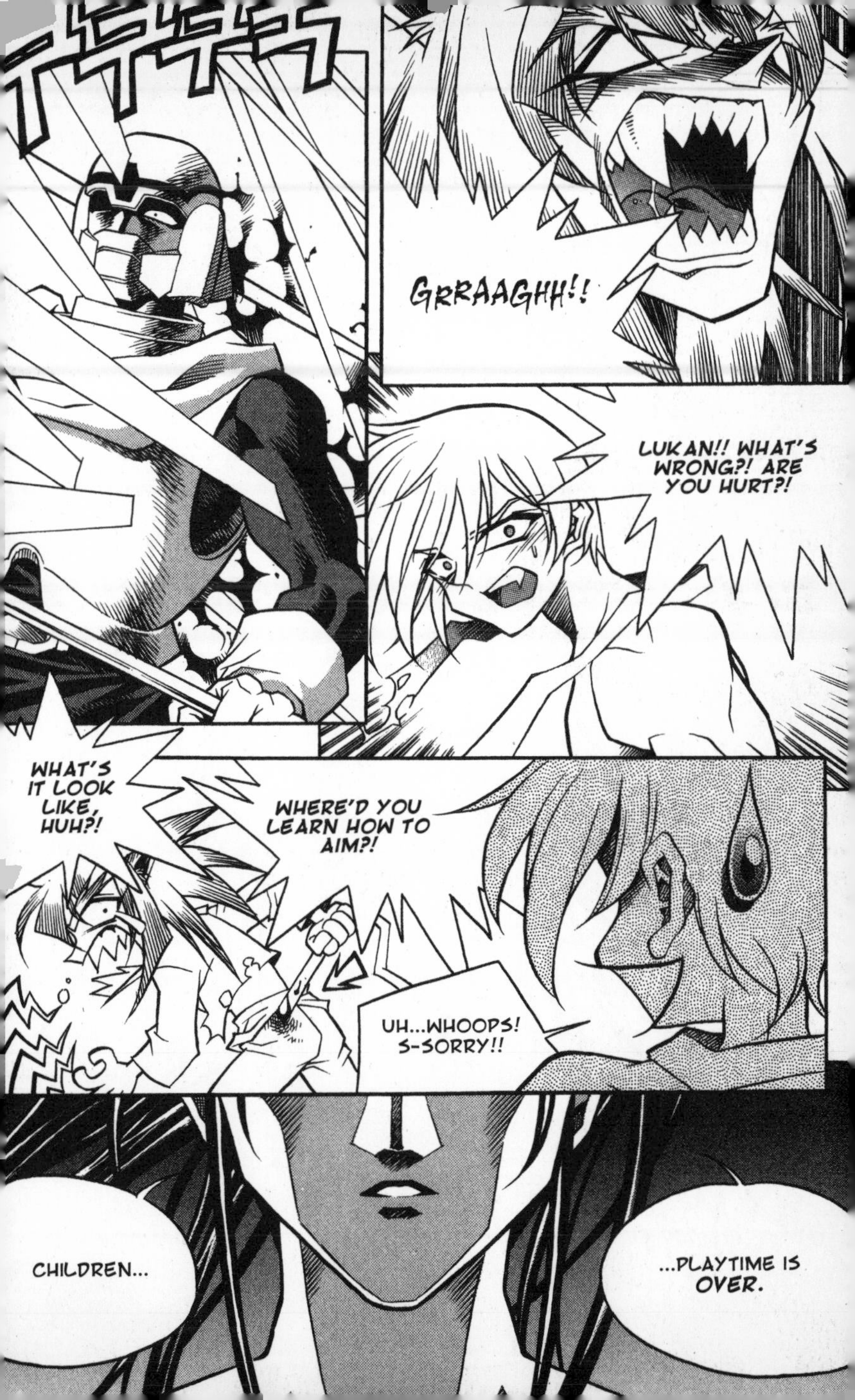
GRRAAGHH!!
LUKAN!! WHAT'S WRONG?! ARE YOU HURT?!
WHAT'S IT LOOK LIKE, HUH?!
WHERE'D YOU LEARN HOW TO AIM?!
UH...WHOOPS! S-SORRY!!
CHILDREN...
...PLAYTIME IS OVER.

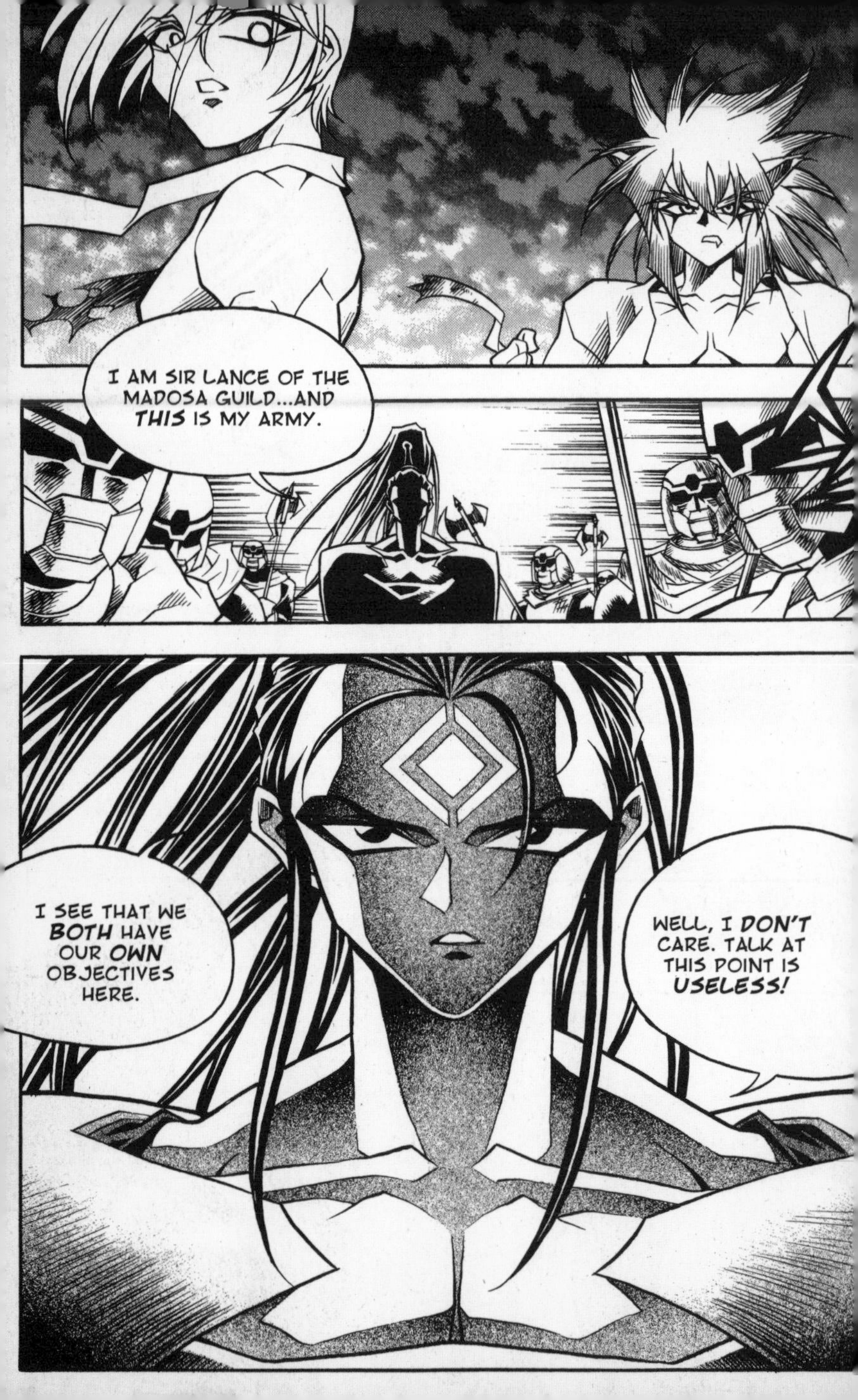
I AM SIR LANCE OF THE MADOSA GUILD...AND THIS IS MY ARMY.
I SEE THAT WE BOTH HAVE OUR OWN OBJECTIVES HERE.
WELL, I DON'T CARE. TALK AT THIS POINT IS USELESS!

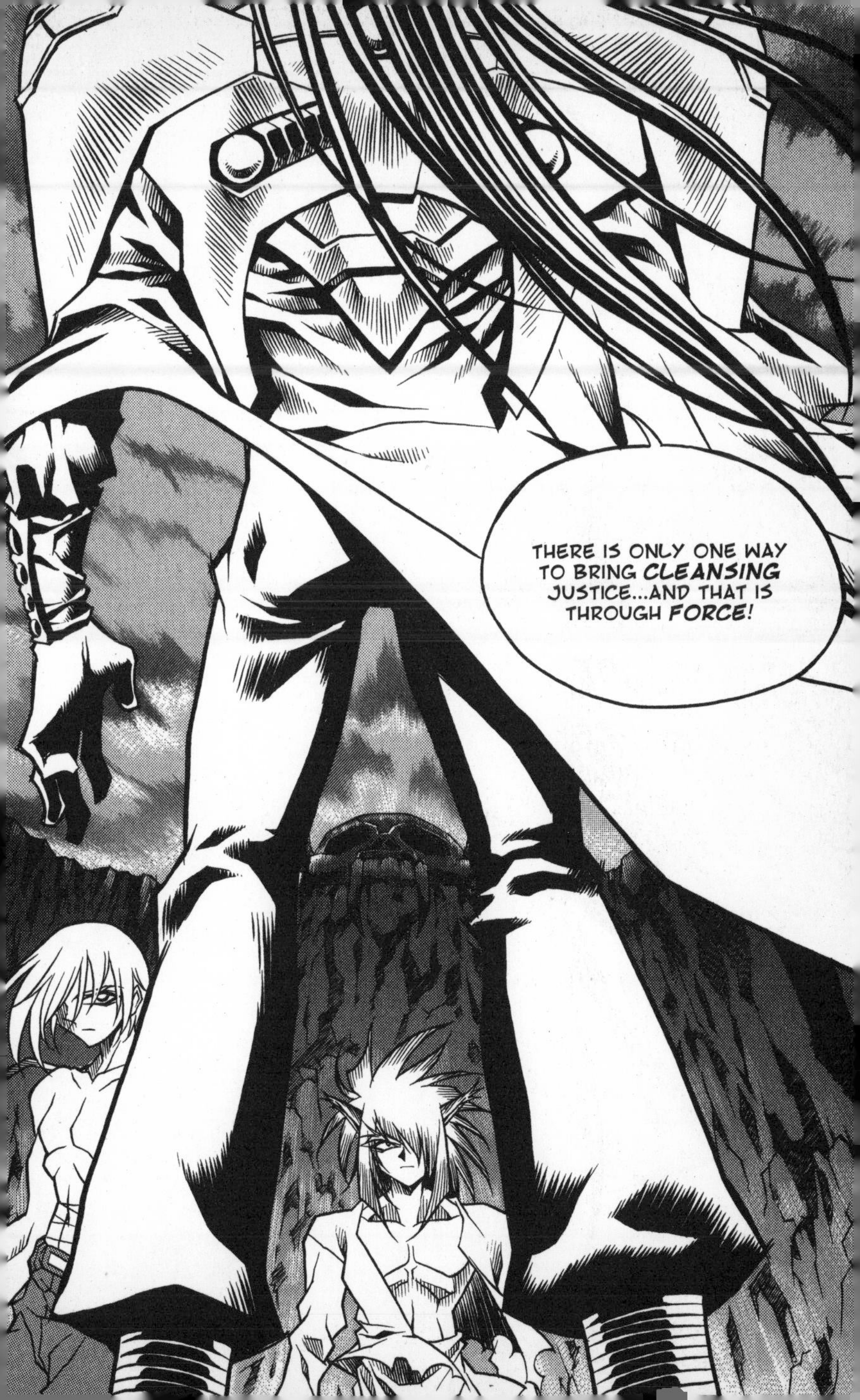
THERE IS ONLY ONE WAY TO BRING CLEANSING JUSTICE...AND THAT IS THROUGH FORCE!

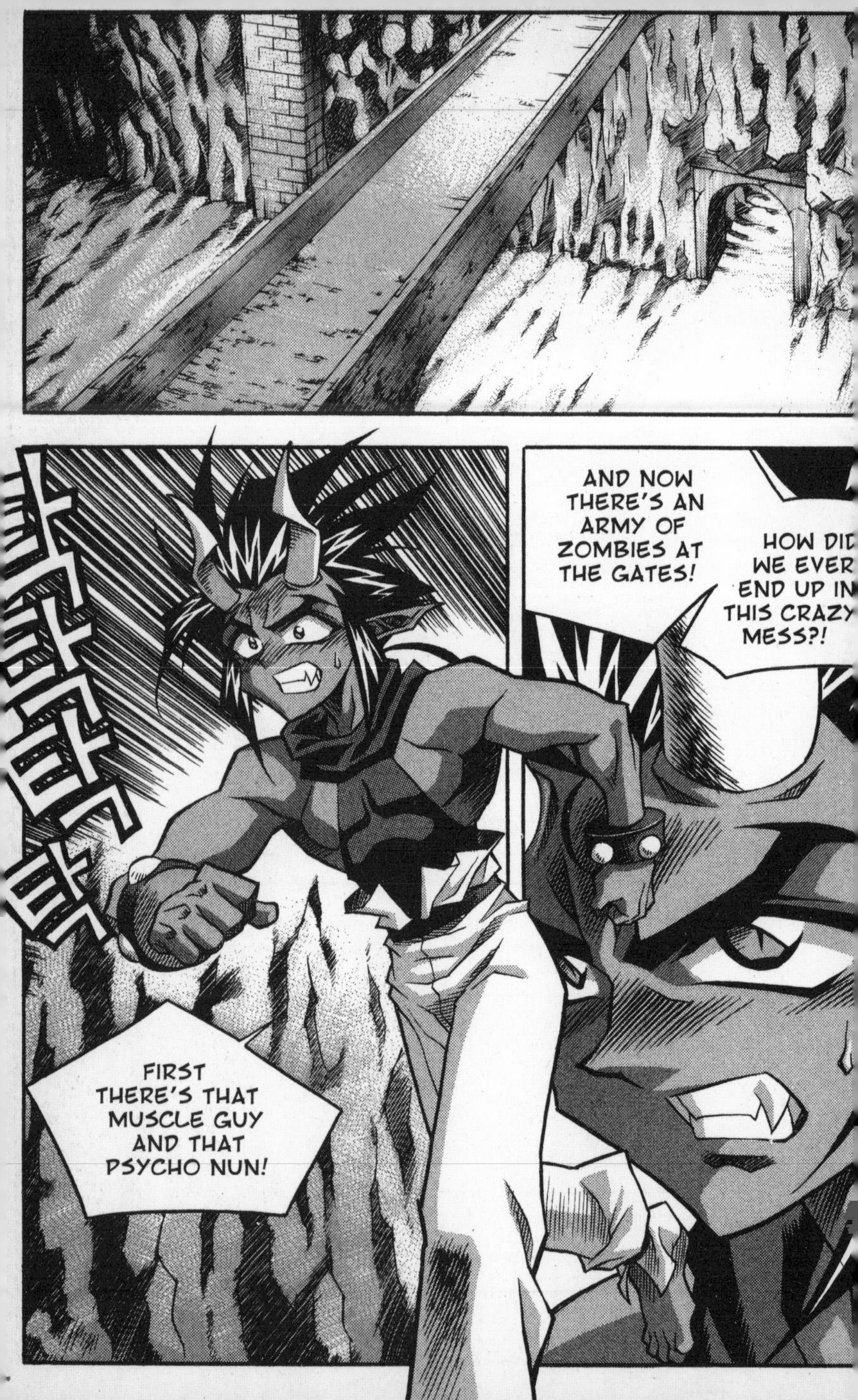
FIRST THERE'S THAT MUSCLE GUY AND THAT PSYCHO NUN!
AND NOW THERE'S AN ARMY OF ZOMBIES AT THE GATES!
HOW DID WE EVER END UP IN THIS CRAZY MESS?!

And those guys, they don't work out. Where'd they get all that power from?!

huff... huff...

But it's not fair! All I'm doing is running. Is this the **most** I can do to help?

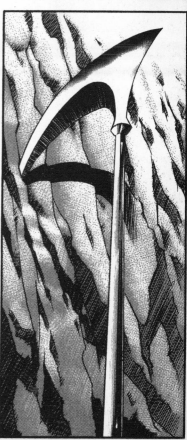

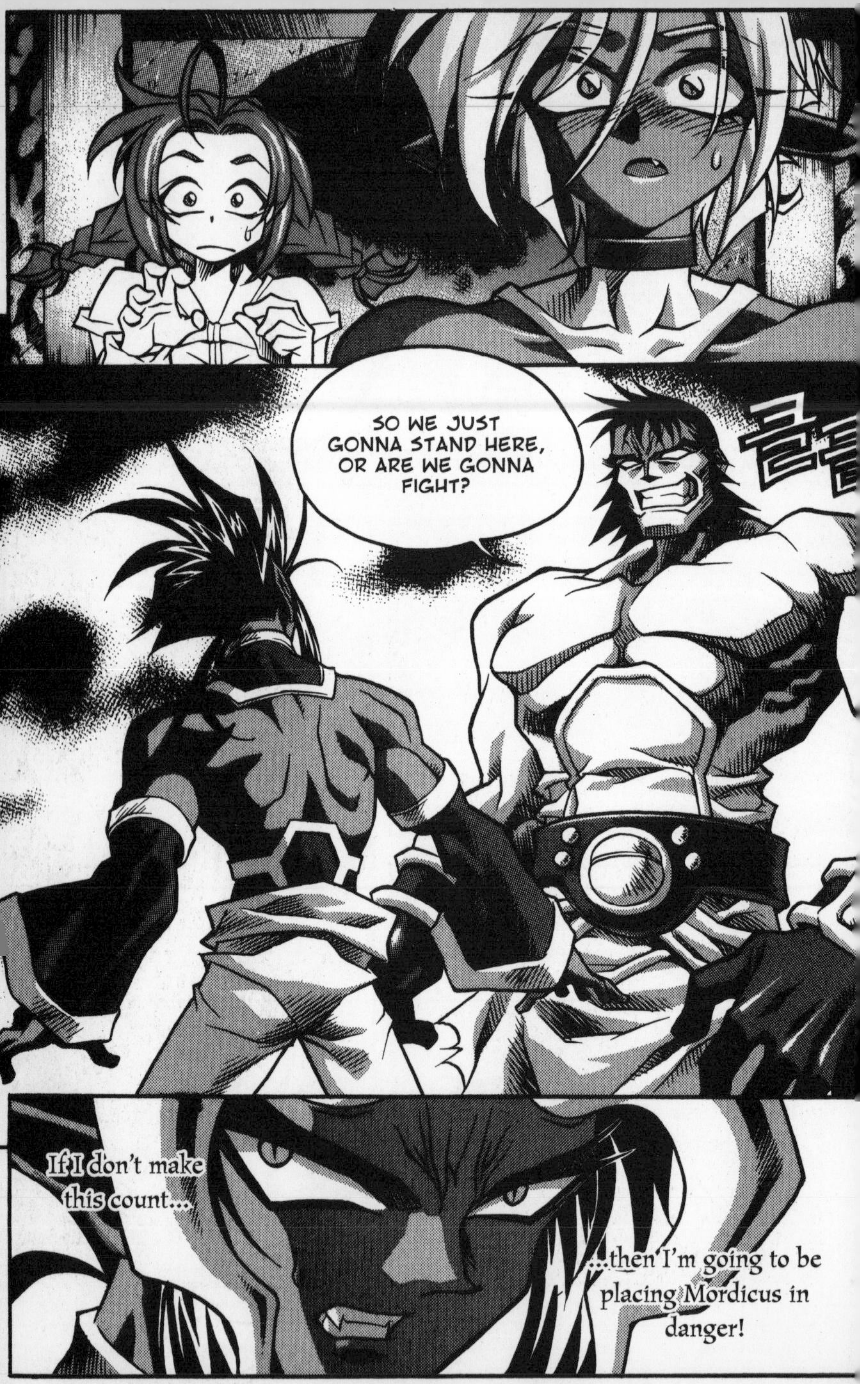
SO WE JUST GONNA STAND HERE, OR ARE WE GONNA FIGHT?
If I don't make this count...
...then I'm going to be placing Mordicus in danger!

Quest 16

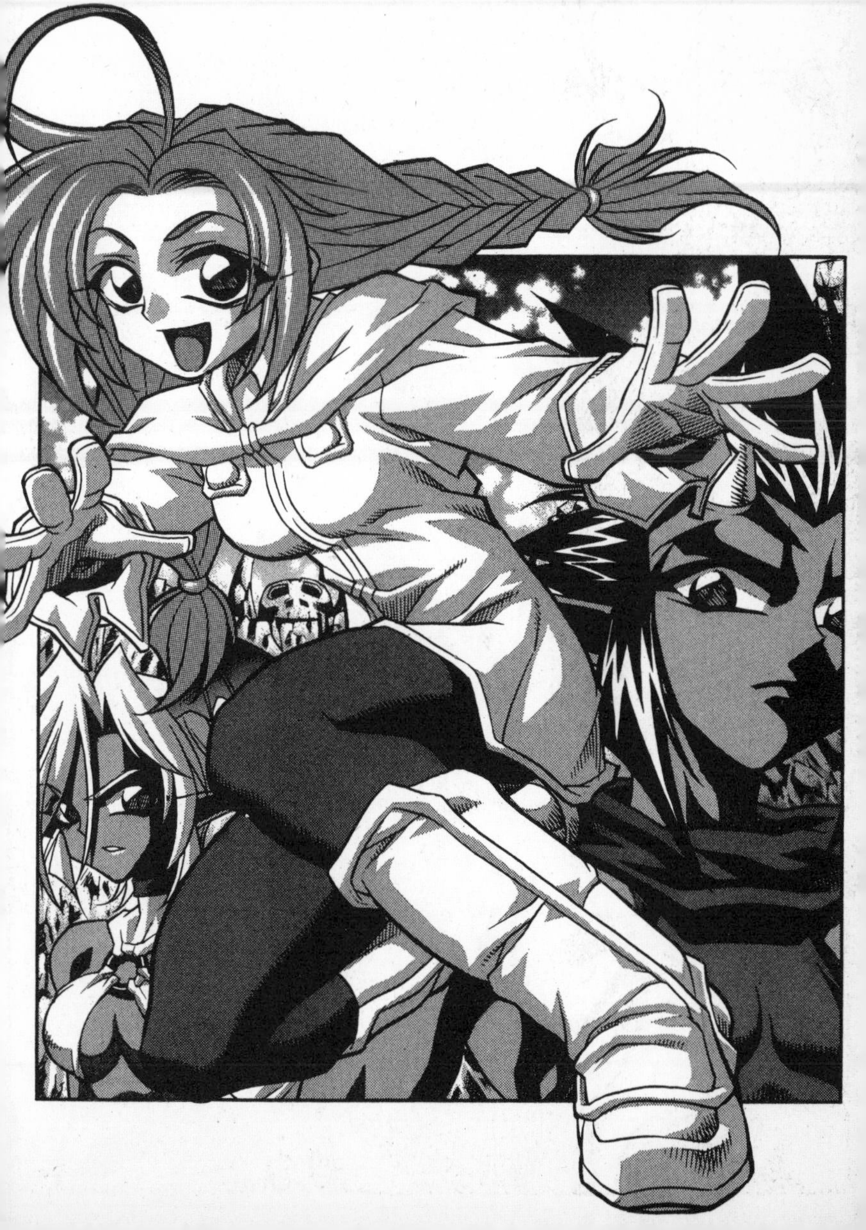

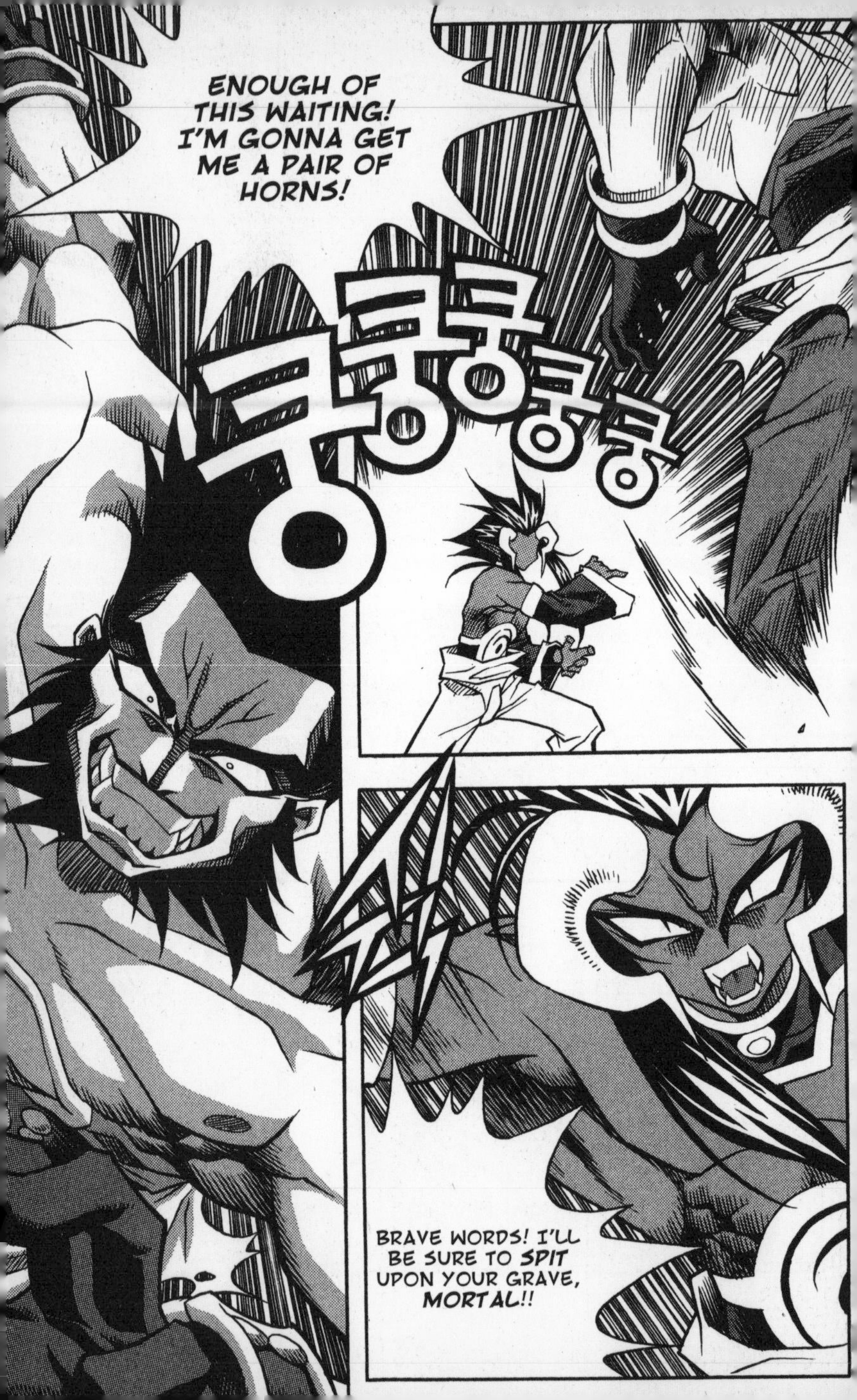
ENOUGH OF THIS WAITING! I'M GONNA GET ME A PAIR OF HORNS!
쿵쿵쿵쿵
BRAVE WORDS! I'LL BE SURE TO SPIT UPON YOUR GRAVE, MORTAL!!

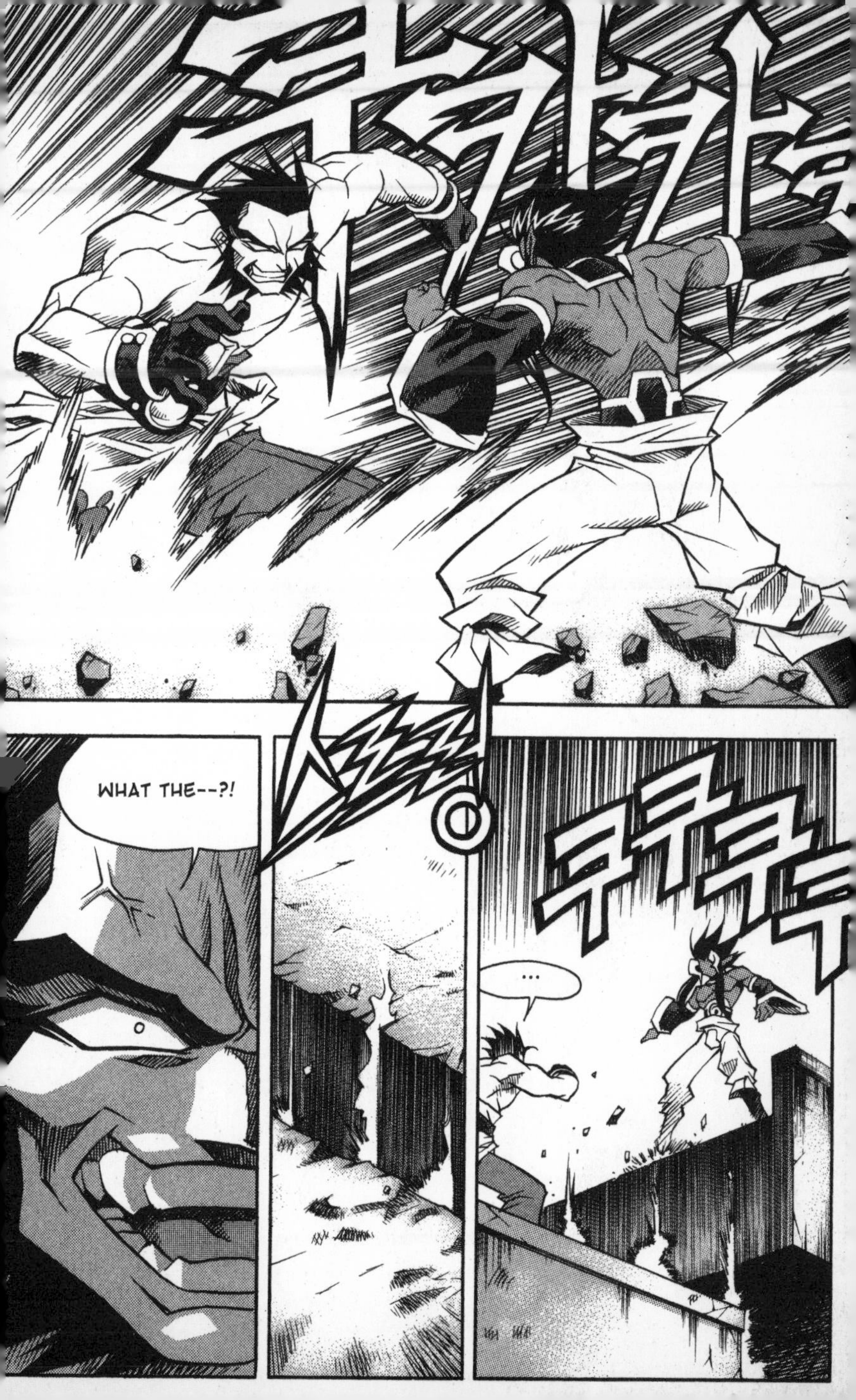
WHAT THE--?!
...

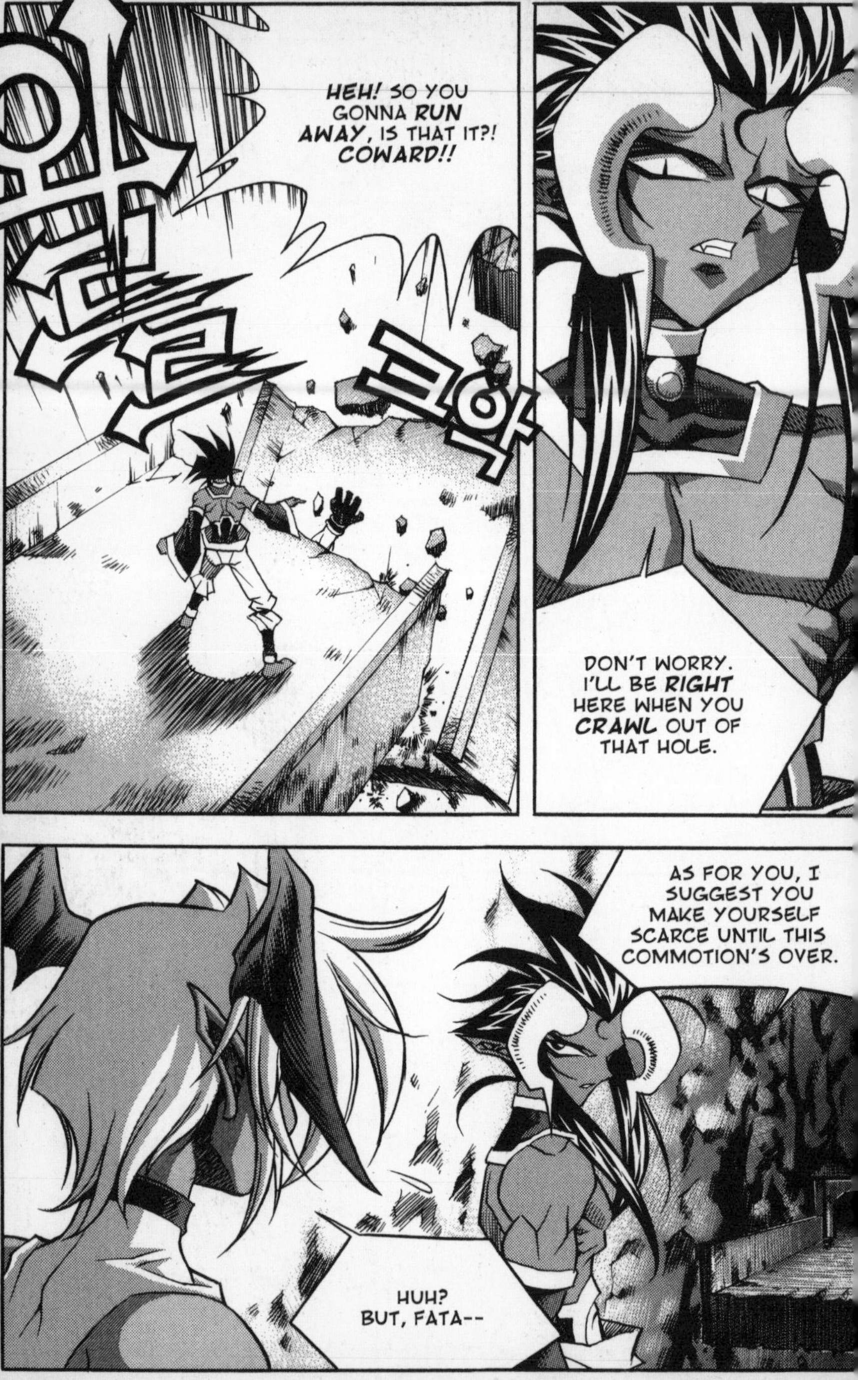
HEH! SO YOU GONNA RUN AWAY, IS THAT IT?! COWARD!!
DON'T WORRY. I'LL BE RIGHT HERE WHEN YOU CRAWL OUT OF THAT HOLE.
AS FOR YOU, I SUGGEST YOU MAKE YOURSELF SCARCE UNTIL THIS COMMOTION'S OVER.
HUH? BUT, FATA--

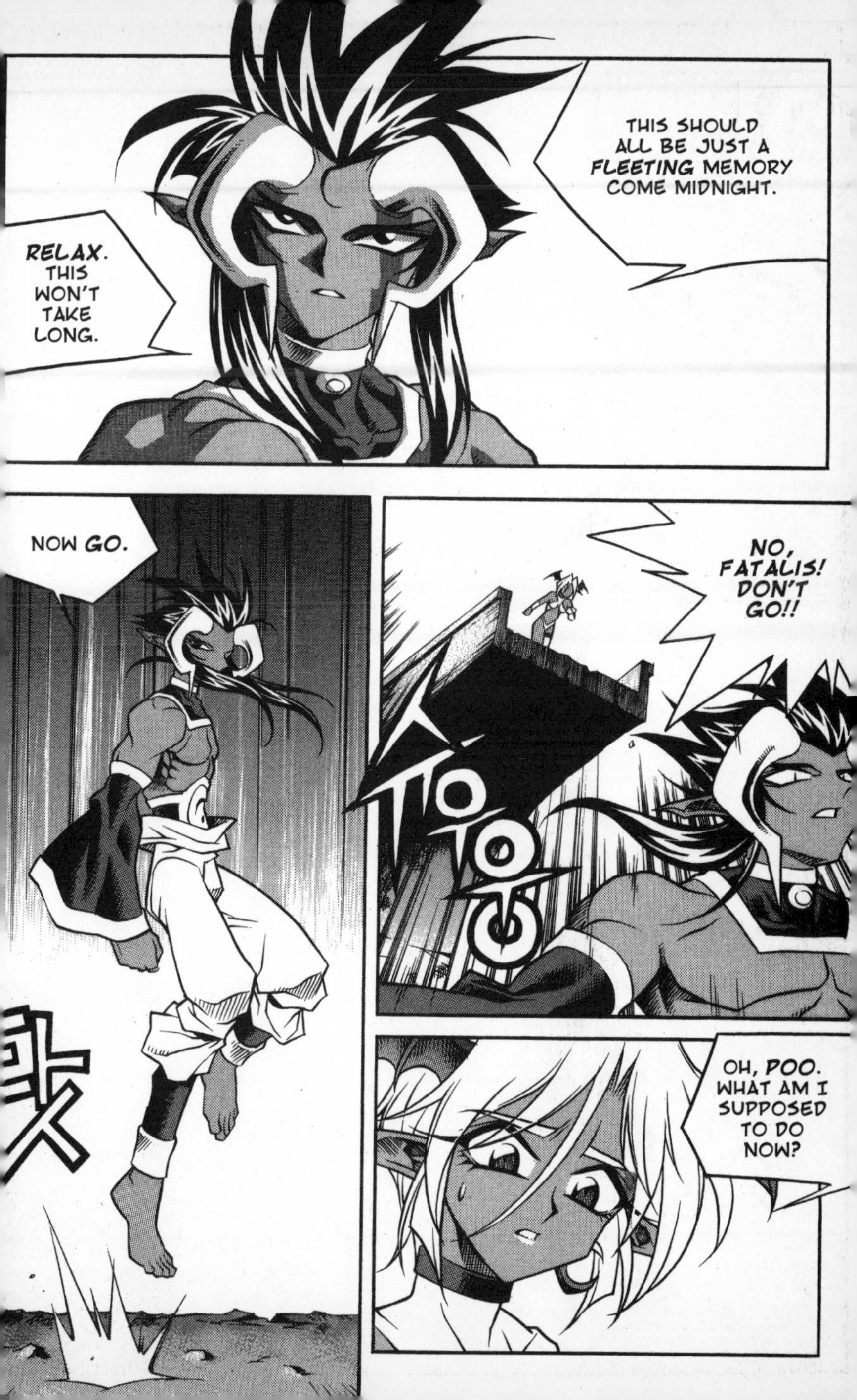
RELAX. THIS WON'T TAKE LONG.
THIS SHOULD ALL BE JUST A FLEETING MEMORY COME MIDNIGHT.
NOW GO.
NO, FATALIS! DON'T GO!!
OH, POO. WHAT AM I SUPPOSED TO DO NOW?

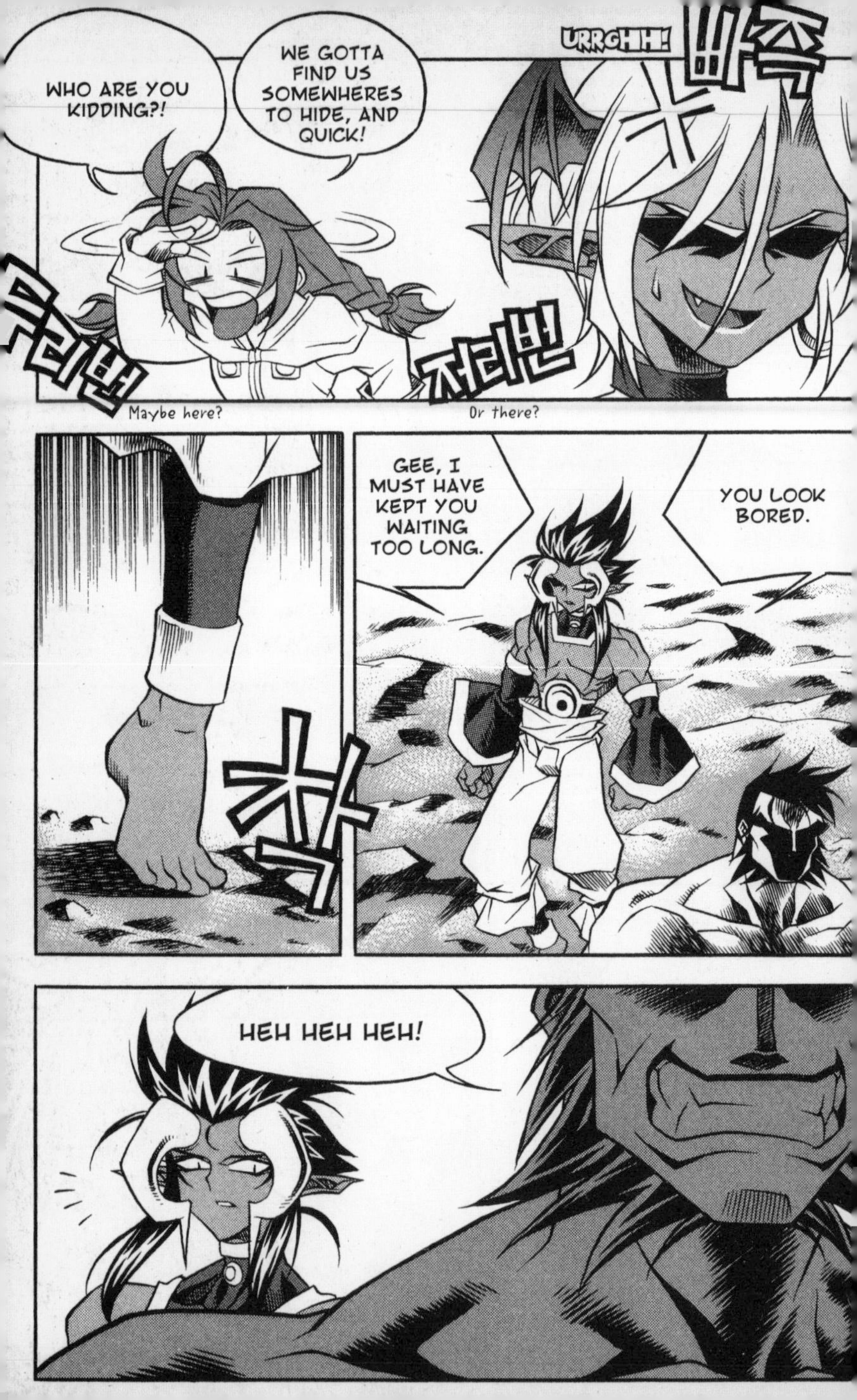
WHO ARE YOU KIDDING?!
WE GOTTA FIND US SOMEWHERES TO HIDE, AND QUICK!
URRGHH!
Maybe here?
Or there?
GEE, I MUST HAVE KEPT YOU WAITING TOO LONG.
YOU LOOK BORED.
HEH HEH HEH!

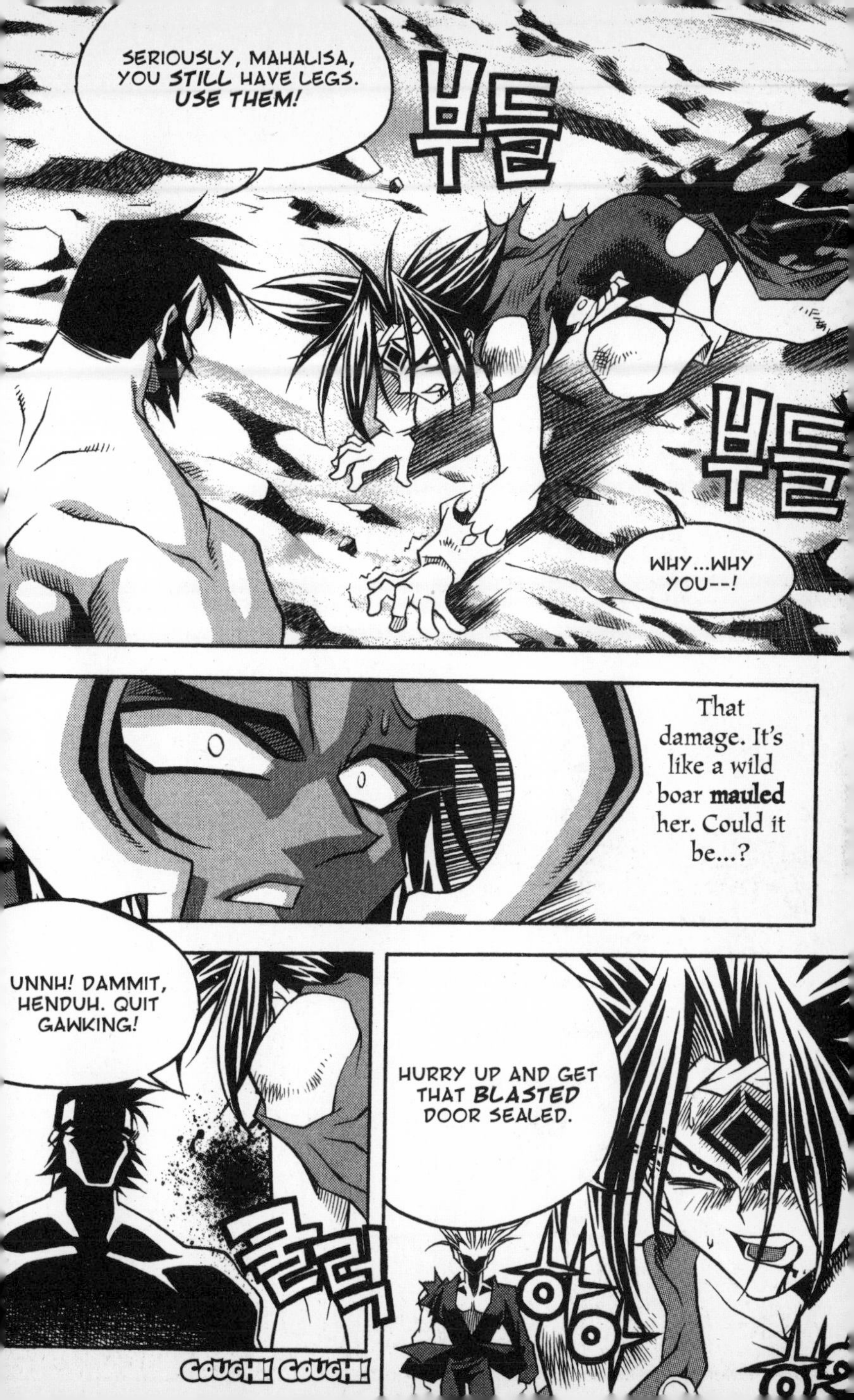
SERIOUSLY, MAHALISA, YOU STILL HAVE LEGS. USE THEM!
부들
부들
WHY...WHY YOU--!
That damage. It's like a wild boar mauled her. Could it be...?
UNNH! DAMMIT, HENDUH. QUIT GAWKING!
COUGH! COUGH!
HURRY UP AND GET THAT BLASTED DOOR SEALED.

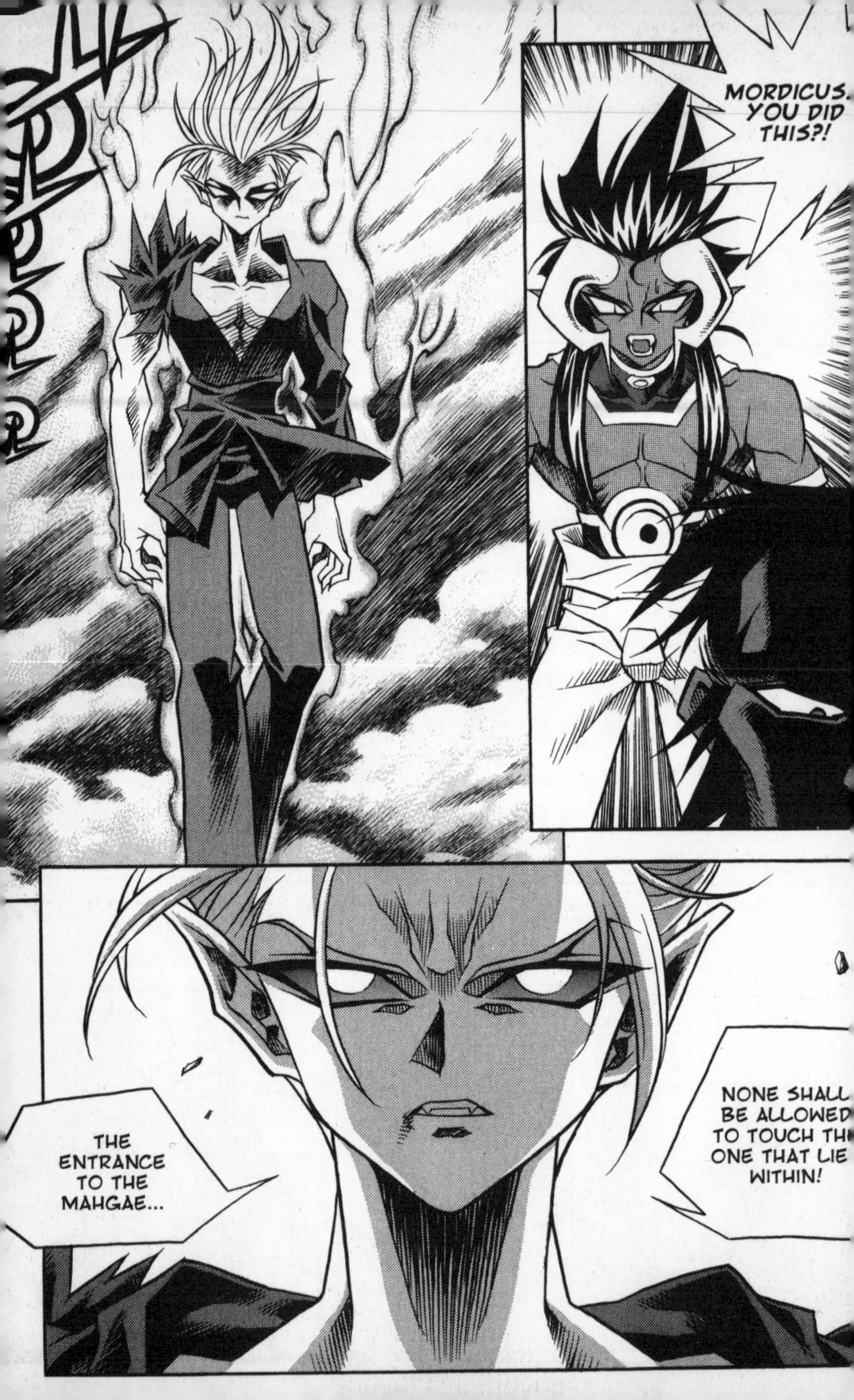
MORDICUS. YOU DID THIS?!
THE ENTRANCE TO THE MAHGAE...
NONE SHALL BE ALLOWED TO TOUCH TH ONE THAT LIE WITHIN!

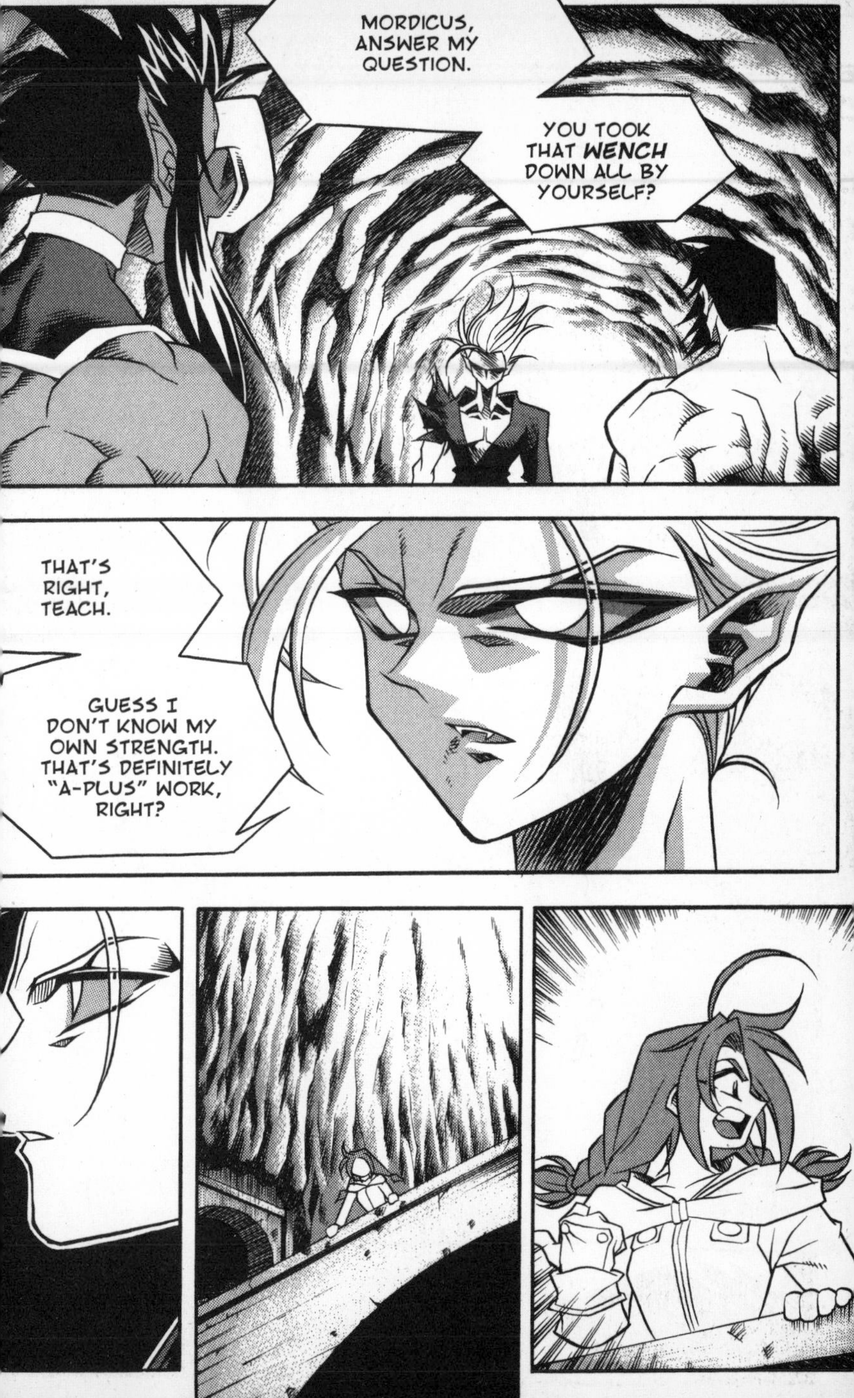
MORDICUS, ANSWER MY QUESTION.
YOU TOOK THAT WENCH DOWN ALL BY YOURSELF?
THAT'S RIGHT, TEACH.
GUESS I DON'T KNOW MY OWN STRENGTH. THAT'S DEFINITELY "A-PLUS" WORK, RIGHT?

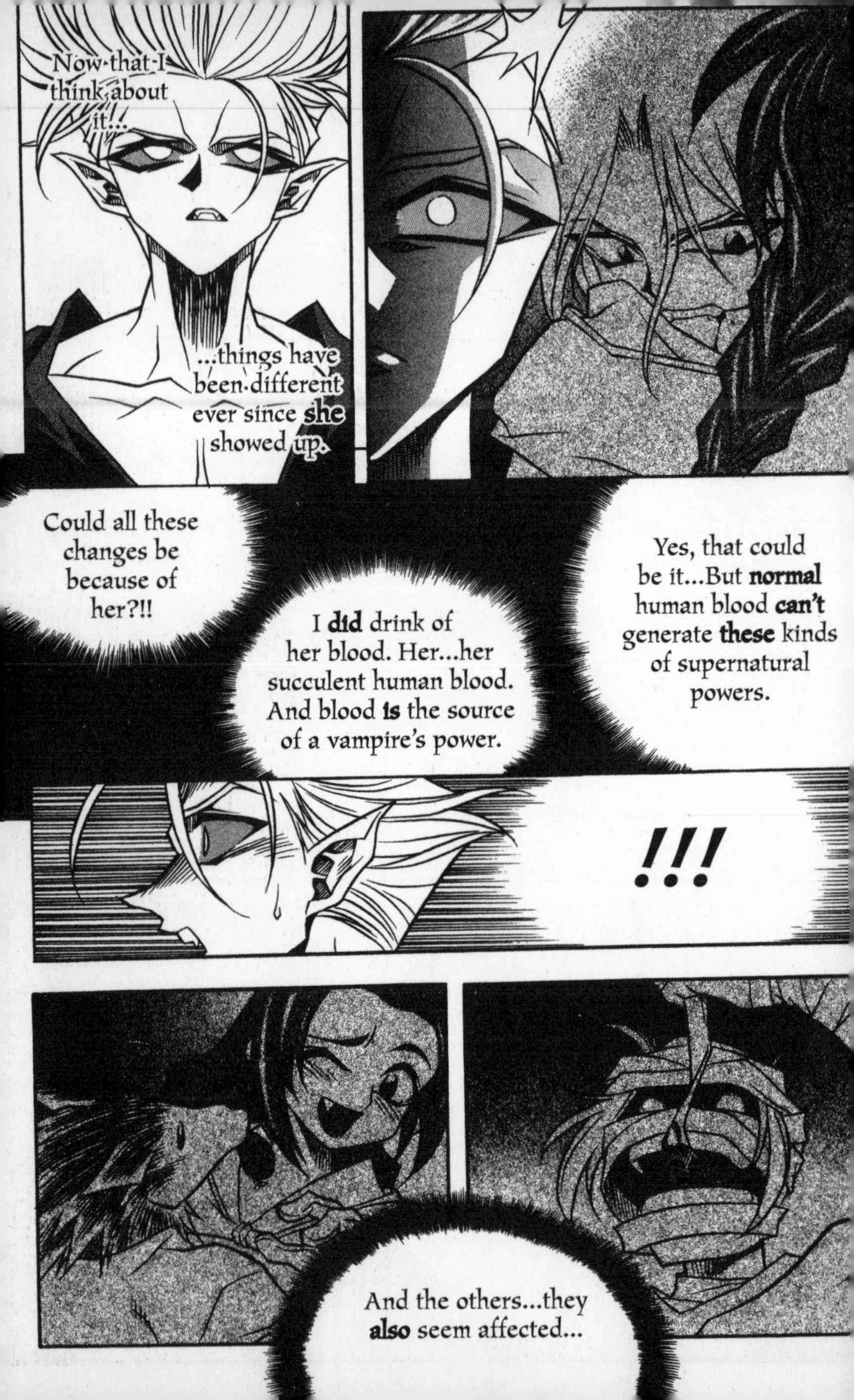
Now that I think about it...
...things have been different ever since she showed up.
Could all these changes be because of her?!!
I did drink of her blood. Her...her succulent human blood. And blood is the source of a vampire's power.
Yes, that could be it...But normal human blood can't generate these kinds of supernatural powers.
!!!
And the others...they also seem affected...

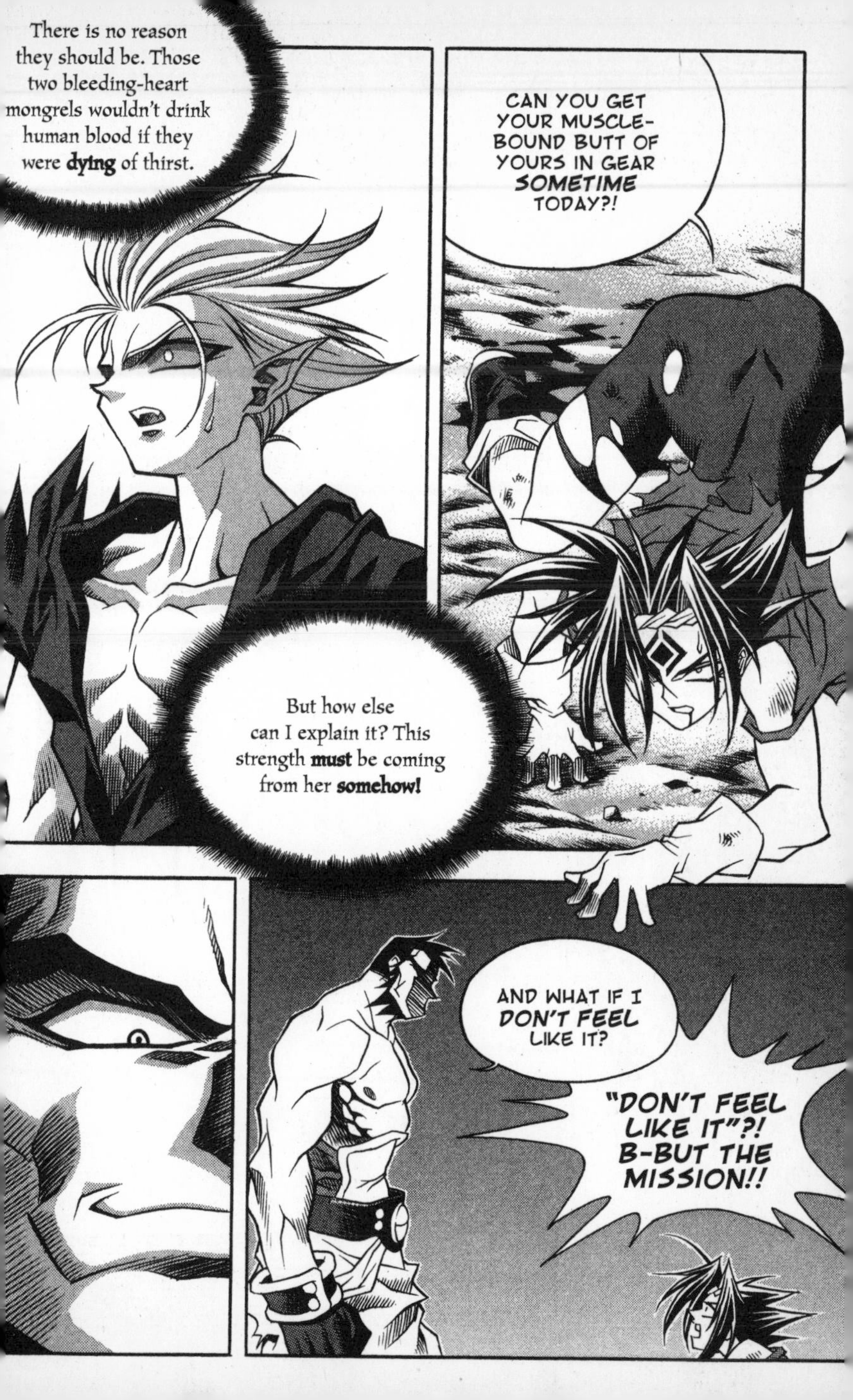
There is no reason they should be. Those two bleeding-heart mongrels wouldn't drink human blood if they were **dying** of thirst.
CAN YOU GET YOUR MUSCLE-BOUND BUTT OF YOURS IN GEAR *SOMETIME* TODAY?!
But how else can I explain it? This strength **must** be coming from her **somehow!**
AND WHAT IF I *DON'T FEEL* LIKE IT?
"DON'T FEEL LIKE IT"?! B-BUT THE MISSION!!

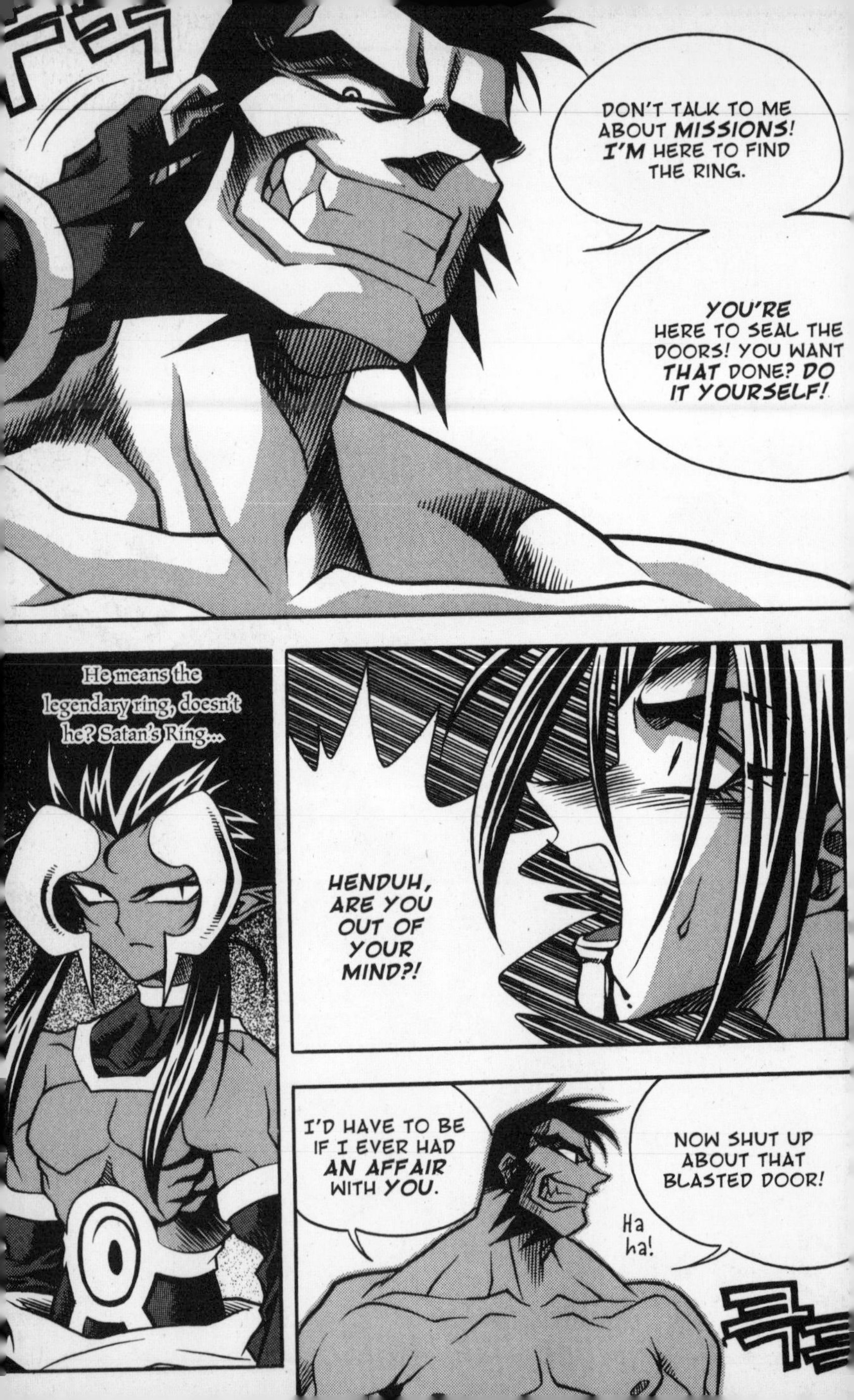
DON'T TALK TO ME ABOUT MISSIONS! I'M HERE TO FIND THE RING.
YOU'RE HERE TO SEAL THE DOORS! YOU WANT THAT DONE? DO IT YOURSELF!
He means the legendary ring, doesn't he? Satan's Ring...
HENDUH, ARE YOU OUT OF YOUR MIND?!
I'D HAVE TO BE IF I EVER HAD AN AFFAIR WITH YOU.
NOW SHUT UP ABOUT THAT BLASTED DOOR!
Ha ha!

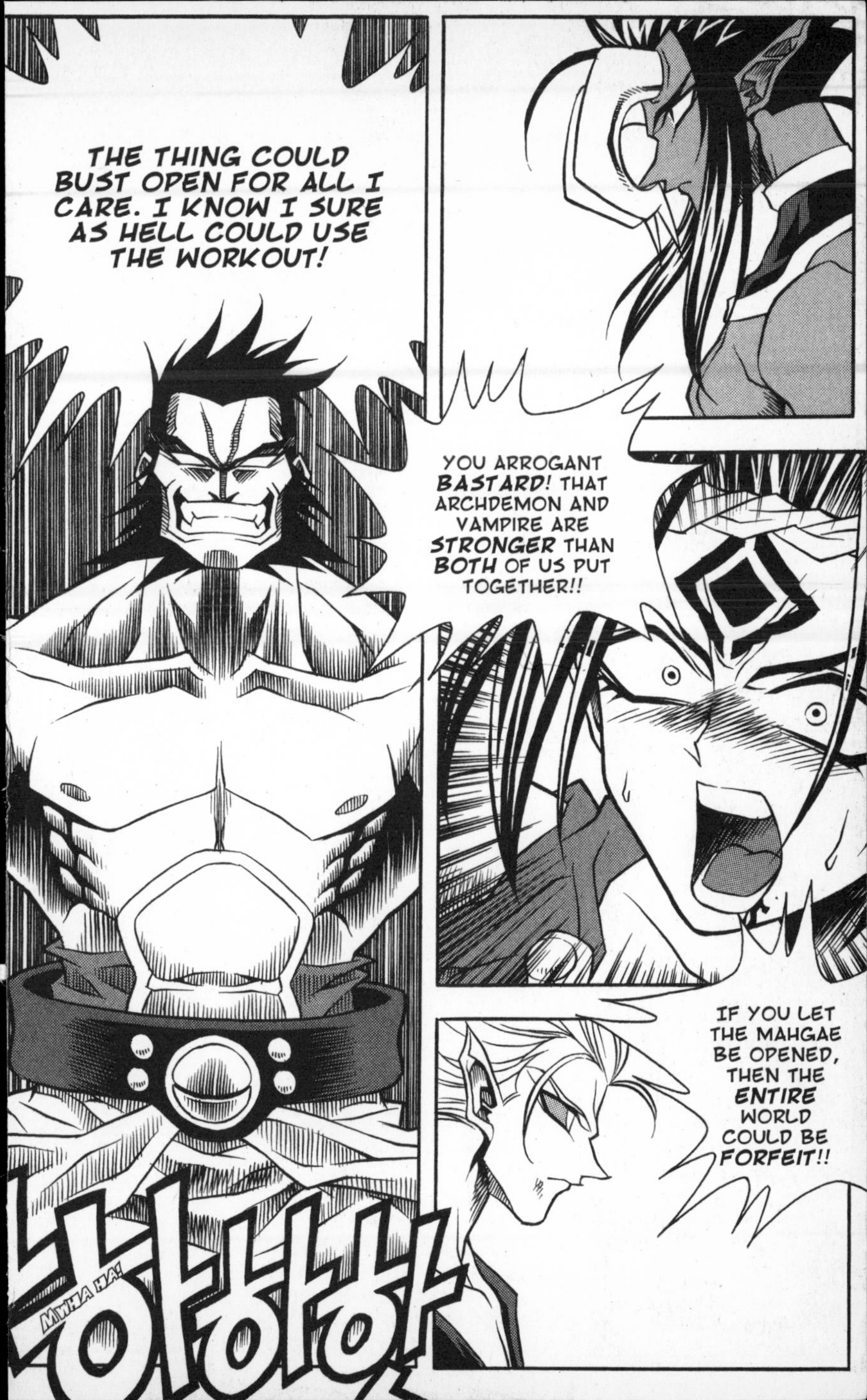
THE THING COULD BUST OPEN FOR ALL I CARE. I KNOW I SURE AS HELL COULD USE THE WORKOUT!
MWHA HA!
YOU ARROGANT BASTARD! THAT ARCHDEMON AND VAMPIRE ARE STRONGER THAN BOTH OF US PUT TOGETHER!!
IF YOU LET THE MAHGAE BE OPENED, THEN THE ENTIRE WORLD COULD BE FORFEIT!!

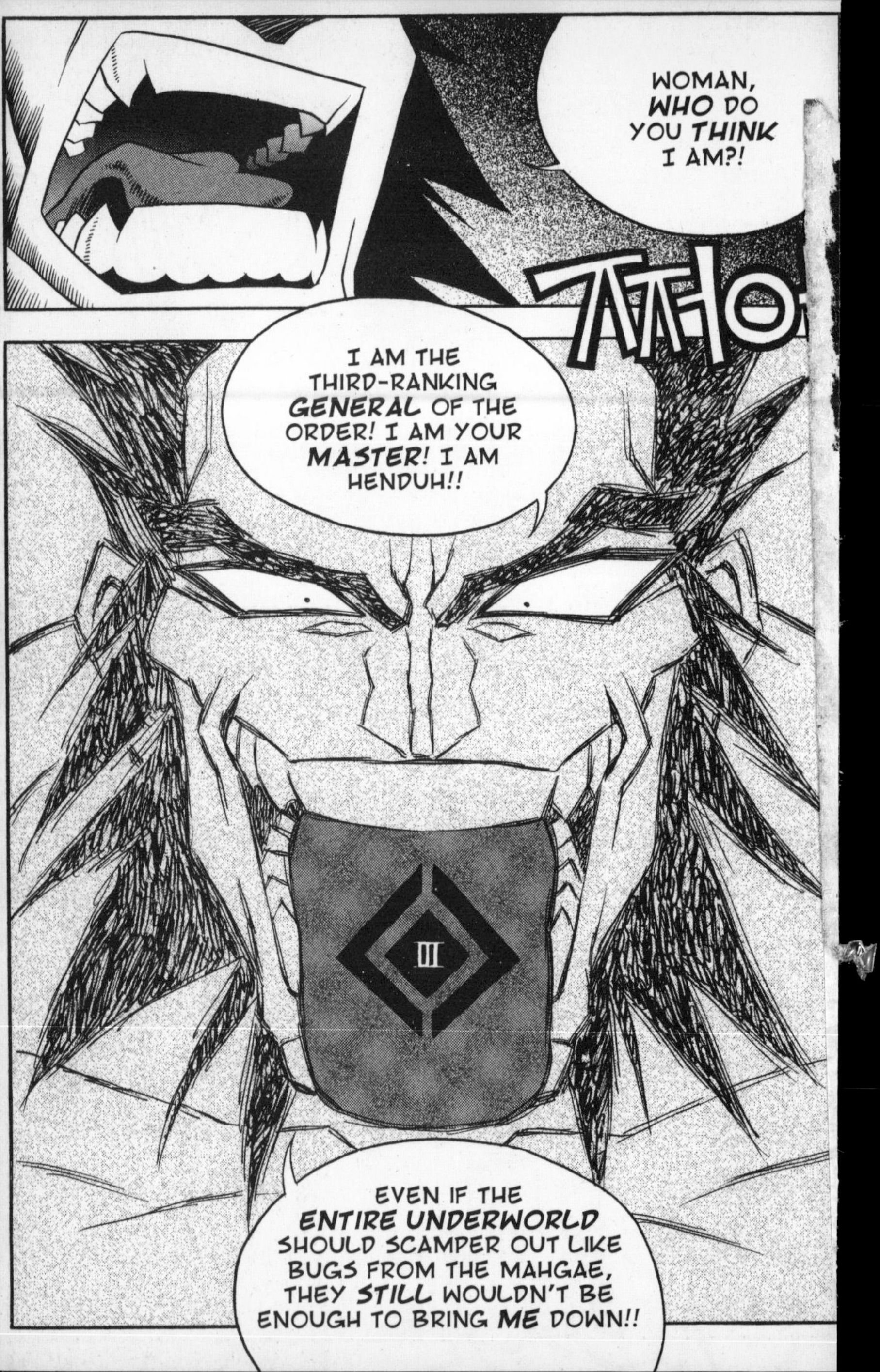
WOMAN, WHO DO YOU THINK I AM?!
I AM THE THIRD-RANKING GENERAL OF THE ORDER! I AM YOUR MASTER! I AM HENDUH!!
EVEN IF THE ENTIRE UNDERWORLD SHOULD SCAMPER OUT LIKE BUGS FROM THE MAHGAE, THEY STILL WOULDN'T BE ENOUGH TO BRING ME DOWN!!

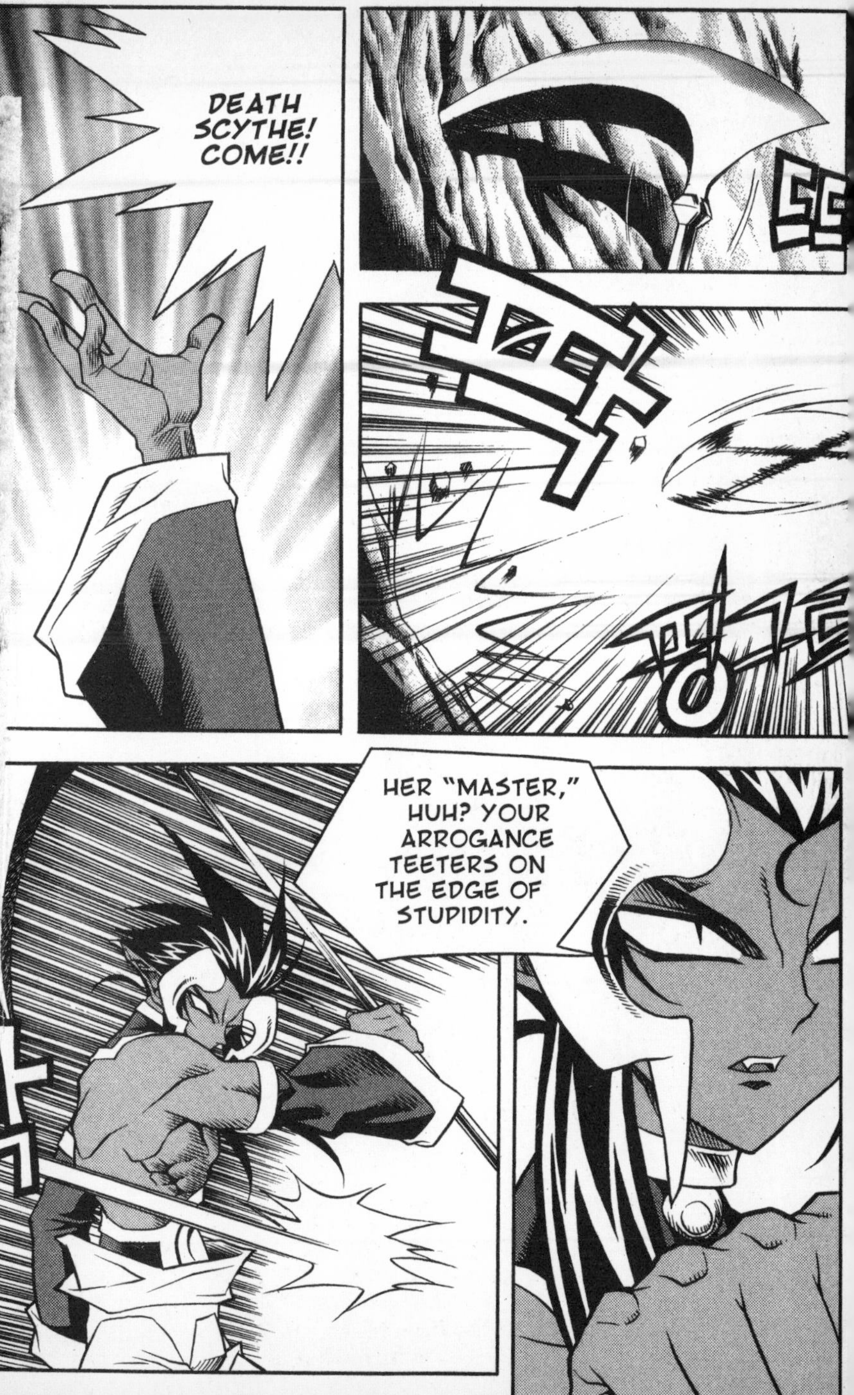
DEATH SCYTHE! COME!!
HER "MASTER," HUH? YOUR ARROGANCE TEETERS ON THE EDGE OF STUPIDITY.

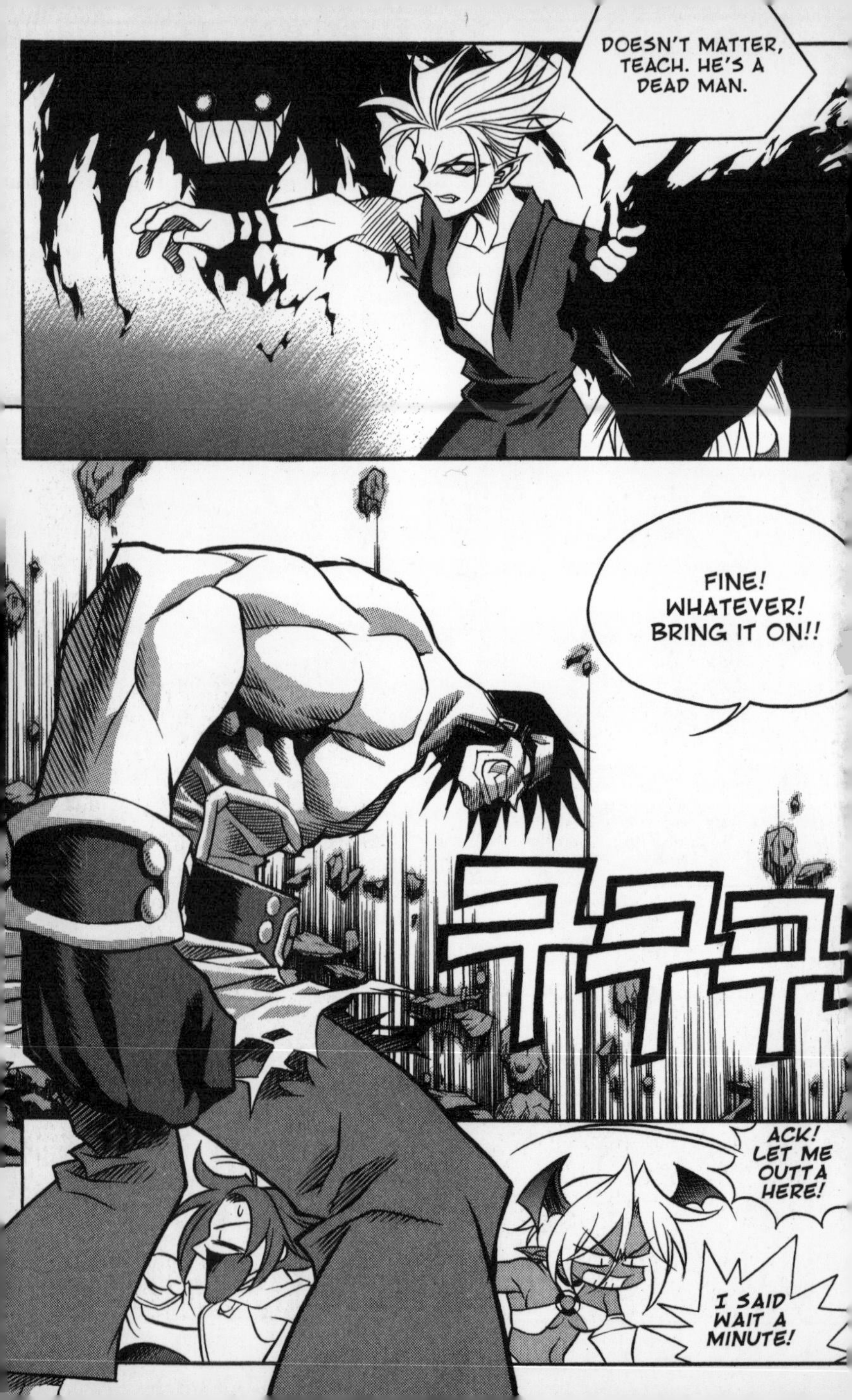
DOESN'T MATTER, TEACH. HE'S A DEAD MAN.
FINE! WHATEVER! BRING IT ON!!
ACK! LET ME OUTTA HERE!
I SAID WAIT A MINUTE!

Quest 17

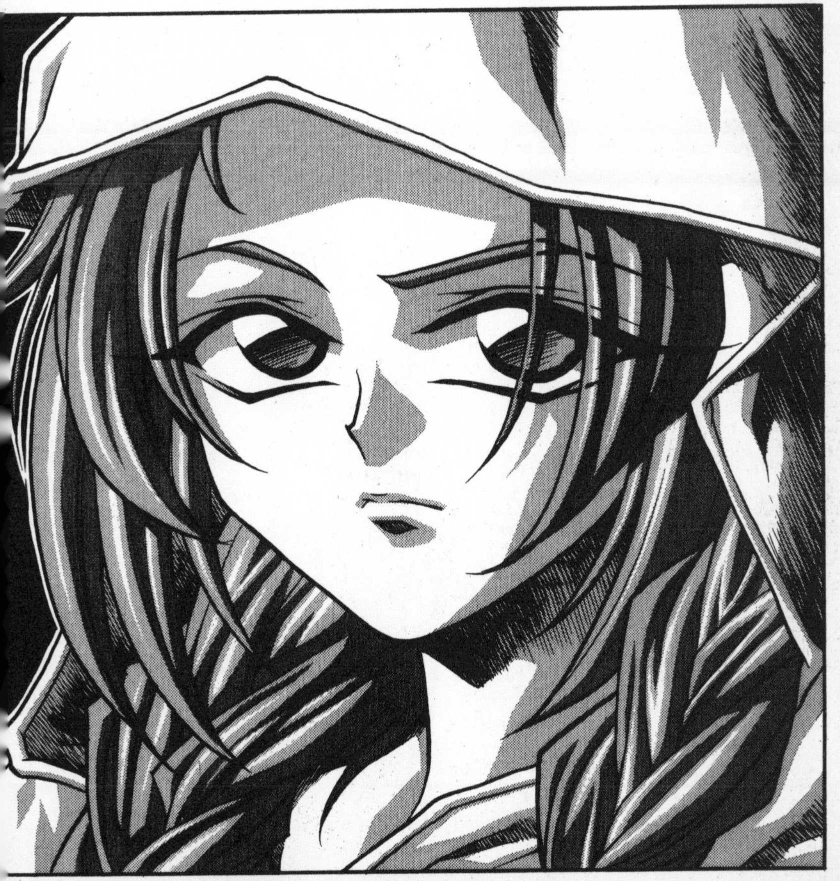

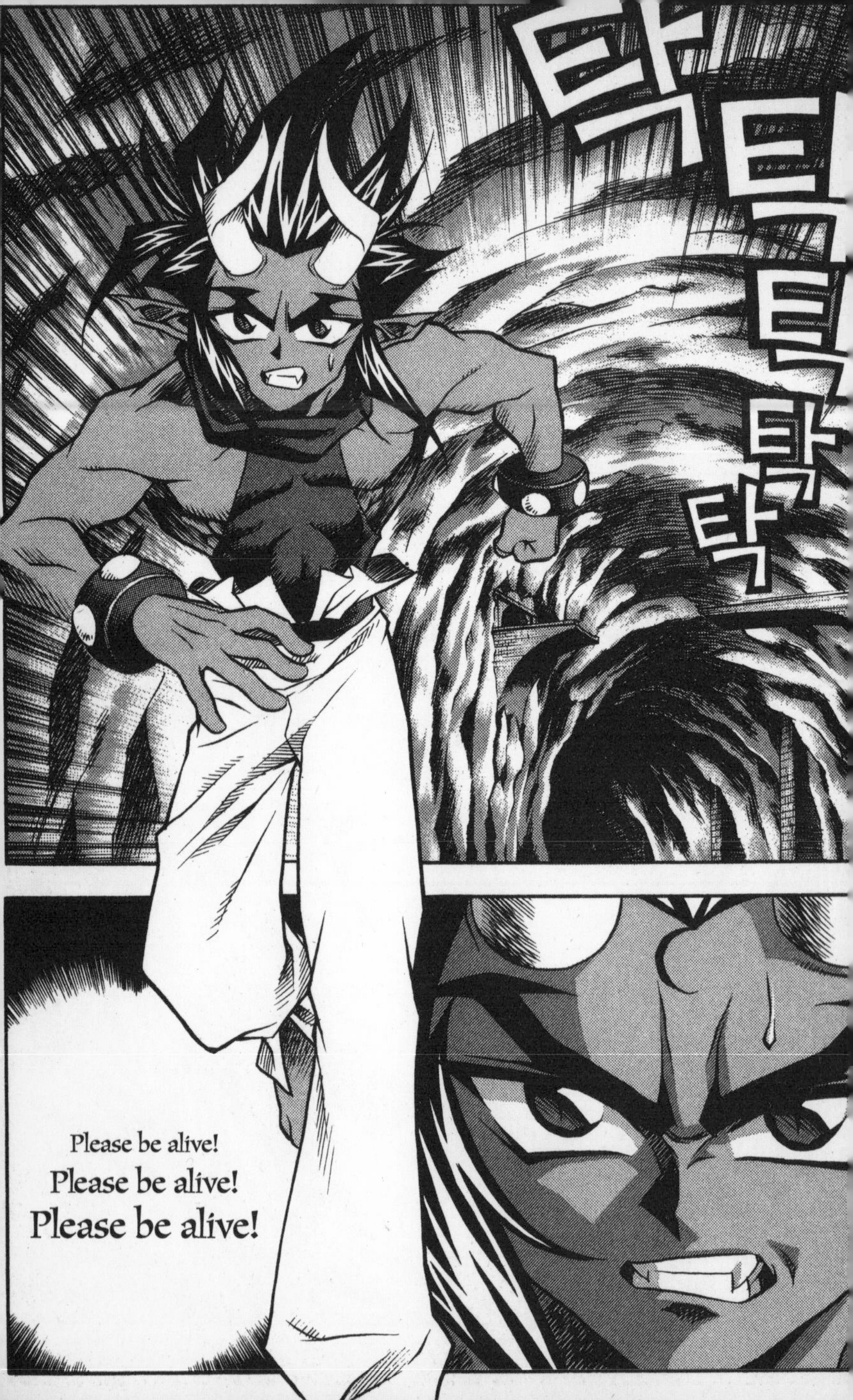

탁
탁
탁
탁
탁
Please be alive!
Please be alive!
Please be alive!

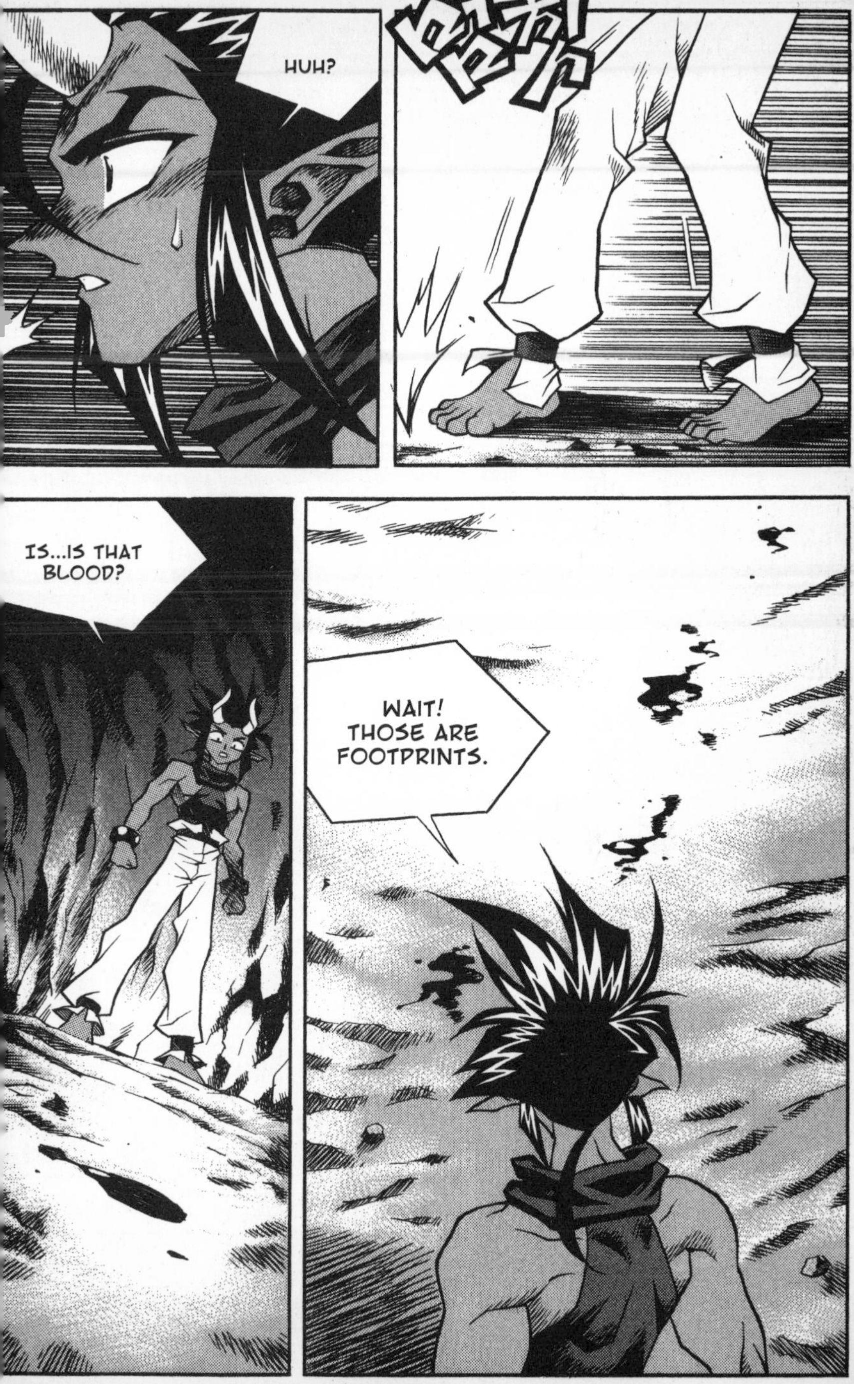
HUH?
IS...IS THAT BLOOD?
WAIT! THOSE ARE FOOTPRINTS.

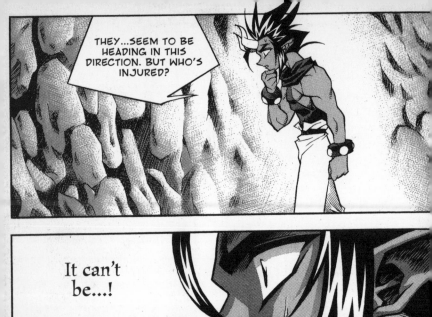

THEY...SEEM TO BE HEADING IN THIS DIRECTION. BUT WHO'S INJURED?

It can't be...!

Not Notra!!

OH, LEAPIN' LUCIFER! WHAT IF IT'S SERIOUS?! THAT'S A LOT OF BLOOD!!

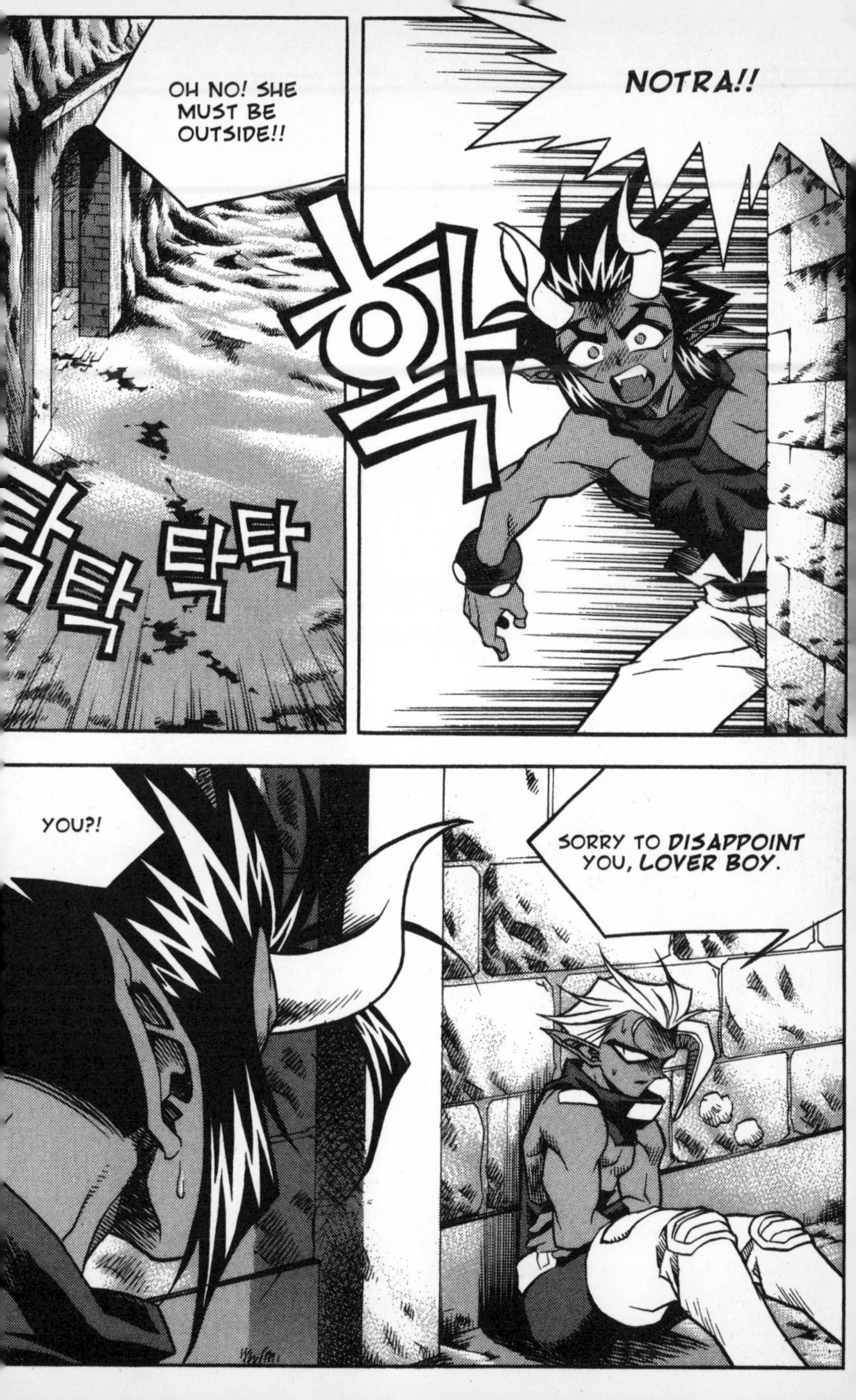
OH NO! SHE MUST BE OUTSIDE!!
탁탁 탁탁
NOTRA!!
왁
YOU?!
SORRY TO DISAPPOINT YOU, LOVER BOY.

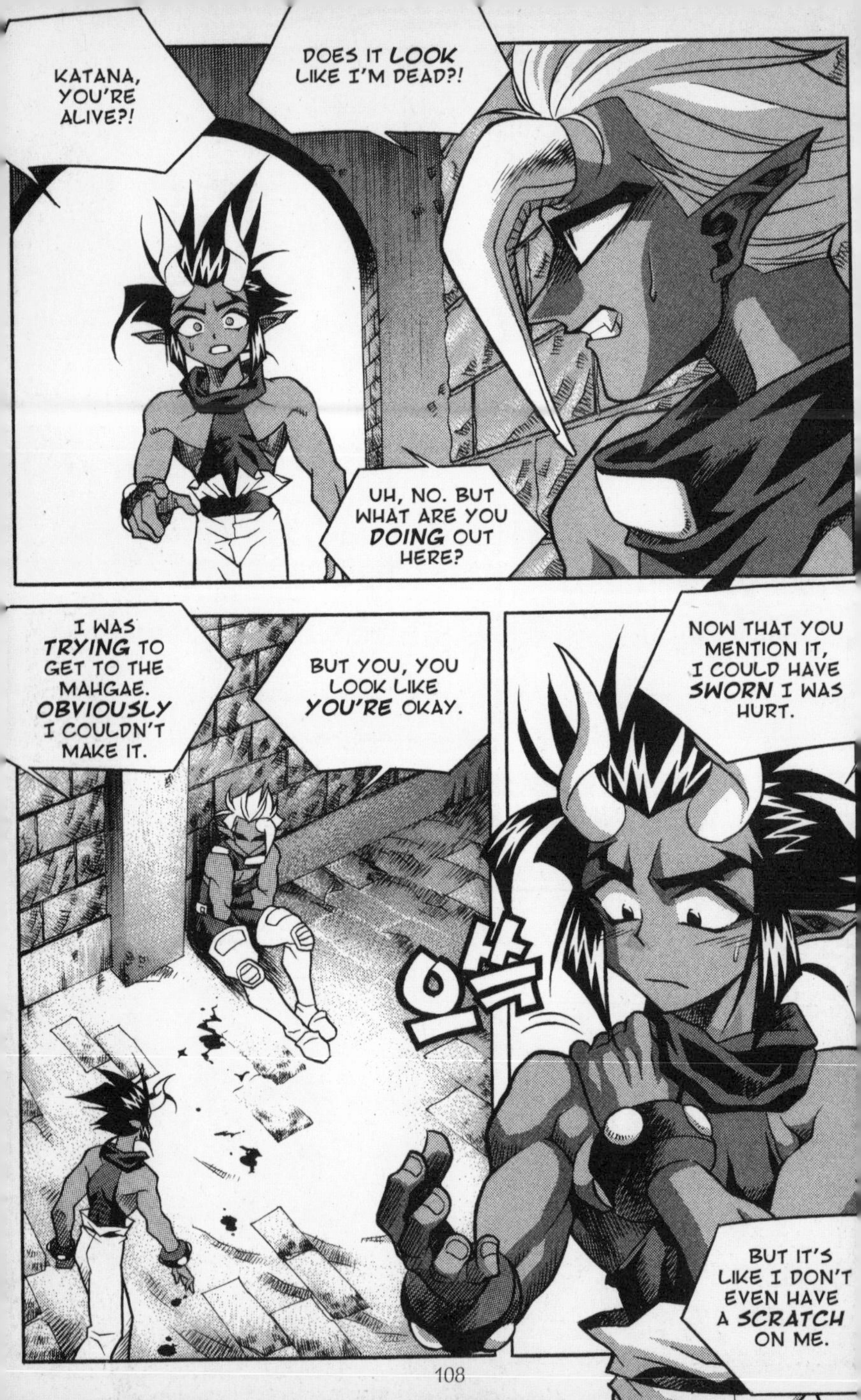
KATANA, YOU'RE ALIVE?!
DOES IT LOOK LIKE I'M DEAD?!
UH, NO. BUT WHAT ARE YOU DOING OUT HERE?
I WAS TRYING TO GET TO THE MAHGAE. OBVIOUSLY I COULDN'T MAKE IT.
BUT YOU, YOU LOOK LIKE YOU'RE OKAY.
NOW THAT YOU MENTION IT, I COULD HAVE SWORN I WAS HURT.
BUT IT'S LIKE I DON'T EVEN HAVE A SCRATCH ON ME.

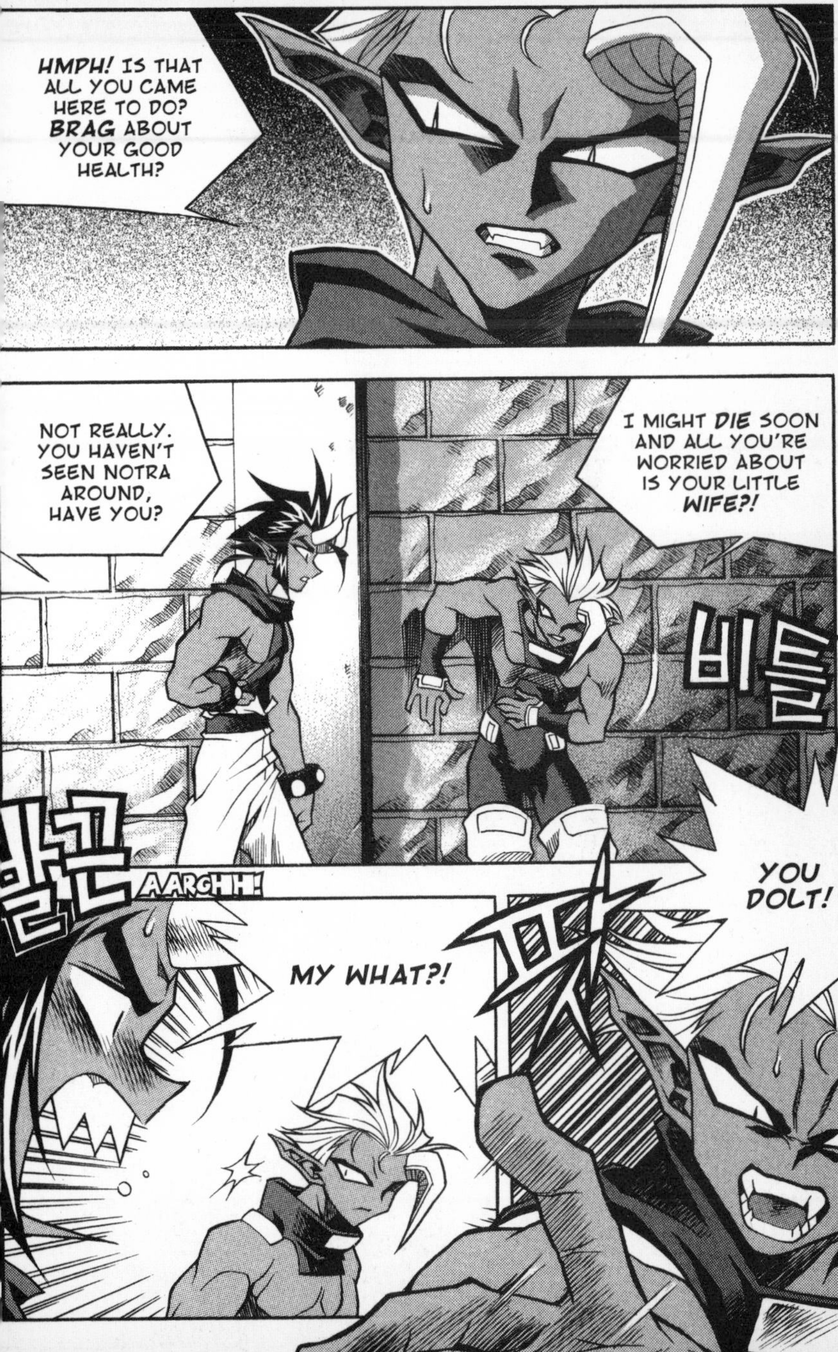
HMPH! IS THAT ALL YOU CAME HERE TO DO? BRAG ABOUT YOUR GOOD HEALTH?
NOT REALLY. YOU HAVEN'T SEEN NOTRA AROUND, HAVE YOU?
I MIGHT DIE SOON AND ALL YOU'RE WORRIED ABOUT IS YOUR LITTLE WIFE?!
비틀
AARGHH!
MY WHAT?!
YOU DOLT!

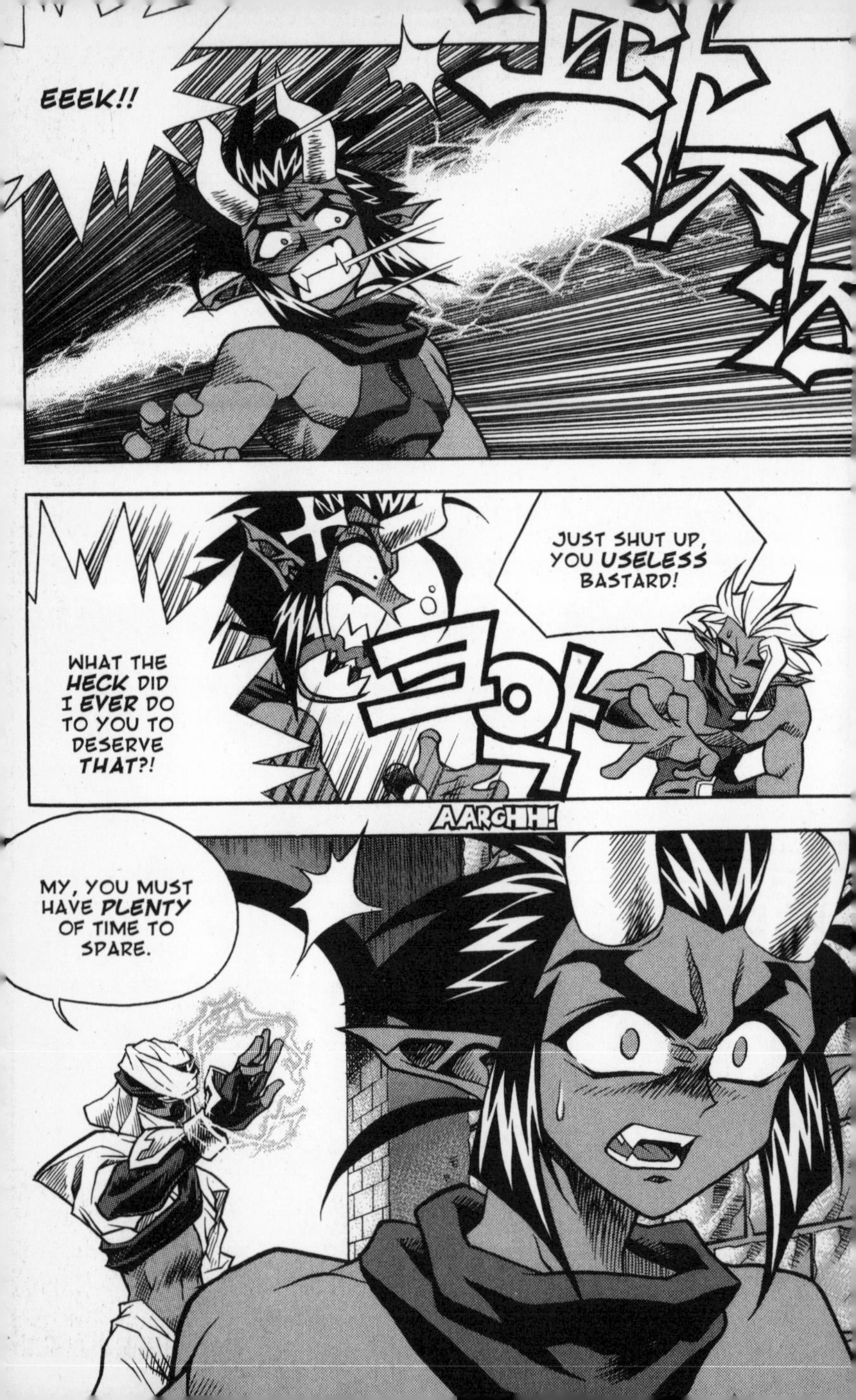
EEEK!!
WHAT THE HECK DID I EVER DO TO YOU TO DESERVE THAT?!
JUST SHUT UP, YOU USELESS BASTARD!
AARGHH!
MY, YOU MUST HAVE PLENTY OF TIME TO SPARE.

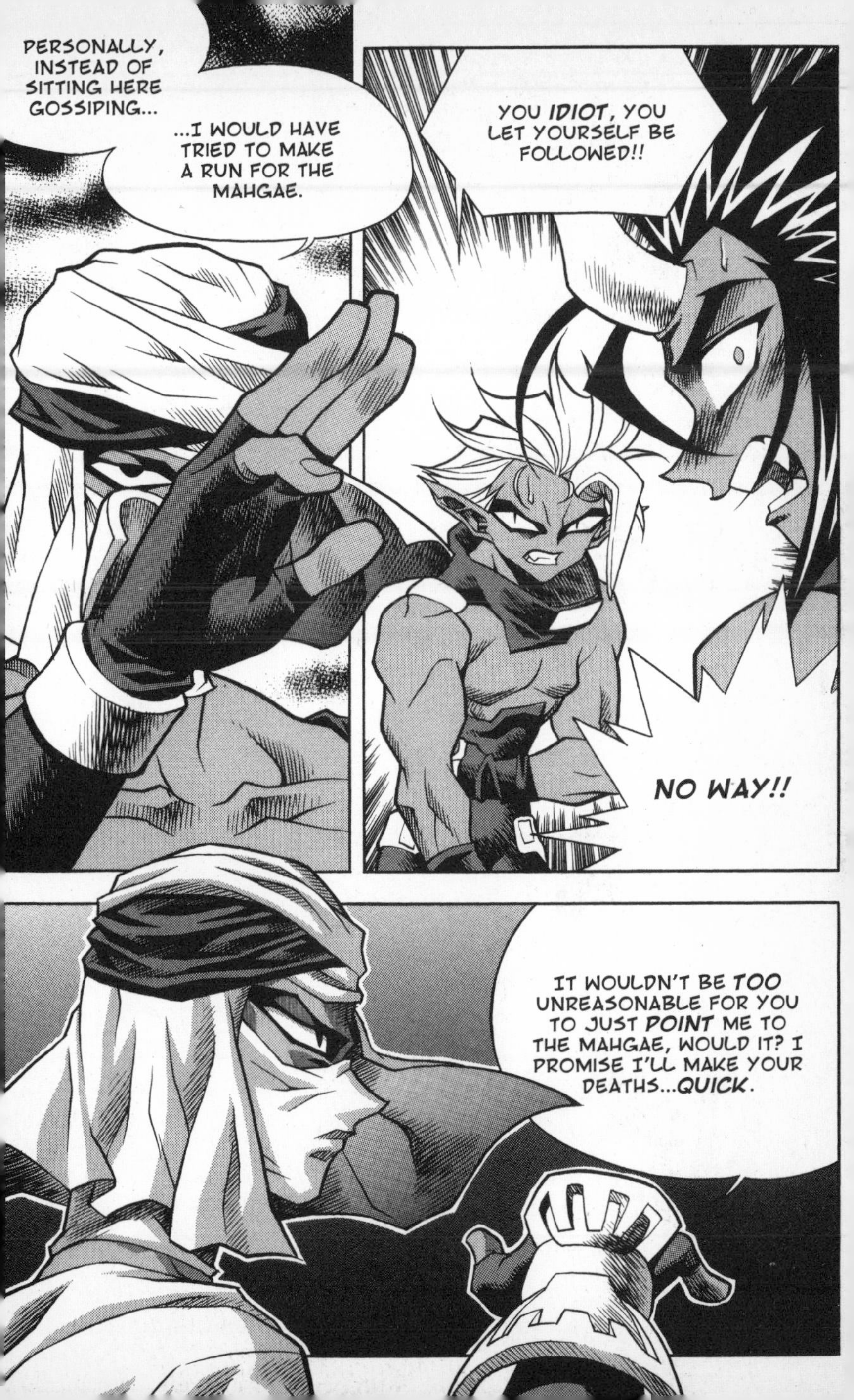
PERSONALLY, INSTEAD OF SITTING HERE GOSSIPING...
...I WOULD HAVE TRIED TO MAKE A RUN FOR THE MAHGAE.
YOU *IDIOT*, YOU LET YOURSELF BE FOLLOWED!!
NO WAY!!
IT WOULDN'T BE *TOO* UNREASONABLE FOR YOU TO JUST *POINT* ME TO THE MAHGAE, WOULD IT? I PROMISE I'LL MAKE YOUR DEATHS...*QUICK*.

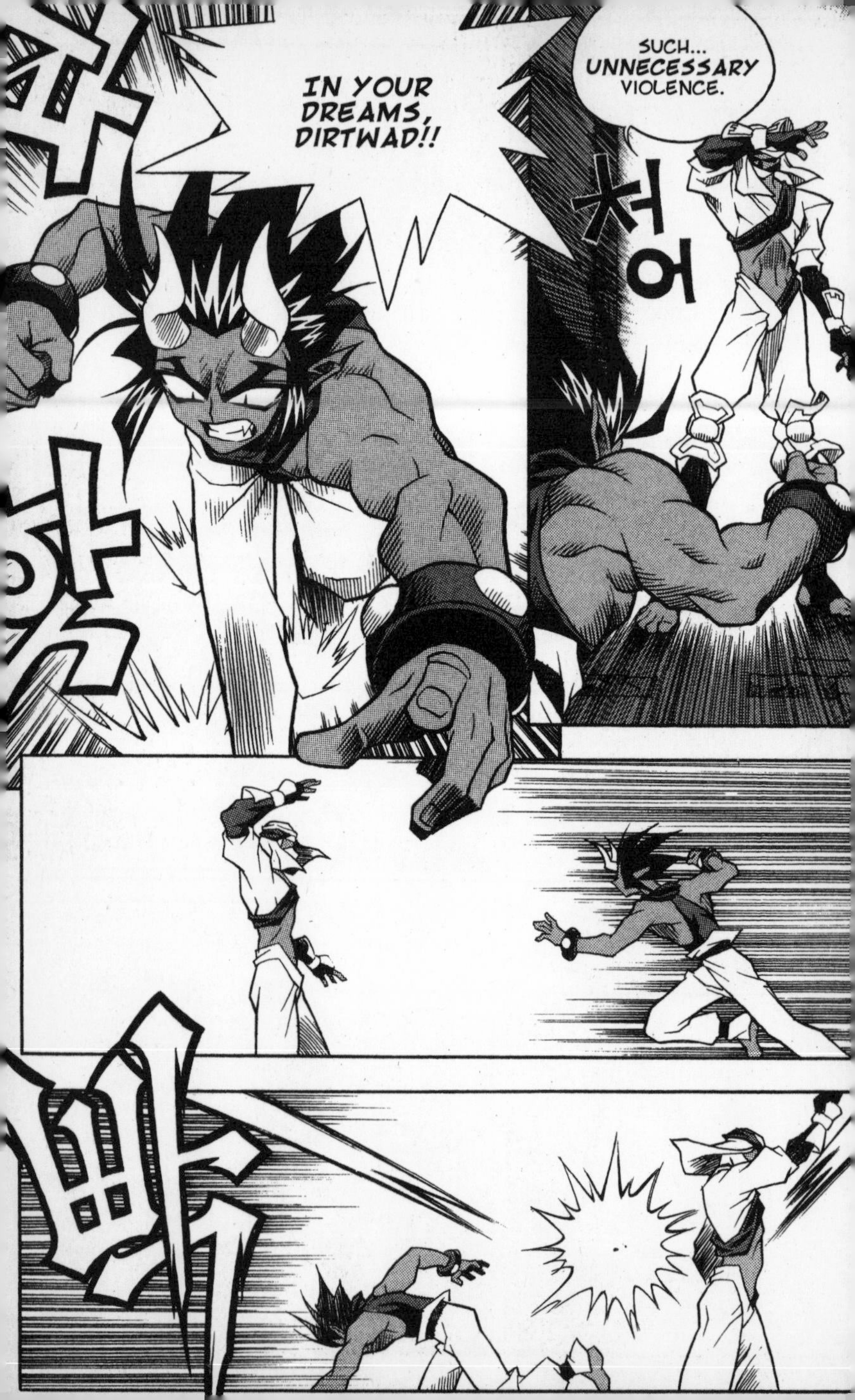
IN YOUR DREAMS, DIRTWAD!!
SUCH... UNNECESSARY VIOLENCE.

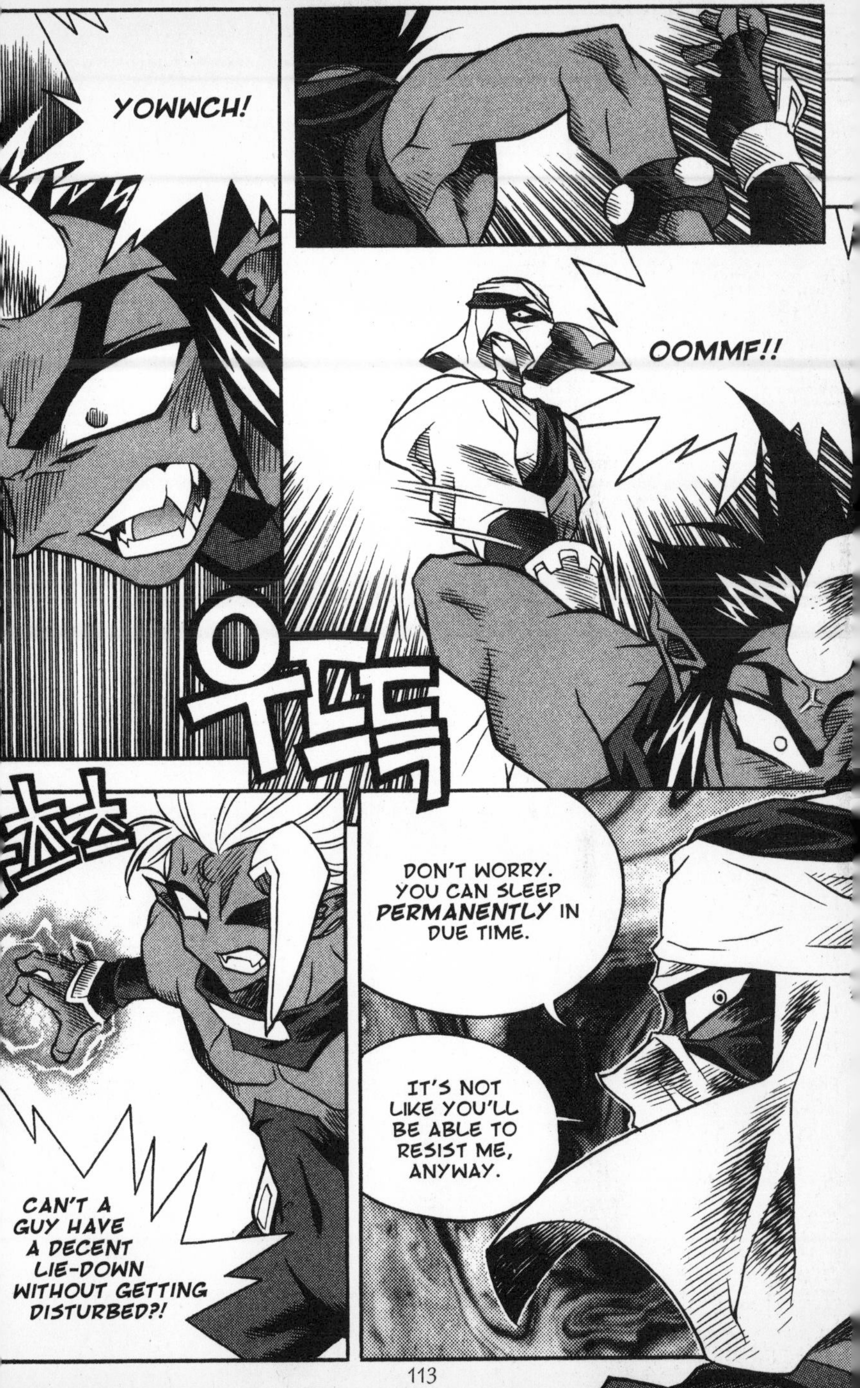
YOWNCH!
OOMMF!!
CAN'T A GUY HAVE A DECENT LIE-DOWN WITHOUT GETTING DISTURBED?!
DON'T WORRY. YOU CAN SLEEP *PERMANENTLY* IN DUE TIME.
IT'S NOT LIKE YOU'LL BE ABLE TO RESIST ME, ANYWAY.

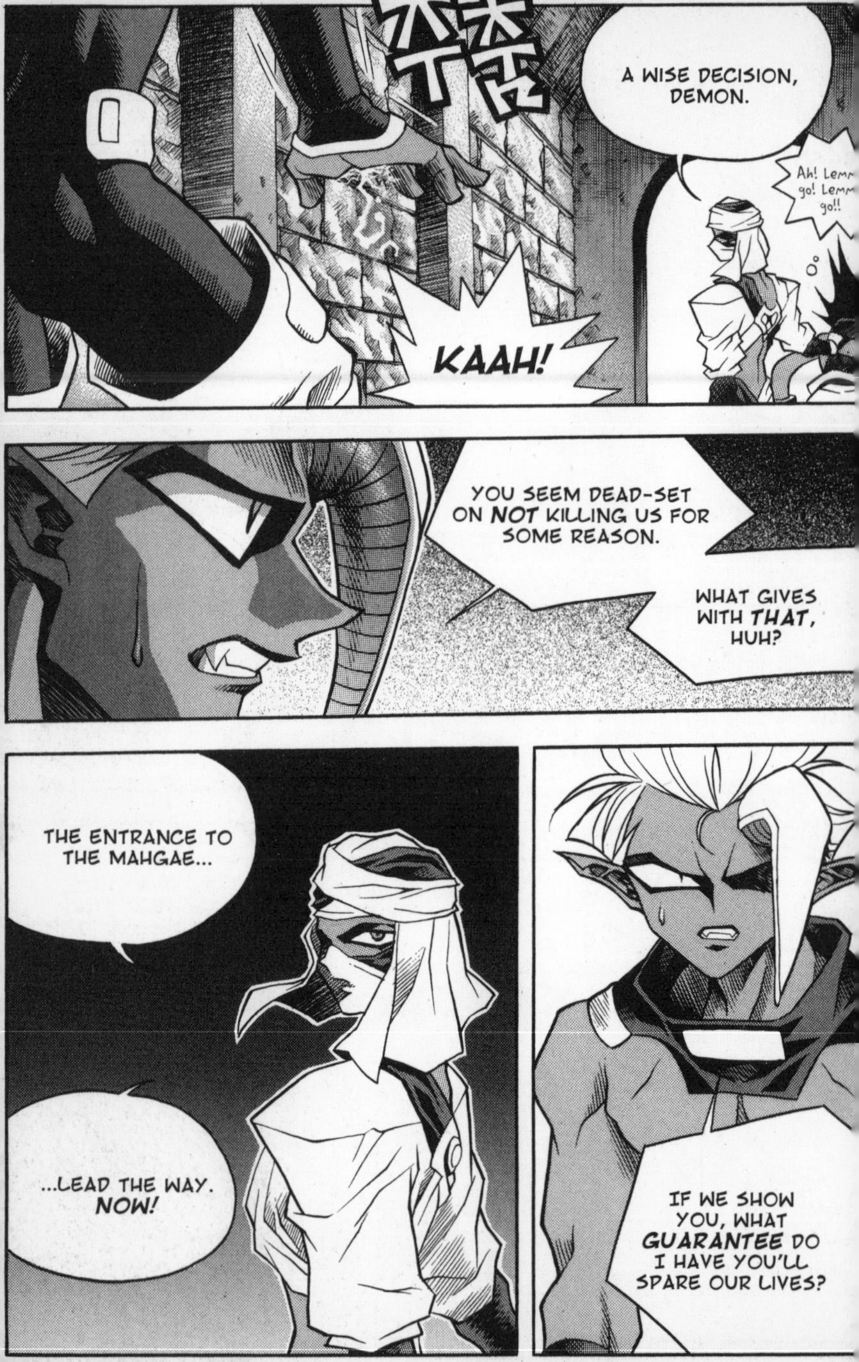
A WISE DECISION, DEMON.
Ah! Lemm go! Lemm go!!
KAAH!
YOU SEEM DEAD-SET ON *NOT* KILLING US FOR SOME REASON.
WHAT GIVES WITH *THAT*, HUH?
THE ENTRANCE TO THE MAHGAE...
...LEAD THE WAY. *NOW!*
IF WE SHOW YOU, WHAT *GUARANTEE* DO I HAVE YOU'LL SPARE OUR LIVES?

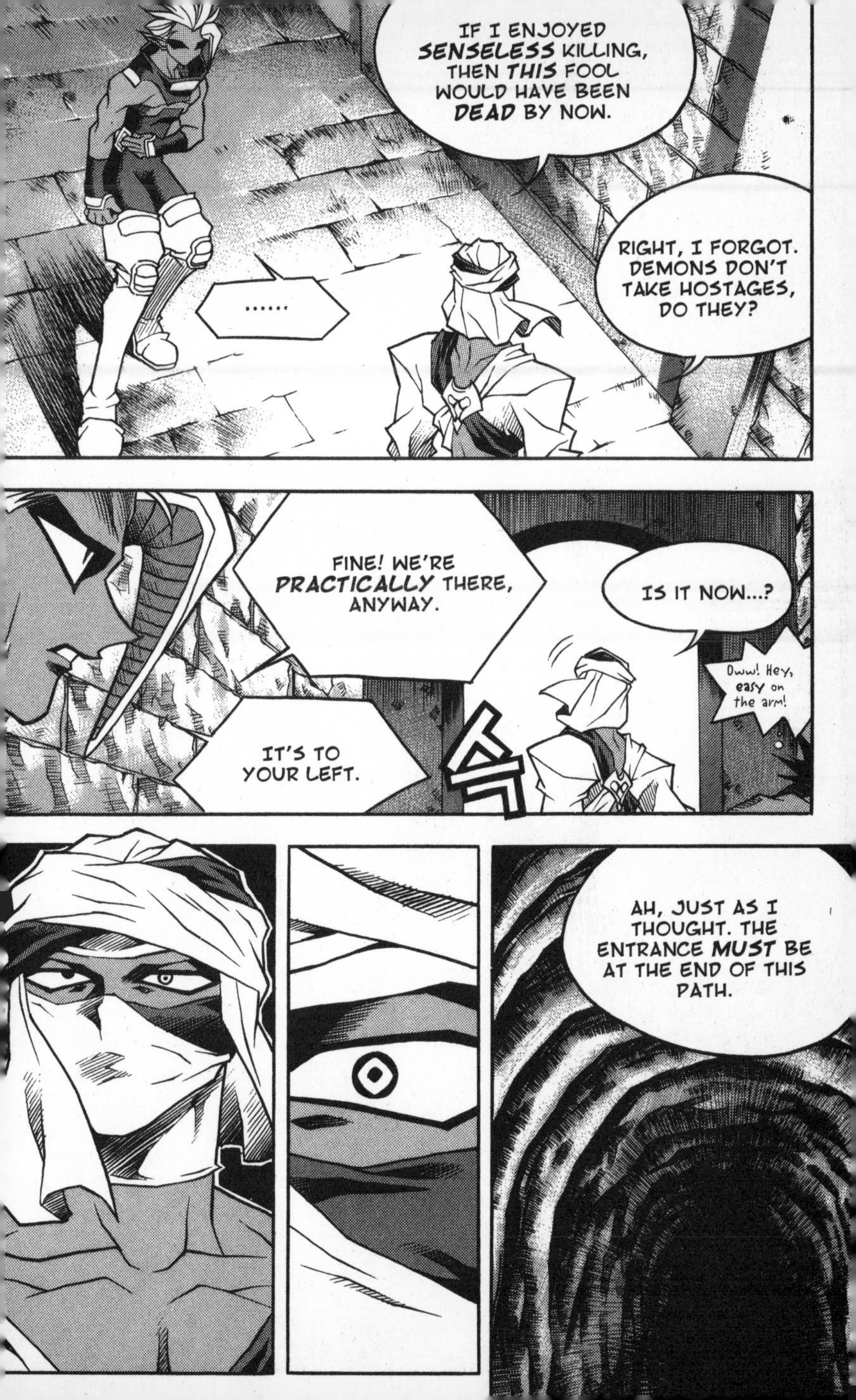

IF I ENJOYED SENSELESS KILLING, THEN THIS FOOL WOULD HAVE BEEN DEAD BY NOW.
......
RIGHT, I FORGOT. DEMONS DON'T TAKE HOSTAGES, DO THEY?
FINE! WE'RE PRACTICALLY THERE, ANYWAY.
IT'S TO YOUR LEFT.
IS IT NOW...?
Oww! Hey, easy on the arm!
AH, JUST AS I THOUGHT. THE ENTRANCE MUST BE AT THE END OF THIS PATH.

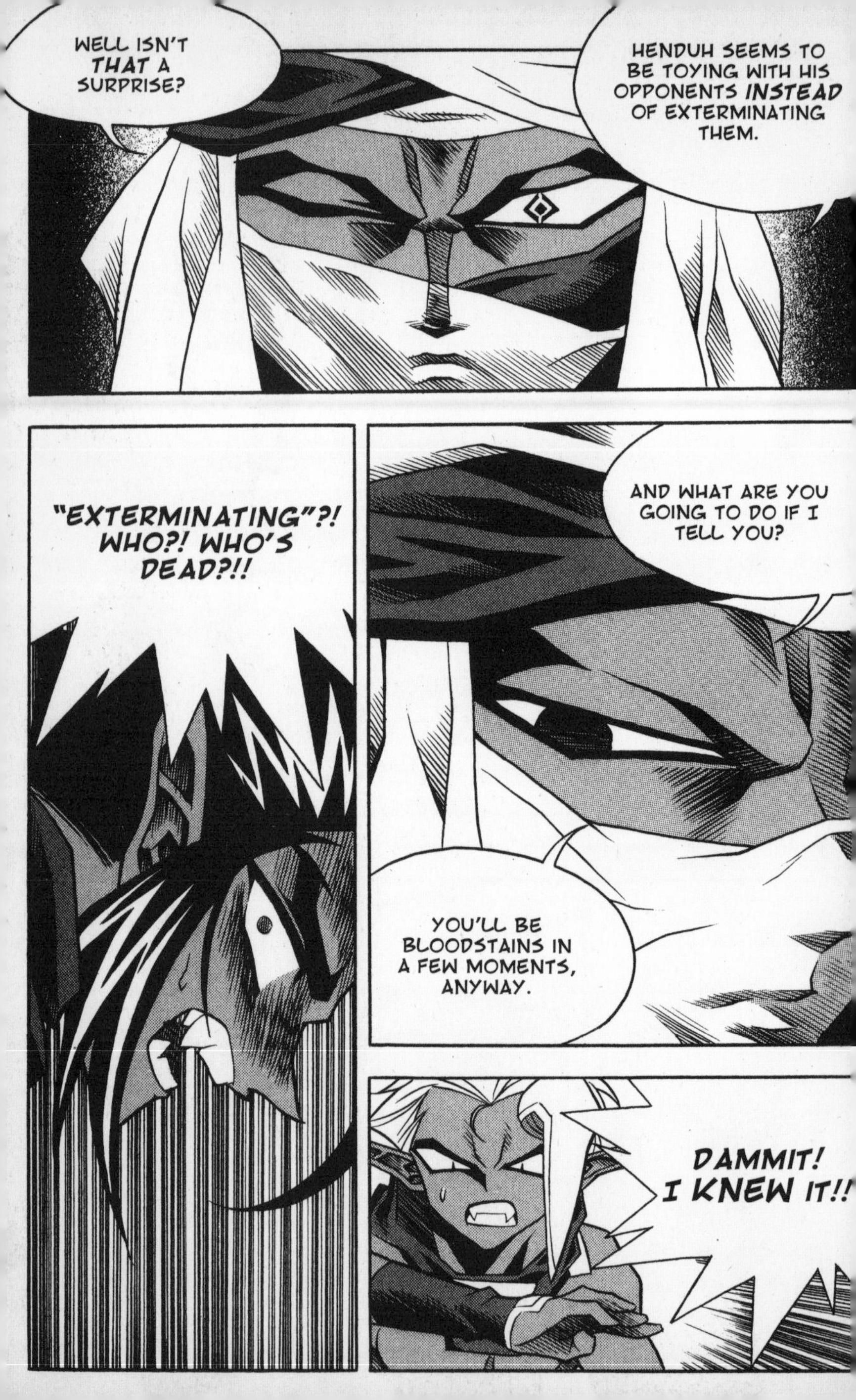
WELL ISN'T *THAT* A SURPRISE?
HENDUH SEEMS TO BE TOYING WITH HIS OPPONENTS *INSTEAD* OF EXTERMINATING THEM.
"EXTERMINATING"?! WHO?! WHO'S DEAD?!!
AND WHAT ARE YOU GOING TO DO IF I TELL YOU?
YOU'LL BE BLOODSTAINS IN A FEW MOMENTS, ANYWAY.
DAMMIT! I KNEW IT!!

Quest 18

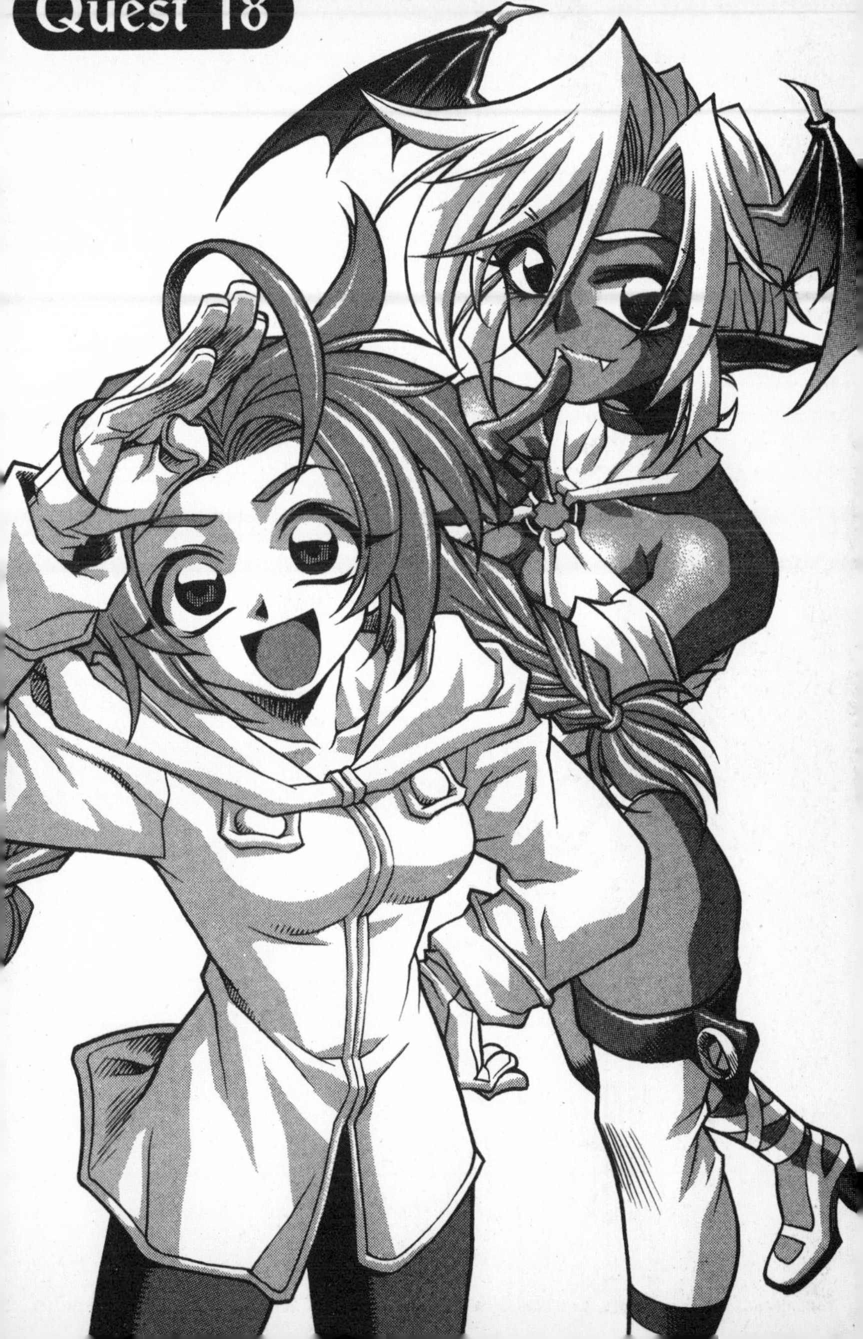

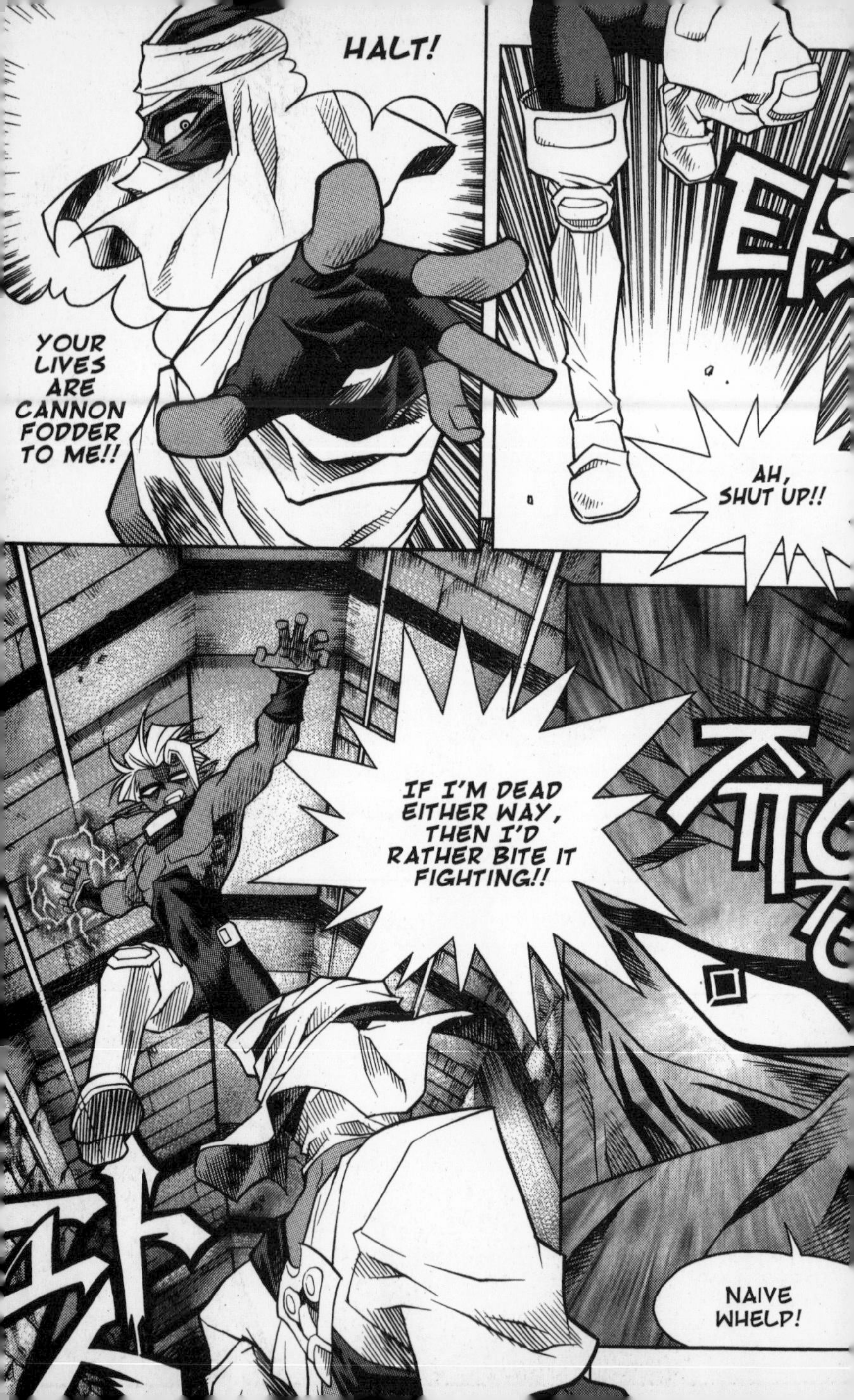
HALT!
YOUR LIVES ARE CANNON FODDER TO ME!!
AH, SHUT UP!!
IF I'M DEAD EITHER WAY, THEN I'D RATHER BITE IT FIGHTING!!
NAIVE WHELP!

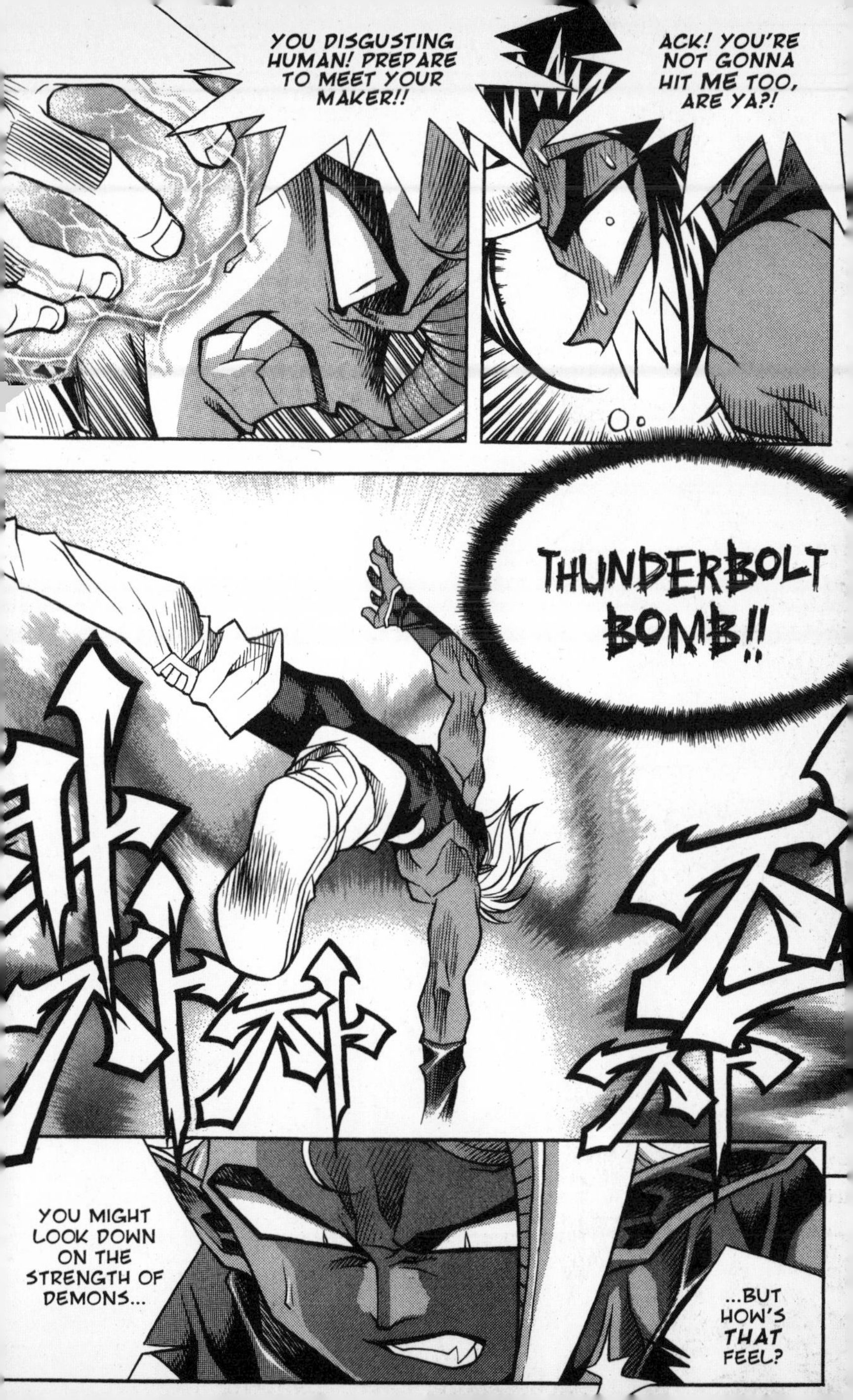
YOU DISGUSTING HUMAN! PREPARE TO MEET YOUR MAKER!!
ACK! YOU'RE NOT GONNA HIT ME TOO, ARE YA?!
THUNDERBOLT BOMB!!
YOU MIGHT LOOK DOWN ON THE STRENGTH OF DEMONS...
...BUT HOW'S THAT FEEL?

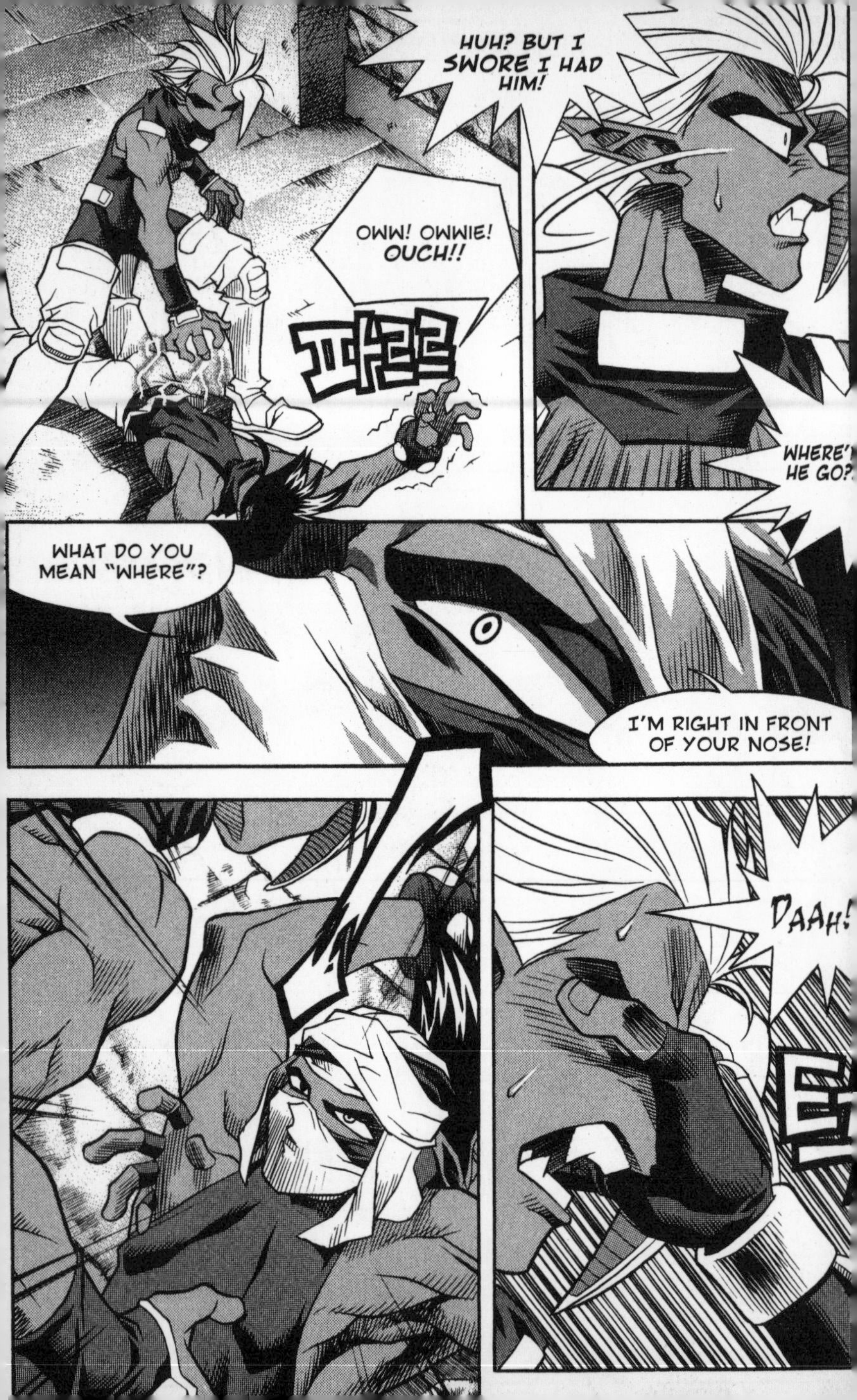
OWW! OWWIE! OUCH!!
HUH? BUT I SWORE I HAD HIM!
WHERE'D HE GO?
WHAT DO YOU MEAN "WHERE"?
I'M RIGHT IN FRONT OF YOUR NOSE!
DAAH!

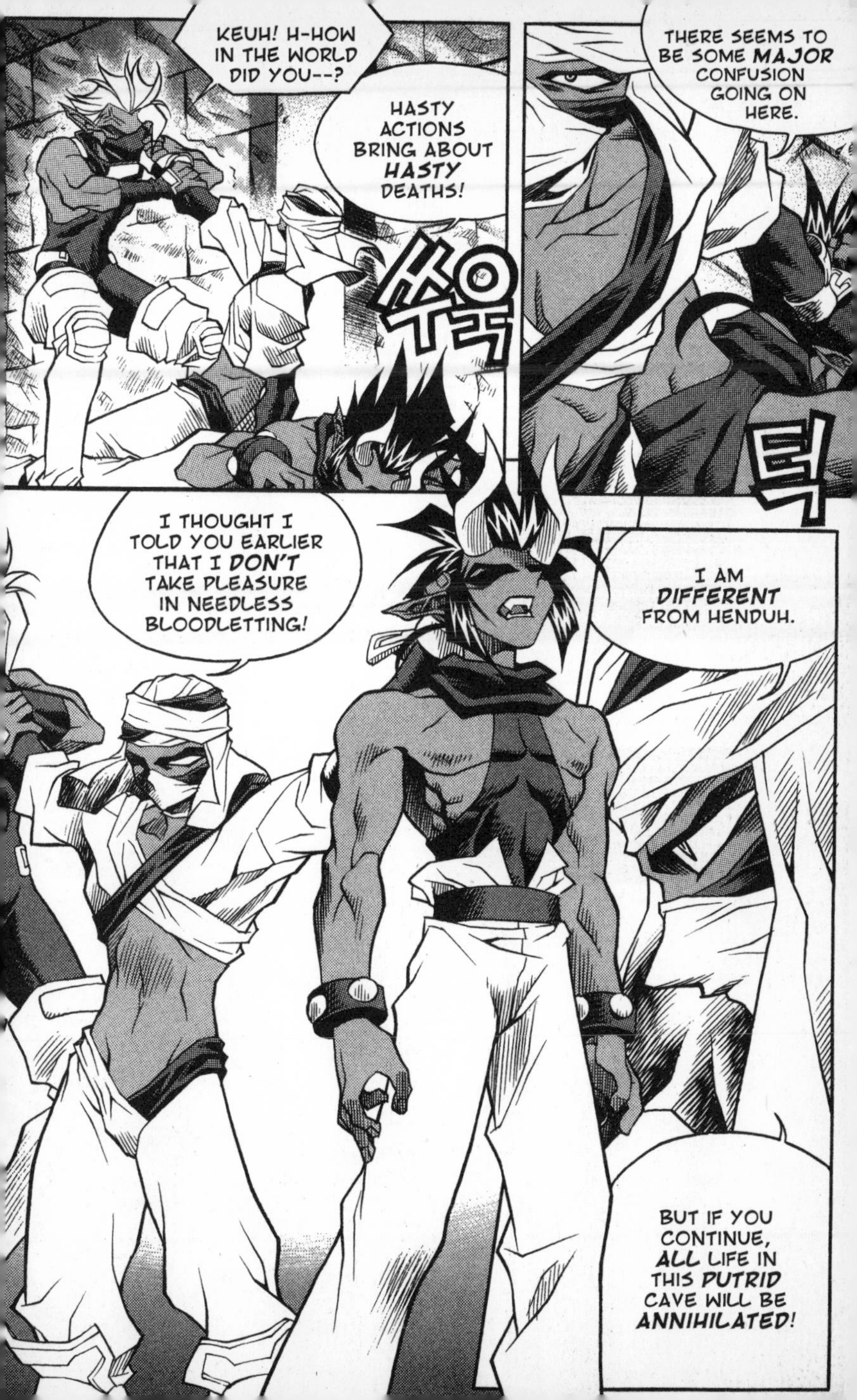
KEUH! H-HOW IN THE WORLD DID YOU--?
HASTY ACTIONS BRING ABOUT **HASTY** DEATHS!
THERE SEEMS TO BE SOME **MAJOR** CONFUSION GOING ON HERE.
턱
I THOUGHT I TOLD YOU EARLIER THAT I **DON'T** TAKE PLEASURE IN NEEDLESS BLOODLETTING!
I AM **DIFFERENT** FROM HENDUH.
BUT IF YOU CONTINUE, **ALL** LIFE IN THIS **PUTRID** CAVE WILL BE **ANNIHILATED**!

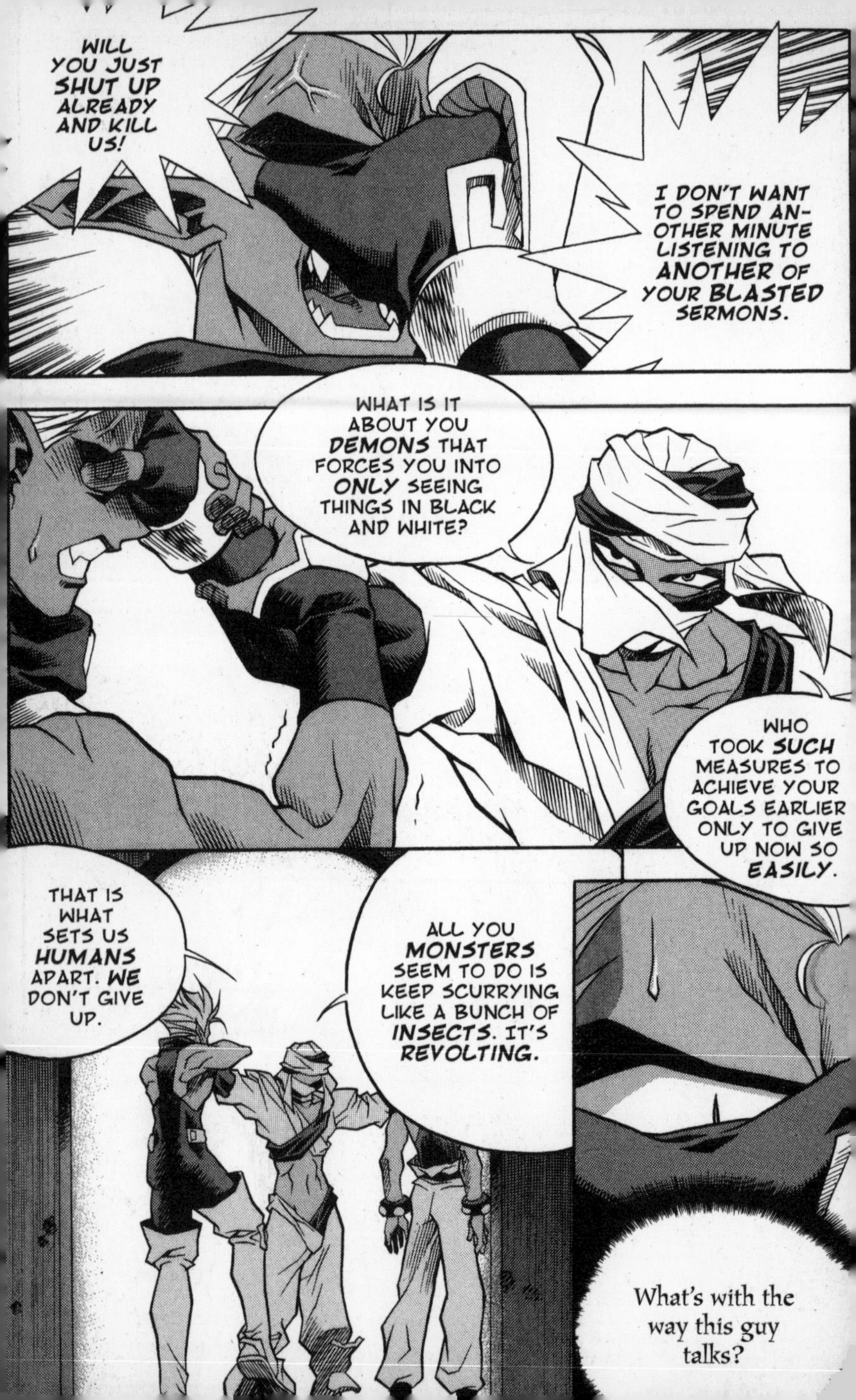
WILL YOU JUST SHUT UP ALREADY AND KILL US!
I DON'T WANT TO SPEND AN-OTHER MINUTE LISTENING TO ANOTHER OF YOUR BLASTED SERMONS.
WHAT IS IT ABOUT YOU DEMONS THAT FORCES YOU INTO ONLY SEEING THINGS IN BLACK AND WHITE?
WHO TOOK SUCH MEASURES TO ACHIEVE YOUR GOALS EARLIER ONLY TO GIVE UP NOW SO EASILY.
THAT IS WHAT SETS US HUMANS APART. WE DON'T GIVE UP.
ALL YOU MONSTERS SEEM TO DO IS KEEP SCURRYING LIKE A BUNCH OF INSECTS. IT'S REVOLTING.
What's with the way this guy talks?

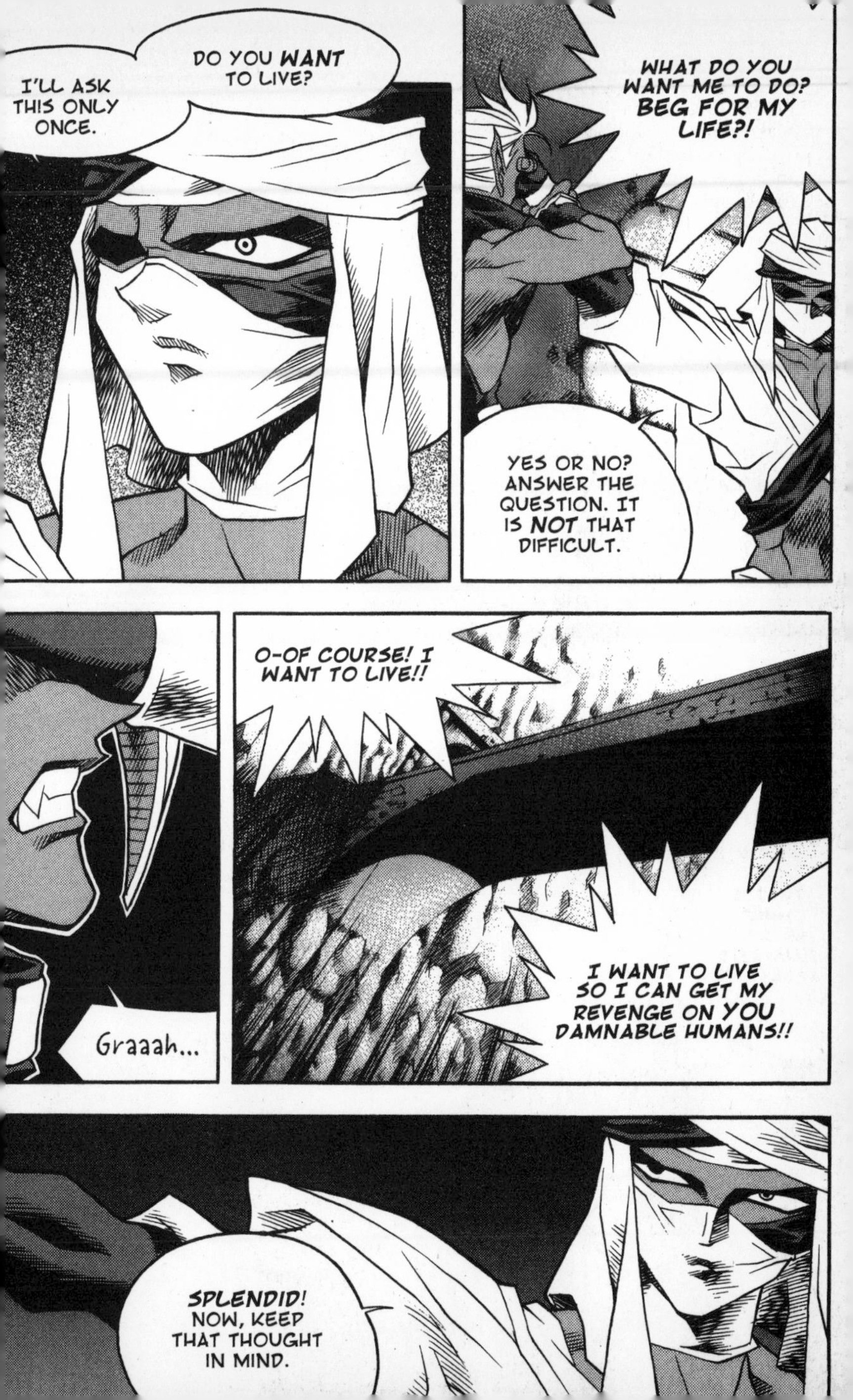
I'LL ASK THIS ONLY ONCE.
DO YOU WANT TO LIVE?
WHAT DO YOU WANT ME TO DO? BEG FOR MY LIFE?!
YES OR NO? ANSWER THE QUESTION. IT IS NOT THAT DIFFICULT.
Graaah...
O-OF COURSE! I WANT TO LIVE!!
I WANT TO LIVE SO I CAN GET MY REVENGE ON YOU DAMNABLE HUMANS!!
SPLENDID! NOW, KEEP THAT THOUGHT IN MIND.

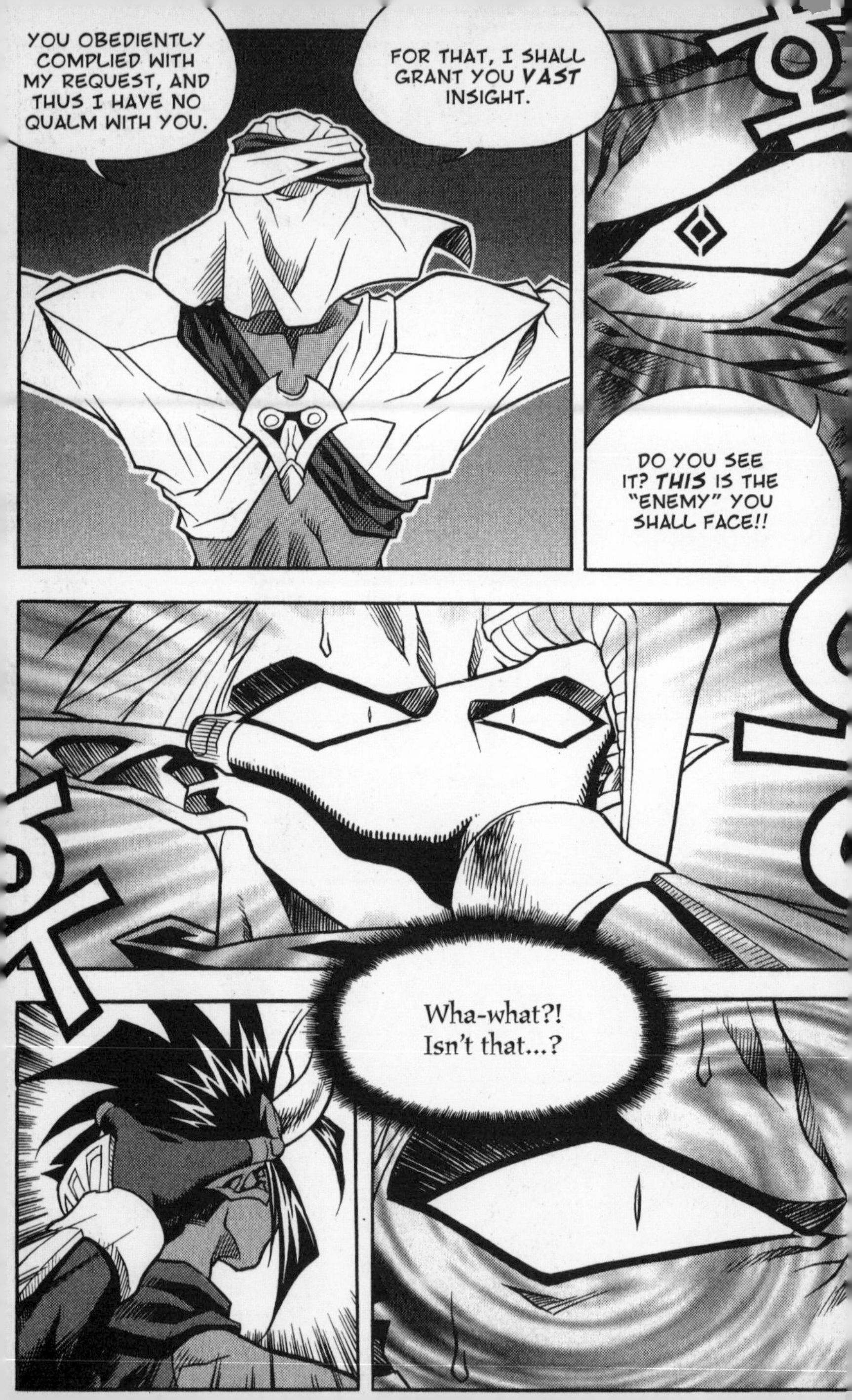
YOU OBEDIENTLY COMPLIED WITH MY REQUEST, AND THUS I HAVE NO QUALM WITH YOU.
FOR THAT, I SHALL GRANT YOU VAST INSIGHT.
DO YOU SEE IT? THIS IS THE "ENEMY" YOU SHALL FACE!!
Wha-what?! Isn't that...?

It is!
That's the school gate.

And that's the Mahgae, but **why** am I seeing all this?

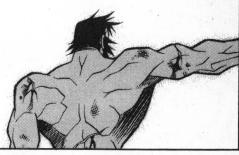

OBSERVE CAREFULLY. THESE TWO ARE OF THE HIGHEST RANKS OF OUR ORDER.

IF THEY ARE NOT DESTROYED, THEN, YES, ALL OF YOU SHALL PERISH HERE TODAY.

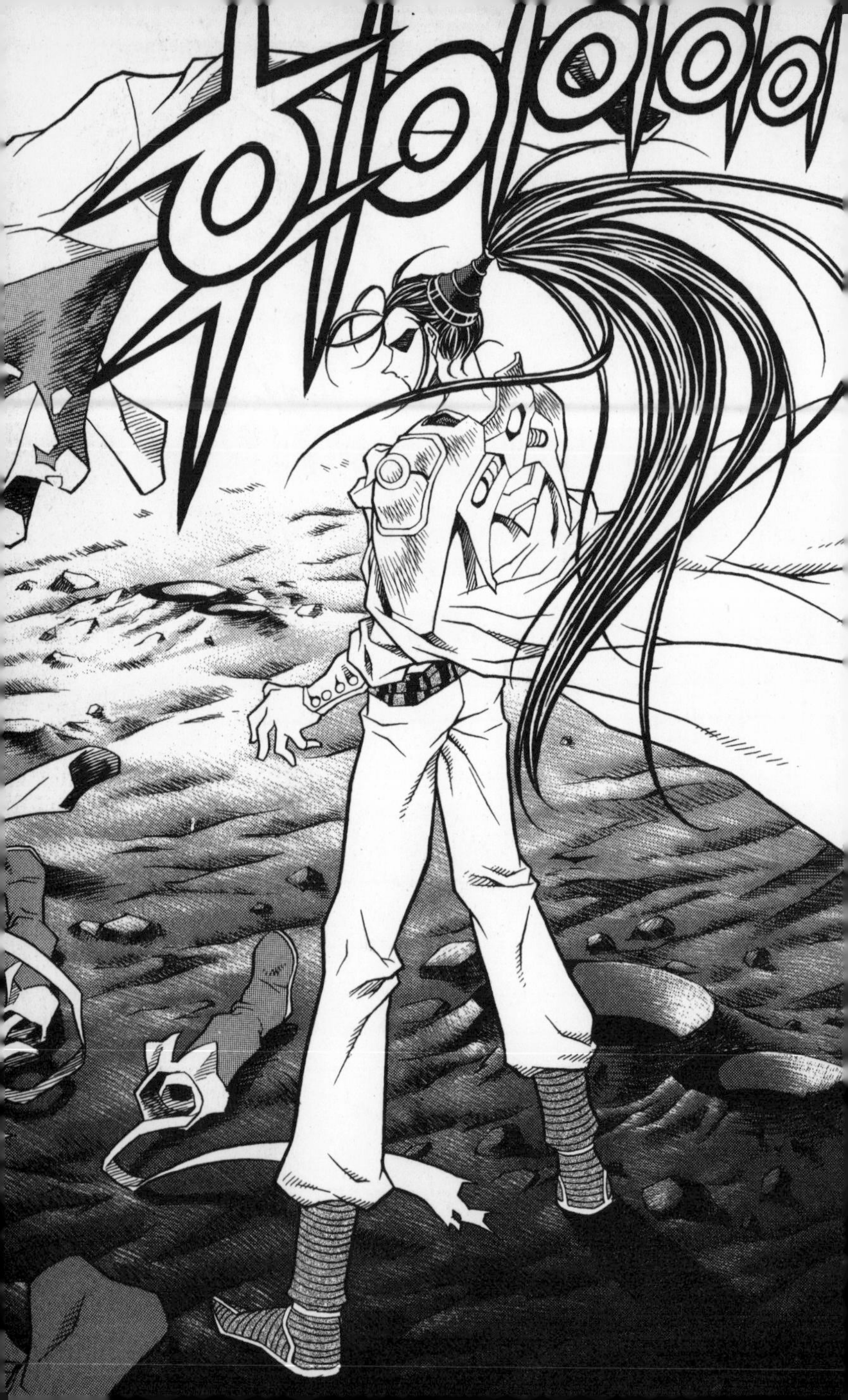

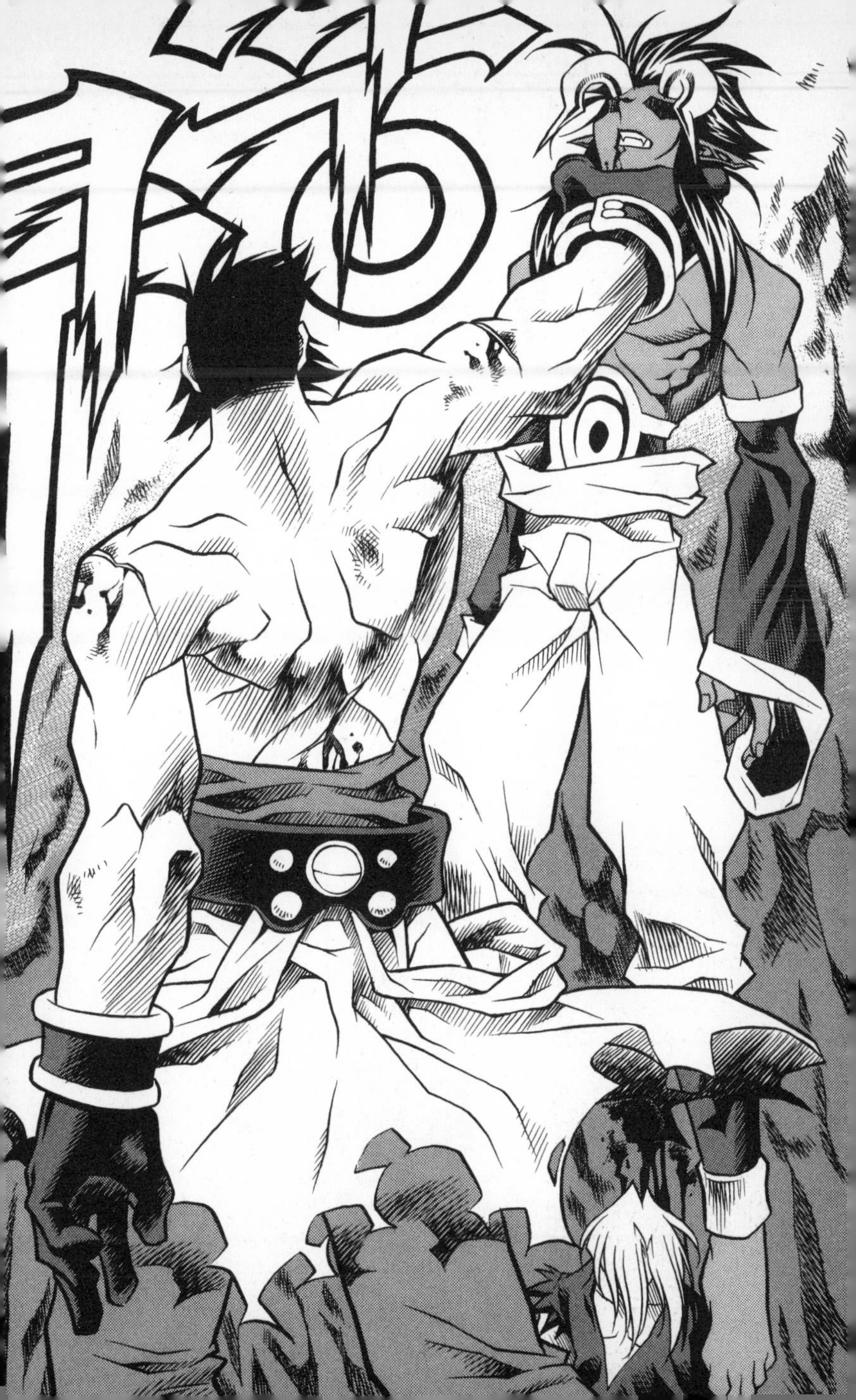

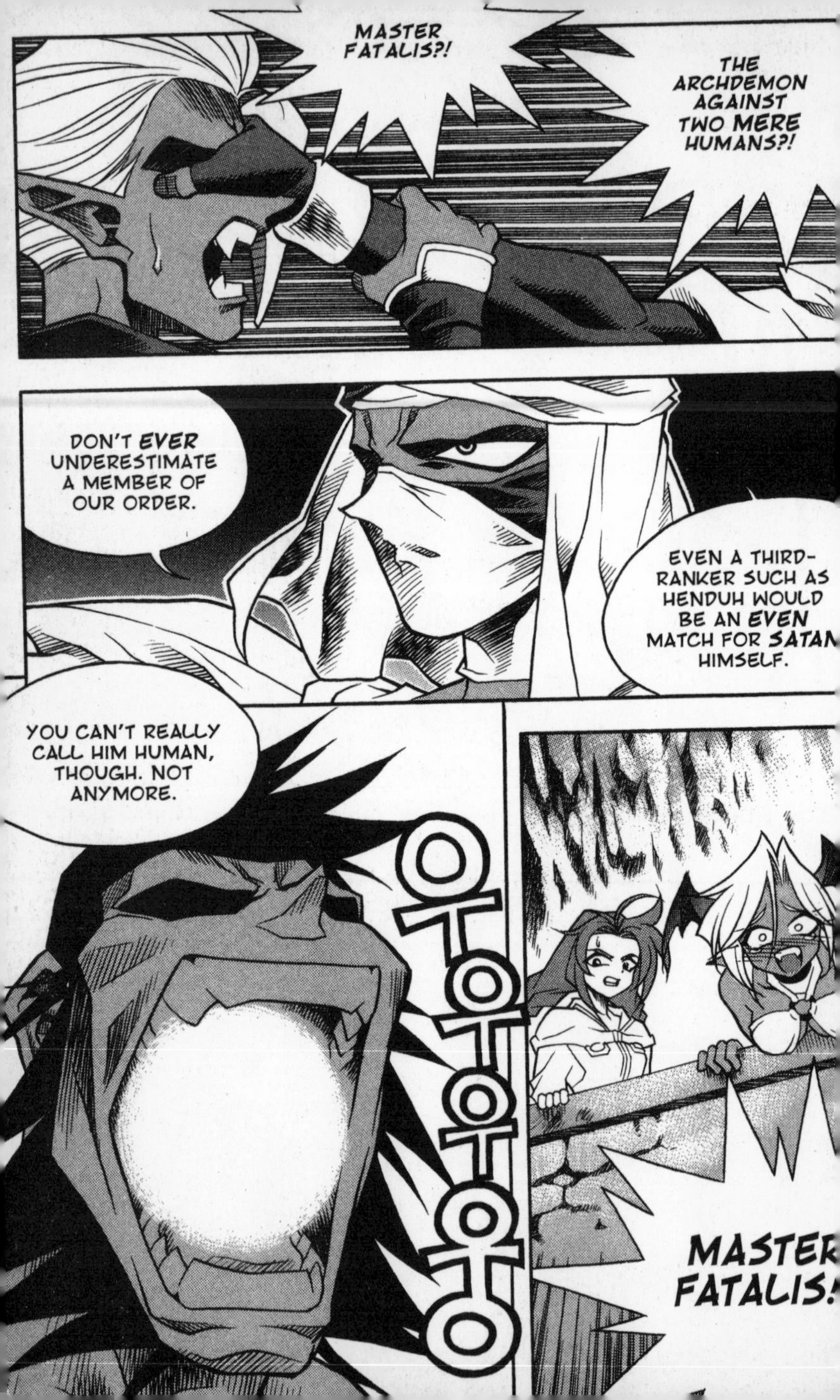
MASTER FATALIS?!
THE ARCHDEMON AGAINST TWO MERE HUMANS?!
DON'T EVER UNDERESTIMATE A MEMBER OF OUR ORDER.
EVEN A THIRD-RANKER SUCH AS HENDUH WOULD BE AN EVEN MATCH FOR SATAN HIMSELF.
YOU CAN'T REALLY CALL HIM HUMAN, THOUGH. NOT ANYMORE.
OOOOOOOO
MASTER FATALIS!

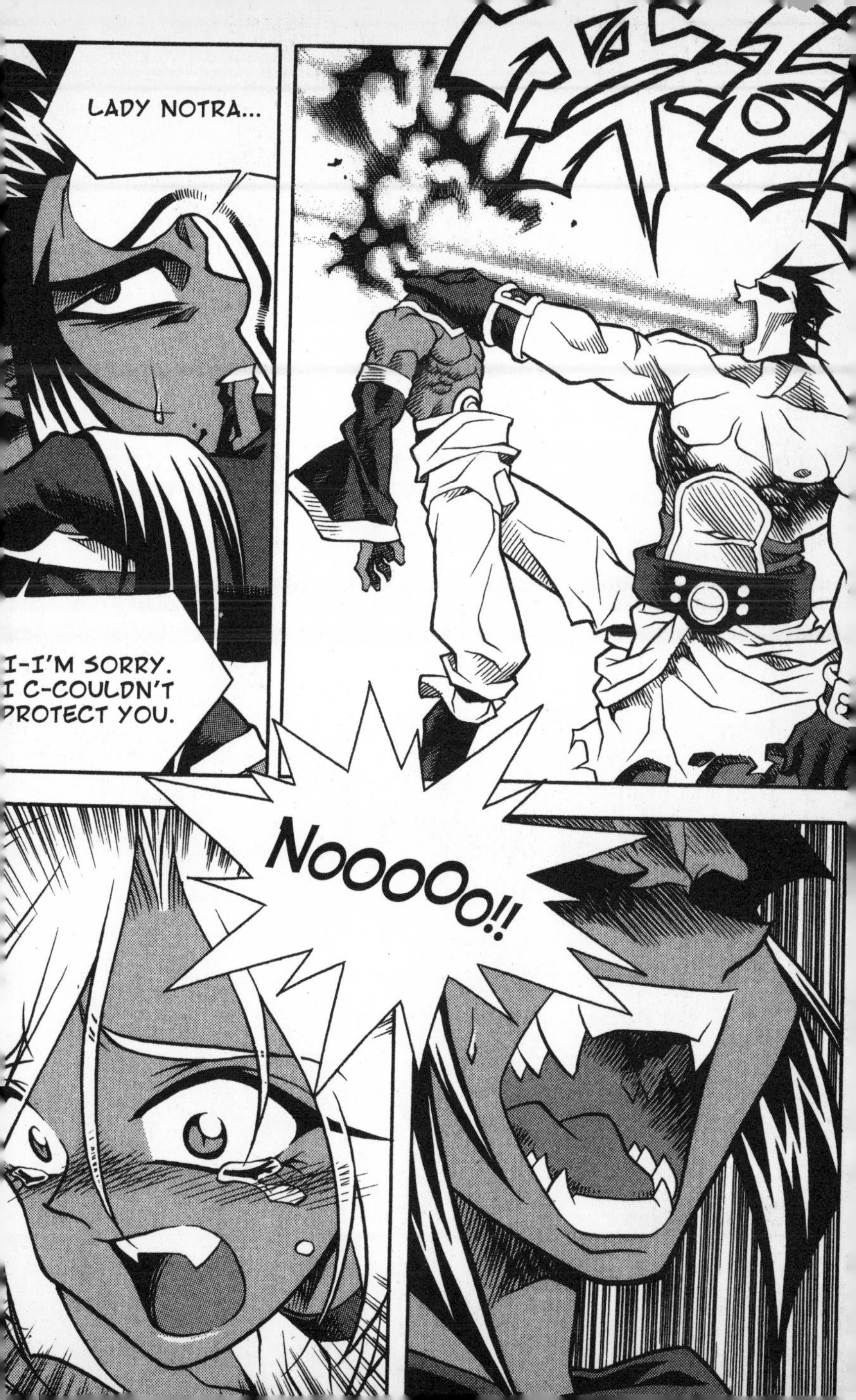
LADY NOTRA...
I-I'M SORRY. I C-COULDN'T PROTECT YOU.
NOOOOOo!!

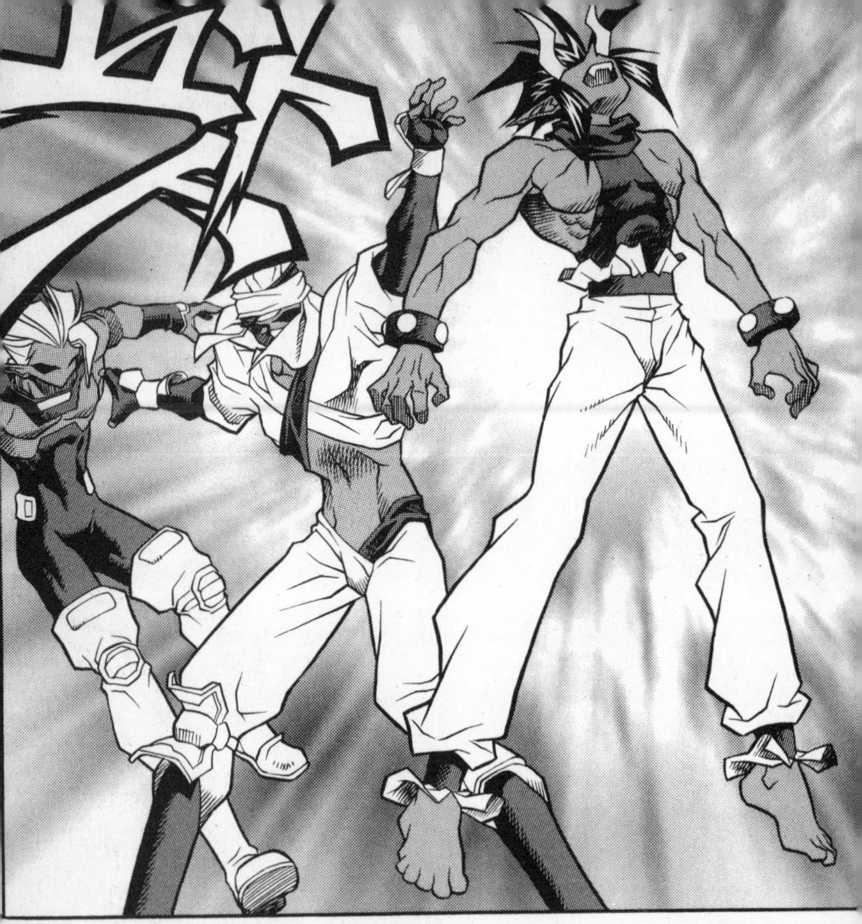

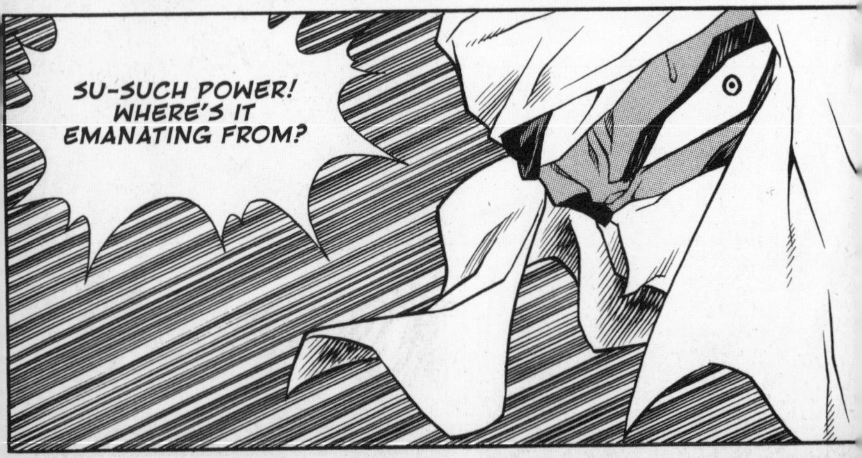
SU-SUCH POWER! WHERE'S IT EMANATING FROM?

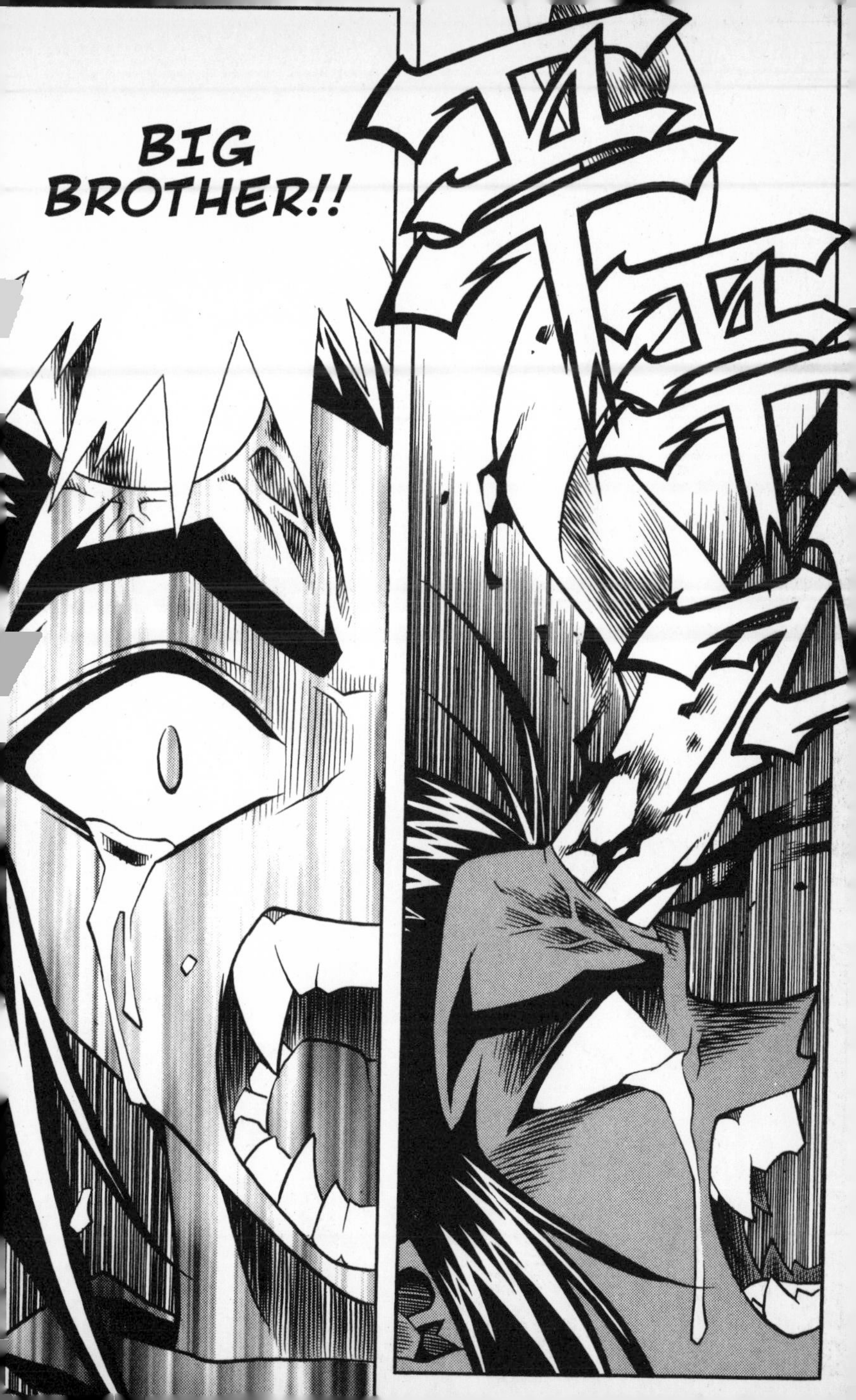
BIG BROTHER!!

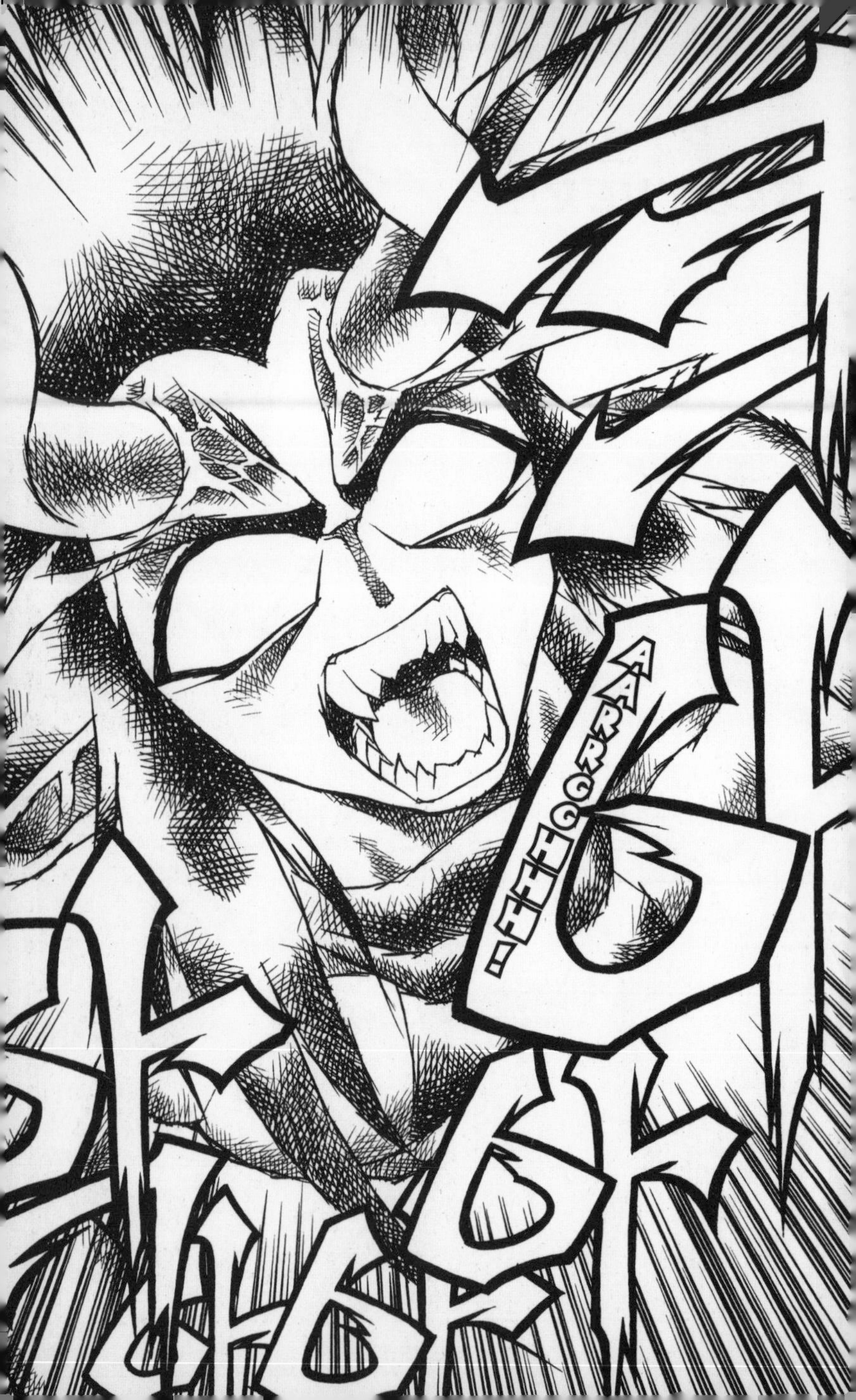
AARRGGHHH!

Quest 19

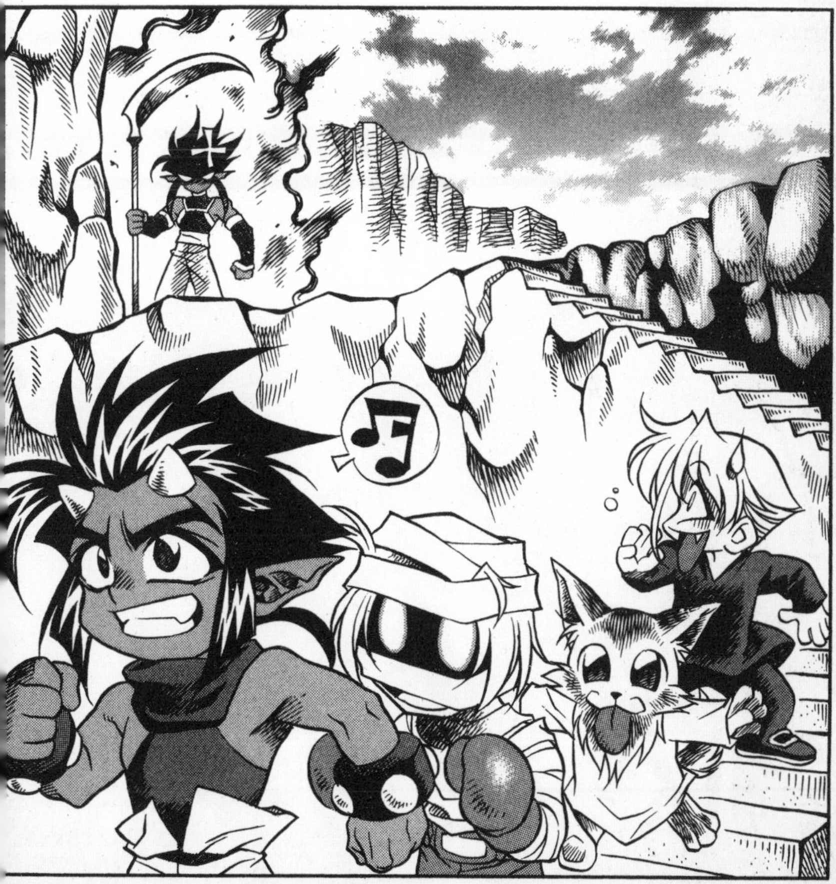

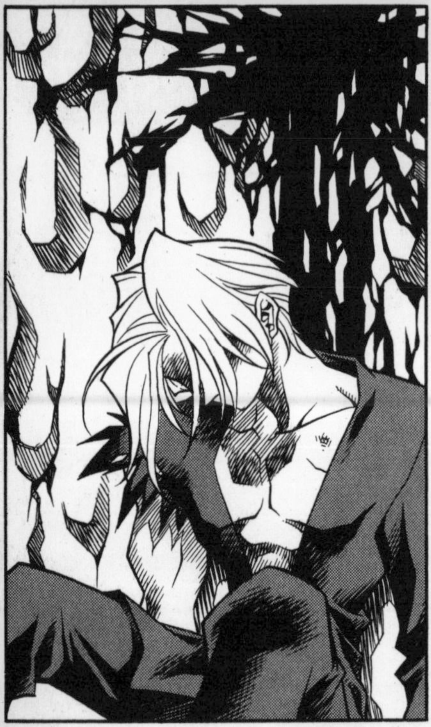

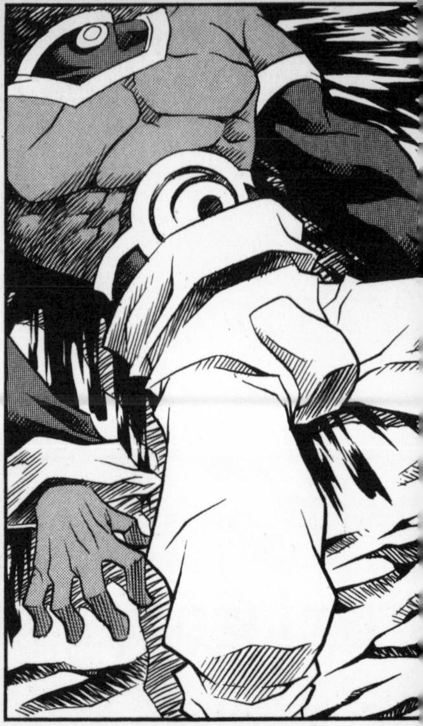

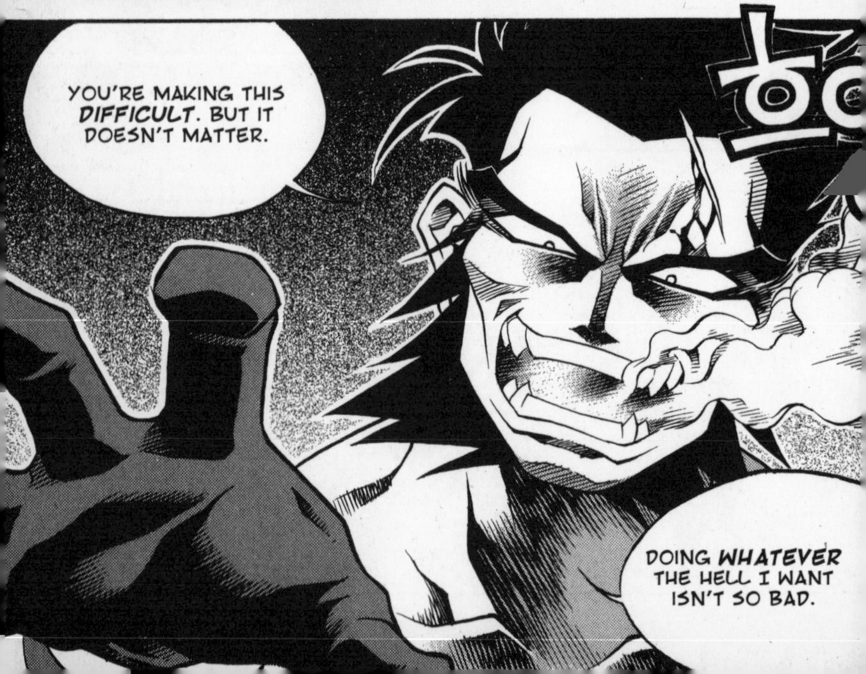
YOU'RE MAKING THIS DIFFICULT. BUT IT DOESN'T MATTER.
DOING WHATEVER THE HELL I WANT ISN'T SO BAD.

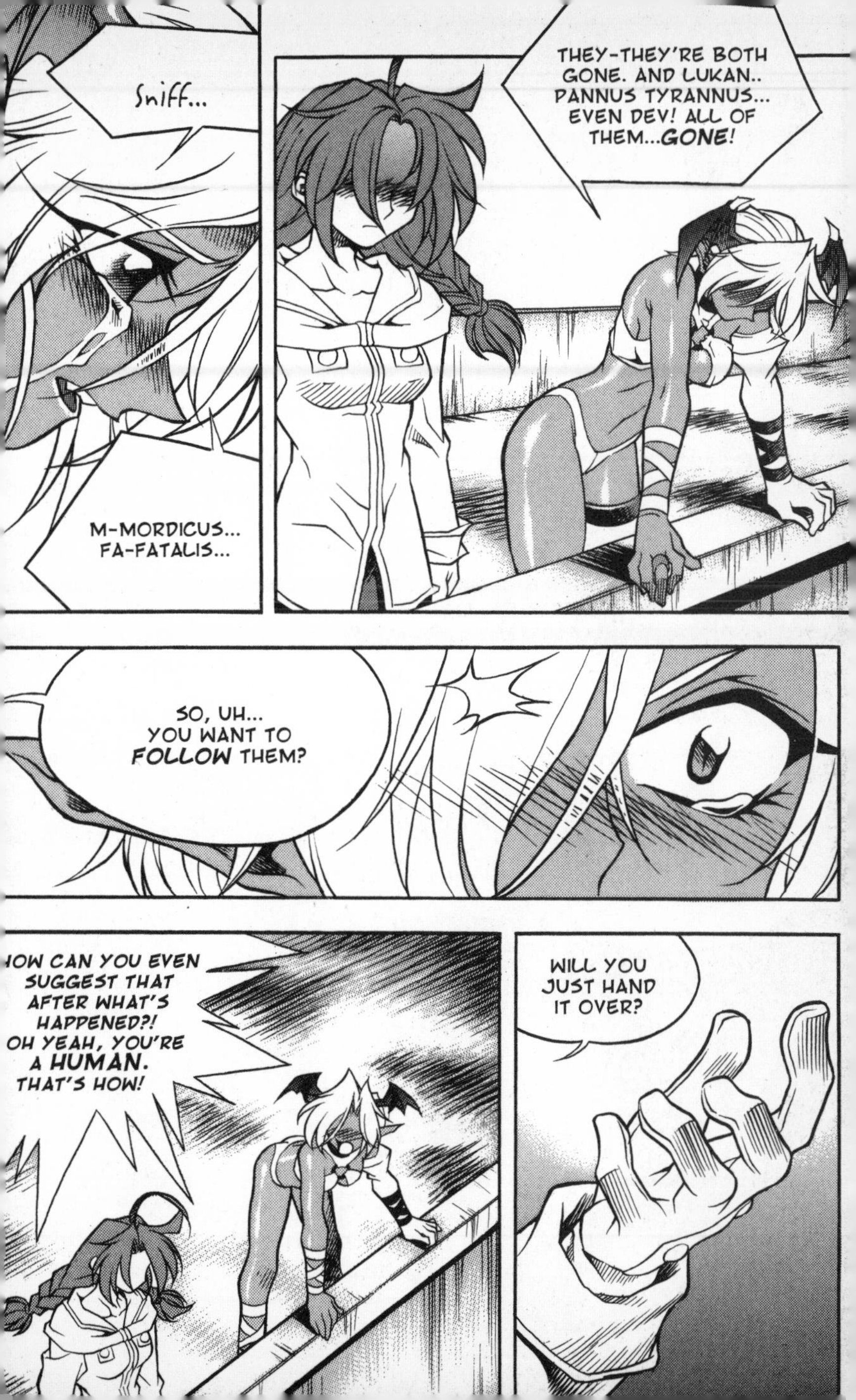
Sniff...
M-MORDICUS...
FA-FATALIS...
THEY-THEY'RE BOTH GONE. AND LUKAN..
PANNUS TYRANNUS...
EVEN DEV! ALL OF THEM...GONE!
SO, UH...
YOU WANT TO FOLLOW THEM?
HOW CAN YOU EVEN SUGGEST THAT AFTER WHAT'S HAPPENED?!
OH YEAH, YOU'RE A HUMAN.
THAT'S HOW!
WILL YOU JUST HAND IT OVER?

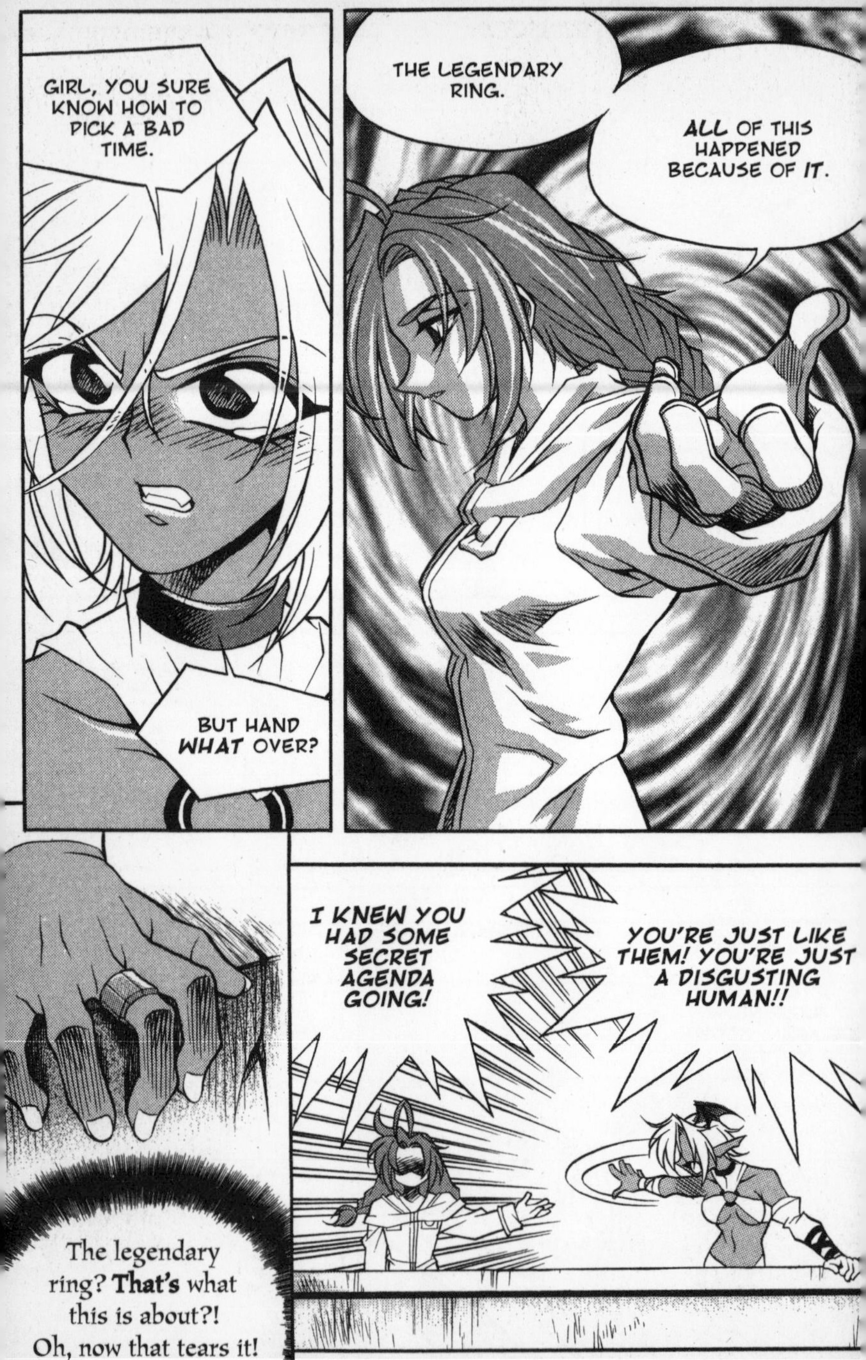
GIRL, YOU SURE KNOW HOW TO PICK A BAD TIME.
BUT HAND **WHAT** OVER?
THE LEGENDARY RING.
ALL OF THIS HAPPENED BECAUSE OF **IT**.
The legendary ring? **That's** what this is about?! Oh, now that tears it!
I KNEW YOU HAD SOME SECRET AGENDA GOING!
YOU'RE JUST LIKE THEM! YOU'RE JUST A DISGUSTING HUMAN!!

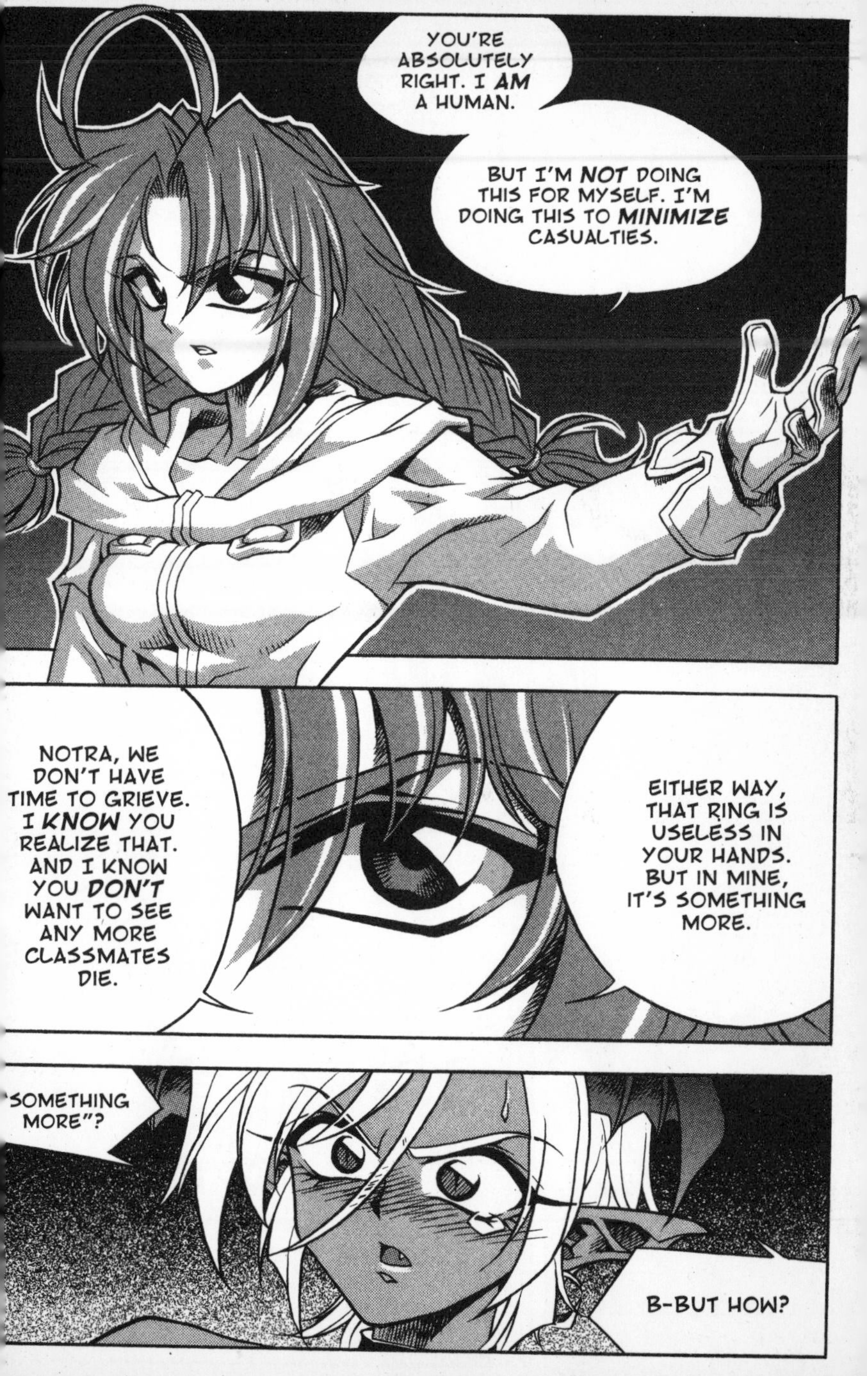
YOU'RE ABSOLUTELY RIGHT. I **AM** A HUMAN.
BUT I'M **NOT** DOING THIS FOR MYSELF. I'M DOING THIS TO **MINIMIZE** CASUALTIES.
NOTRA, WE DON'T HAVE TIME TO GRIEVE. I **KNOW** YOU REALIZE THAT. AND I KNOW YOU **DON'T** WANT TO SEE ANY MORE CLASSMATES DIE.
EITHER WAY, THAT RING IS USELESS IN YOUR HANDS. BUT IN MINE, IT'S SOMETHING MORE.
"SOMETHING MORE"?
B-BUT HOW?

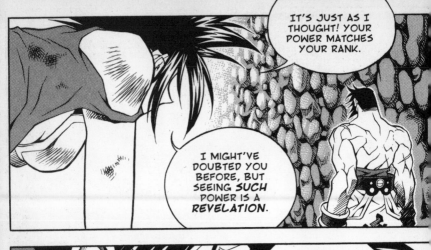

IT'S JUST AS I THOUGHT! YOUR POWER MATCHES YOUR RANK.

I MIGHT'VE DOUBTED YOU BEFORE, BUT SEEING *SUCH* POWER IS A *REVELATION*.

AND NOW THAT YOU'VE ELIMINATED ALL YOUR OPPONENTS, WE STILL HAVE SOME TIME.

HURRY, HENDUH, *SEAL* THE MAHGAE'S ENTRANCE!

HOW MUCH TIME IS THERE UNTIL IT AUTOMATICALLY OPENS?

...

I'M NOT SURE. MAYBE HALF AN HOUR?

IT'LL TAKE FAR LESS THAN THAT TO SEAL IT.

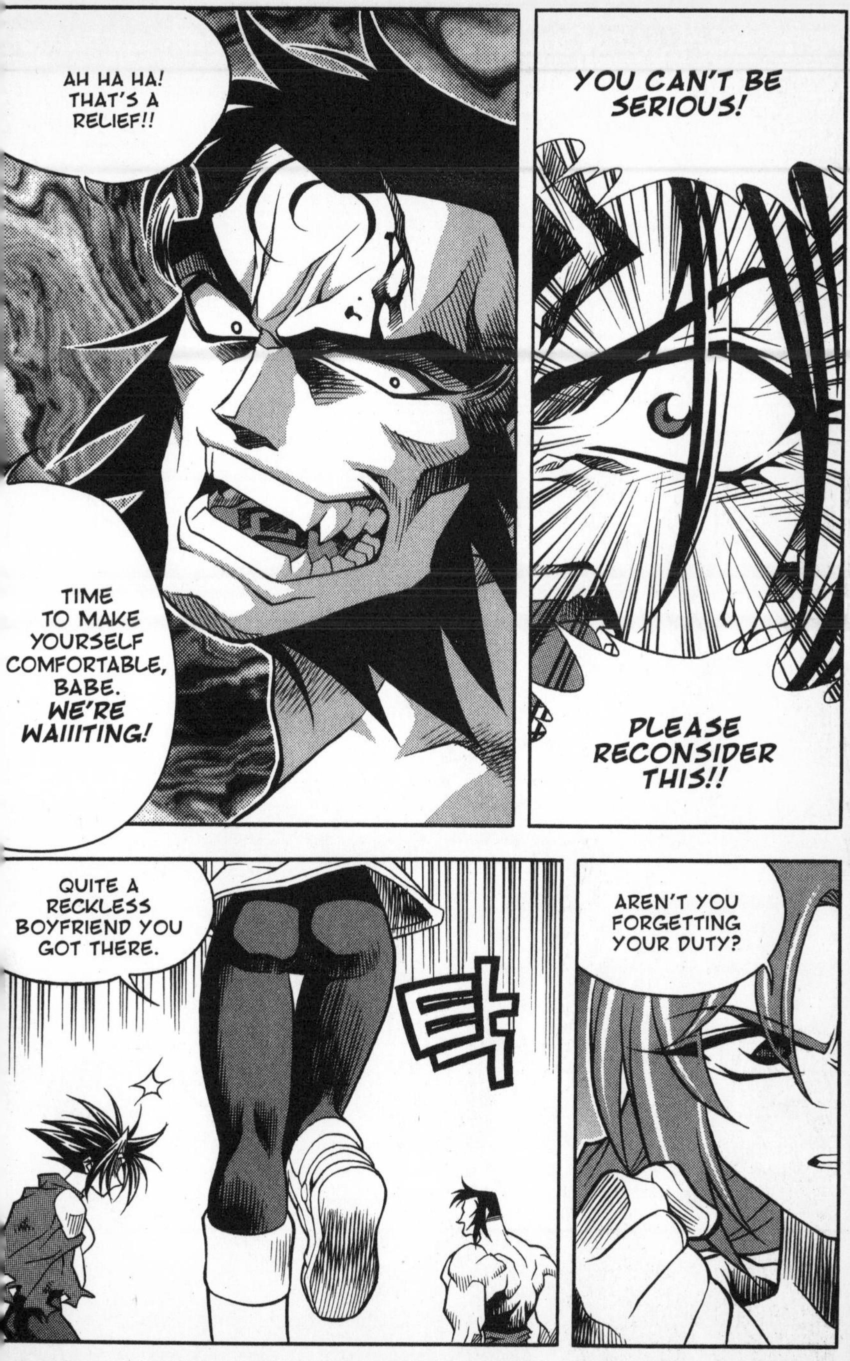
AH HA HA! THAT'S A RELIEF!!
TIME TO MAKE YOURSELF COMFORTABLE, BABE. WE'RE WAIIITING!
YOU CAN'T BE SERIOUS!
PLEASE RECONSIDER THIS!!
QUITE A RECKLESS BOYFRIEND YOU GOT THERE.
AREN'T YOU FORGETTING YOUR DUTY?

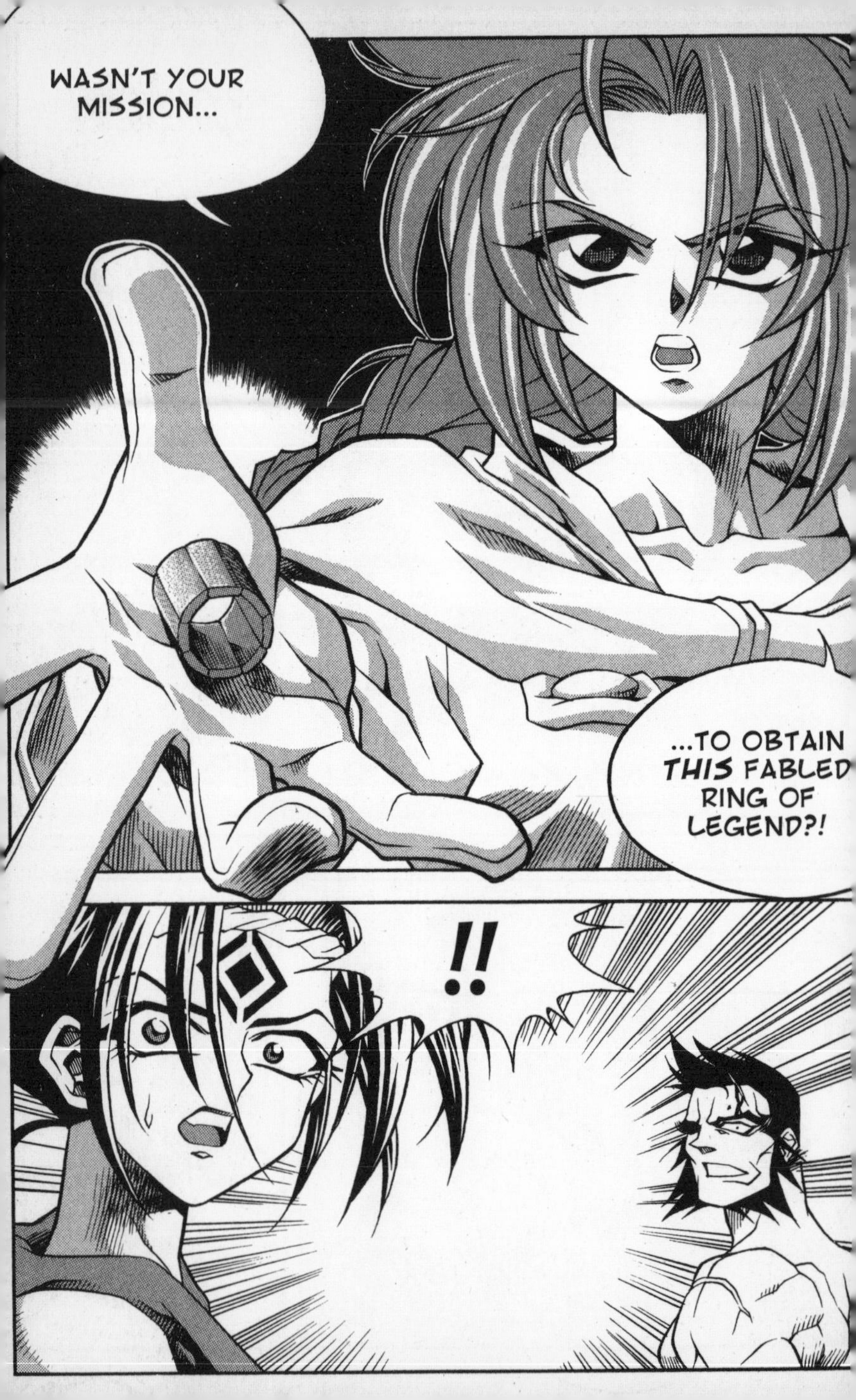
WASN'T YOUR MISSION...
...TO OBTAIN THIS FABLED RING OF LEGEND?!
!!

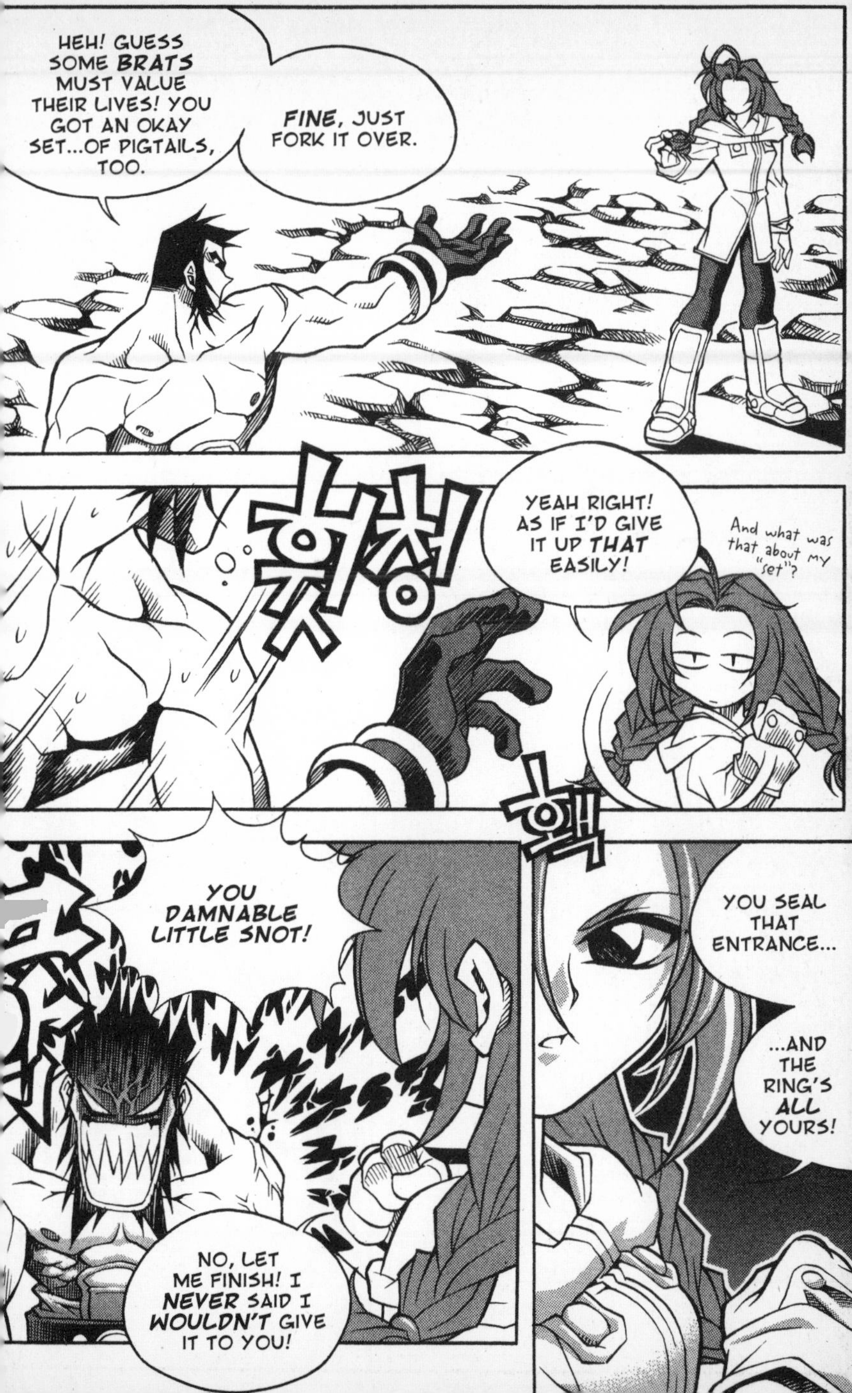

HEH! GUESS SOME BRATS MUST VALUE THEIR LIVES! YOU GOT AN OKAY SET...OF PIGTAILS, TOO.
FINE, JUST FORK IT OVER.
훼액
YEAH RIGHT! AS IF I'D GIVE IT UP THAT EASILY!
And what was that about my "set"?
YOU DAMNABLE LITTLE SNOT!
NO, LET ME FINISH! I NEVER SAID I WOULDN'T GIVE IT TO YOU!
YOU SEAL THAT ENTRANCE...
...AND THE RING'S ALL YOURS!

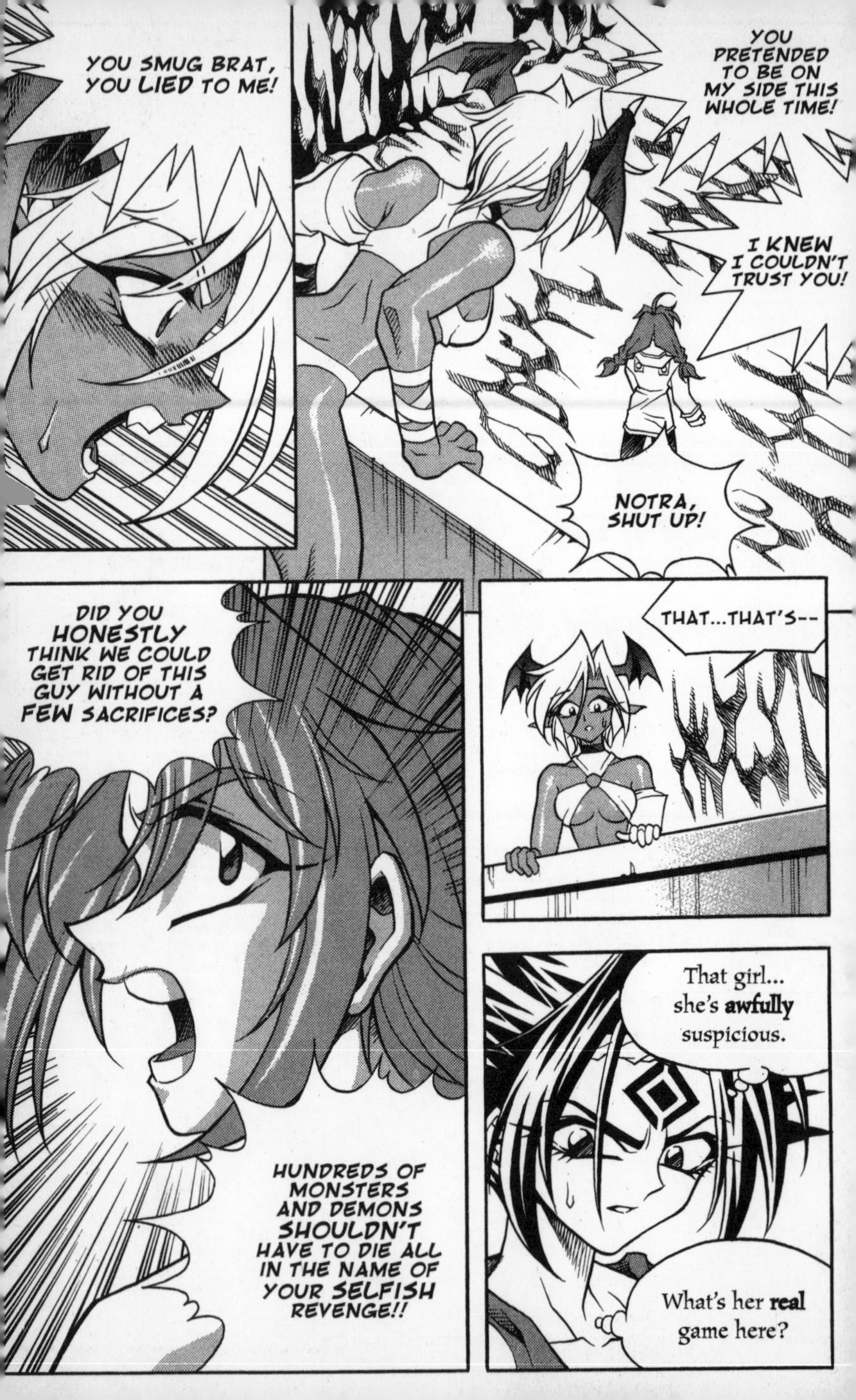
YOU SMUG BRAT, YOU LIED TO ME!
YOU PRETENDED TO BE ON MY SIDE THIS WHOLE TIME!
I KNEW I COULDN'T TRUST YOU!
NOTRA, SHUT UP!
DID YOU HONESTLY THINK WE COULD GET RID OF THIS GUY WITHOUT A FEW SACRIFICES?
HUNDREDS OF MONSTERS AND DEMONS SHOULDN'T HAVE TO DIE ALL IN THE NAME OF YOUR SELFISH REVENGE!!
THAT...THAT'S--
That girl... she's awfully suspicious.
What's her real game here?

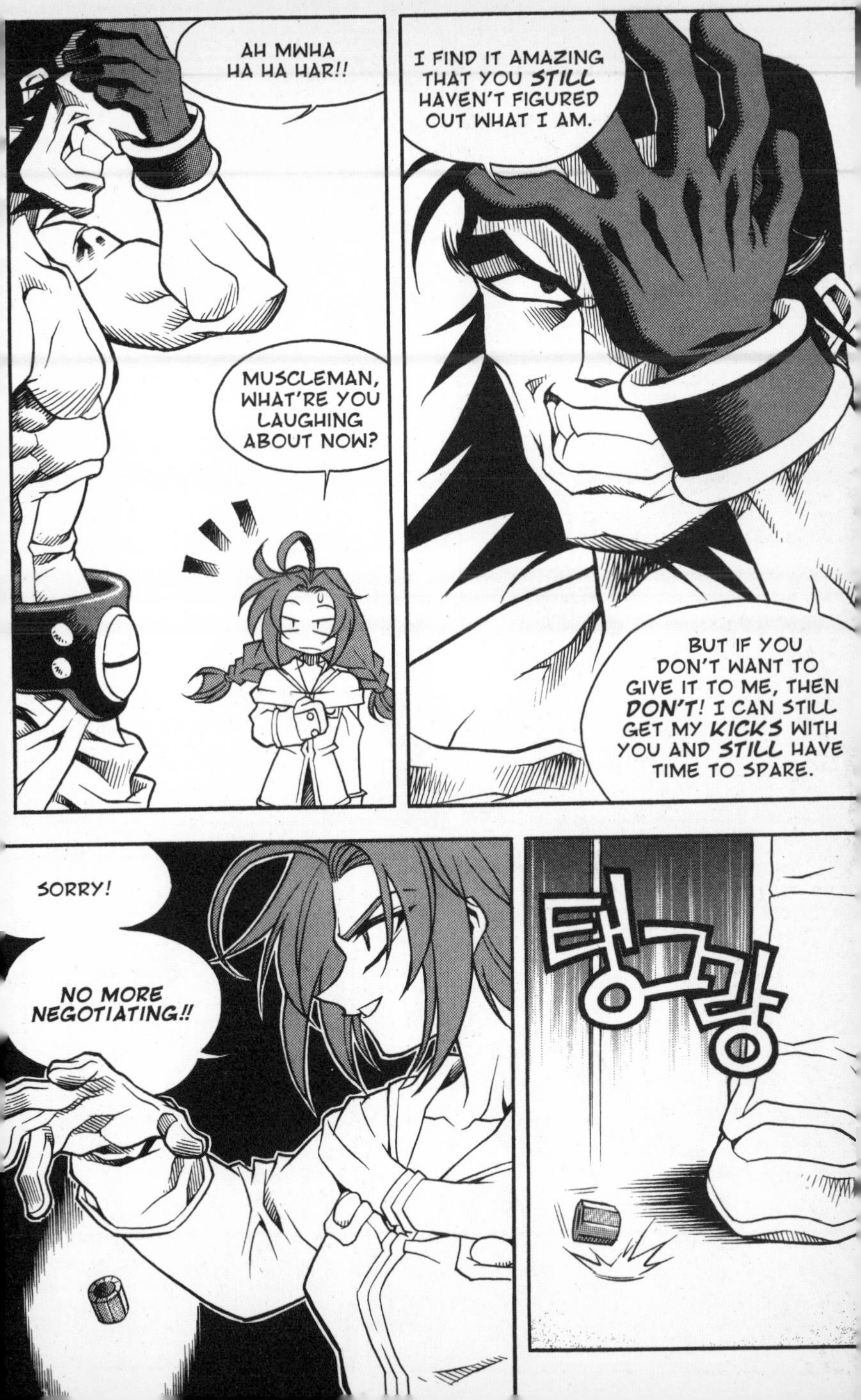
AH MWHA HA HA HAR!!
MUSCLEMAN, WHAT'RE YOU LAUGHING ABOUT NOW?
I FIND IT AMAZING THAT YOU *STILL* HAVEN'T FIGURED OUT WHAT I AM.
BUT IF YOU DON'T WANT TO GIVE IT TO ME, THEN *DON'T*! I CAN STILL GET MY *KICKS* WITH YOU AND *STILL* HAVE TIME TO SPARE.
SORRY!
NO MORE NEGOTIATING!!
탕그랑

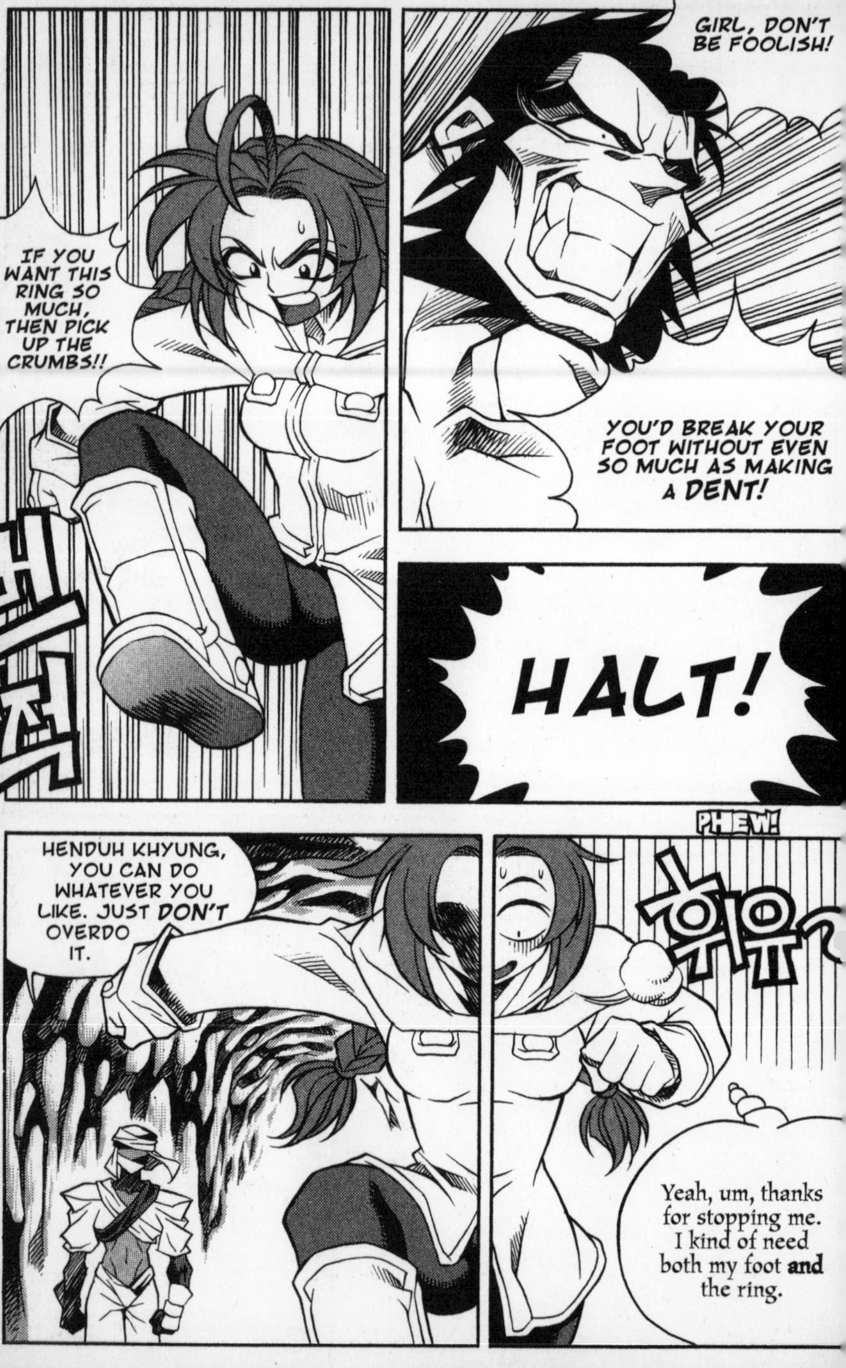
IF YOU WANT THIS RING SO MUCH, THEN PICK UP THE CRUMBS!!
GIRL, DON'T BE FOOLISH!
YOU'D BREAK YOUR FOOT WITHOUT EVEN SO MUCH AS MAKING A **DENT!**
HALT!
HENDUH KHYUNG, YOU CAN DO WHATEVER YOU LIKE. JUST **DON'T** OVERDO IT.
PHEW!
Yeah, um, thanks for stopping me. I kind of need both my foot **and** the ring.

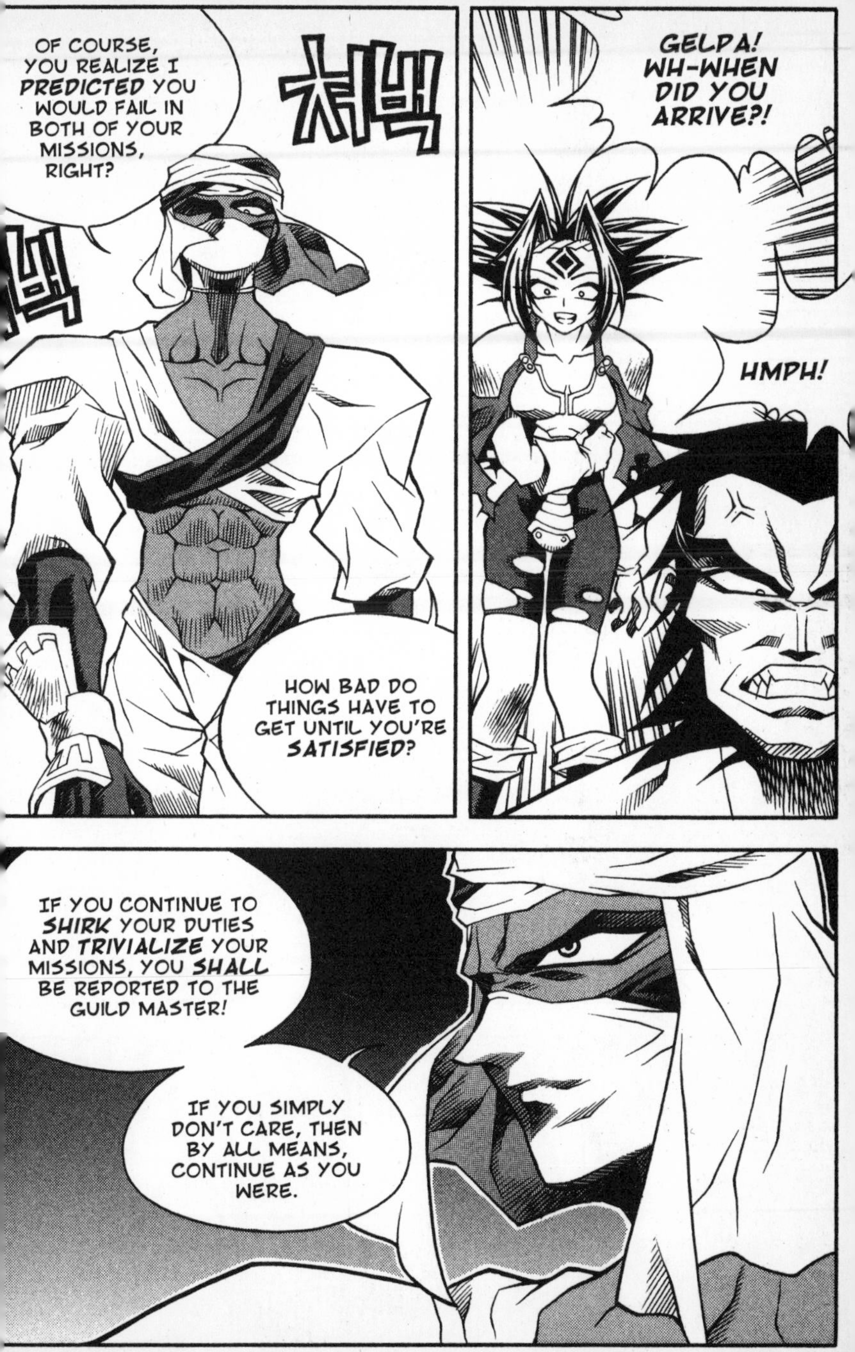
OF COURSE, YOU REALIZE I PREDICTED YOU WOULD FAIL IN BOTH OF YOUR MISSIONS, RIGHT?
HOW BAD DO THINGS HAVE TO GET UNTIL YOU'RE SATISFIED?
GELPA! WH-WHEN DID YOU ARRIVE?!
HMPH!
IF YOU CONTINUE TO SHIRK YOUR DUTIES AND TRIVIALIZE YOUR MISSIONS, YOU SHALL BE REPORTED TO THE GUILD MASTER!
IF YOU SIMPLY DON'T CARE, THEN BY ALL MEANS, CONTINUE AS YOU WERE.

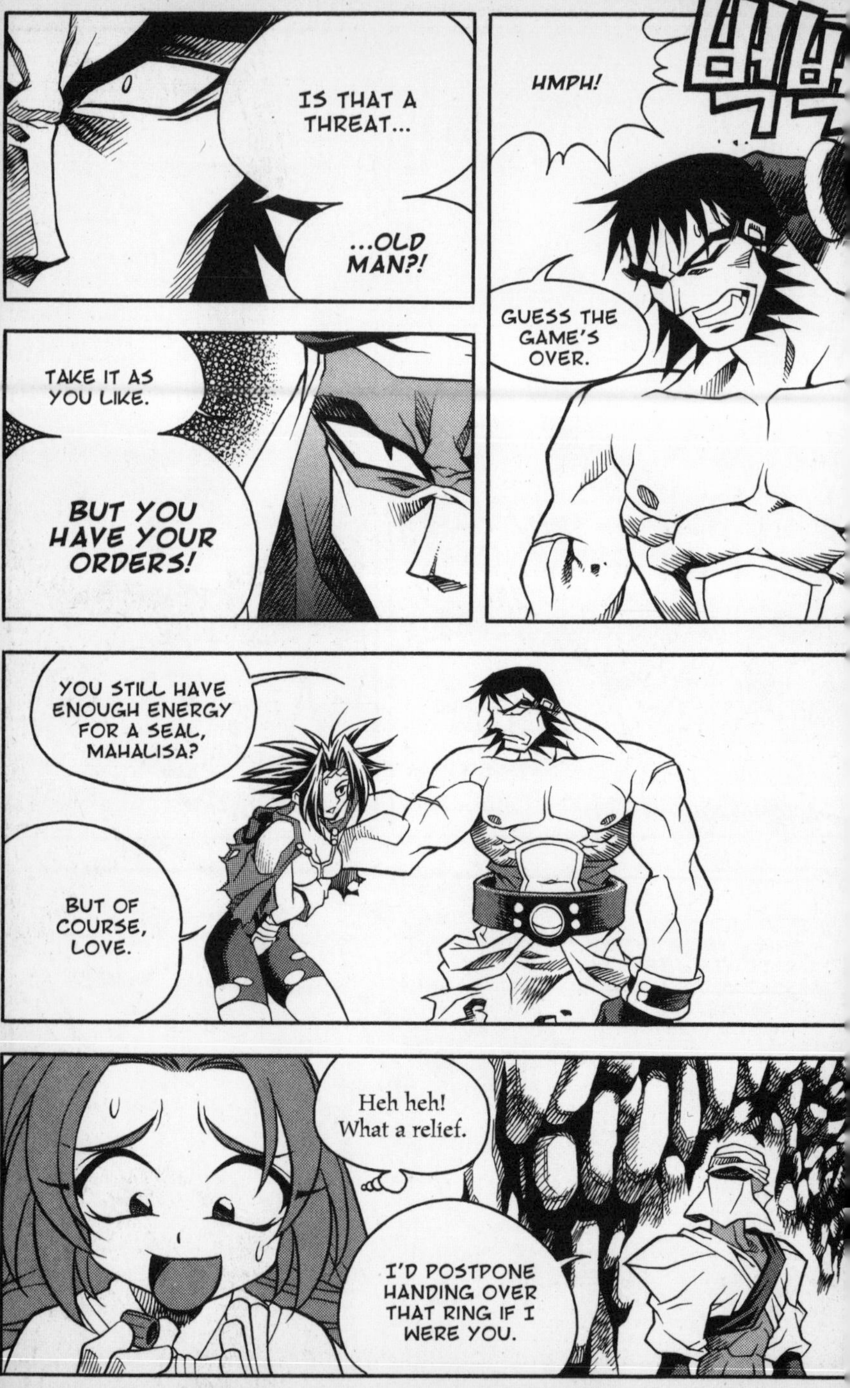
IS THAT A THREAT...
...OLD MAN?!
TAKE IT AS YOU LIKE.
BUT YOU HAVE YOUR ORDERS!
HMPH!
GUESS THE GAME'S OVER.
YOU STILL HAVE ENOUGH ENERGY FOR A SEAL, MAHALISA?
BUT OF COURSE, LOVE.
Heh heh! What a relief.
I'D POSTPONE HANDING OVER THAT RING IF I WERE YOU.

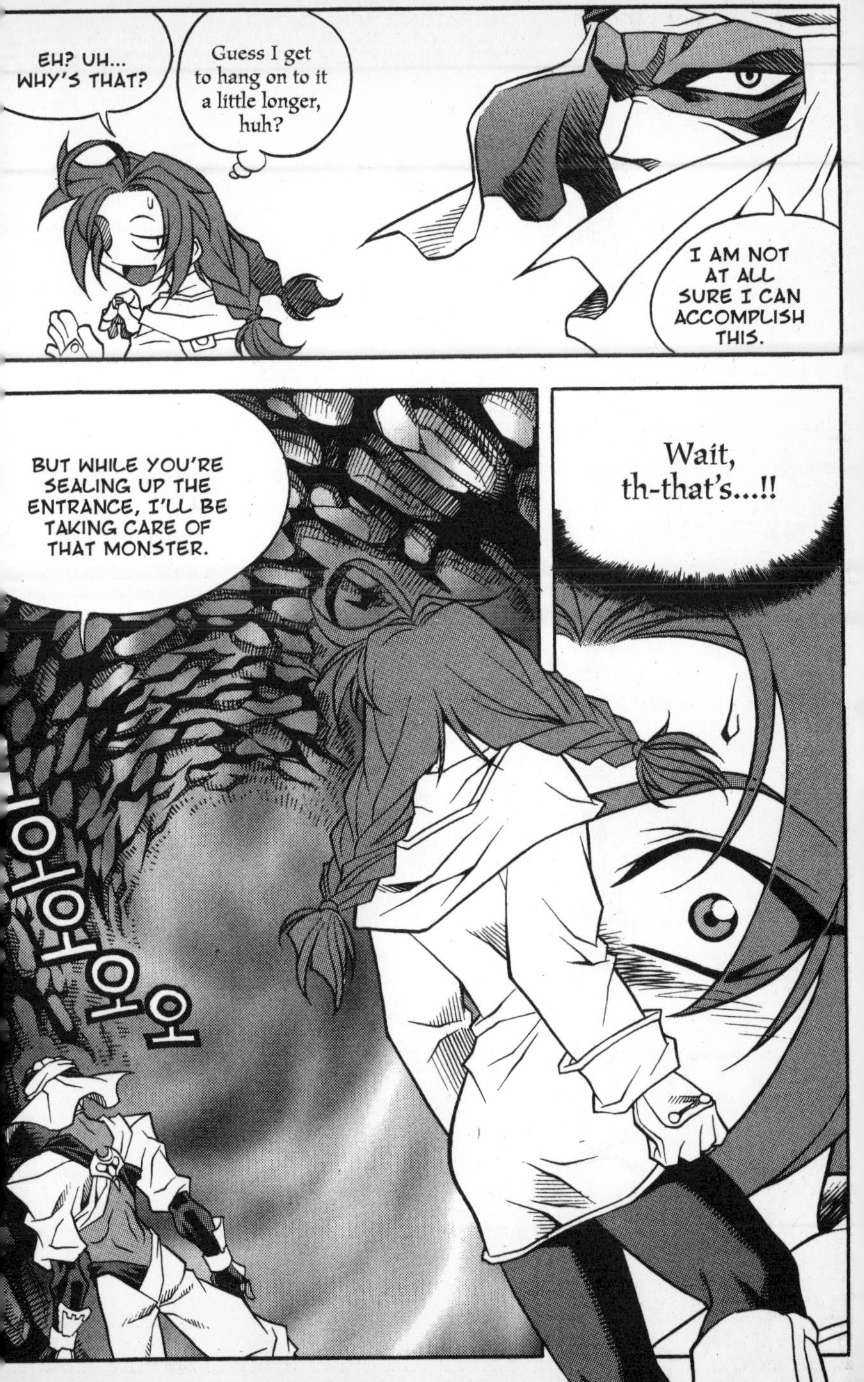

EH? UH... WHY'S THAT?
Guess I get to hang on to it a little longer, huh?
I AM NOT AT ALL SURE I CAN ACCOMPLISH THIS.
BUT WHILE YOU'RE SEALING UP THE ENTRANCE, I'LL BE TAKING CARE OF THAT MONSTER.
Wait, th-that's...!!

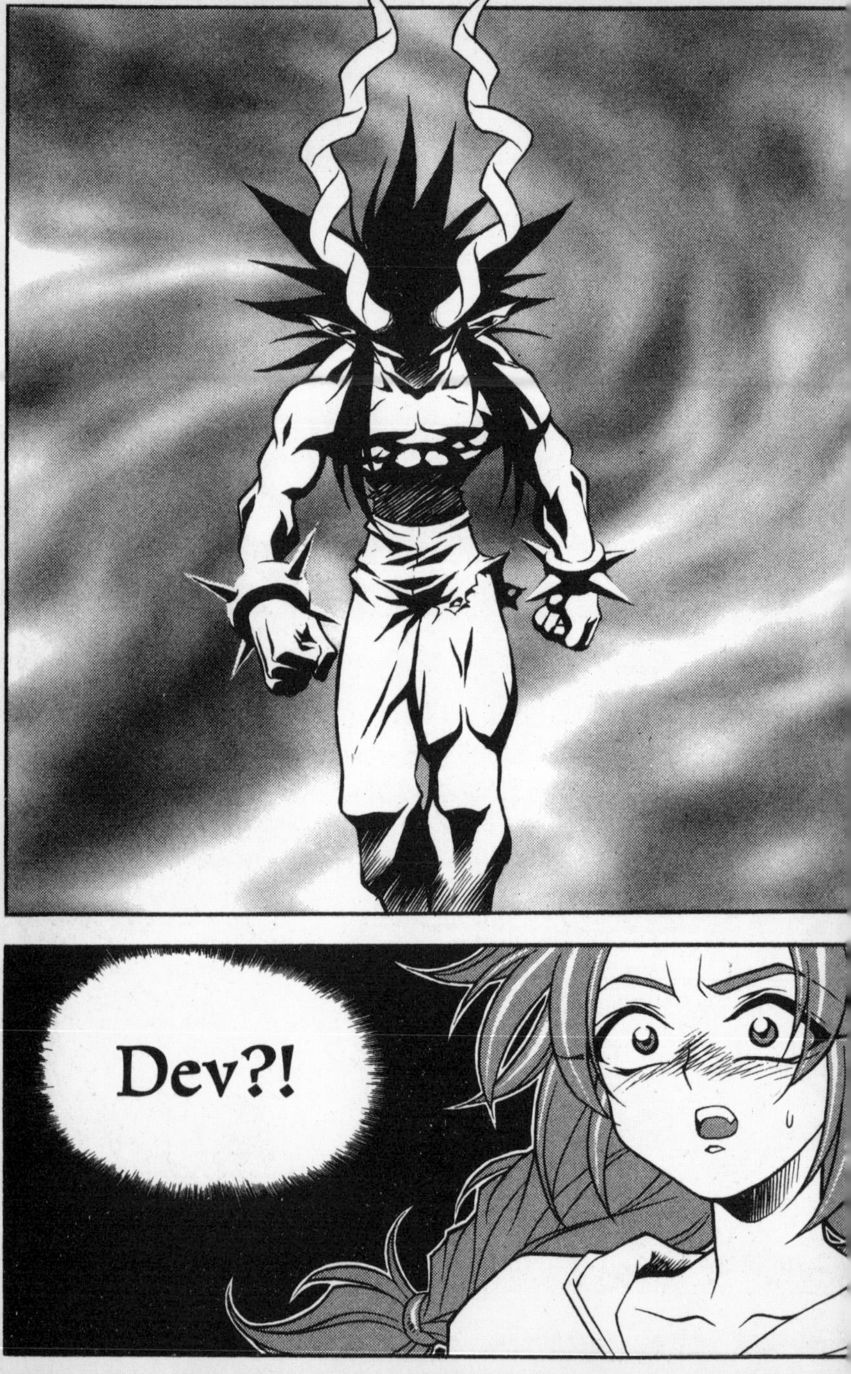
Dev?!

Quest 20

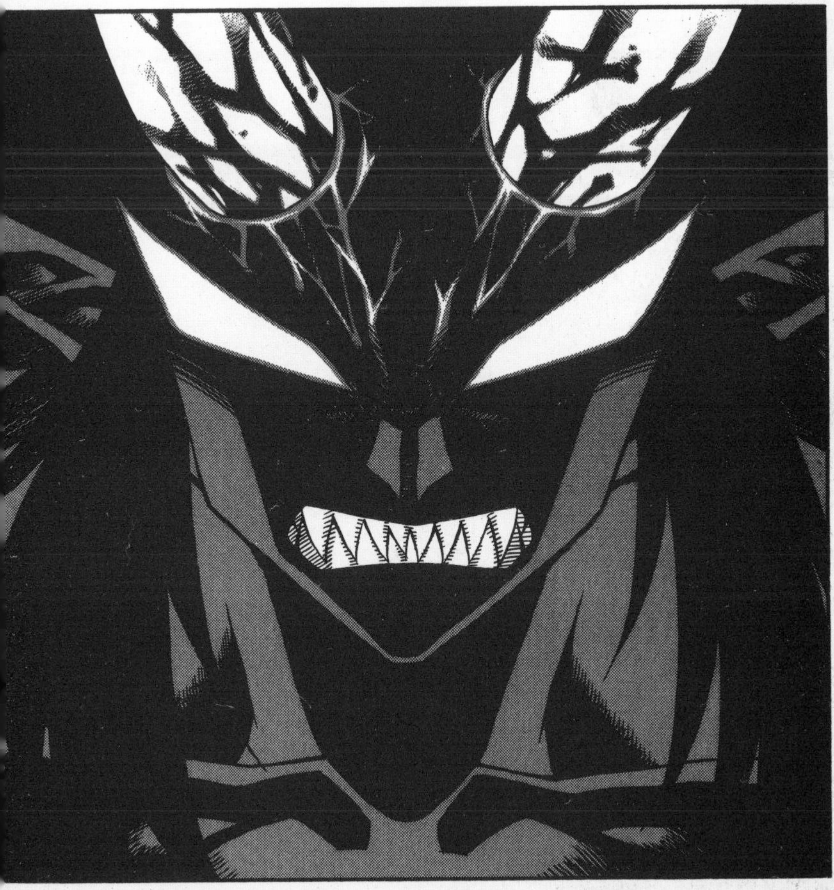

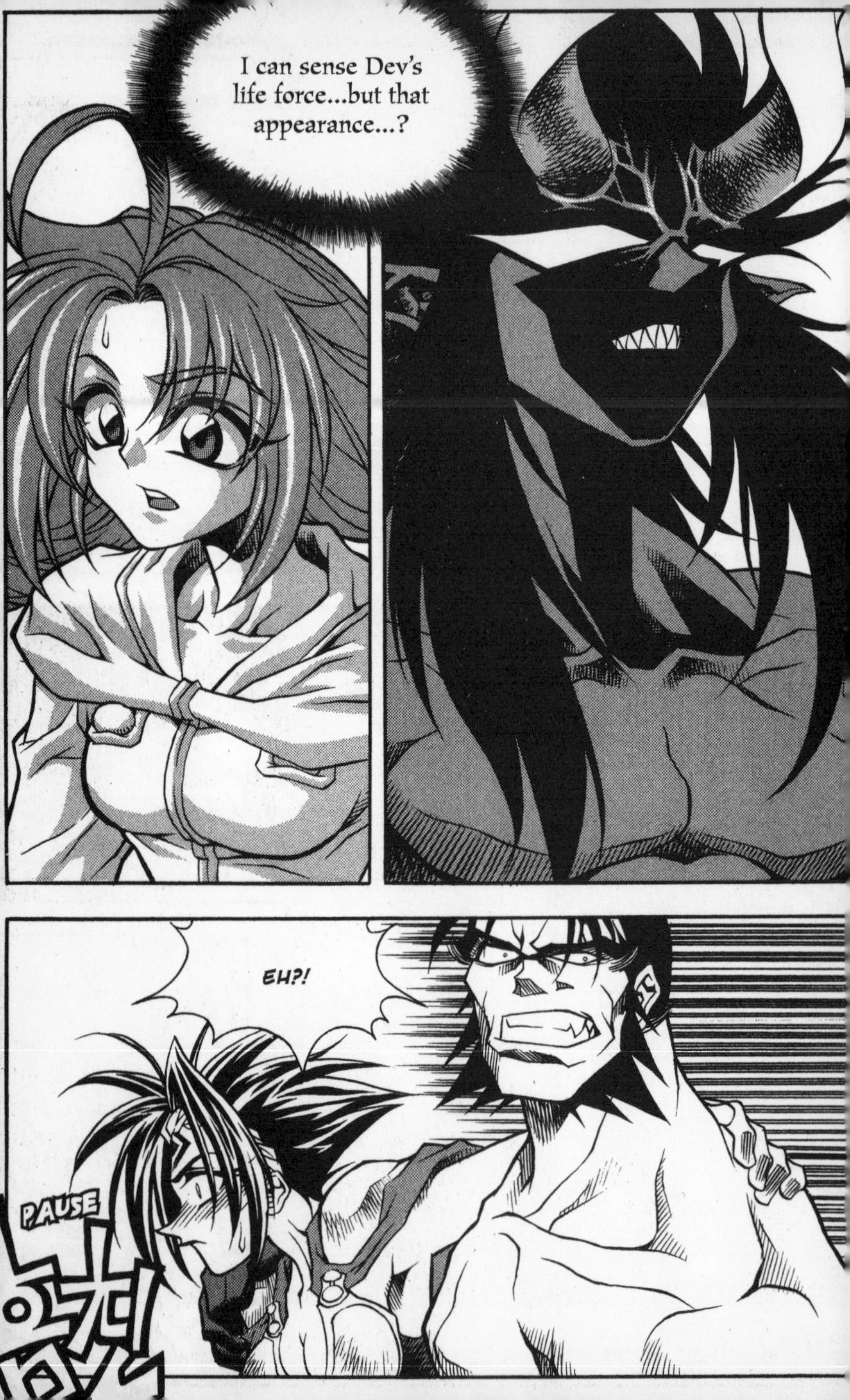
I can sense Dev's life force...but that appearance...?
EH?!
PAUSE

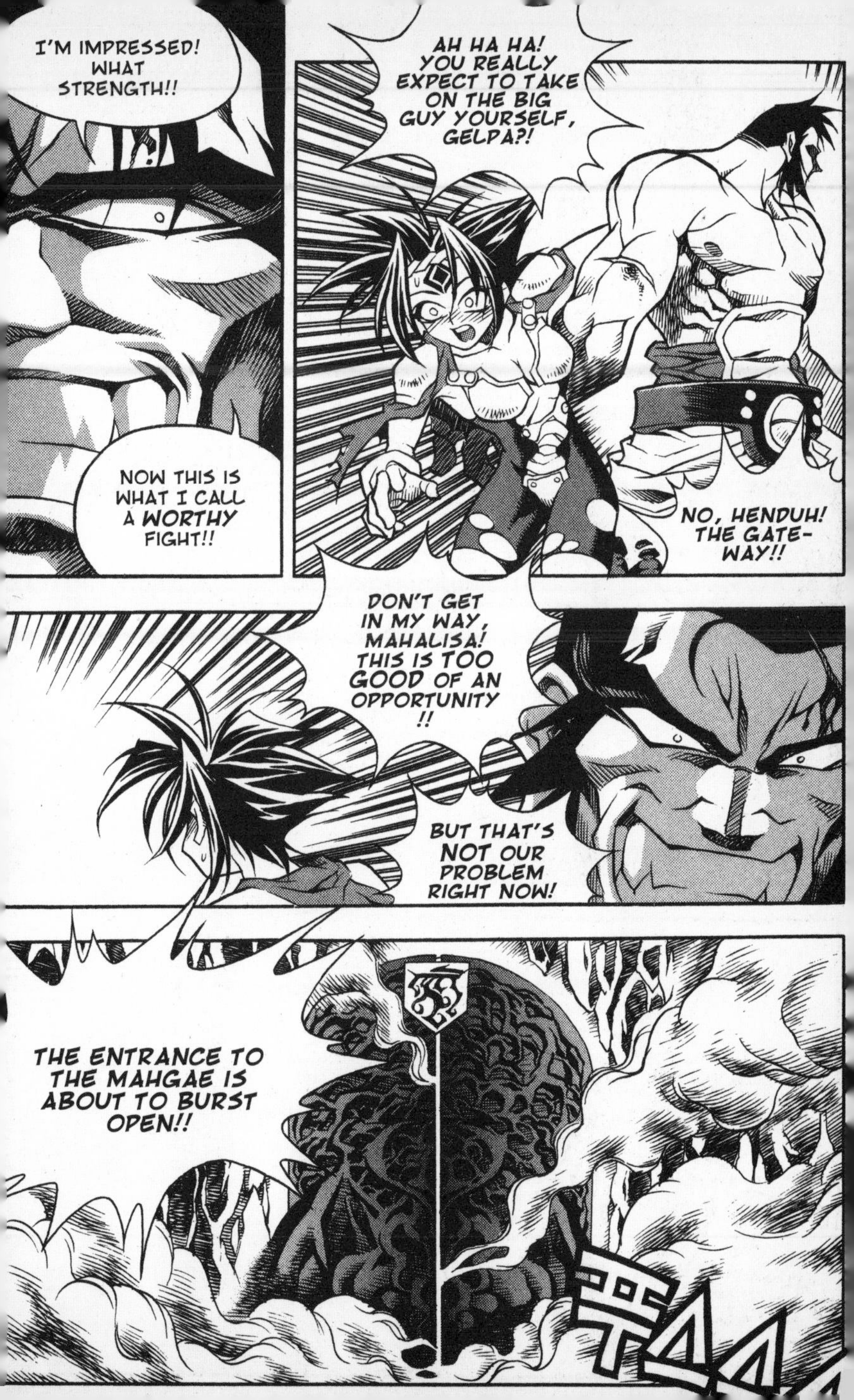
I'M IMPRESSED! WHAT STRENGTH!!
NOW THIS IS WHAT I CALL A WORTHY FIGHT!!
AH HA HA! YOU REALLY EXPECT TO TAKE ON THE BIG GUY YOURSELF, GELPA?!
NO, HENDUH! THE GATE-WAY!!
DON'T GET IN MY WAY, MAHALISA! THIS IS TOO GOOD OF AN OPPORTUNITY!!
BUT THAT'S NOT OUR PROBLEM RIGHT NOW!
THE ENTRANCE TO THE MAHGAE IS ABOUT TO BURST OPEN!!

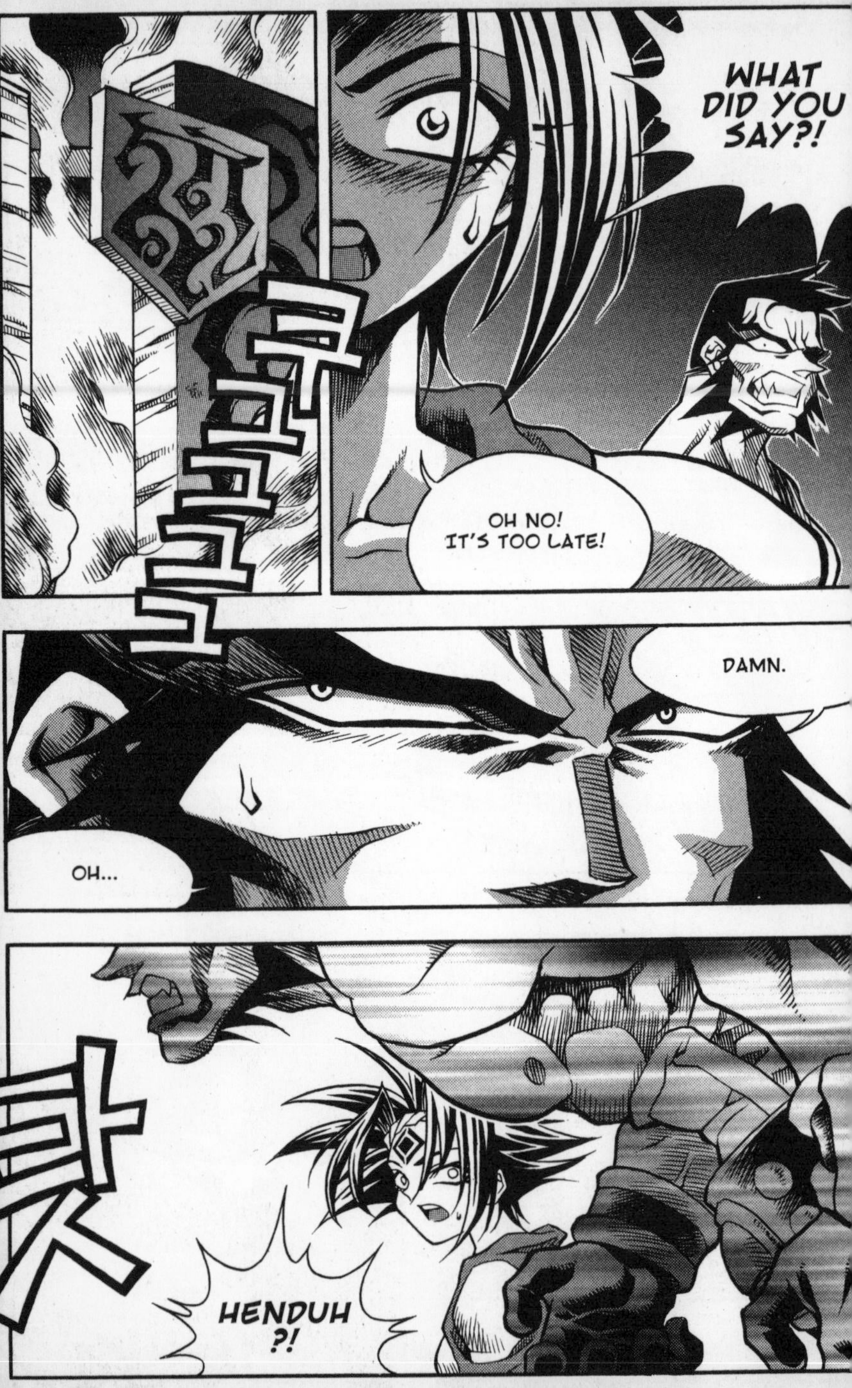
WHAT DID YOU SAY?!
OH NO! IT'S TOO LATE!
OH...
DAMN.
HENDUH ?!

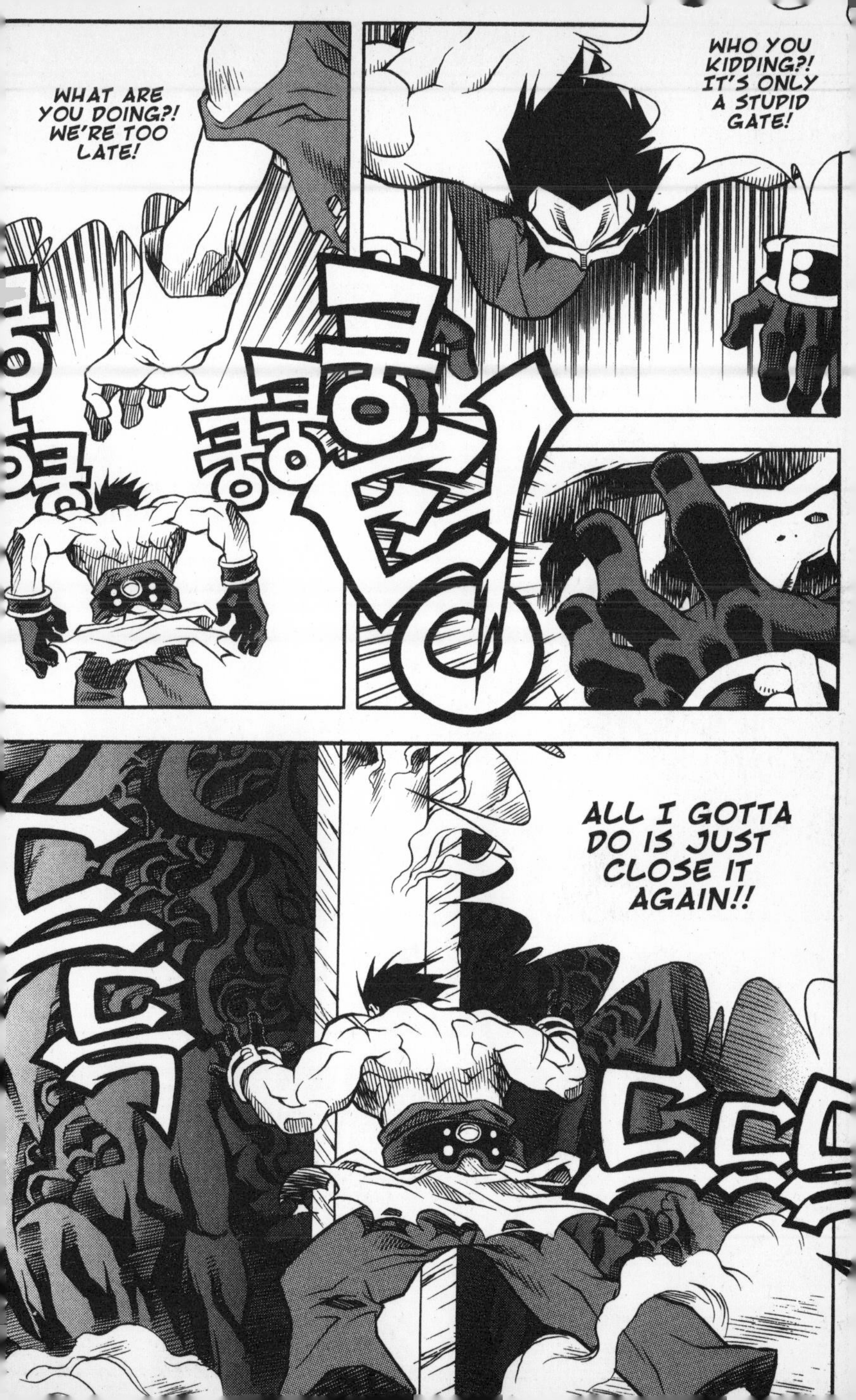
WHAT ARE YOU DOING?! WE'RE TOO LATE!
WHO YOU KIDDING?! IT'S ONLY A STUPID GATE!
ALL I GOTTA DO IS JUST CLOSE IT AGAIN!!

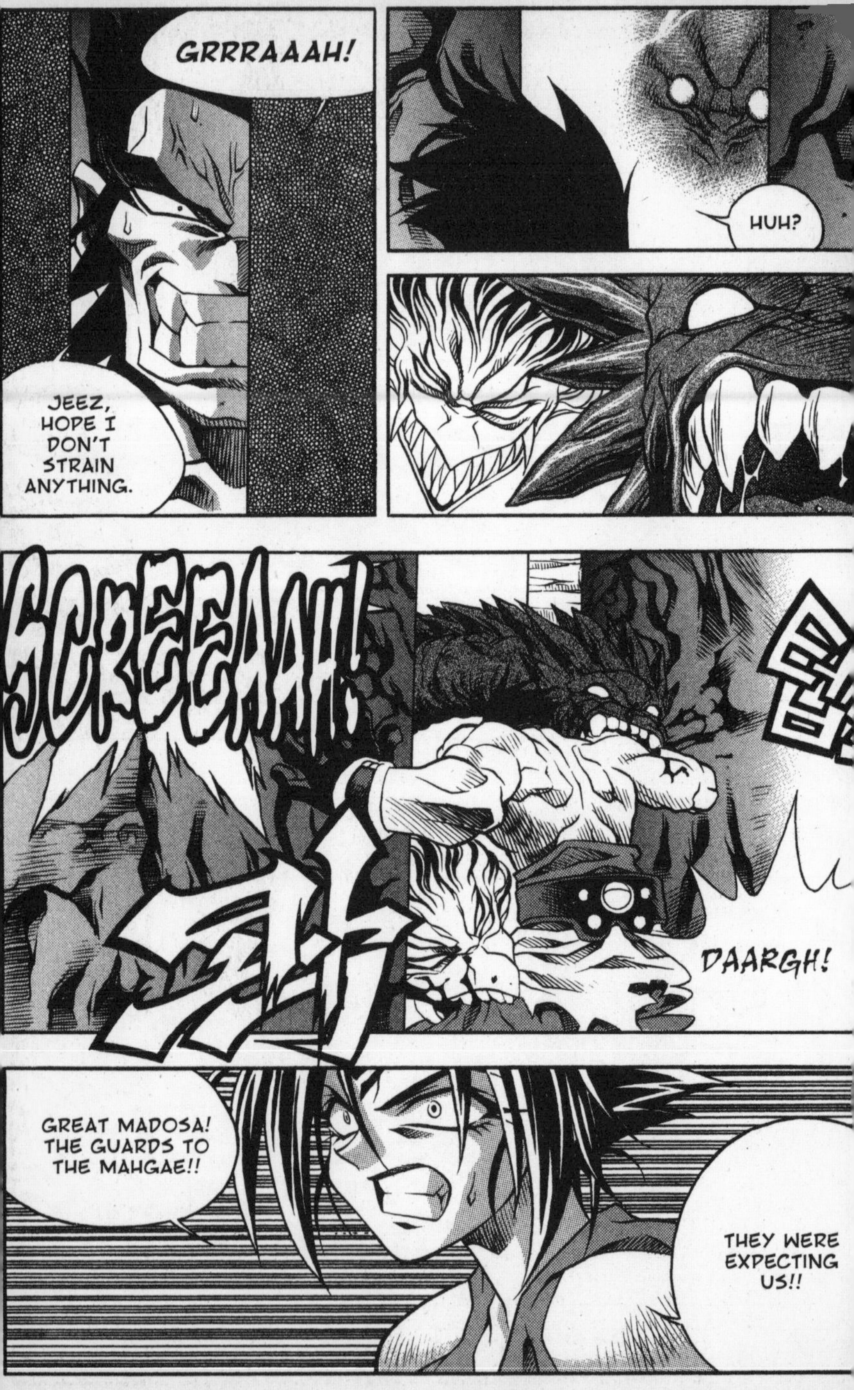
GRRRAAAH!
JEEZ, HOPE I DON'T STRAIN ANYTHING.
HUH?
SCREEAAH!
DAARGH!
GREAT MADOSA! THE GUARDS TO THE MAHGAE!!
THEY WERE EXPECTING US!!

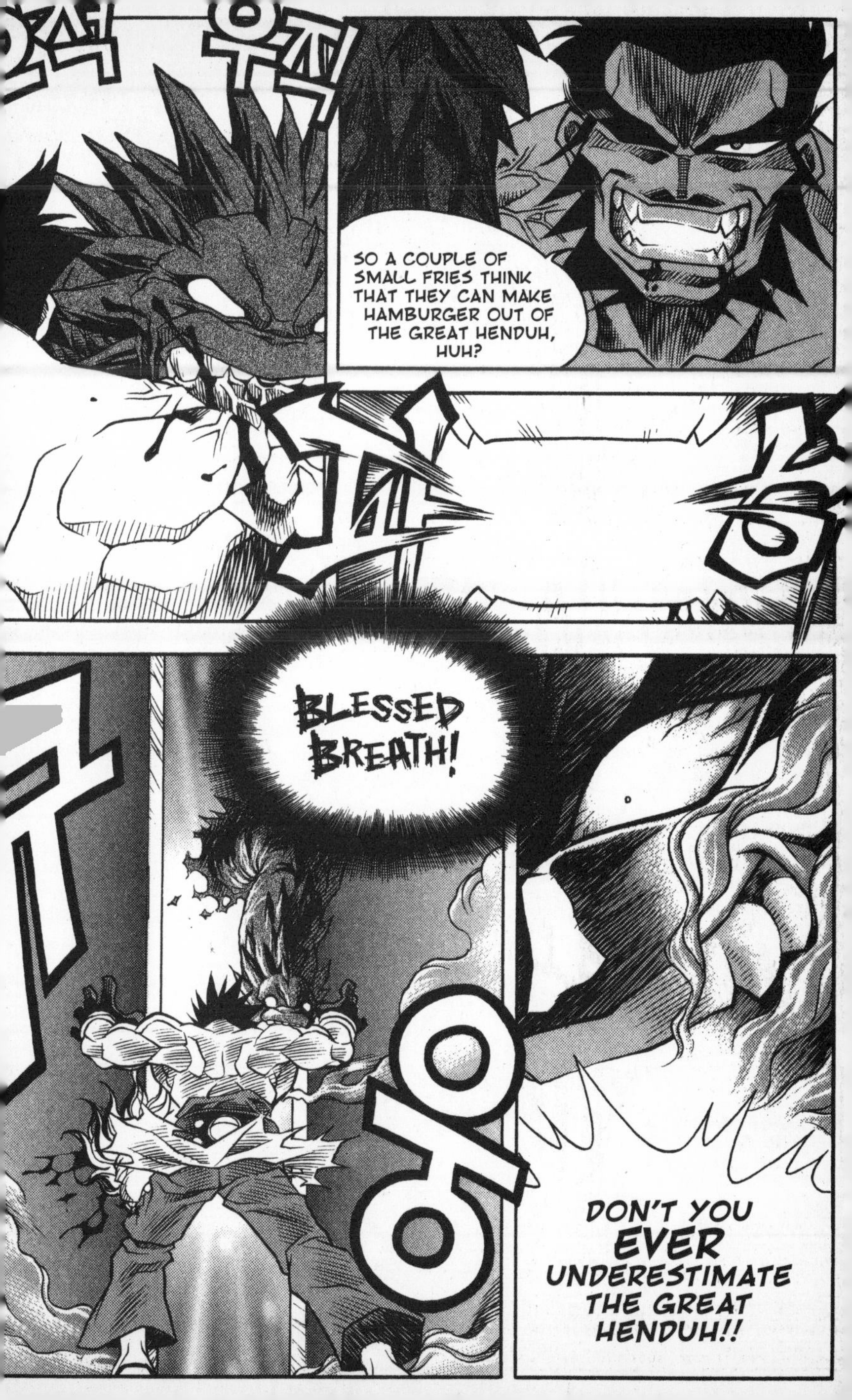

SO A COUPLE OF SMALL FRIES THINK THAT THEY CAN MAKE HAMBURGER OUT OF THE GREAT HENDUH, HUH?
BLESSED BREATH!
DON'T YOU EVER UNDERESTIMATE THE GREAT HENDUH!!

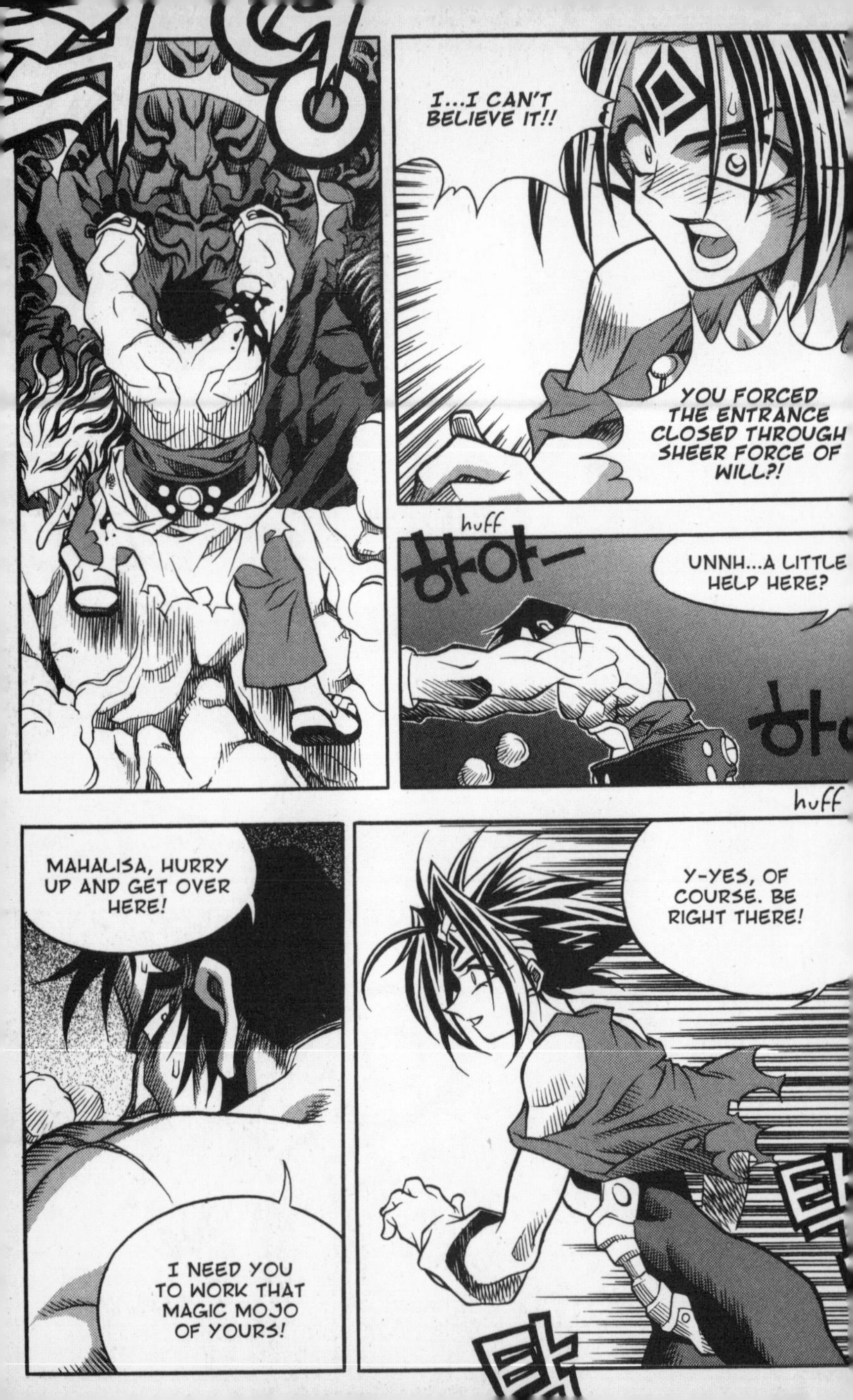
I...I CAN'T BELIEVE IT!!
YOU FORCED THE ENTRANCE CLOSED THROUGH SHEER FORCE OF WILL?!
huff
하아—
UNNH...A LITTLE HELP HERE?
huff
MAHALISA, HURRY UP AND GET OVER HERE!
I NEED YOU TO WORK THAT MAGIC MOJO OF YOURS!
Y-YES, OF COURSE. BE RIGHT THERE!

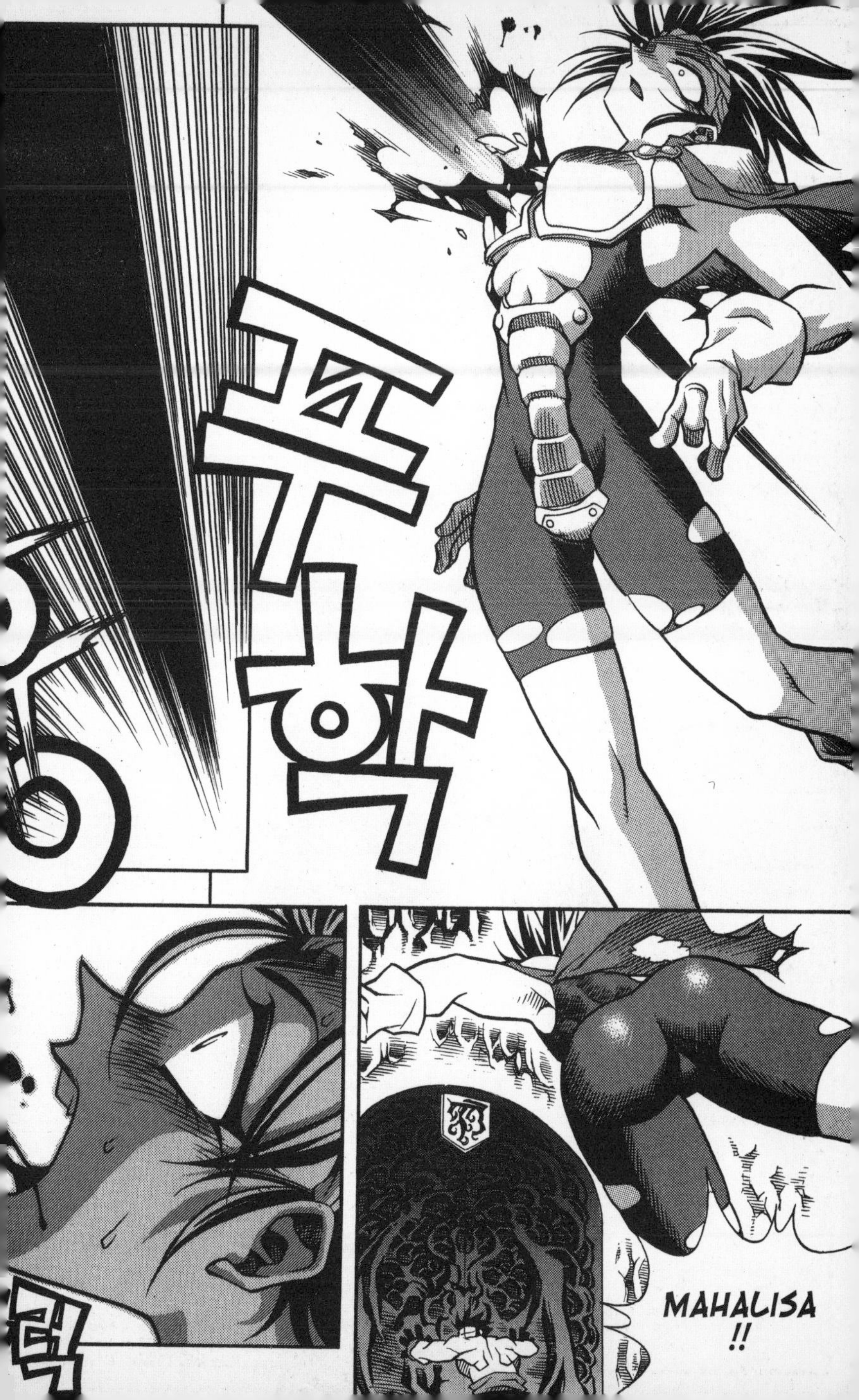

푸확
MAHALISA
!!

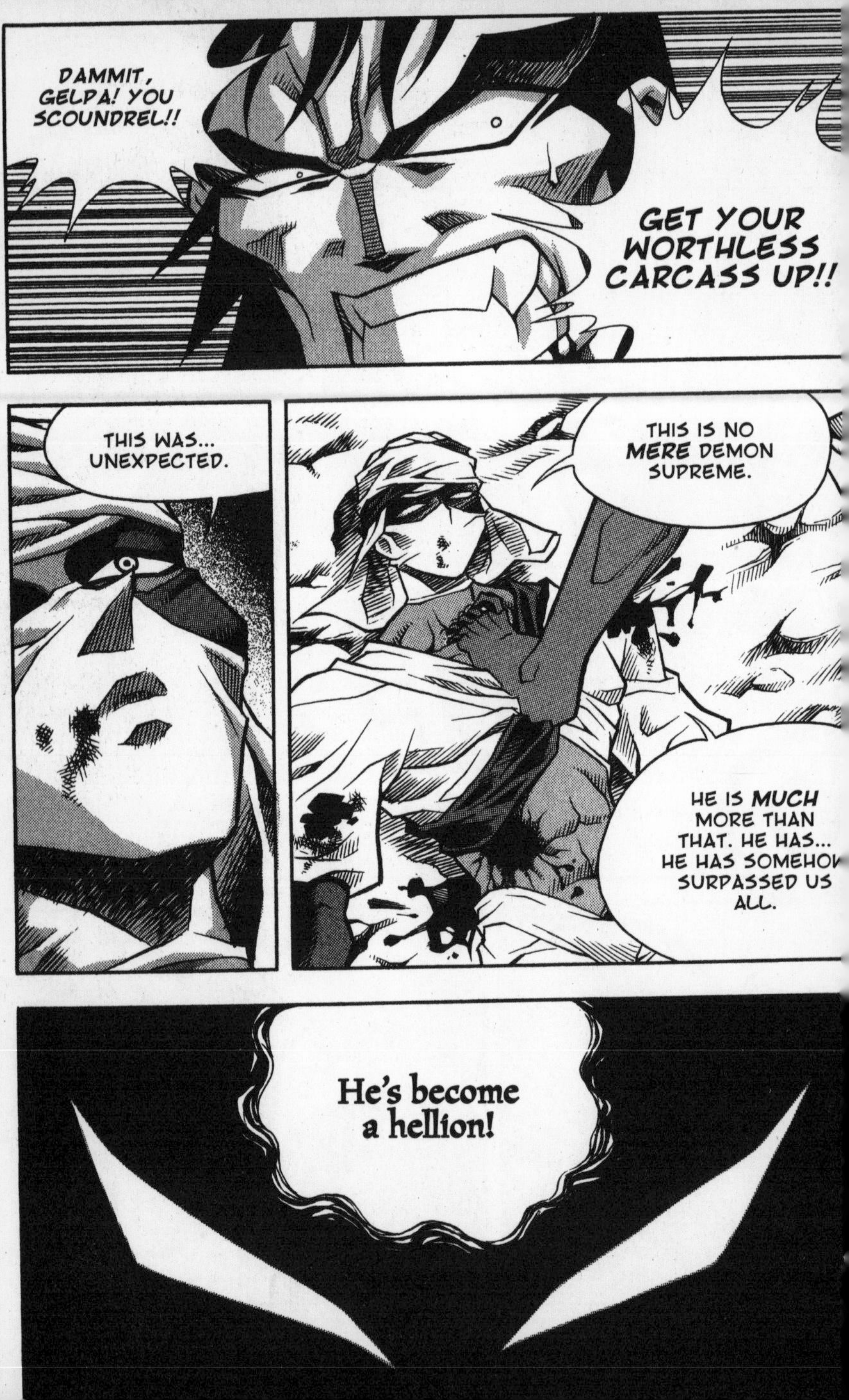
DAMMIT, GELPA! YOU SCOUNDREL!!
GET YOUR WORTHLESS CARCASS UP!!
THIS WAS... UNEXPECTED.
THIS IS NO MERE DEMON SUPREME.
HE IS MUCH MORE THAN THAT. HE HAS... HE HAS SOMEHOW SURPASSED US ALL.
He's become a hellion!

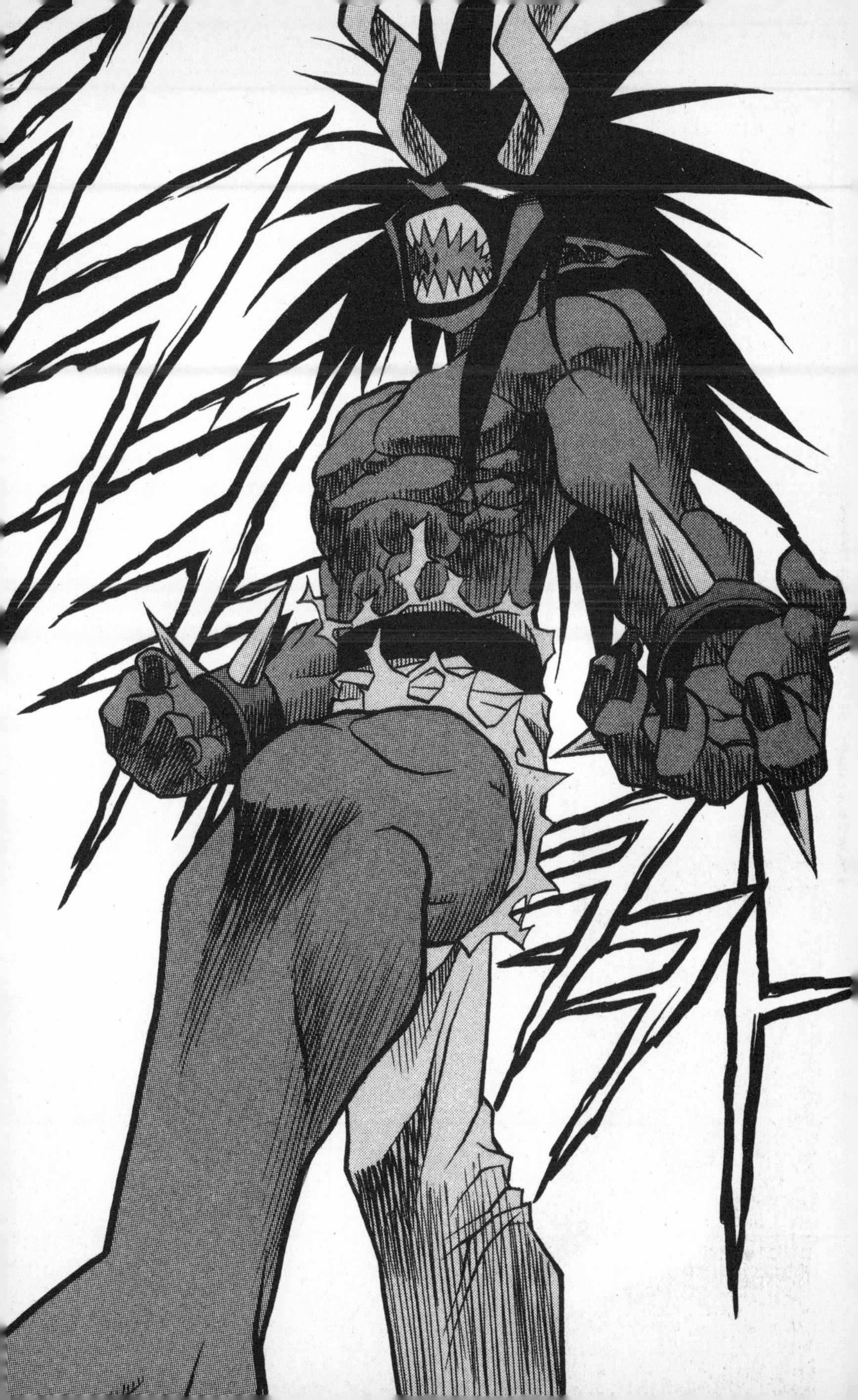

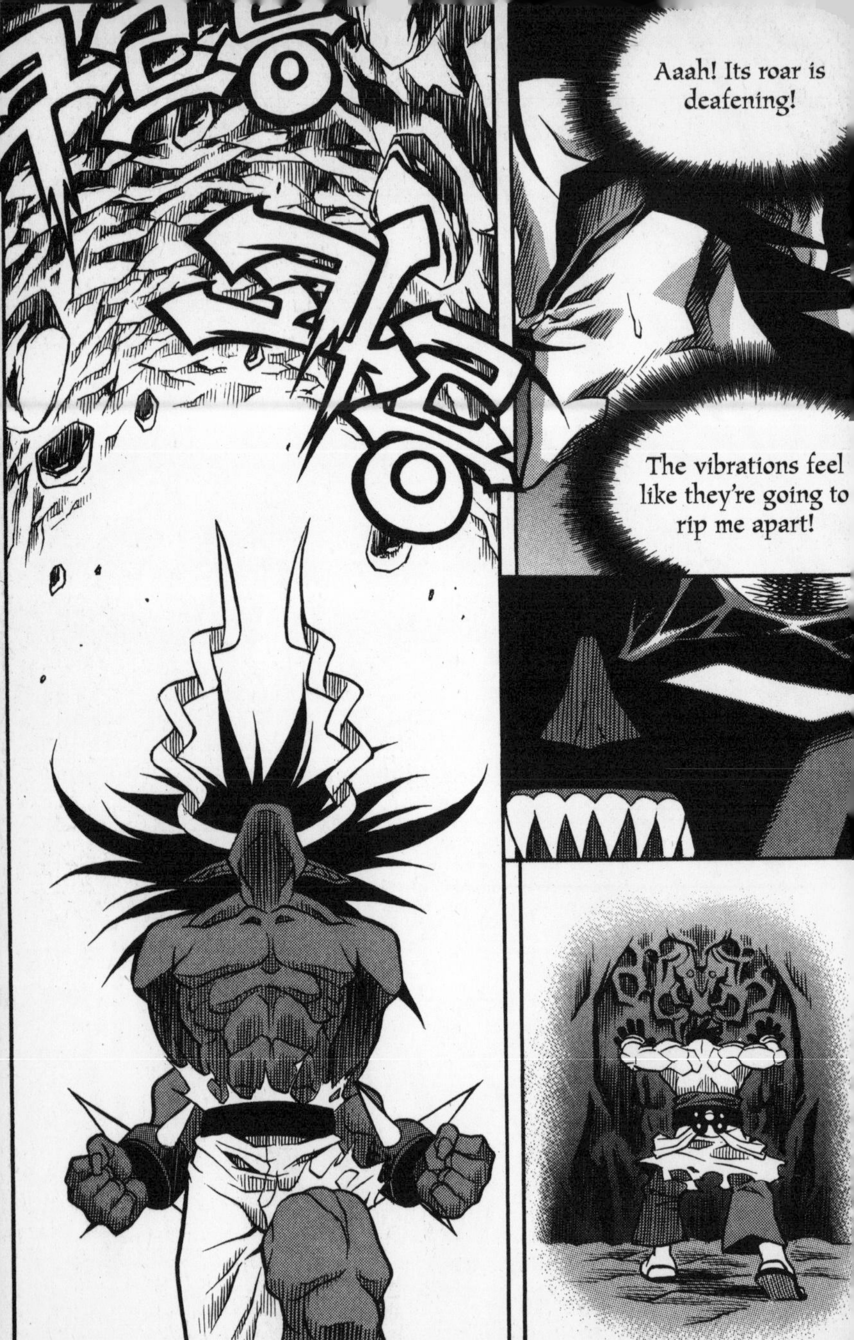
Aaah! Its roar is deafening!
The vibrations feel like they're going to rip me apart!

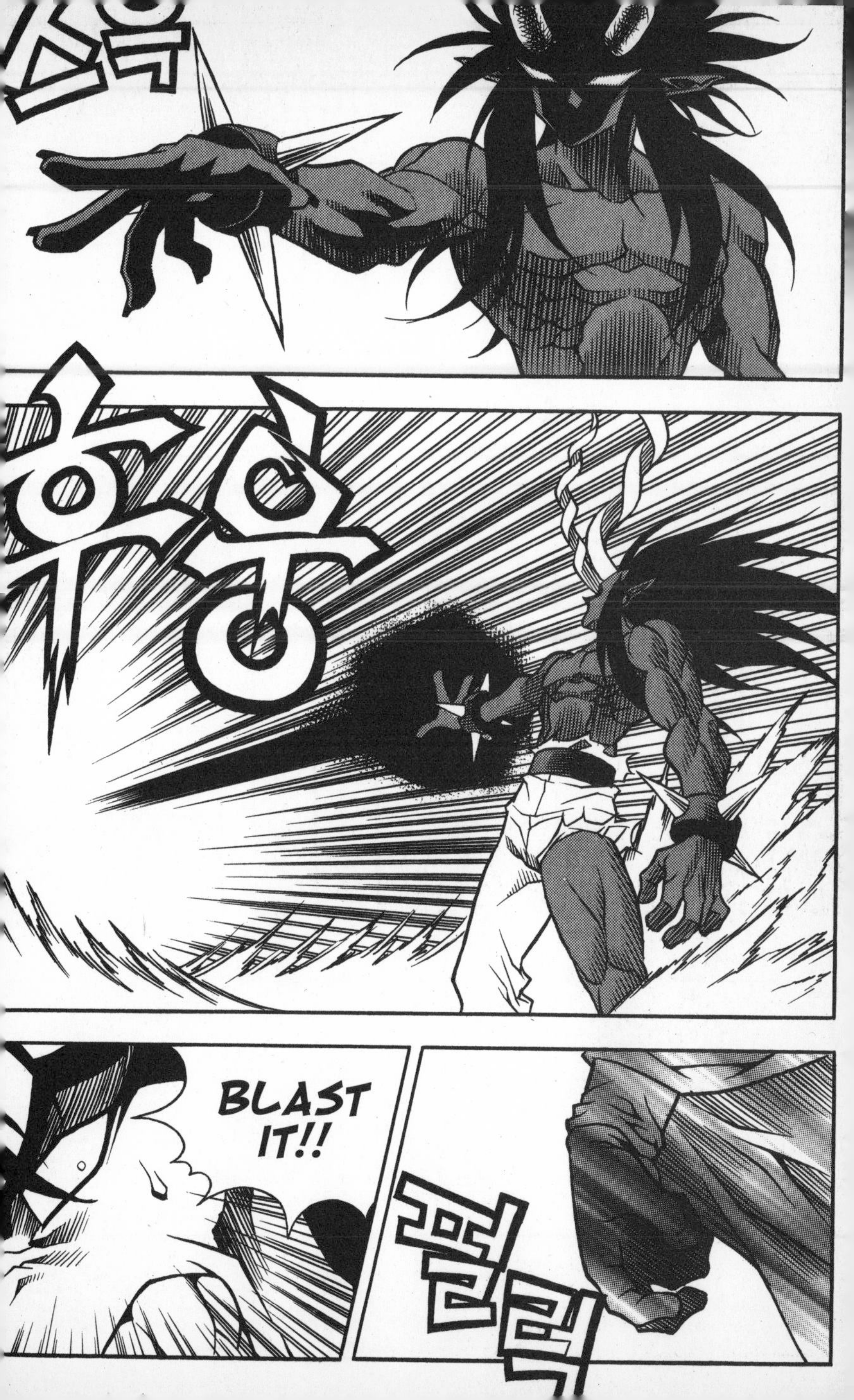
스윽
화아앙
BLAST IT!!
펄럭

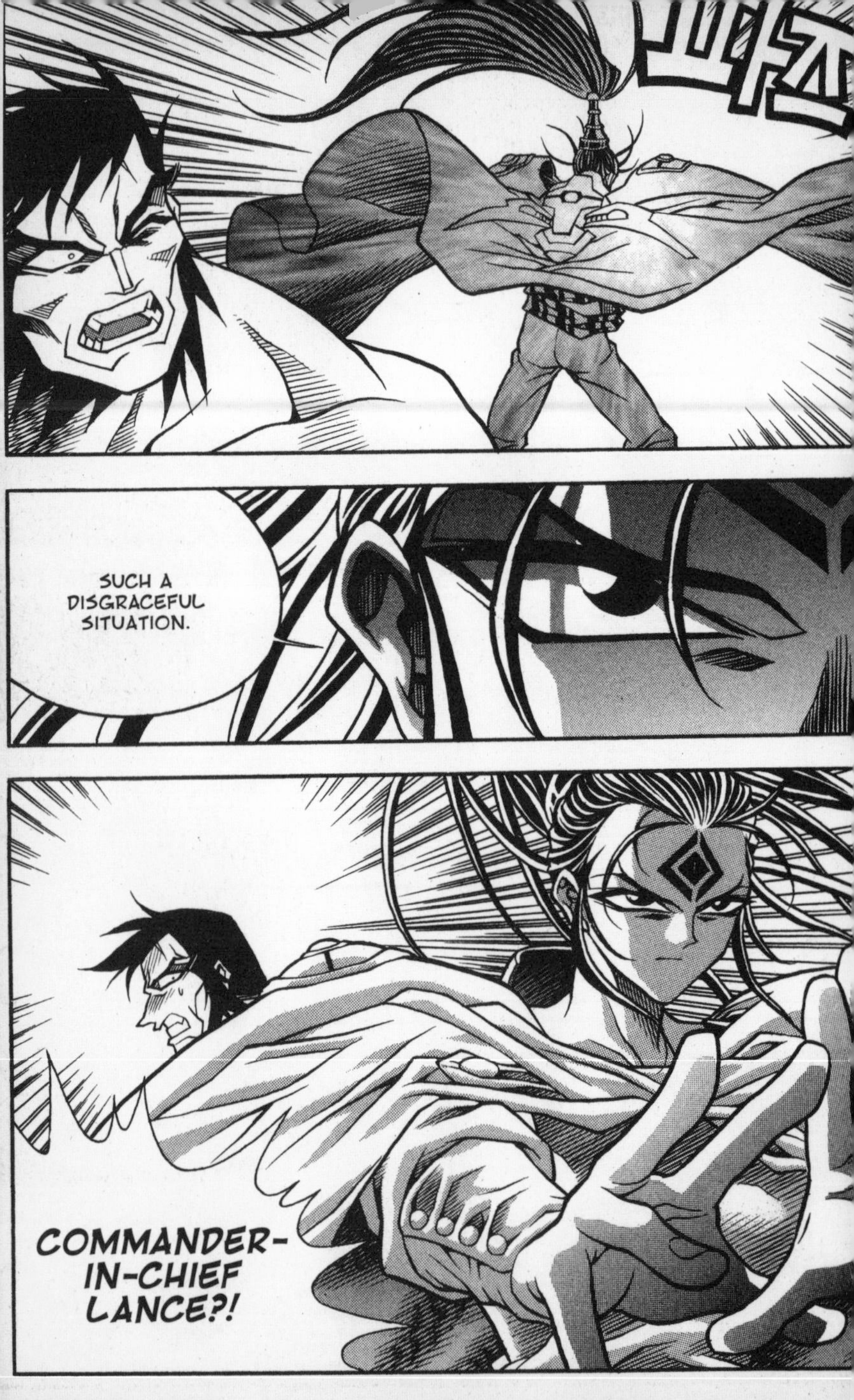
SUCH A DISGRACEFUL SITUATION.
COMMANDER-IN-CHIEF LANCE?!

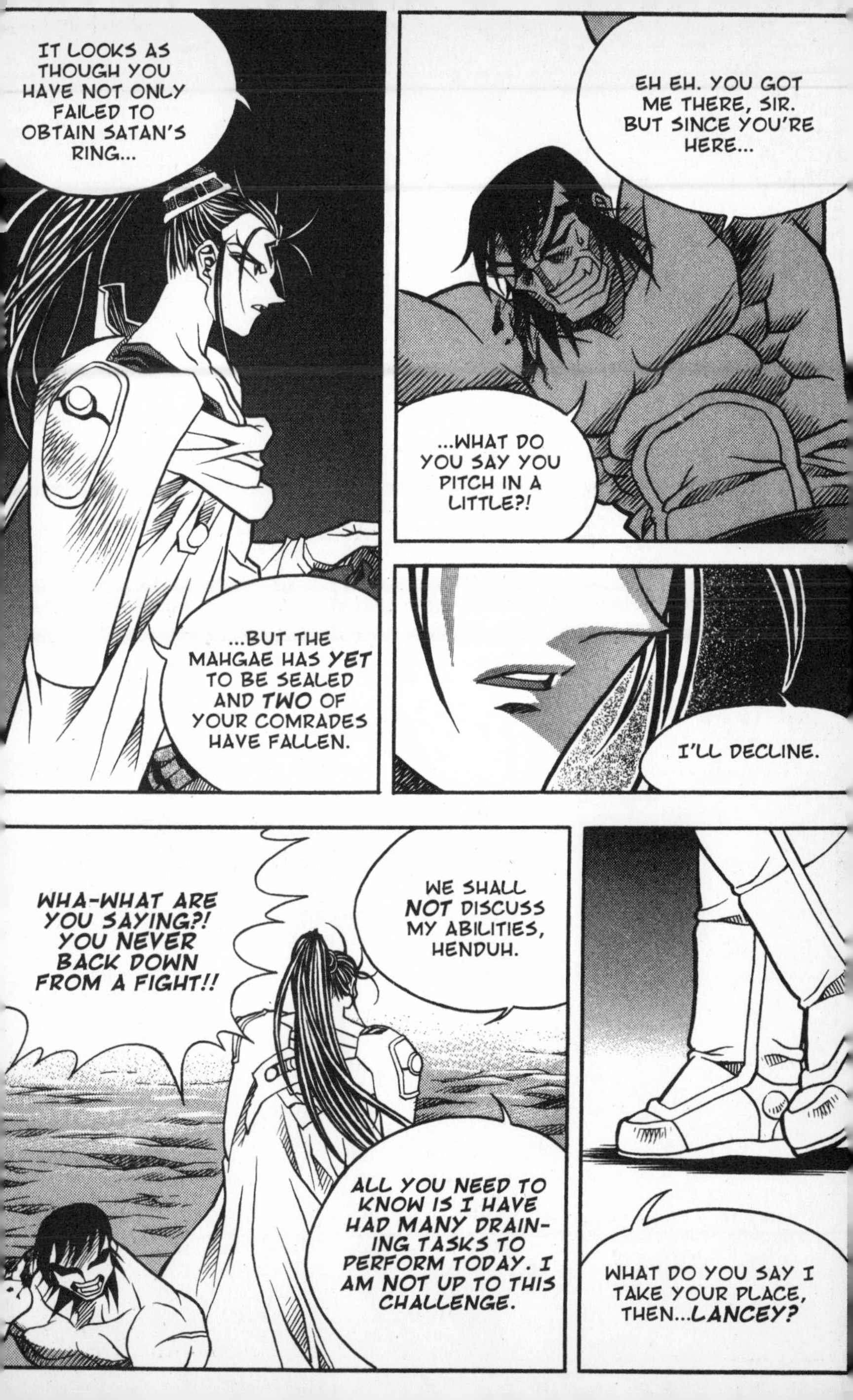
IT LOOKS AS THOUGH YOU HAVE NOT ONLY FAILED TO OBTAIN SATAN'S RING...
...BUT THE MAHGAE HAS YET TO BE SEALED AND TWO OF YOUR COMRADES HAVE FALLEN.
EH EH. YOU GOT ME THERE, SIR. BUT SINCE YOU'RE HERE...
...WHAT DO YOU SAY YOU PITCH IN A LITTLE?!
I'LL DECLINE.
WHA-WHAT ARE YOU SAYING?! YOU NEVER BACK DOWN FROM A FIGHT!!
WE SHALL NOT DISCUSS MY ABILITIES, HENDUH.
ALL YOU NEED TO KNOW IS I HAVE HAD MANY DRAINING TASKS TO PERFORM TODAY. I AM NOT UP TO THIS CHALLENGE.
WHAT DO YOU SAY I TAKE YOUR PLACE, THEN...LANCEY?

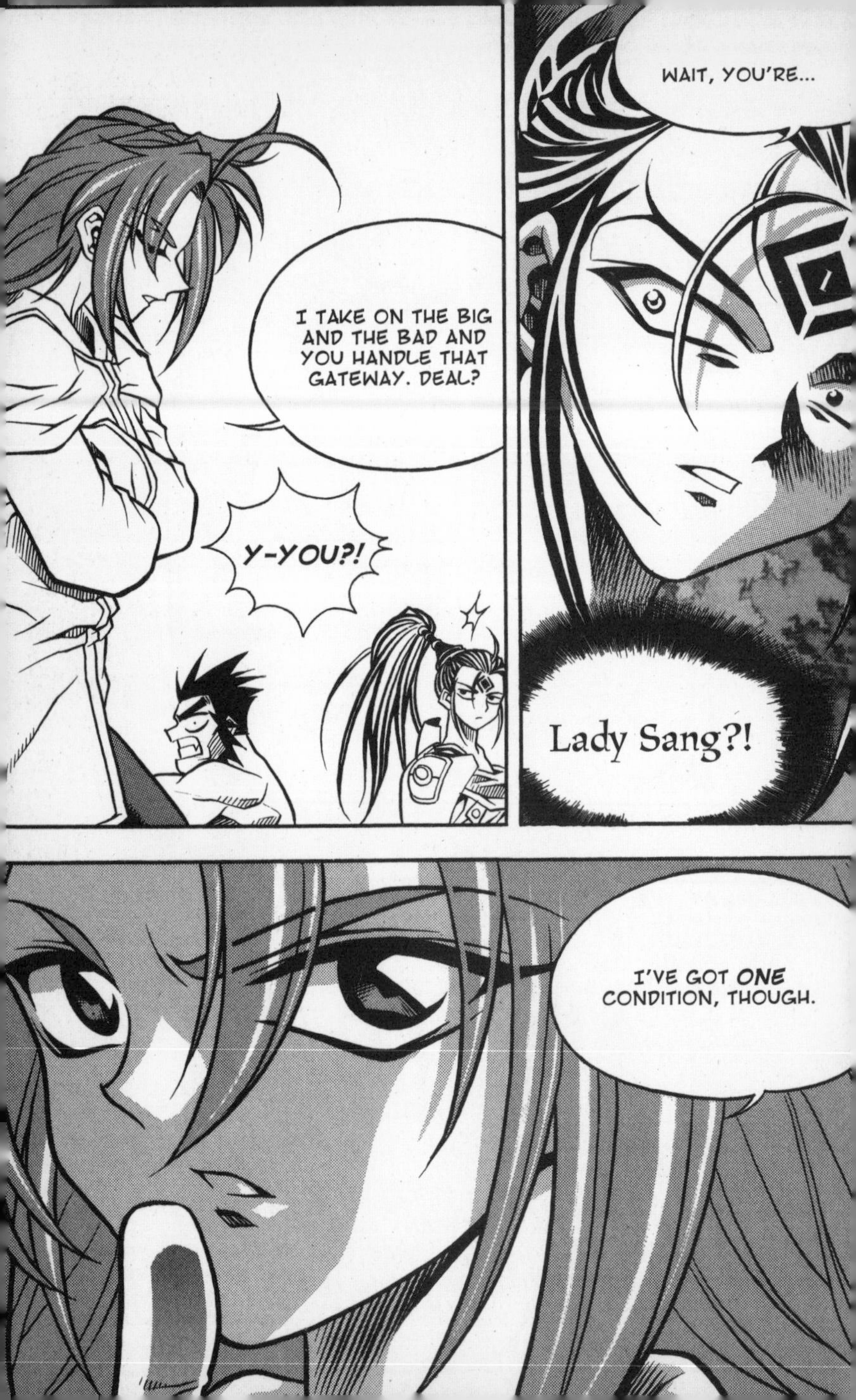
I TAKE ON THE BIG AND THE BAD AND YOU HANDLE THAT GATEWAY. DEAL?
Y-YOU?!
WAIT, YOU'RE...
Lady Sang?!
I'VE GOT ONE CONDITION, THOUGH.

Quest 21

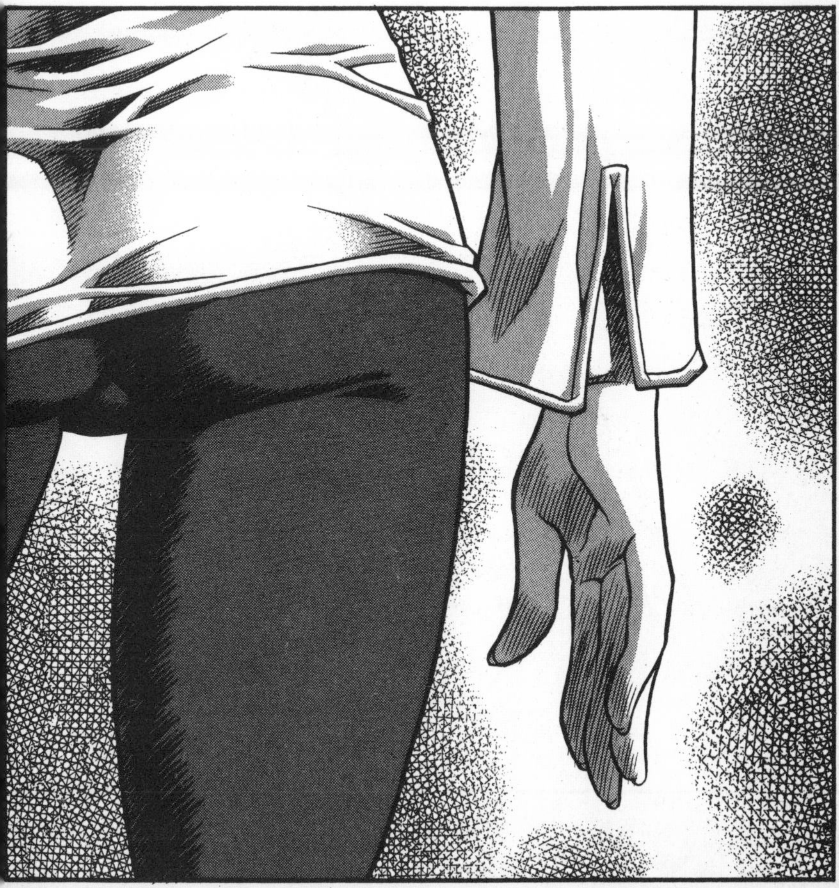

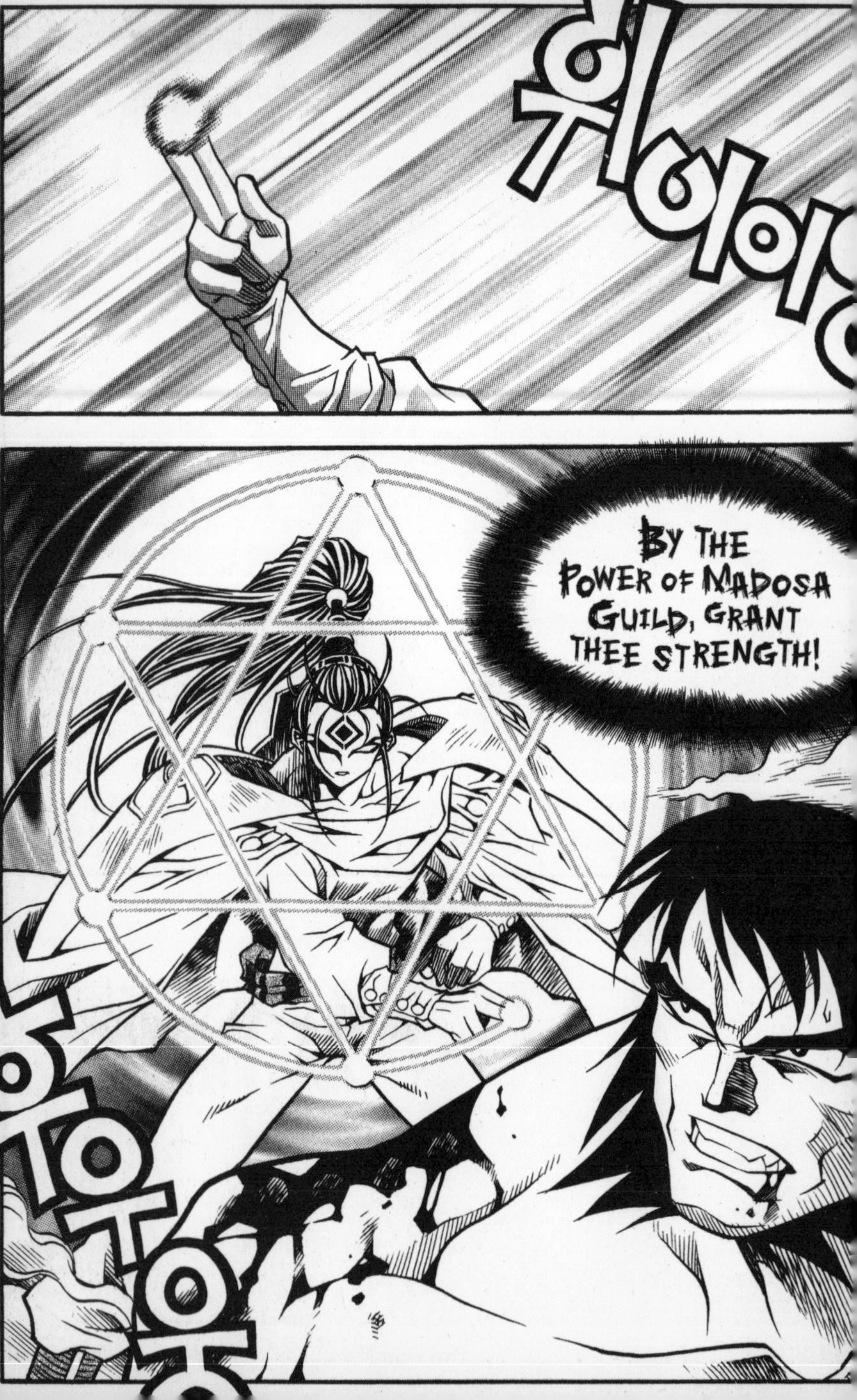
BY THE POWER OF MADOSA GUILD, GRANT THEE STRENGTH!

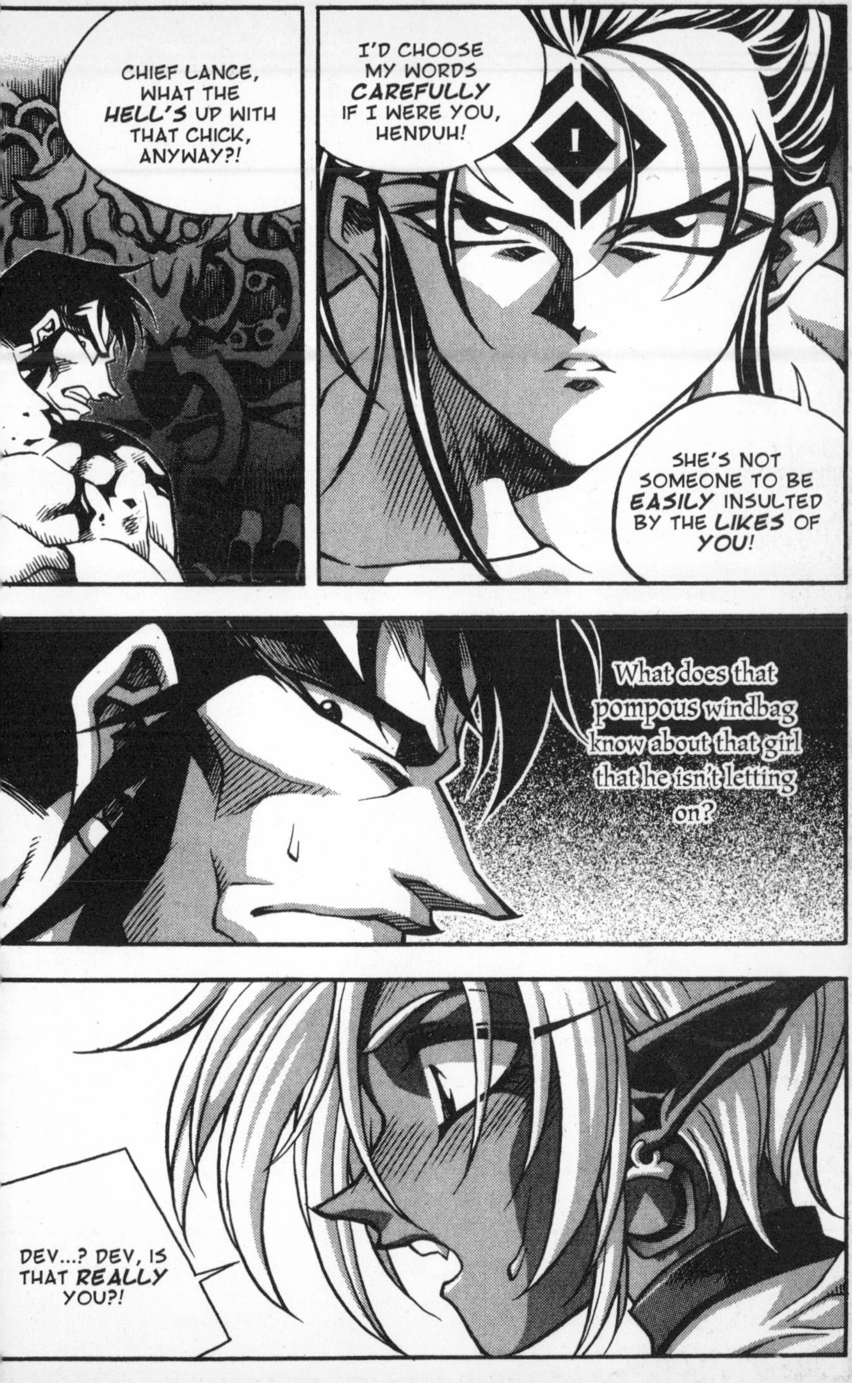
CHIEF LANCE, WHAT THE HELL'S UP WITH THAT CHICK, ANYWAY?!
I'D CHOOSE MY WORDS CAREFULLY IF I WERE YOU, HENDUH!
SHE'S NOT SOMEONE TO BE EASILY INSULTED BY THE LIKES OF YOU!
What does that pompous windbag know about that girl that he isn't letting on?
DEV...? DEV, IS THAT REALLY YOU?!

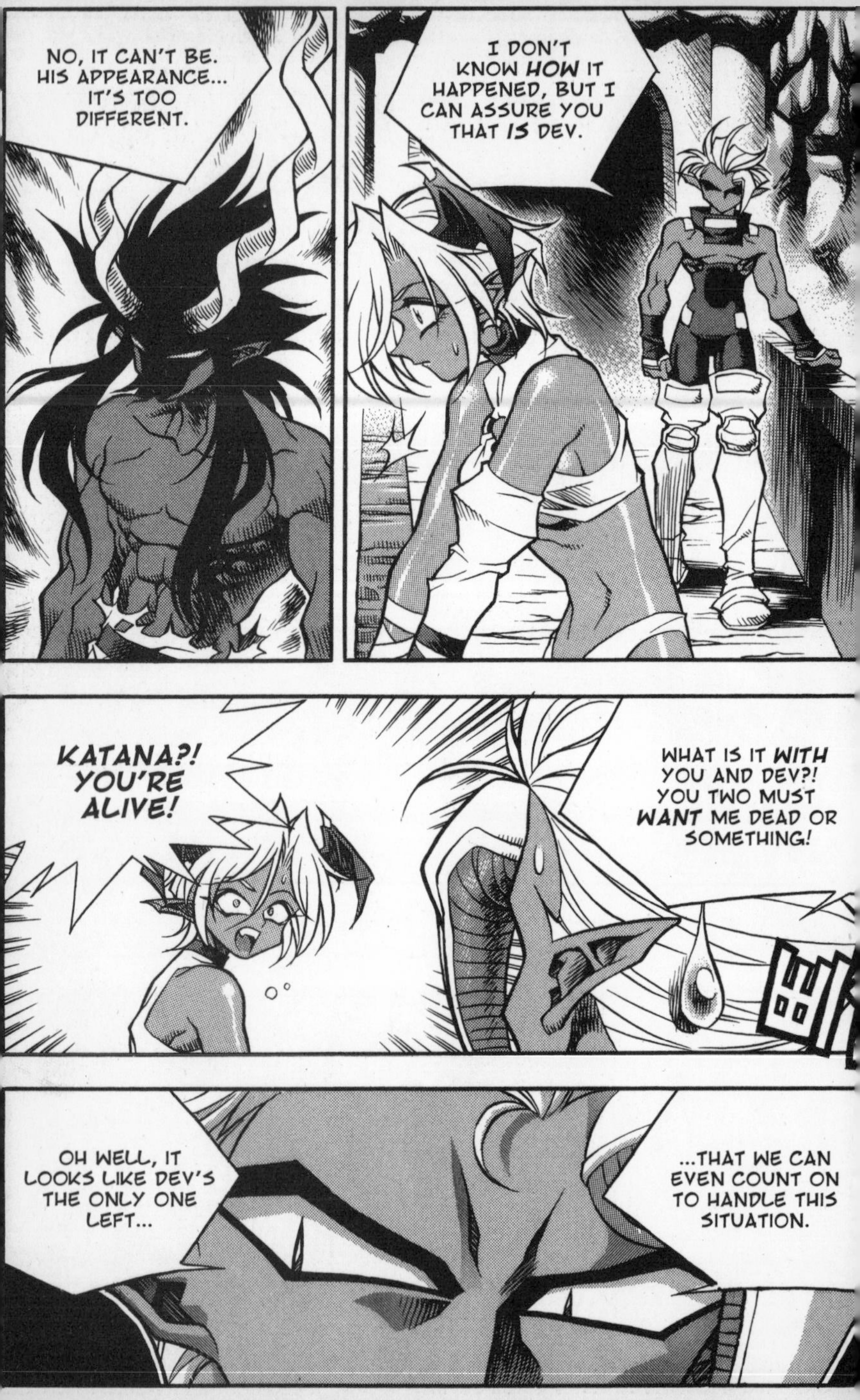
NO, IT CAN'T BE. HIS APPEARANCE... IT'S TOO DIFFERENT.
I DON'T KNOW HOW IT HAPPENED, BUT I CAN ASSURE YOU THAT IS DEV.
KATANA?! YOU'RE ALIVE!
WHAT IS IT WITH YOU AND DEV?! YOU TWO MUST WANT ME DEAD OR SOMETHING!
OH WELL, IT LOOKS LIKE DEV'S THE ONLY ONE LEFT...
...THAT WE CAN EVEN COUNT ON TO HANDLE THIS SITUATION.

UNLESS *YOU* WANT TO GO OUT THERE, THAT IS.

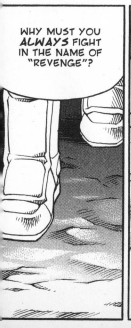

WHY MUST YOU *ALWAYS* FIGHT IN THE NAME OF "REVENGE"?

YOU KNOW IT'S *POINTLESS*, RIGHT? ALL THIS FIGHTING.

I THINK YOU JUST WANT TO FIGHT BECAUSE YOU *CAN*.

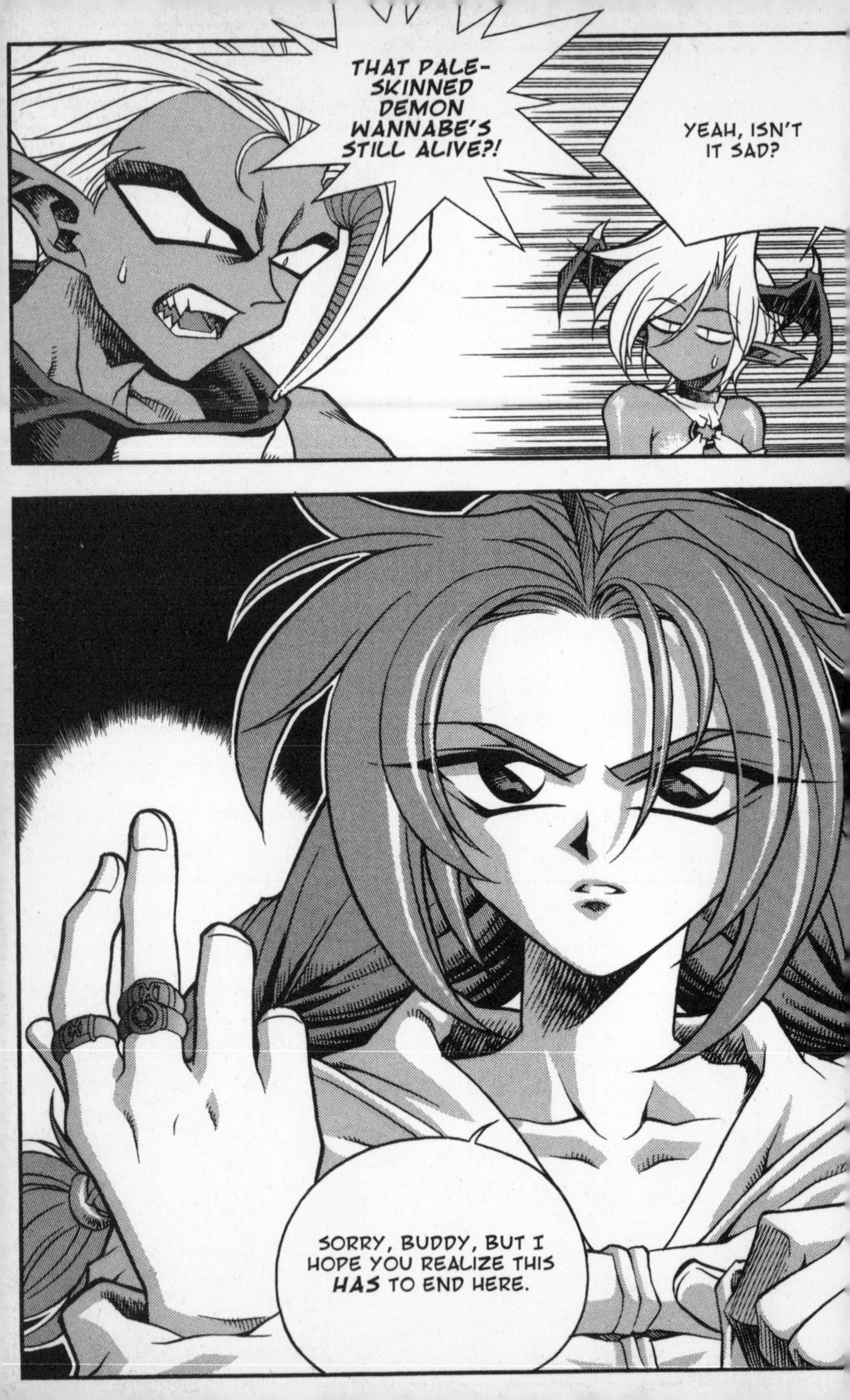
THAT PALE-SKINNED DEMON WANNABE'S STILL ALIVE?!
YEAH, ISN'T IT SAD?
SORRY, BUDDY, BUT I HOPE YOU REALIZE THIS **HAS** TO END HERE.

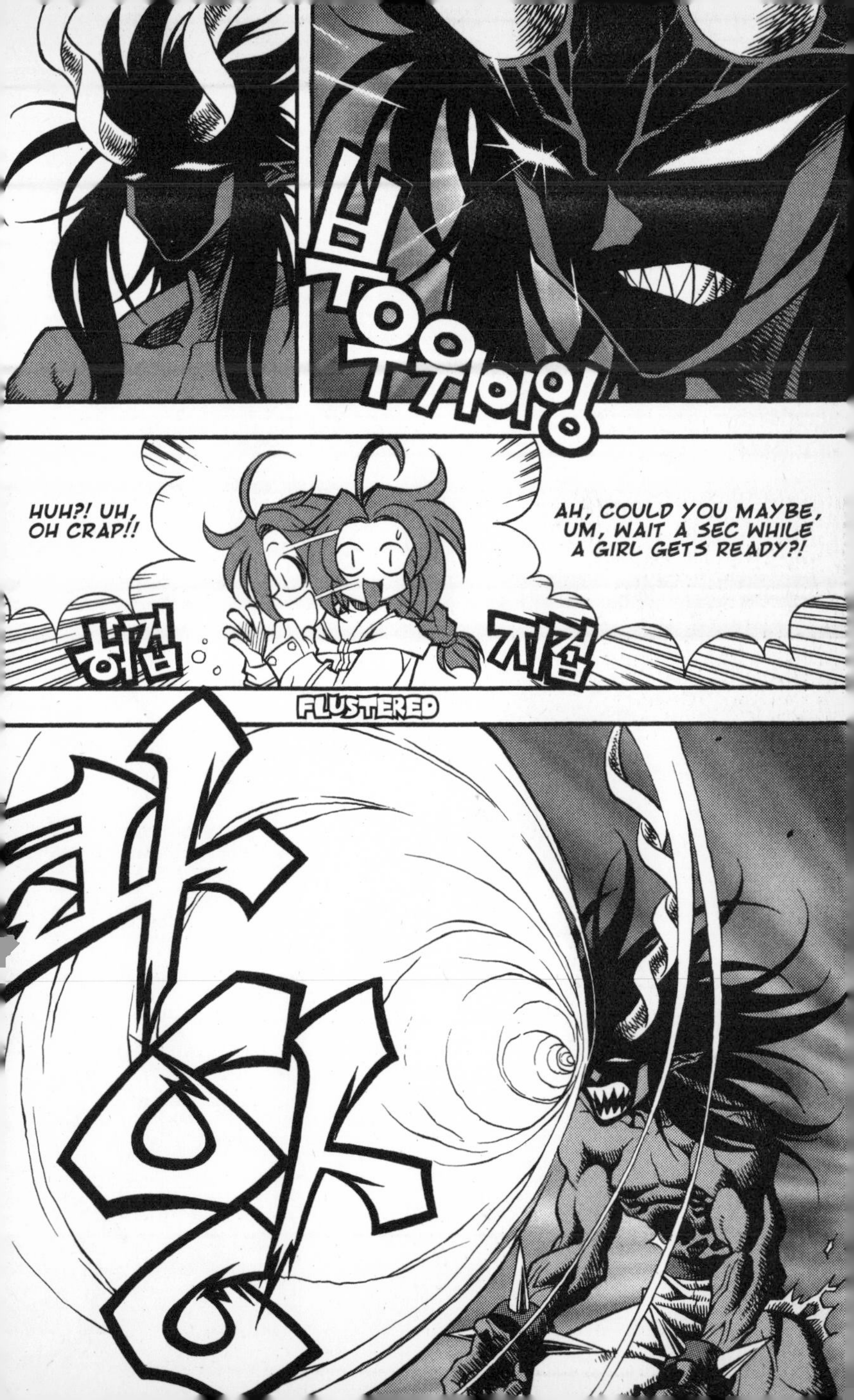
HUH?! UH,
OH CRAP!!
AH, COULD YOU MAYBE,
UM, WAIT A SEC WHILE
A GIRL GETS READY?!
허겁
지겁
FLUSTERED

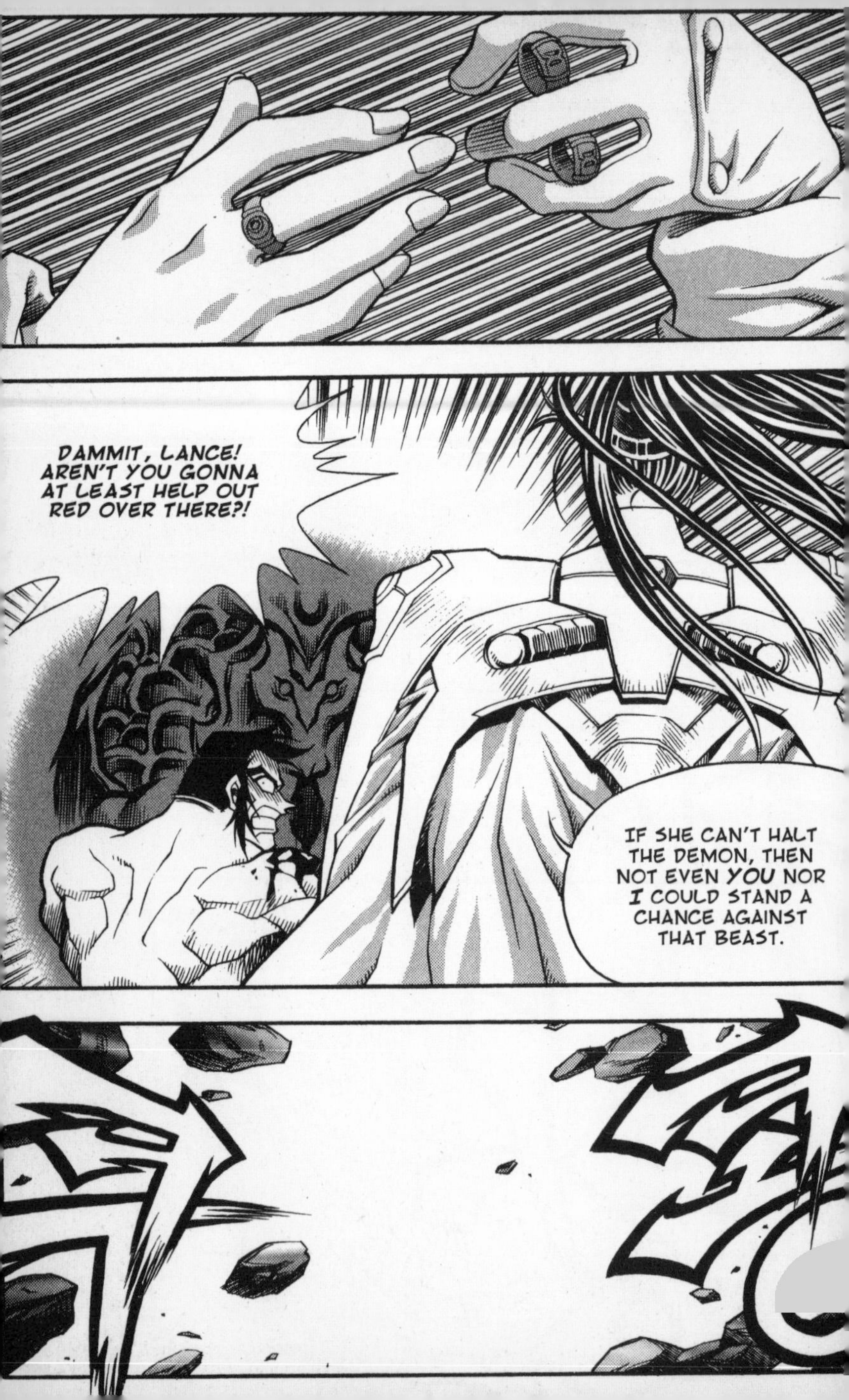
DAMMIT, LANCE! AREN'T YOU GONNA AT LEAST HELP OUT RED OVER THERE?!
IF SHE CAN'T HALT THE DEMON, THEN NOT EVEN YOU NOR I COULD STAND A CHANCE AGAINST THAT BEAST.

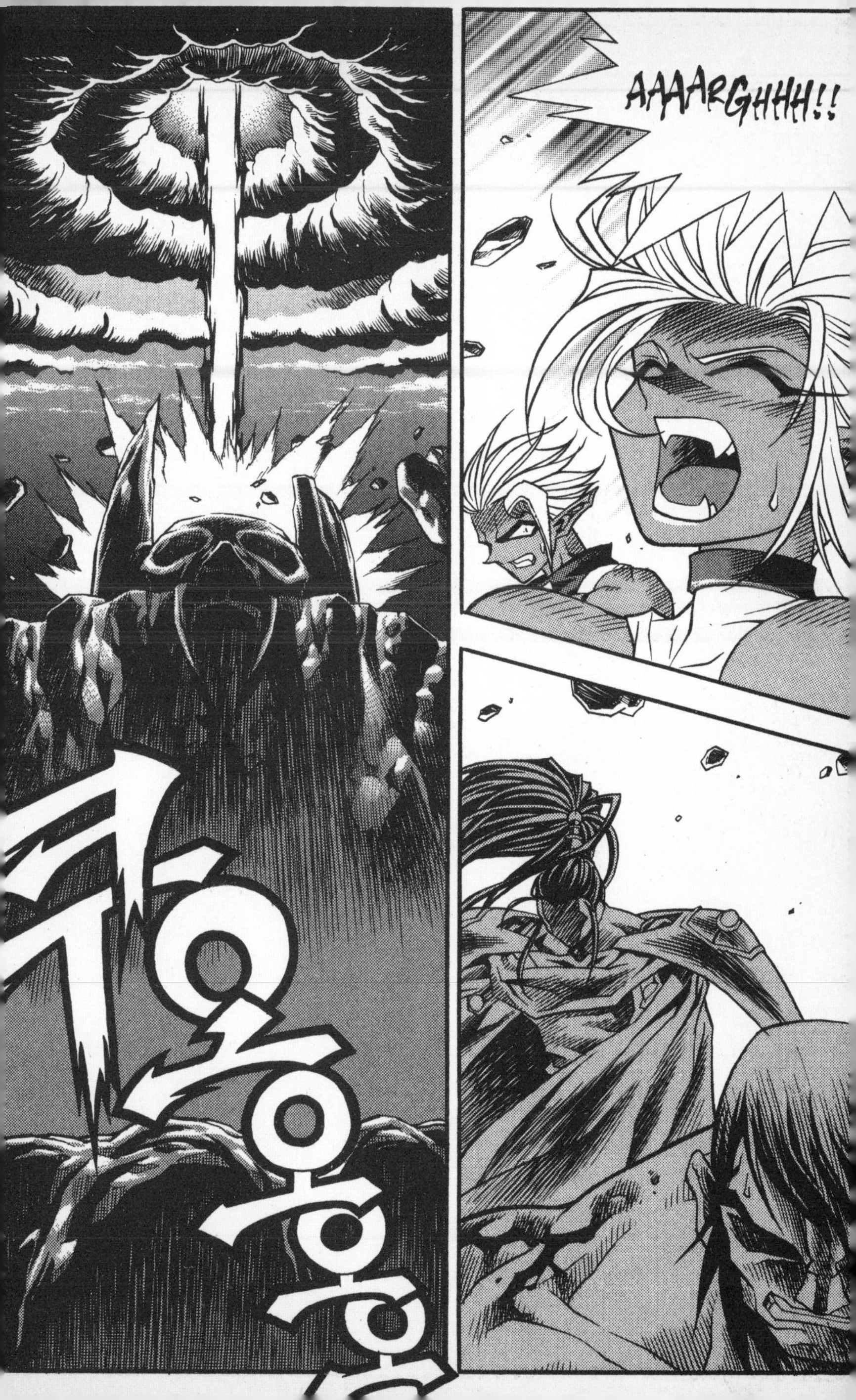
AAAARGHHH!!

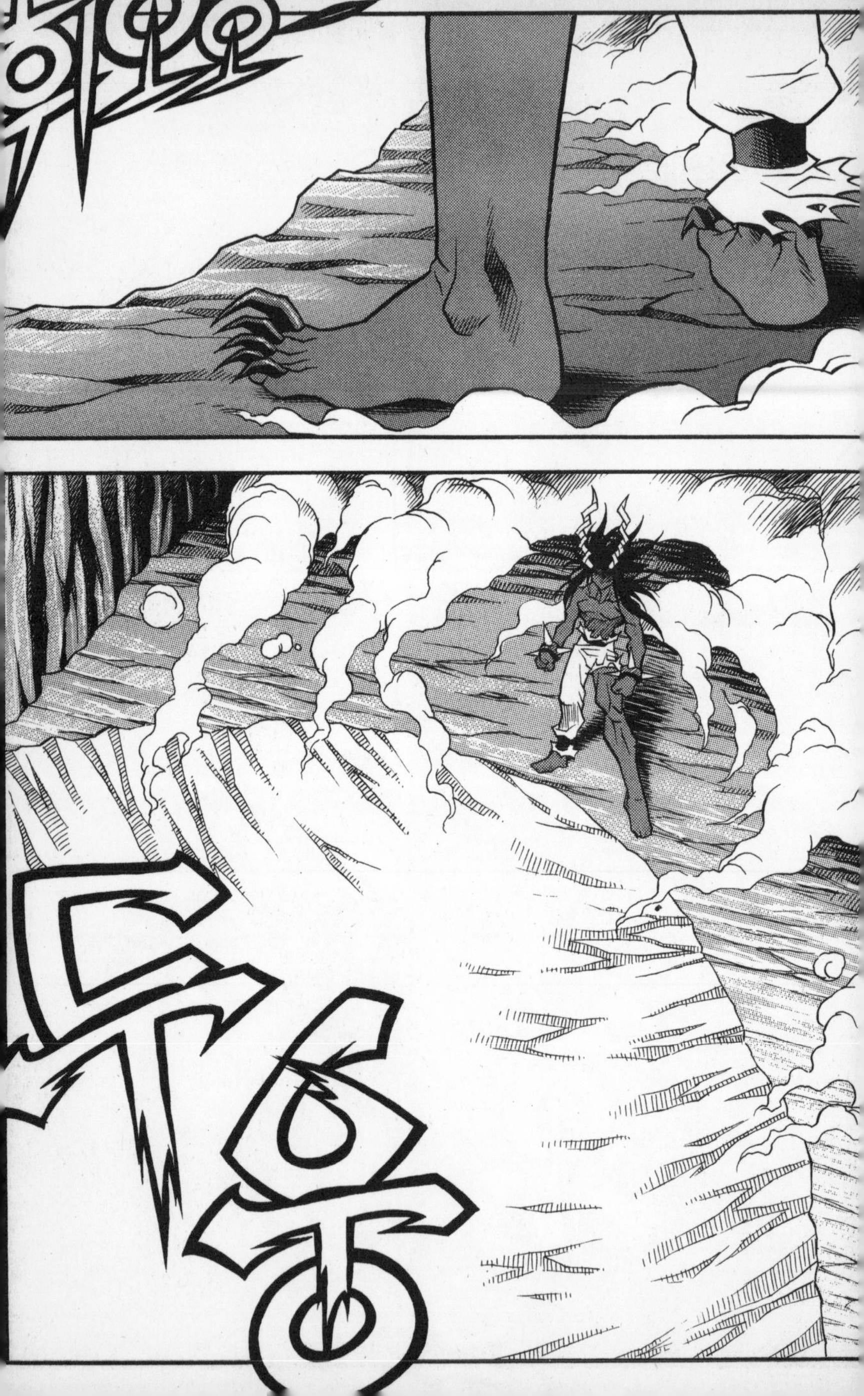
두웅

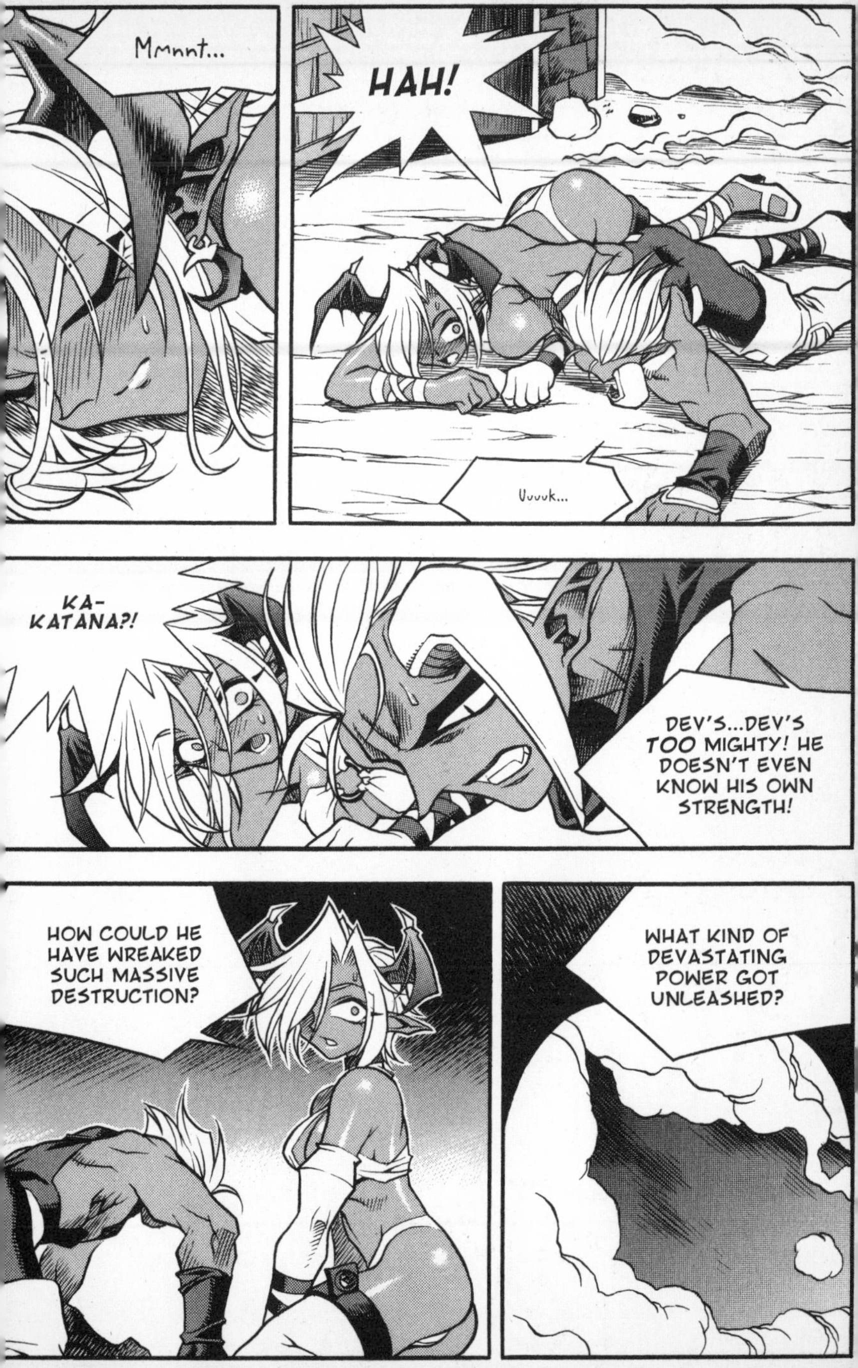
Mmnnt...
HAH!
Uuuuk...
KA-
KATANA?!
DEV'S...DEV'S TOO MIGHTY! HE DOESN'T EVEN KNOW HIS OWN STRENGTH!
HOW COULD HE HAVE WREAKED SUCH MASSIVE DESTRUCTION?
WHAT KIND OF DEVASTATING POWER GOT UNLEASHED?

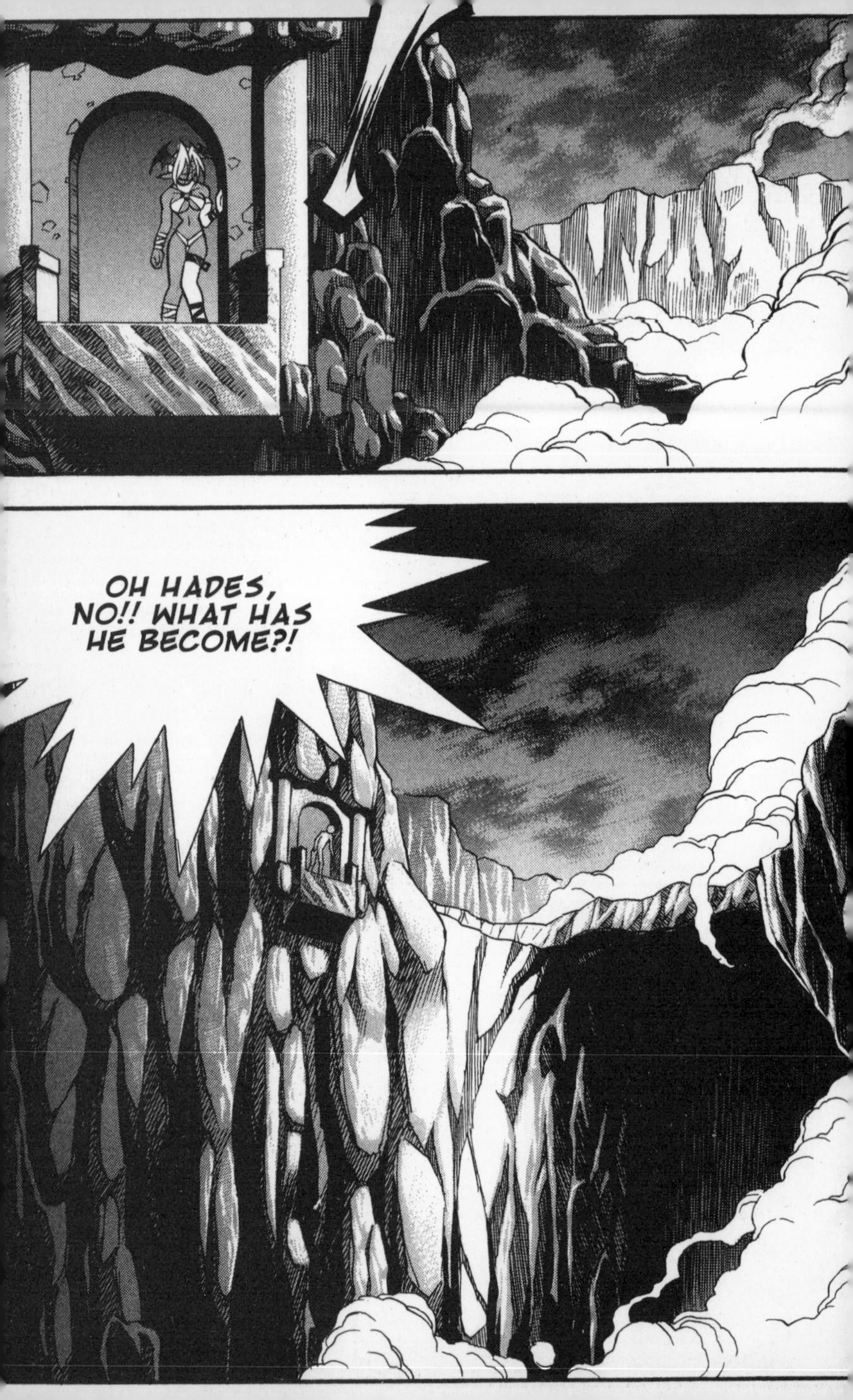
OH HADES, NO!! WHAT HAS HE BECOME?!

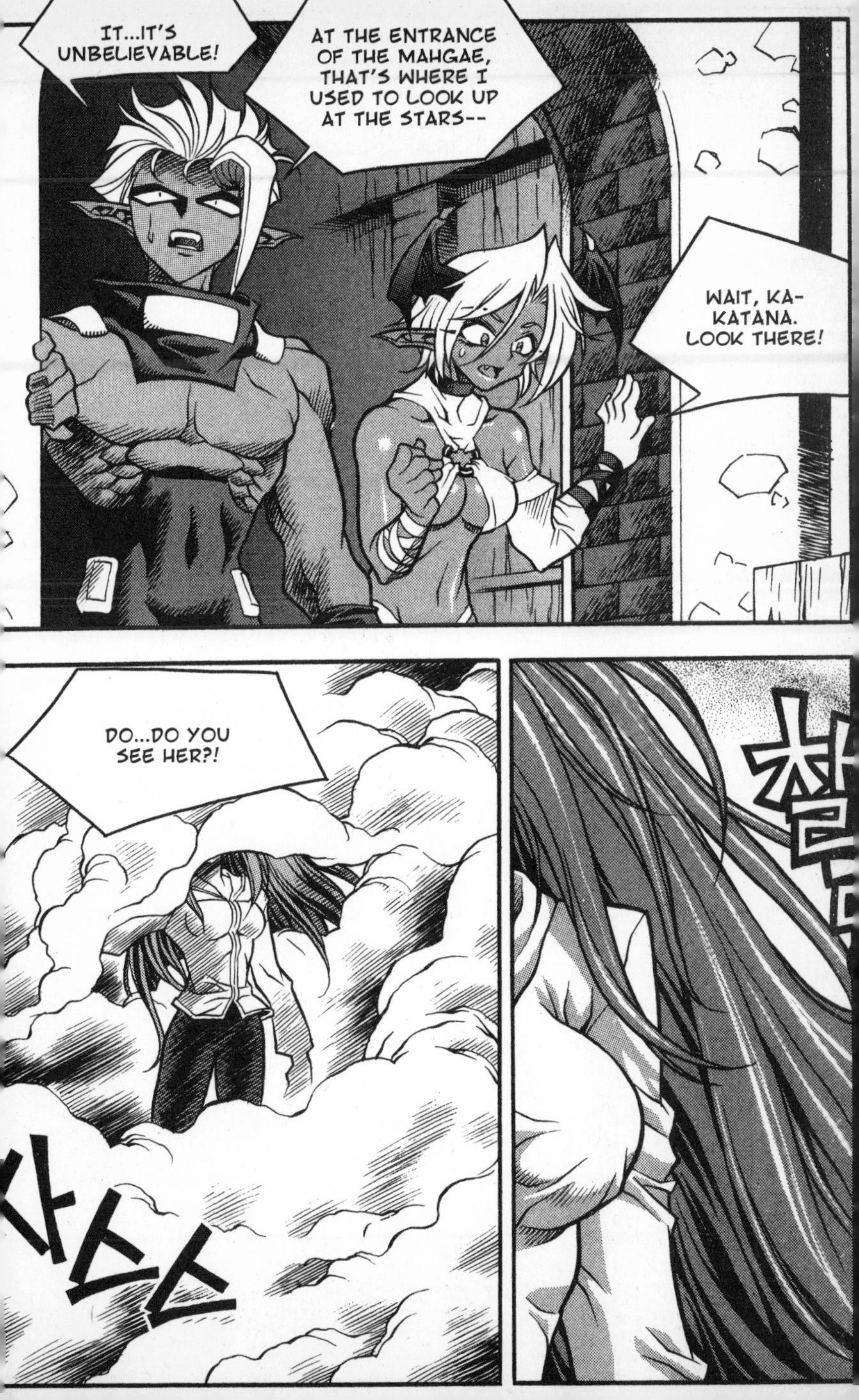
IT...IT'S UNBELIEVABLE!
AT THE ENTRANCE OF THE MAHGAE, THAT'S WHERE I USED TO LOOK UP AT THE STARS--
WAIT, KA-KATANA. LOOK THERE!
DO...DO YOU SEE HER?!

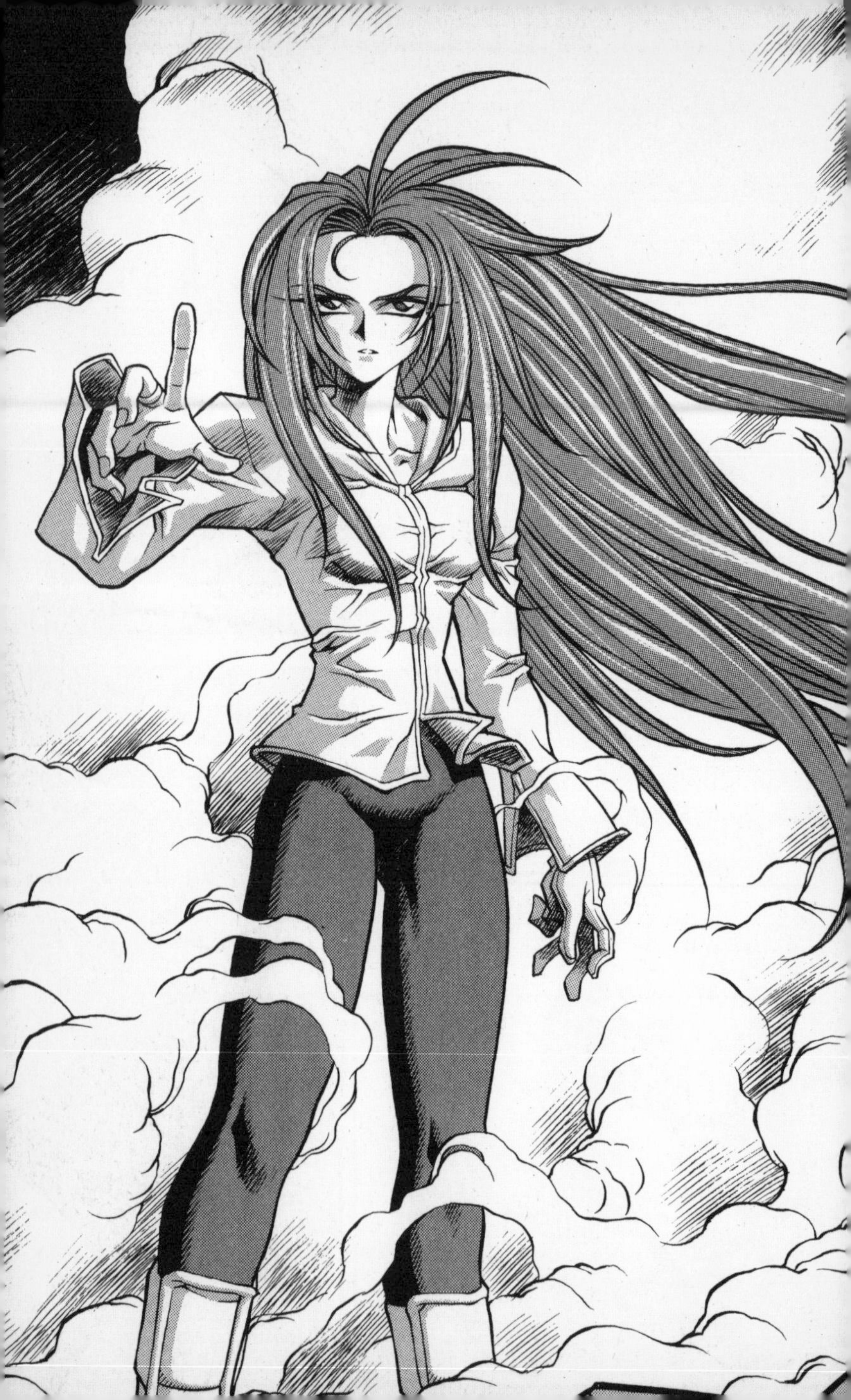

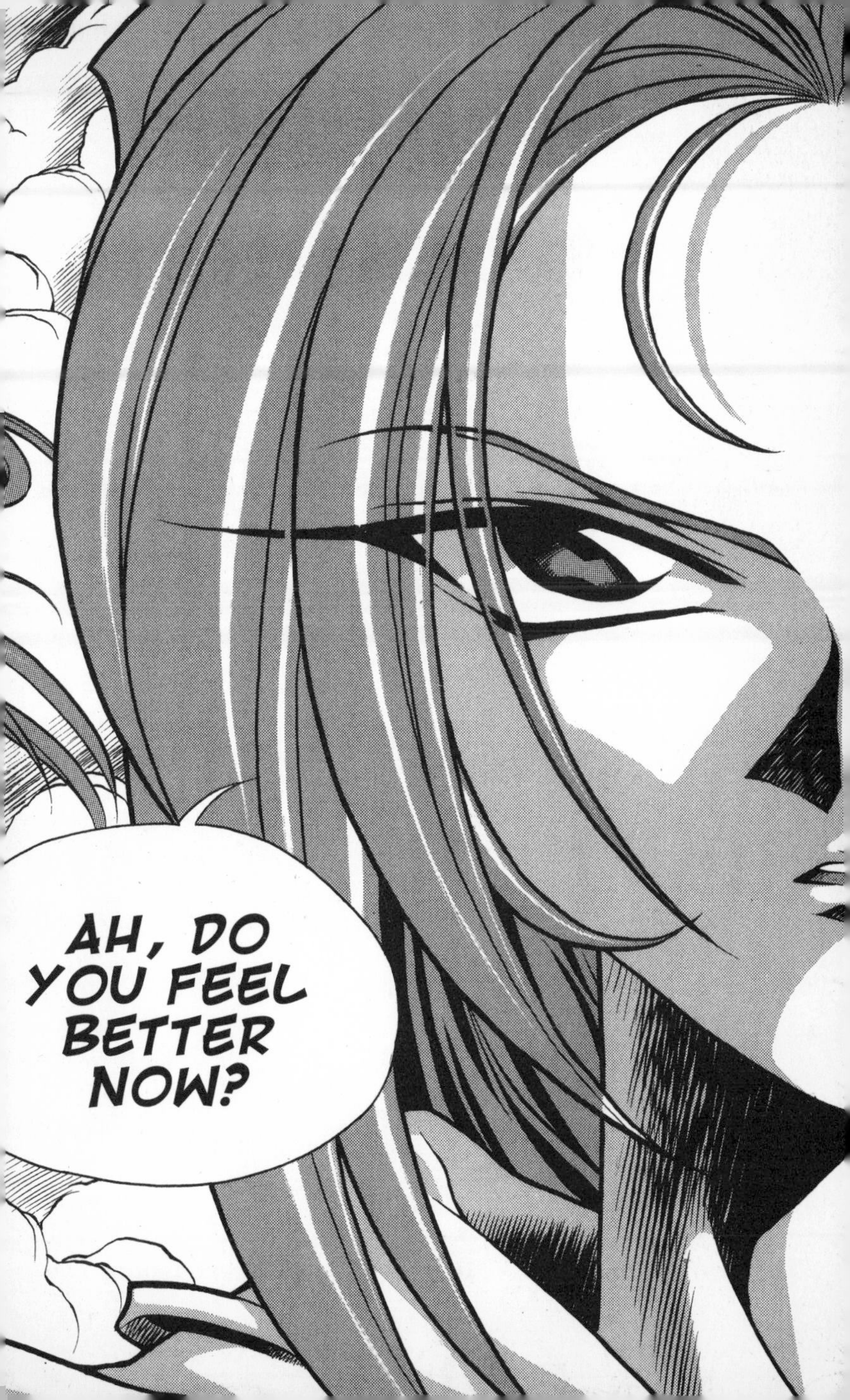
AH, DO YOU FEEL BETTER NOW?

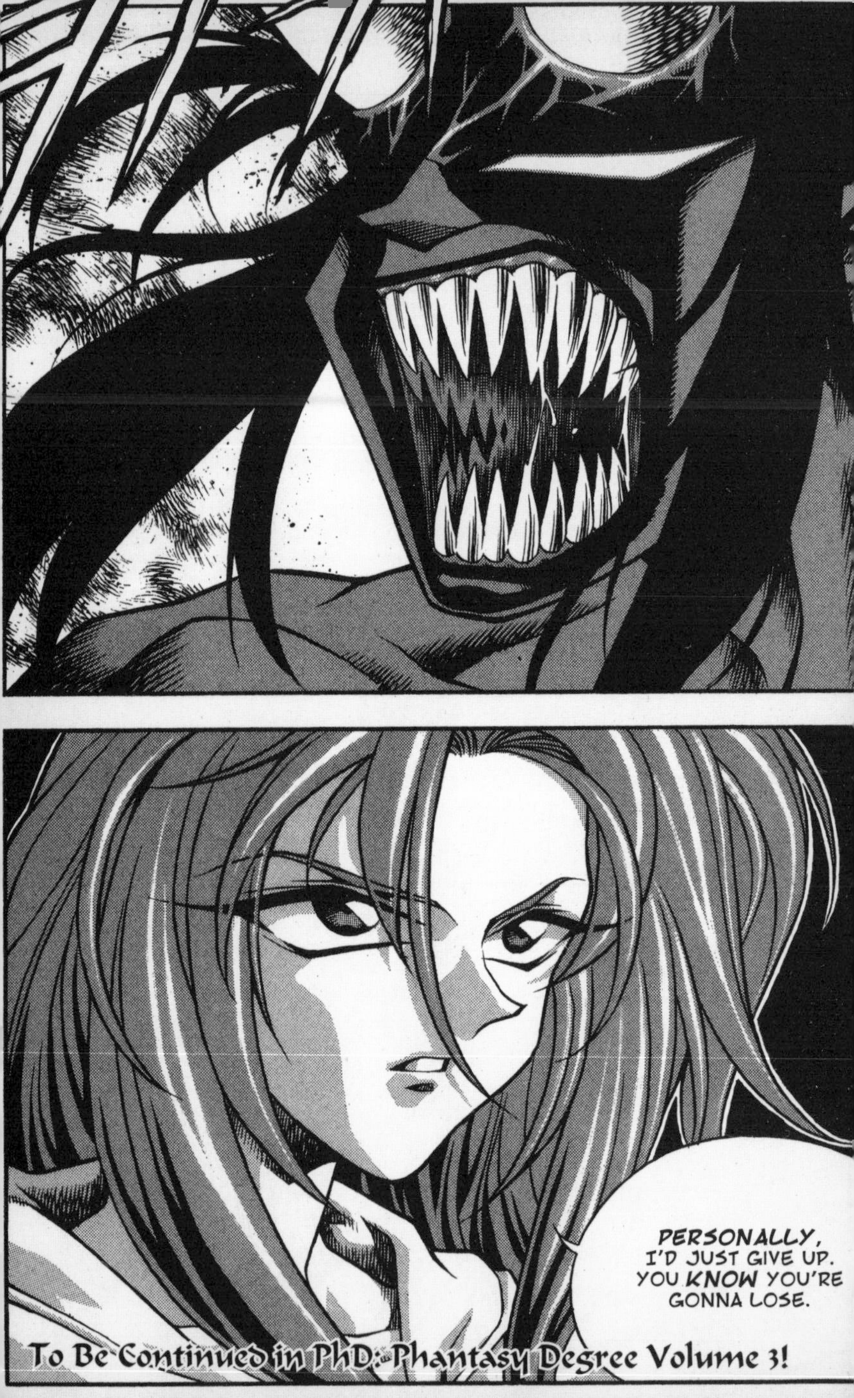
PERSONALLY, I'D JUST GIVE UP. YOU KNOW YOU'RE GONNA LOSE.
To Be Continued in PhD: Phantasy Degree Volume 3!

In the Next Volume of...

PhD
PHANTASY DEGREE

While the Madosa Guild tries to seal the doors to the Mahgae before all Hades breaks loose, Sang protects everyone by battling a savage Dev. But who's that hulking hunk who has entered the fray? And why is he wearing Sang's tattered clothes? Holy gender-bender defender! Is that...**Sang?!** Do her rings have the power of sex-swap sorcery?! Can the Madosa Guild handle two versions of Sang? Can *you*? Find out in Volume 3 of "PhD: Phantasy Degree"!

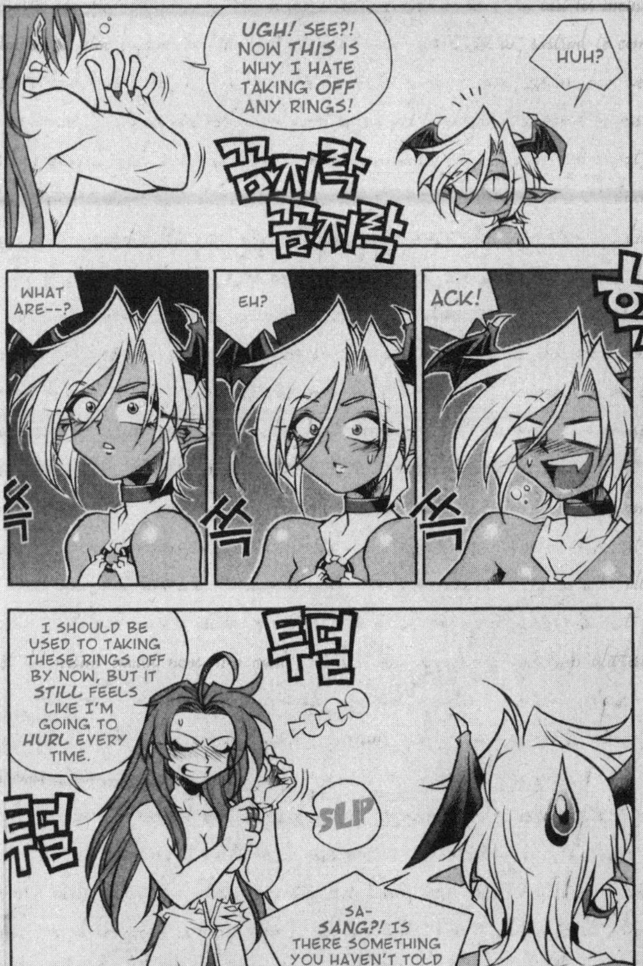
UGH! SEE?! NOW THIS IS WHY I HATE TAKING OFF ANY RINGS!
HUH?
WHAT ARE--?
쓱
EH?
쓱
ACK!
쓱
헉!
I SHOULD BE USED TO TAKING THESE RINGS OFF BY NOW, BUT IT STILL FEELS LIKE I'M GOING TO HURL EVERY TIME.
투덜
투덜
SLIP
SA-SANG?! IS THERE SOMETHING YOU HAVEN'T TOLD US YET?

Available July 2005

TOKYOPOP SHOP

WWW.TOKYOPOP.COM/SHOP

HOT NEWS!
Check out
TOKYOPOP.COM/SHOP
The world's best
collection of manga in
English is now available
online in one place!

SOKORA REFUGEES

PLANET BLOOD

THE TAROT CAFÉ

EVIL NEVER DIES...
BUT EVIL STUFF DOES!

FROM THE
WINNERS OF
TOKYOPOP'S FIRST
RISING STARS OF
MANGA™
COMPETITION

VAN VON HUNTER ™

In the dark ages long ago, in a war-torn land where tranquility and harmony once blossomed, tyranny ruled with a flaming fist! At last, a hero arose to defeat the evildoers and returned hope to the people and peace to the countryside. Now...the sinister forces are back with a vengeance, and in their hour of direst-est need, the commoners once again seek a champion to right wrongs and triumph over villainy! Unfortunately, they could only get the mighty warrior Van Von Hunter, Hunter of Evil...Stuff!

Together with his loyal, memory-challenged sidekick, Van Von Hunter is on a never-ending quest to smite the bad guys—and believe us, they're real bad!

Preview the manga at:

www.TOKYOPOP.com/vanvonhunter
www.VanVonHunter.com

T TEEN AGE 13+

EDITORS' PICKS TOKYOPOP MANGA SUPPLEMENT

SGT FROG

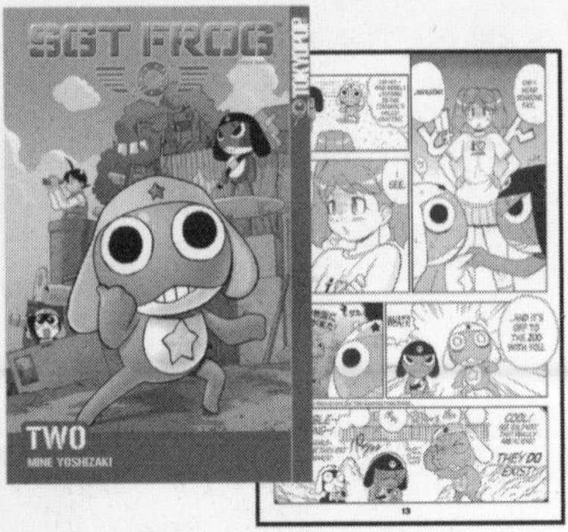
SGT FROG
TWO
MINE YOSHIZAKI

BY MINE YOSHIZAKI

Sgt. Frog is so absurdly comical, it has me in stitches every time I edit it. Mine Yoshizaki's clever sci-fi spoof showcases the hijinks of Sergeant Keroro, a cuddly looking alien, diabolically determined to oppress our planet! While some E.T.s phone home, this otherworldly menace has your number! Abandoned on Earth, Keroro takes refuge in the Hinata home, whose residents quickly take advantage of his stellar cleaning skills. But between scrubbing, vacuuming and an unhealthy obsession with Gundam models, Keroro still finds time to plot the subjugation of humankind!

~ Paul Morrissey, Editor

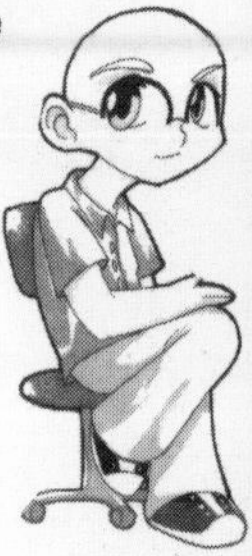

@LARGE

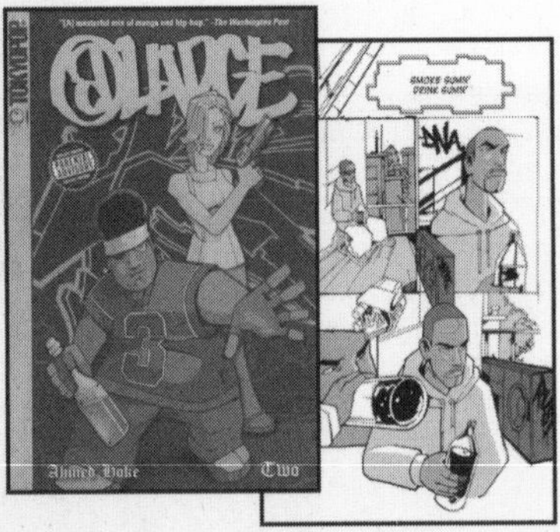
Ahmed Hoke
Two

BY AHMED HOKE

Ahmed Hoke's revolutionary hip-hop manga is a groundbreaking graphic novel. While at first glace this series may seem like a dramatic departure from traditional manga styles, on a deeper level one will find a rich, lyrical world full of wildly imaginative characters, intense action and heartfelt human emotions. This is a truly unique manga series that needs to be read by everyone—whether they are fans of hip-hop or not.

~Rob Valois, Editor

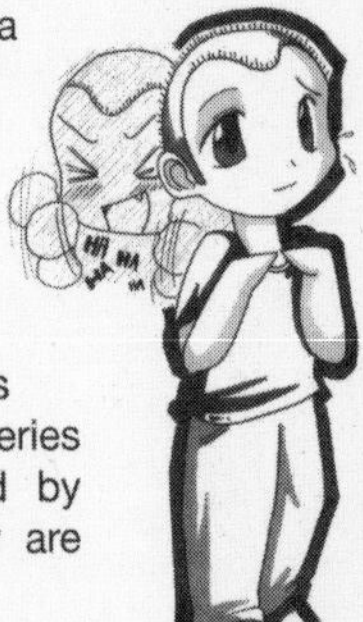

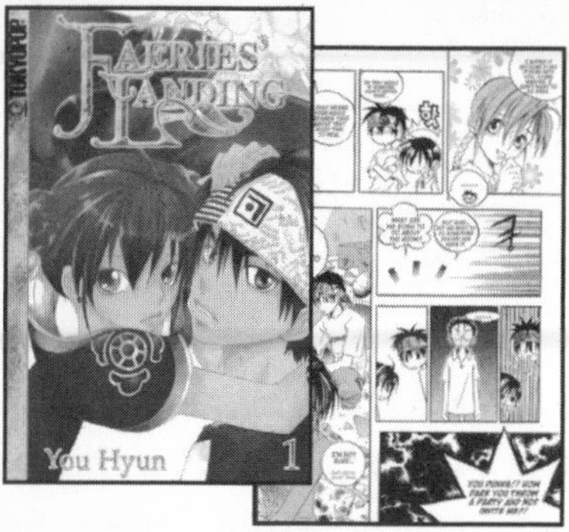
Faeries' Landing
You Hyun
1

BY YOU HYUN

FAERIES' LANDING

Following the misadventures of teenager Ryang Jegal and Fanta, a faerie who has fallen from the heavens straight into South Korea, *Faeries' Landing* is both a spoof of modern-day teen romance and a lighthearted fantasy epic. Imagine if Shakespeare's *A Midsummer Night's Dream* had come from the pen of Joss Whedon after about a dozen shots of espresso, and you have an idea of what to expect from You Hyun's funny little farce. Bursting with sharp wit, hip attitude and vibrant art, *Faeries' Landing* is guaranteed to get you giggling.
~Tim Beedle, Editor

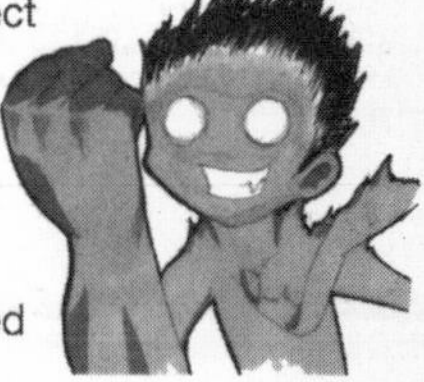

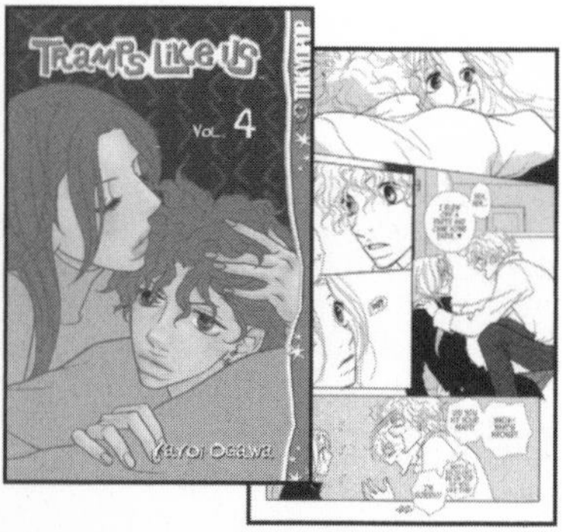
Tramps Like Us
Vol. 4
Yayoi Ogawa

BY YAYOI OGAWA

TRAMPS LIKE US

Yayoi Ogawa's *Tramps Like Us*—known as *Kimi wa Pet* in Japan—is the touching and humorous story of Sumire, a woman whose striking looks and drive for success alienate her from her friends and co-workers...until she takes in Momo, a cute homeless boy, as her "pet." As sketchy as the situation sounds, it turns out to be the sanest thing in Sumire's hectic life. In his quiet way, Momo teaches Sumire how to care for another being while also caring for herself...in other words, how to love. And there ain't nothin' wrong with that.
~Carol Fox, Editor

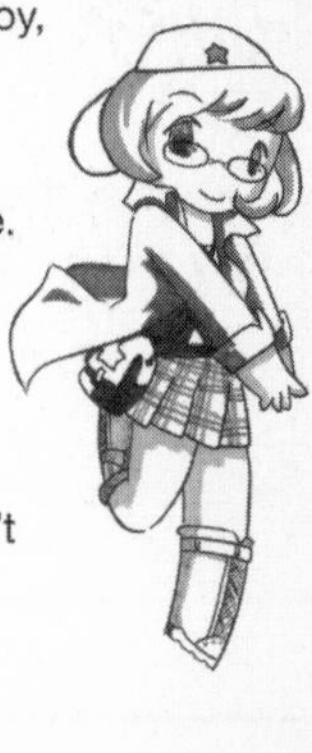

PASSION FRUIT
BY MARI OKAZAKI

Passion Fruit is a unique, unforgettable collection of stylish stories that touch upon our most private inhibitions and examine our deepest desires. This uncompromising blend of realism and raw emotion focuses on women exploring the vulnerability and frailty of the human condition. With uninhibited authenticity and pathos, passion proves to be stranger than fiction.

OT OLDER TEEN AGE 16+

© Mari Okazaki

PLANET BLOOD
BY TAE-HYUNG KIM

Universal Century 0091. The Mars and Moon colonies fight for repatriation rights over the newly restored Earth. Amidst the bloody battle, one soldier, is rendered unconscious—only to awaken in an entirely different world enmeshed in an entirely different war...

T TEEN AGE 13+

© KIM TAE-HYUNG, DAIWON C.I. Inc.

LILING-PO
BY AKO YUTENJI

Master thief Liling-Po has finally been captured! However, the government offers a chance for Liling-Po to redeem himself. All he has to do is "retrieve" some special items—eight mystic treasures that are fabled to grant their owners any wish!

T TEEN AGE 13+

© Ako Yutenji

The breakout manga that put CLAMP on the map!

RG VEDA
聖伝

At the dawn of creation, the world was a beautiful and tranquil place. When a powerful warlord rebelled against the king, a violent, chaotic age began.... Three hundred years later, a group of noble warriors embarks on a quest to find the prophesied Six Stars before the land is torn apart!

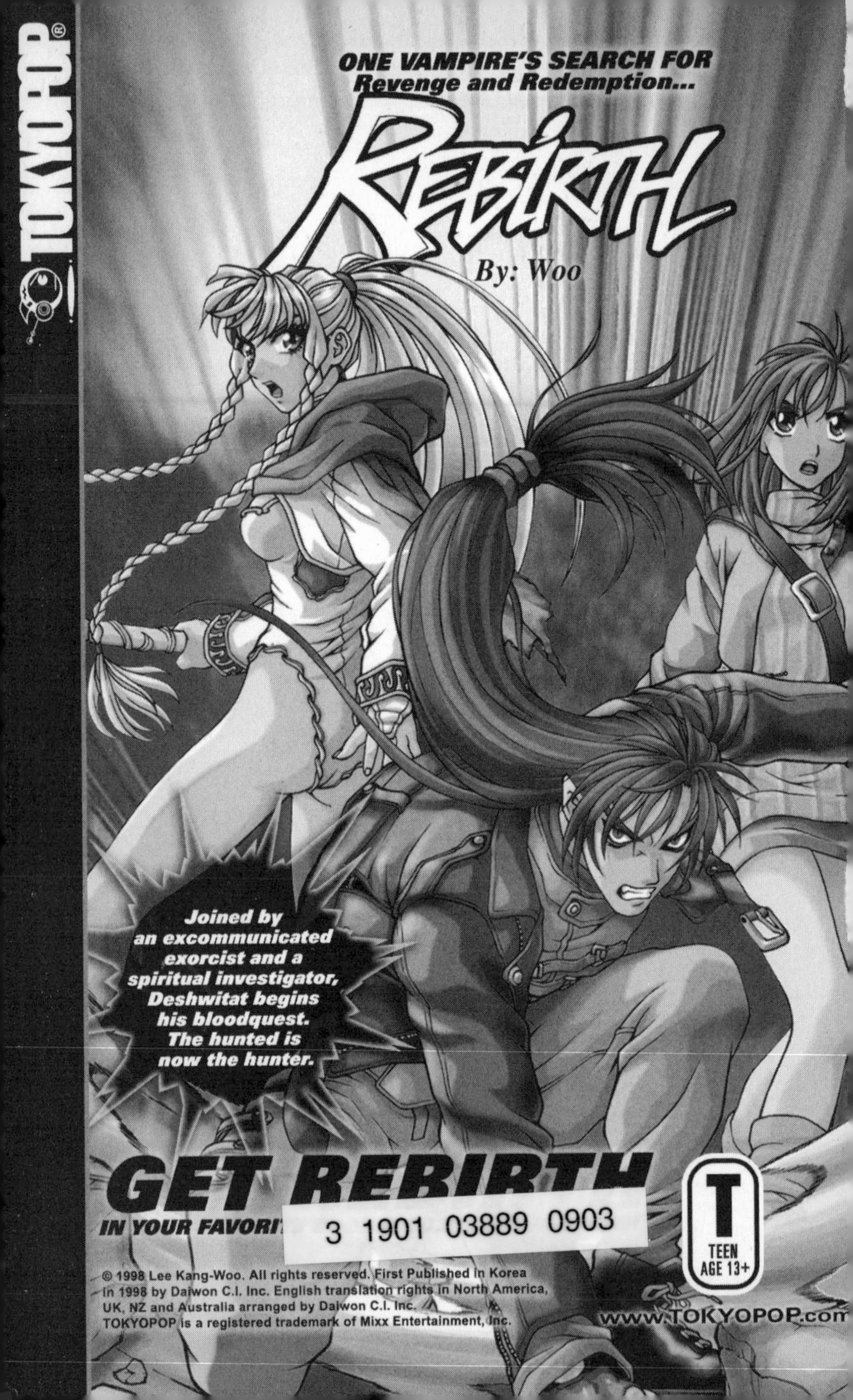
TOKYOPOP
ONE VAMPIRE'S SEARCH FOR Revenge and Redemption...
REBIRTH
By: Woo
Joined by an excommunicated exorcist and a spiritual investigator, Deshwitat begins his bloodquest. The hunted is now the hunter.
GET REBIRTH
IN YOUR FAVORIT
3 1901 03889 0903
T
TEEN AGE 13+
© 1998 Lee Kang-Woo. All rights reserved. First Published in Korea in 1998 by Daiwon C.I. Inc. English translation rights in North America, UK, NZ and Australia arranged by Daiwon C.I. Inc.
TOKYOPOP is a registered trademark of Mixx Entertainment, Inc.
www.TOKYOPOP.com